The *Revels* History of Drama in English

GENERAL EDITOR
Lois Potter

The *Revels* History of Drama in English

VOLUME I Medieval Drama

A. C. Cawley

Marion Jones

Peter F. McDonald

& David Mills

Methuen

London and New York

First published in 1983 by
Methuen & Co. Ltd
11 New Fetter Lane, London EC4P 4EE

Published in the USA by
Methuen & Co.
in association with Methuen, Inc.
733 Third Avenue, New York, NY 10017

Printed in Great Britain by
the University Press, Cambridge

British Library Cataloguing in Publication Data

The Revels history of Drama in English.
  Vol. I: Medieval drama
  1. English drama—History and criticism
  I. Cawley, A. C.
  822'.009   PR625

  ISBN 0-416-13020-8

Library of Congress Cataloging in Publication Data

(Revised for vol. 1)
Main entry under title:

The Revels history of drama in English.

  Vol. 1: 1983.
  Bibliography: v. 3, p.
  Includes intend.
      CONTENTS:—v. 1. A. C. Cawley et al. Medieval drama.—v. 2.—Norman
Sanders et al. 1500–1576.—v. 3.—Barroll, J. L. et al. 1576–1613.
      1. English drama—History and criticism.   2. American drama—History and
criticism.   3. Theaters—Great   Britain.   4. Theaters—United   States.   I.
Leech,   Clifford.   II. Craik,   Thomas   Wallace.   III. Barroll,   John   Leeds,
1928–   .   IV. Booth, Michael R.
  PR625.R44   822'.009   75-321430
  ISBN 0-416-13040-2 (v. 3)
  ISBN 0-416-81380-1 (v. 3: pbk.)

Contents

List of illustrations

Acknowledgements

The authors and publishers would like to thank the following for their permission to reproduce the illustrations: the Austrian National Library, Vienna, for no. 28; the Biblioteca Nazionale, Venice, for no. 3; the Bibliothèque Nationale, Paris, for nos 1, 7, 23, 25, 29; the Bodleian Library, Oxford, for no. 26; the Borthwick Institute of Historical Research and the University of York for no. 13; Brassai for no. 22; the British Library for the photographs of nos 4, 10, 15; Corpus Christi College, Cambridge, and the Courtauld Institute of Art, London, for no. 27; the Folger Shakespeare Library, Washington, DC, and the Council of the Early English Text Society for no. 5; Fürstlich Fürstenbergische Hofbibliothek, Donaue-schingen, for no. 10; the Huntington Library, San Marino, California, for no. 24; the Koninklijk Museum, Antwerp, for no. 19; the Musée Condé de Chantilly and Photographie Giraudon for nos 8, 20; the Pierpont Morgan Library, New York, for no. 21; the Church of St Peter Mancroft, Norwich, and Jarrolds for no. 12; the Master and Fellows of Trinity College, Cambridge, for no. 30; the photographic department of the University of Leeds for the photographs of nos 1, 2, 3, 5, 6, 9; the University of Wisconsin Press and the University of London for no. 14; the Victoria and Albert Museum, London, for nos 11, 16, 17, 18; and the Zentralbibliothek, Lucerne, for no. 9.

Preface

That the first chronological volume in the Revels History should be the last one to be published has a certain appropriateness, in view of medieval drama's fascination with all aspects of circularity, from the God who is Alpha et Omega to the drama whose end is its beginning. In fact, its late appearance is due less to any such sense of symbolic fitness than to the workings of the Wheel of Fortune. Professor Cawley's essay was substantially completed in 1968, though revised in 1980; Dr Mills and Mr McDonald, who replaced a previous contributor, also submitted theirs in 1980. I should like to thank them for having so patiently borne with the difficulties of compiling a work by several authors over a long period, and for doing their best to ensure that the finished product would be as up-to-date as possible. I am particularly grateful to Professor Cawley, who has taken a consistent interest in the volume for many years. At his suggestion, I asked Professor Ian Lancashire, the bibliographer of *REED* (*Records of Early English Drama*), University of Toronto, to undertake the revision of the appendix on recorded performances in the period, which Professor Cawley himself had originally compiled. The result turned out to be of such massive proportions that the volume could not find room for it, but it has been published separately by the University of Toronto Press as *A Guide to*

Dramatic Texts and Records to 1558 in England, Scotland and Ireland. The chronological table, originally compiled by Professor Cawley, has been supplemented by me with reference to Professor Lancashire's work. I am glad that the Revels History has been associated with this important research tool, thanks to the help given to us by the *REED* project under its director, Professor Alexandra Johnston.

The contributors have also been helpful in their suggestions for the illustrations to this volume. In addition, I should like to thank the Huntington Library, San Marino, for assistance in compiling the illustrations. The copy editor was Della Couling. The index was compiled by me, with help from the contributors. Professor T. W. Craik's cheerfulness, in his role as general editor of other volumes in this series, has provided a model for us all.

Lois Potter

Chronological table

Because of the different nature of the period considered, this table takes a somewhat different form from the others in this series. It is highly selective, and mainly orientated towards the early drama in England. It gives no indication of the wealth of quasi-dramatic activity, in the form of civic pageants and court revels, which went on throughout the period, but which are too numerous to list. Dates of dramatic works have been checked with those given by Ian Lancashire in *A Guide to Dramatic Texts and Records to 1558 in England, Scotland and Ireland* (Toronto, 1983); dates of non-dramatic works are taken from *Annals of English Literature, 1475–1950* (Oxford, 1961).

Reigns	Public events	Drama and dramatic records
	597 Landing of St Augustine in Kent	
871–99 Alfred		
959–75 Edgar		*c.*950 Monastery of St Gall, Bavaria: earliest example of *Quem quaeritis* dialogue *c.*965 *Regularis Concordia*: monastic code for Benedictine communities in England, attributed to Æthelwold, Bishop of Winchester (gives detailed directions for performances of *Quem quaeritis* ceremony)
979–1013 Ethelred I		*c.*980 Winchester troper containing text of *Quem quaeritis*

	*c.*700 *Lindisfarne Gospels*: finest example of Anglo–Saxon MS illumination
731 Bede, *Ecclesiastical History of the English People* *c.*891 *Anglo–Saxon Chronicle* first compiled; continued in one text until 1154	
	*c.*980 *Benedictional of Æthelwold*: later Anglo-Saxon MS illumination, Winchester school *c.*980 Earl's Barton Church, Northants, tower
*c.*990–94 Ælfric, *Catholic Homilies* *c.*991 *The Battle of Maldon* *c.*1000 Date of MSS of Old English poetry: Junius MS, *Vercelli Book*, *Beowulf* MS, *Exeter Book*	

Reigns	Public events	Drama and dramatic records
1066–87 William I	1066 Battle of Hastings	
1087–1100 William II	1085 Domesday Book 1096 First Crusade	
1100–35 Henry I		1100 Play of St Katherine at Dunstable
1135–54 Stephen		*c*.1146–75 *Ordo representacionis Ade* (*Mystère d'Adam*) (earliest surviving Norman play in England)
1154–89 Henry II		
1189–99 Richard I		*c*.1180 *La Seinte Resureccion* (revised *c*.1275) *c*.1188–98 'Shrewsbury Fragments', Christmas and Easter plays, preserved in a fifteenth–century MS (liturgical plays in Latin and English, consisting of one actor's part and cues in each of the plays)
1199–1216 John	Late twelfth–early thirteenth century; beginning of collegiate system at Oxford and Cambridge	Thirteenth century. *Dame Sirith*, dramatic *fabliau*
	1215 Magna Carta	

1079–93
Winchester Cathedral, crypt
and transepts, rebuilt

1096–1120
Norwich Cathedral, choir
and transepts (nave
completed, 1145)

1132
Fountains Abbey founded
1133
Durham Cathedral, nave
vault completed

*c.*1150–70
Winchester Bible: finest
achievement of
twelfth-century MS
illumination
1175–8
Canterbury Cathedral, choir

*c.*1189
The Owl and the Nightingale

1192
Rebuilding of Lincoln
Cathedral begun

*c.*1200
Ancrene Riwle
Layamon, *The Brut*

Reigns	Public events	Drama and dramatic records
1216–72 Henry III		
		c.1220 Easter play acted outside Beverley Minster
	1221–4 Dominican and Franciscan orders established in England	
		1244 Bishop Grosseteste of Lincoln attacks 'ludos quos vocant miracula'
		c.1255 Latin liturgical plays at York
1272–1307 Edward I	1275 Marco Polo at the court of Kublai Khan c.1285–95 Hereford World Map	

Other literature	Art and architecture
	*c.*1218–1315 Chester Cathedral, choir *c.*1220–25 Beverley Minster, choir
	*c.*1225–53 Lincoln Cathedral, nave *c.*1226–55 York Minster, transepts
*c.*1237 Guillaume de Lorris begins *Le Roman de la Rose* (finished by Jean de Meun, *c.*1275)	
*c.*1250 *Havelok the Dane, King Horn*	*c.*1250 Bishop's Palace, Chichester, wall painting of Virgin and Child Mid-thirteenth century. Southwell Minster, chapter-house
1265–73 St Thomas Aquinas, *Summa Theologica*	*c.*1270 Westminster Abbey, panel depicting the miracles of Christ
	*c.*1290 Exeter Cathedral, carved corbels of choir

Reigns	Public events	Drama and dramatic records
		*c.*1300 *Manuel des Péchés*, written by William of Wadington and translated into English verse by Robert Mannyng in *Handlyng Synne* (1303), approves of religious plays acted reverently in church but condemns outdoor performance of 'miracles'
		*c.*1300–25 *Dux Moraud*: part of a single actor (Dux Moraud) in an English moral play
1307–27 Edward II		*Interludium de Clerico et Puella*: fragmentary secular play in English
	1311 Feast of Corpus Christi established	
	1314 Battle of Bannockburn	
		*c.*1317 Latin liturgical plays at Lincoln
1327–77 Edward III	1338–1453 Hundred Years' War with France	
	1346 Battle of Crécy	
	1348 Black Death	

Other literature	*Art and architecture*
	1291–1345 York Minster, nave rebuilt
*c.*1300 Dante begins *Divina Commedia*	
*c.*1300–49 Richard Rolle of Hampole, *Meditations on the Passion,* *The Form of Living*	Early fourteenth century. *Queen Mary's Psalter*: MS illuminations of biblical and apocryphal subjects
	*c.*1323–75 Chester Cathedral, nave (part) *c.*1326–31 *Holkham Bible Picture Book*: sequence of biblical pictures from Creation to Last Judgement; possibly shows influence of drama
1341 Petrarch crowned poet laureate at Rome	
	*c.*1342–50 Chapel of St Mary on the Bridge, Wakefield

Reigns	Public events	Drama and dramatic records
		*c.*1350 'The Pride of Life' (moral play fragment), preserved in MS of *c.* 1400–25.
	1356 Battle of Poitiers	
1377–99 Richard II		*c.*1375 Cornish *Origo Mundi, Passio Domini Nostri*, and *Resurrexio Domini Nostri* (in fifteenth-century MS) 1376 Earliest record of Corpus Christi pageants (at York) 1377 First mention of Corpus Christi play at Beverley (now lost) – 36 pageants 1378 Reference in the English translation of Wycliffe's *De Officio Pastorali* to the Paternoster play of York (now lost)

Reigns	Public events	Drama and dramatic records
	1381 Peasants' Revolt	
		1384 Cycle of biblical plays performed at Skinners Well (Clerkenwell) by London clerics in minor orders
		1392 First mention of Corpus Christi play at Coventry
1399–1413 Henry IV		1397 Allegorical pageants at York to welcome Richard II Fifteenth century. Date of MS of Cornish *Ordinalia*: dramatic trilogy consisting of *Origo Mundi,* *Passio Domini, Resurrexio* *Domini* *c.*1400 *A tretise of miraclis pleyinge*: sermon against miracle plays *c.*1405–10 *Dives et Pauper* (first printed in 1493): English handbook of religious instruction in which miracle plays are defended

Other literature	*Art and architecture*
	1379–1405 Canterbury Cathedral, nave and south transept *c.*1380–1400 York Minster, choir (part)
*c.*1385 Wycliffe, translation of Bible *c.*1385 Chaucer, *Troilus and Criseyde* *c.*1387–1400 Chaucer, *The Canterbury Tales* (allusions to religious plays in *Miller's Tale* and *Wife of Bath's Prologue*) 1390 Gower, *Confessio Amantis*	
	1394–*c.*1450 Winchester Cathedral, nave and aisles rebuilt Late fourteenth century. *Wilton Diptych*: painting on two panels of Richard II adoring Virgin and Child First half of fifteenth century. Book of Hours 'of Elizabeth the Queene' (Elizabeth Woodville) 1405–8 York Minster, east window

Reigns	Public events	Drama and dramatic records
1413–22 Henry V	1415 Battle of Agincourt	1415 York Proclamation concerning Corpus Christi play and procession; pageants for Henry V's triumphant entry into London
1422–61 Henry VI		1422 First mention of Corpus Christi play at Chester 1424–30 Lydgate, 'mumming at Bishopwood' and 'Bicorne and Chychevache' 1424 Lydgate, 'Mumming at Eltham' after 1426 Corpus Christi play and procession separated at York, the procession being postponed to the day after the Feast of Corpus Christi 1427–1589 Corpus Christi plays at Newcastle-upon-Tyne (lost, except for The Shipwrights' Play of Noah) c.1427–30 Lydgate, 'Mummings' for London, Hertford, and Windsor

Other literature	Art and architecture
*c.*1411 Hoccleve, *De Regimine* *Principum* *c.*1412–20 Lydgate, *Troy Book*	
*c.*1420–1500 *Paston Letters*	*c.*1420 Alabaster panels, carved in relief, representing scenes from Christ's life and Passion (Hildburgh Collection, Victoria and Albert Museum) *c.*1420 Wakefield Cathedral, tower *c.*1421 York Minster, St William window
*c.*1424 James I of Scotland, *The* *Kingis Quair*	
	*c.*1430–40 Great Malvern Priory, east window depicting scenes from the Passion

Reigns	Public events	Drama and dramatic records
		c.1440 Earliest record of Corpus Christi Passion play in Scotland: 'ludo de ly Haliblude' at Aberdeen
		c.1440 Date of MS of *The Castle of Perseverance*: moral play
		1441 First mention of Beverley Paternoster play
		1446 First mention of Creed play performed every tenth year by the Corpus Christi guild at York
		c.1450–85 Date of MS of *Towneley Plays*, i.e. Wakefield Corpus Christi play (32 plays)
		c.1450–1500 Date of MS of *Mankind* and of *Mind, Will, and Understanding* (or *Wisdom*): moral plays
	1453 Fall of Constantinople	
	1455–85 Wars of the Roses	1455 First reference to Whitsun plays at Henley-on-Thames; later references – 1499, 1520 – mention Robin Hood
		1457 Queen Margaret visits Coventry to see Corpus Christi play
1461–83 Edward IV		*c*.1457–61 Thomas Chaundler, *Liber Apologeticus*

*c.*1438
The Book of Margery Kempe

.

1446–1515
Chapel of King's College
Cambridge

Mid-fifteenth century.
Wakefield Cathedral, nave
remodelled

*c.*1455
Jean Fouquet's miniature of
the martyrdom of St
Apollonia

Reigns	Public events	Drama and dramatic records
		c.1461–1500 *Croxton Play of The Sacrament* 1461 Reference to an Abraham and Isaac play at Northampton 1465–83 Corpus Christi play (11 pageants) at Stamford, Lincolnshire (lost) 1467–1584 Pageants at Hocktide in Worcester *c*.1468 Date of MS of *Ludus Coventriae*, also known as Hegge plays or N-town plays; possibly the Corpus Christi play of Lincoln *c*.1470–80 Date of Brome MS of *Abraham and Isaac* *c*.1475 Date of MS of York Corpus Christi play (48 plays) *c*.1475–6 Earliest text of a Robin Hood play (MS fragment, 'Robin Hood and the Sheriff of Nottingham') *c*.1475–1500 Possible date of earliest MS of Chester Corpus Christi play, a fragment of 41 lines; oldest nearly complete MS is dated 1591 (25 plays)
	1476 Caxton sets up his press at Westminster	

*c.*1464
Biblia Pauperum: one of
earliest block books showing
system of typology by which
Old Testament episodes
prefigure people and events
in the New Testament

1469–70
Malory, *Le Morte Darthur*
(printed by Caxton, 1485)

Reigns	Public events	Drama and dramatic records
		1478 First mention of Corpus Christi play at Norwich (the Grocers' Play of the Fall, only extant play, is preserved in an eighteenth-century transcript) *c.*1480 'Occupation and Idleness' and 'Lucidus and Dubius' (interludes)
1483 Edward V 1483–95 Richard III 1485–1509 Henry VII	**1488** Duke Humphrey's Library opened at Oxford **1492** First voyage of Columbus	**1490–1500** Medwall's *Nature* **1494–1617** Many references to performances at Shrewsbury, sometimes in the quarry **1495–1501** *The Life of St Meriasek* **1497** Medwall's *Fulgens and Lucrece* acted at Christmas **1498–1569** 16 Corpus Christi pageants in Dublin Sixteenth century. Stage plan for Donaueschingen passion play **1501** Directors' copies, or *Abregiés*, of *Le Mystère de la Passion* at Mons **1503** References to Corpus Christi plays in Hereford (lost) **1504–16** Skelton, *Magnificence*

Other literature	Art and architecture
*c.*1478 Caxton's first edn of *The Canterbury Tales* (2nd edn *c.*1484)	
	1479–88 Series of wall-paintings in Eton College Chapel representing miracles of the Virgin
*c.*1482 Caxton's first edn of *Troilus and Creseyde* *c.*1483 Caxton's *Golden Legend*	
	1492–1505 Tower of Magdalen College, Oxford 1495–98 Leonardo da Vinci, 'Last Supper' 1498 Dürer, engravings of *The Apocalypse*
*c.*1500 Scottish 'Pleugh Song'	Early sixteenth century. Roof bosses in transept of Norwich cathedral, representing Christ's Nativity and early years of his ministry
*c.*1503 Dunbar, *The Golden Targe*	

Reigns	Public events	Drama and dramatic records
		1507 In connection with Corpus Christi celebrations, the Edinburgh Hammermen's Book gives details of payments to actors playing Herod and his knights c.1507–8 *Mundus et Infans* (*The World and the Child*)
1509–47 Henry VIII		
		c.1510–20 Date of MS of *Mary Magdalen*, *The Conversion of St Paul*, and *The Killing of the Children* c.1510–25 *Everyman* printed c.1512–16 *Fulgens and Lucrece*, first printed secular play 1512–13 *Palamades*, a Latin comedy by Remaclus Arduenne, printed in London c.1513 *The Interlude of Youth* c.1513–21 John Heywood, *The Pardoner and the Friar* c.1515 *Hick Scorner* first printed

Reigns	Public events	Drama and dramatic records
	1517 Luther breaks away from the Church 1519–22 First circumnavigation of the globe	
		c.1523–5 *Calisto and Melebea*
	1529 Calvin begins to preach	c.1530 Skelton's *Magnificence* printed c.1530–65 Pageants and plays at Norwich in Pentecost week
	1534 Act of Supremacy; Henry VIII establishes himself as supreme head of church in England	1534 Date of MS of Coventry Weavers' pageant, revised by Robert Croo
	1536–9 Suppression of monasteries 1536 Pilgrimage of Grace	

Other literature	Art and architecture
1520 Machiavelli, *La Mandragola* 1525 Tyndale, trans. of New Testament	1520 Henry VII's chapel, Westminster Abbey
	1526 Holbein's first visit to England
1531 Elyot, *The Book Named The Governor* 1532 Henryson, *The Testament of Cresseid*, pub. along with other spurious works as by Chaucer	1532 Holbein's second visit to England
	1533 Painting of subjects apart from portraits and allegories forbidden in England
1535 and 1537 Coverdale trans. of the Bible	
1539 The 'Great' Bible	

Reigns	Public events	Drama and dramatic records
		1540 Statute prevents the printing or performance of all plays contrary to religious doctrine as prescribed in 1540 Lindsay, *Ane Satyre of the Thrie Estaitis* performed as an indoor interlude; later enlarged and performed in the open (1552, 1554)
	1545–63 Council of Trent	
1547–53 Edward VI	1547 Corpus Christi procession suppressed	1547 Hubert Cailleau's design for Valenciennes Passion play
1553–8 Mary		
		1554, 1556 Wakefield Burgess Court records containing references to Corpus Christi play
1558–1603 Elizabeth I		1560 *A Play of Robin Hood for May Games* pub. 1569 Last performance of York plays 1575 Last performance of Chester plays 1575–1612 Corpus Christi play at Kendal, Westmorland

1542
Hall's *Chronicle*
1543
More's *History of Richard III* pub.

1549
First Book of Common
Prayer

Reigns	Public events	Drama and dramatic records
		1576 Diocesan Court of High Commission at York prohibits Wakefield plays; Burbage builds The Theatre: first permanent theatre building in England
	1577–80 Drake's voyage round the world	1580 Last performance of Coventry plays 1583 Stage plans for first and second days of Lucerne Passion play
	1588 Spanish Armada	
1603–25 James I		1609 David Rogers' *Breviary of Chester* (in two versions) gives account of pageant-wagons at Chester and includes a late copy of Chester Banns 1610–25 A fragmentary cycle of 18 Old Testament pageants ('the Stoneyhurst pageants')
1625–49 Charles I		1639 Last performance of Corpus Christi plays in Kilkenny, Ireland

Abbreviations used in the footnotes

Baker, *Digby Plays*	Donald C. Baker, John L. Murphy and Louis B. Hall, Jr (eds), *The Late Medieval Religious Plays of Bodleian MSS Digby 133 and E Museo 160* (Oxford, EETS, 1982)
Block	K. S. Block (ed.), *Ludus Coventriae* (London, EETS, 1923)
Chambers	E. K. Chambers, *The Mediaeval Stage*, 2 vols (Oxford, 1903)
Craig	Hardin Craig, *Two Corpus Christi Plays* (London, EETS, 1902, 2nd edn, 1957)
EETS	Early English Texts Society
ELN	*English Language Notes*
Hardison	O. B. Hardison, Jr, *Christian Rite and Christian Drama in The Middle Ages* (Baltimore, Md, 1965)
Kolve	V. A. Kolve, *The Play Called Corpus Christi* (London, 1966)
LSE	*Leeds Studies in English*
MED	*Middle English Dictionary*
METh	*Medieval English Theatre*

MLR	*Modern Language Review*
MP	*Modern Philology*
MSC	*Malone Society Collections*
NCPF	Norman Davis (ed.), *Non-Cycle Plays and Fragments* (London, EETS, 1970)
OED	*Old English Dictionary*
PMLA	*Publications of the Modern Language Association of America*
REED, Chester	Lawrence M. Clopper (ed.), *Records of Early English Drama: Chester* (Toronto, 1979)
REED, Coventry	R. W. Ingram (ed.), *Records of Early English Drama: Coventry* (Toronto and Buffalo, N.Y., 1981)
REED, York	Alexandra F. Johnston and Margaret Rogerson (eds), *Records of Early English Drama: York*, 2 vols (Toronto, 1978)
RORD	*Research Opportunities in Renaissance Drama*
Salter	F. M. Salter, *Mediaeval Drama in Chester* (Toronto, 1955).
SP	*Studies in Philology*
TN	*Theatre Notebook*
Wickham	Glynne Wickham, *Early English Stages 1300–1660*: I (*1300–1576*), II, Pts 1 and 2 (*1576–1660*), and III (*Plays and Their Makers to 1576*) (London, 1959, 1963, 1972, and 1981)
Young	Karl Young, *The Drama of the Medieval Church*, 2 vols (Oxford, 1933)

I The staging of medieval drama

A. C. Cawley

Good speeche fine playes with Apparell comlye

Chester Banns 1608–9

1 Introduction

This account of medieval staging is concerned mainly with the religious
and moral drama of medieval England. It attempts to give a conspectus
of the different types of staging, to indicate how the Corpus Christi plays
in general were organized, to study the production of one particular Corpus
Christi pageant (*The Purification of Mary*) at Chester and Coventry, and
to examine the evidence for the presentation of the Wakefield plays.
Throughout the chapter an emphasis is laid on the evidence of medieval
documents and iconography.

Religious plays in the vernacular held the interest of all sections of English
society for more than two centuries. At one end of the social scale they
earned the praise of King Henry VII, who saw and 'much commended'
the Coventry plays in 1493.[1] At the other end of the scale they served as
a kind of *biblia pauperum* and, as far as one old man at Cartmel in 1644
was concerned, were the only source of his knowledge of Christ:

> 'Oh, sir,' said he, 'I think I heard of that man you speak of once in
> a play at Kendall, called Corpus-Christ's play, where there was a man

[1] Chambers, II, 358; *REED, Coventry*, 77.

on a tree and blood run down, &c.' And afterwards he professed he could not remember that he ever heard of salvation by Jesus, but in that play.[1]

It is to the old man's credit that the dramatization of the Crucifixion had made such a strong impression on him. But the villains of religious drama also made an impression; they insinuated themselves into the language of the people, so that Chaucer's Miller could cry out 'in Pilates voys',[2] and J. Whetley writing to John Paston in 1478 could say sarcastically of the Duke of Suffolk: 'ther was never no man that playd Herrod in Corpus Crysty play better and more agreable to hys pageaunt then he dud [did].'[3] Even today we can still play the devil and out-Herod Herod.

In view of the wide appeal of the religious plays, it is reasonable to assume that the medieval theatre-goer found them entertaining as well as edifying, dramatically interesting as well as soul-saving. It can also be assumed that the staging of the plays, elementary though it may seem by modern illusionistic standards, was adequate enough to embody the dramatic qualities of the plays in appropriate spectacle, sound, and action.

These assumptions would hardly be tenable if there were evidence that medieval men and women were content to accept a lower standard in dramatic art than in the other arts. However, the evidence seems to point the other way: we know that precautions were taken to prevent bad acting (see p. 38), and that penalties were imposed if the production of a play fell below the required standard. So Glynne Wickham is surely right to be indignant that

> no one has seen fit to credit mediaeval actors and technicians with a mental age of more than seven. Quaint, primitive, naive, childish, simple: we are told they were all of this. Yet they were men and women like ourselves, who built cathedrals, stained glass, painted frescoes, illuminated manuscripts, wove tapestry, composed music, all of a design and taste and skill in execution which are envied and admired today. Why, then, in their theatre should they have been so cretinous and inept as to deserve the patronizing and at times contemptuous epithets so liberally bestowed on them by posterity?[4]

---

[1] I. D'Israeli, *Curiosities of Literature*, 13th edn (London, 1843), 539.

[2] *Miller's Prologue*, 3124. Jean Palsgrave, *L'Eclaircissement de la Langue Française* (1530), ed. F. Génin (Paris, 1852), 837, has 'In a pylates voyce, *a haulte voyx*'. See R. E. Parker, 'Pilates Voys', *Speculum*, XXV (1950), 237–44.

[3] *Paston Letters and Papers of the Fifteenth Century*, Pt II, ed. Norman Davis (Oxford, 1976), 426.

[4] Wickham, I, 151.

The drama, if its staging is taken into consideration, can be *seen* to have affinities in choice and treatment of subject with the other visual arts of the Middle Ages. Without going into the vexed problem of which influenced which, we can recognize that these arts, especially of the fourteenth to early sixteenth centuries, help us to see religious drama as medieval man must have seen it. The art historians have discovered numerous visual counterparts to the properties, costumes, and effects indicated in the text and stage directions of medieval plays or in civic and ecclesiastical records. No one can begin to visualize Hell-Mouth who has not looked at the monstrous head on the right of the Valenciennes miniature (Plate 1) or at the gaping jaws on the Carcassonne alabaster panel of the Harrowing of Hell.[1] The grotesque masks worn by stage devils,[2] the feathered tights of angels, the 'furres fyne' of the Doctors (Plate 2), the horned head-dress of a woman of fashion, and the workaday costume of Noah and his wife – all these details are best seen through the eyes of the medieval artist in painted window, roof boss, or misericord.

But medieval drama also makes use of the speaking and singing voice and of instrumental music; these, too, are part of its total staging. In order to do justice to the drama of medieval England, a modern reader must try to recapture some of its visual and sound effects, and be deliberately curious about the contribution they make to the dramatic interest of the text.

---

[1] W. L. Hildburgh, 'English alabaster carvings as records of the medieval religious drama', *Archaeologia*, XCIII (1949), 67–8.

[2] Masks ('vesernes') for three devils, each mask bearing two faces, are specified in an inventory of the properties of the York Mercers' Doomsday pageant. For this important document see Alexandra F. Johnston and Margaret Dorrell, 'The Doomsday pageant of the York Mercers, 1433', *LSE*, n.s., V (1971), 29–45; also *REED, York*, I, 55.

2 Symbolism of the medieval theatre

It is of first importance to realize that medieval staging was symbolic rather than realistic. This does not mean that the medieval producer was barred from attempting realistic effects; but it does mean that medieval staging should not be thought of as simply a primitive precursor of modern realistic staging. The medieval theatre readily invites the imagination to see it as a symbol of the universe in miniature. It embraces Heaven, Hell and Middle Earth, and the dramatic action moves freely between them.

The 'stage as universe' is seen most clearly in relation to a fixed playing area, and especially the circular playing area represented by the Cornish 'round'. In this type of theatre, the east is traditionally associated with God or Heaven, the north with Belial or Hell, so that (looking towards the east) Hell is always to the left of Heaven.

Although the location of Heaven and Hell in the east and north respectively is traditional, this tradition does not derive from the liturgy, where positional symbolism requires Heaven to be on the left (that is, north) as we face the high altar in the east, while Hell is on the right (that is, south).[1] The relative positions of Heaven and Hell in the medieval circular theatre

[1] See Hardison, 50.

are, however, reminiscent of a medieval *mappa mundi*, where the known habitable world is represented diagrammatically as a circle, with the east often shown at the top of the map and the north on the left. A comparison of the fourteenth-century *mappa mundi* (Plate 3) with the staging plans of the Cornish *Origo mundi*, *c*.1375 (Plate 4) and *The Castle of Perseverance*, 1400–25 (Plate 5) will illustrate the parallelism.

The resemblance between map and plans is strengthened by the location of the east at the top of the *mappa mundi*, corresponding to Heaven (*Celum*) at the top of the Cornish plan; by the double circle, representing the surrounding 'River of Ocean' on the map and the 'water about the place' on the *Castle* plan; and by the central position of the castellated Jerusalem on the map and of the Castle of Perseverance on the plan of the *Castle*.

In short, there are similarities between a typical *mappa mundi* and the staging plans for the Cornish plays and *The Castle of Perseverance*. Whether or not they have been influenced by *mappae mundi*, at least it can be said that the 'geographical' features of the plans heighten the effectiveness of their stage-as-universe symbolism. Fittingly, they are cosmic plans for actions which reach from the Creation to the Judgement, or from birth to death and beyond. 'The medieval map-maker was interested first in providing a guide to readers of Biblical history';[1] the medieval religious playwright was similarly motivated.

[1] G. R. Crone, *The Hereford World Map* (London, 1949), 5.

3 Different types of staging

(i) The church as theatre

The earliest Latin liturgical drama had the church as a theatre: more precisely, the original Easter dialogue was mimed, intoned and sung in the chancel of the church. The oldest of all tenth-century texts which both gives the words and describes the actions of the *Visitatio Sepulchri* (Visit to the Sepulchre) dialogue is that preserved in the *Regularis Concordia* of St Ethelwold (*c*.965), a monastic code for Benedictine religious houses in England. This dialogue, which was dramatized at the end of matins on Easter Sunday, has been described as 'our earliest surviving music–drama, with costumes, properties, and careful directions as to action and gesture':[1]

> While the third lesson is being read, four of the brethren shall vest, one of whom, wearing an alb as though for some different purpose, shall enter and go stealthily to the place of the 'sepulchre' and sit there quietly, holding a palm in his hand. Then, while the third respond is being sung, the other three brethren, vested in copes and holding

[1] W. L. Smoldon, 'Liturgical drama', in Dom Anselm Hughes (ed.), *Early Medieval Music up to 1300* (London, 1955; rev. 1961), 181.

thuribles in their hands, shall enter in their turn and go to the place of the 'sepulchre', step by step, as though searching for something. Now these things are done in imitation of the angel seated on the tomb and of the women coming with perfumes to anoint the body of Jesus. When, therefore, he that is seated shall see these three draw nigh, wandering about as it were and seeking something, he shall begin to sing softly and sweetly, *Quem quaeritis*. As soon as this has been sung right through, the three shall answer together, *Ihesum Nazarenum*. Then he that is seated shall say *Non est hic. Surrexit sicut praedixerat. Ite, nuntiate quia surrexit a mortuis*. At this command the three shall turn to the choir saying *Alleluia. Resurrexit Dominus*. When this has been sung he that is seated, as though calling them back, shall say the antiphon *Venite et videte locum*, and then, rising and lifting up the veil, he shall show them the place void of the Cross and with only the linen in which the Cross had been wrapped. Seeing this the three shall lay down their thuribles in that same 'sepulchre' and, taking the linen, shall hold it up before the clergy; and, as though showing that the Lord was risen and was no longer wrapped in it, they shall sing this antiphon: *Surrexit Dominus de sepulchro*. They shall then lay the linen on the altar.

When the antiphon is finished the prior, rejoicing in the triumph of our King in that He had conquered death and was risen, shall give out the hymn *Te Deum laudamus*, and thereupon all the bells shall peal.[1]

The setting is the chancel: the localities referred to are the altar at the eastern end of the chancel, 'the place of the sepulchre' (a curtained part of the altar), and the choir where the clergy are.

The most important property is the Easter sepulchre ('a representation as it were of a sepulchre, hung about with a curtain').[2] Other properties are the palm held by the brother acting the part of the angel, the thuribles carried by the brethren impersonating the three Marys, and the linen in which the Cross representing the crucified Christ had been wrapped.

The costumes mentioned are the alb for the angel and the copes for the three Marys. So we see that the brother who acts the part of the angel is

---

[1] T. Symons (ed. and tr.), *Regularis Concordia* (London, 1953), 49–50. The Latin text translated above is given by Karl Young, *The Drama of the Medieval Church*, 2 vols (Oxford, 1933), I, 249 (with a facsimile facing p. 250). The *Visitatio Sepulchri* dialogue printed in italic in the above extract is in a slightly abbreviated form. A similar but rather fuller version is found in the eleventh-century *Winchester Troper*, ed. W. H. Frere, Henry Bradshaw Society, VIII (London, 1894), 17 (with a facsimile); see also Young, I, 587.

[2] Symons, *Regularis Concordia*, 44.

distinguished by his white vestment and by the palm he holds, while the other three brethren are distinguished by their copes and thuribles.

The singing serves to mark the beginning, climax and end of this ceremony. The words of the angel's opening question are sung 'softly and sweetly', the dialogue which follows is apparently spoken or intoned, and then the three Marys, singing together, once more declare the Resurrection. The ceremony ends with the singing of *Te Deum laudamus* and with the sudden pealing of the bells after their silence during Holy Week.

There are several movements by the actors towards the sepulchre. The angel goes to the place of the sepulchre as unobtrusively as possible. The three Marys make their way to the sepulchre 'step by step, as though searching for something'. After the angel has dismissed them with the command to announce Christ's Resurrection, they turn to the choir and say that the Lord has risen. Then the angel summons them back in order to convince them that the Lord has indeed risen from the dead: this he does by drawing aside the veil of the sepulchre and calling attention to the absence of the Cross but not of the linen in which it had been wrapped. Thus the three Marys are shown advancing to the sepulchre, withdrawing from it to make their first announcement of the Resurrection, and returning again at the angel's command. The final movement brings them to the altar itself, on which they lay the grave-cloths of the risen Christ.

It is not too fanciful to imagine that these repeated movements towards the altar symbolize the culmination of faith in three human beings upon hearing the news of the Resurrection. Their search for the body of the crucified Christ ends in the discovery that he has risen from the dead; their first acceptance of the angel's message is confirmed by their being shown the empty tomb; the strength of their faith, expressed in song, finally takes them from the sepulchre to the altar, where the whole plan of redemption is renewed each day in the drama of the Mass 'through the re-creation of the "life, death, and resurrection" of Christ'.[1]

Already in this miniature music-drama, bounded by altar, sepulchre and choir, one can observe certain conventions of staging which underlie all later forms of medieval stage practice. One of these conventions is the use of symbols of locality (here a curtained part of the altar to represent Christ's tomb) known as *loca* and, at various times, as *domus*, *aedes*, *sedes*, *tenti*, *pulpita*, *lieux*, *estals*, *mansions*, 'houses', or 'scaffolds'. Another is the use of the ground space surrounding the symbol of locality as a neutral acting

---

[1] Hardison, 39.

area, known as the *platea* or *placea* or, in English, 'place'. A third is the
movement of the actors towards or away from the symbol of locality; this
may be a physical journey or, as in the Easter play, a journey of the spirit
as well. No less important than these conventions of staging is the close
connection between 'actors' and 'audience': here the audience is the clergy
seated in the choir to whom the three Marys turn once to announce the
Resurrection and again to display the empty grave-linen. This is a fairly
simple production, but even in the later and more elaborate forms of
medieval staging the conventions remain the same. They are the conventions
of an emblematic, non-illusionistic stage.

(ii) Outside the church

In the words of Professor F. M. Salter, 'the church was never designed as
a theatre; and performances within it must always have been difficult for
the whole audience to see. The reasonable thing to do was to move the
liturgical play outside to the great west door and place it on stands. That
was done.'[1] Although this is the traditional view of what happened, the fact
is that there are examples from France of quite elaborately staged liturgical
plays within the church. One of these is the *Presentation of the Virgin Mary
in the Temple*, acted at Avignon in 1385, for which detailed stage directions
have survived.[2] Whatever difficulties were encountered in staging the play
were overcome by careful organization, including a skilful use of both choir
and nave. Apart from lavish spectacles of this sort, it is questionable
whether liturgical plays in general were intended to be seen by large
audiences, even though the reference in the *Regularis Concordia* to the value
of dramatic ceremonies in strengthening the faith of 'unlearned common
persons and neophytes'[3] may imply an audience of some size. In other
words, it is not at all certain that the increasing length and elaborateness
of dramatic liturgical sequences or the audience's difficulty in seeing and
hearing them were factors which forced them to be produced outside the
church. It seems just as likely that open-air production was a method
devised for presenting *vernacular* plays to the people at large. According
to this view, the first vernacular religious plays were not liturgical plays

[1] Salter, 8.
[2] Grace Frank, *The Medieval French Drama* (Oxford, 1954; corrected 1967), 64.
[3] Symons, *Regularis Concordia*, 44.

driven out of church by lack of space or vision inside, and simultaneously translated into the vernacular. Rather they were written as vernacular plays for open-air presentation to the laity, while the liturgical plays remained where they had always been – inside the church – and continued to be acted there until as late as the sixteenth century.

The earliest vernacular plays to have survived are the twelfth-century *Jeu d'Adam (Ordo representacionis Ade)* and *La Seinte Resureccion*, both written in Anglo-Norman. The first of these was probably intended for staging in front of a church;[1] there is some doubt about *La Seinte Resureccion*, which has 'no reference indicating that it was performed in or near a church'.[2]

The *Adam* play is in three sections: the first dramatizes the story of Adam and Eve, the second that of Cain and Abel, and the third is a *Prophetae* in which figures from the Old Testament foretell the coming of Christ. Fortunately, the text has comprehensive stage directions in Latin which describe not only the setting of the action but the costumes, expressions and movements of the actors, and even their manner of speaking. The play begins with the following stage direction:

> Paradise shall be constructed on a raised place, with curtains and silk hangings surrounding it at such a height that the persons who are in Paradise can be seen from the shoulders upwards; there shall be ferns and sweet scented flowers and varied trees with fruit hanging from them, so that it appears a very pleasant place. Then shall come the Saviour wearing a dalmatic, and Adam and Eve shall take their places before him, Adam wearing a red tunicle, but Eve in the white garments proper to a woman, with a white silk headdress. And they shall both stand before the Figure, Adam however nearer, with a calm expression and Eve more humbly. And let Adam be carefully instructed when he is to speak, that he reply neither too soon nor too late. Not only he, but all the actors shall be so taught that they speak calmly and with gestures suited to what they are saying. And in the verse they shall neither add nor omit a syllable but pronounce all clearly and say in proper order what they have to say. Whoever names Paradise shall point to it with his hand.[3]

[1] W. Noomen, 'Le *Jeu d'Adam*: Étude descriptive et analytique', *Romania*, 89 (1968), 190–3, argues in support of performance inside a church.

[2] Hardison, 254.

[3] P. Studer (ed.), *Le Mystère d'Adam* (Manchester, 1918; repr. 1962), 1; English translation by Lynette R. Muir, in *Proceedings of the Leeds Philosophical and Literary Society, Literary and Historical Section*, XIII, Pt V, 166. See also Lynette R. Muir's *Liturgy and Drama in the Anglo-Norman Adam*, Medium Ævum Monographs, n.s., III (Oxford, 1973).

Grace Frank, in her account of the staging of this play, imagines that the church itself symbolized Heaven, with 'a raised place' outside the church representing the earthly paradise. From this raised place Adam and Eve descend after the fall to the level of the audience, which was also the level of the *infernus* from which the demons emerge to claim their first human victims:

> Then comes the Devil with three or four demons carrying iron chains and fetters, which they put round the necks of Adam and Eve. Some push and some pull them towards Hell. Others come to meet them, rejoicing in their damnation. Some point at them, then throw themselves on them and drag them into Hell. A great smoke rises and there are noisy rejoicings and a clattering of pots and pans so that it can be heard outside. After a time the demons come out and run about [*discurrentes per plateas*] but others stay in Hell.[1]

A point of interest in the staging is the positioning of Heaven and Hell, both of which seem to have been fairly elaborate structures, even at this early date. Almost certainly Heaven was placed to the left and Hell to the right of the acting area as seen by the audience. This positional symbolism may have derived from the placing and movement of the clergy during Mass – the left side of the altar (from the point of view of the congregation) being associated with Heaven, the right side with Hell (see p. 6).

The earliest account of a churchyard performance in England is of an Easter play performed *c.*1220 outside Beverley Minster. It is worth quoting for its own sake and also because it might, at least on chronological grounds, be a description of a performance of *La Seinte Resureccion*:

> It happened one summer in the churchyard of St John's church, on the north side, there was a representation as usual by players [*larvatorum*, masked performers] of the Lord's Ascension in words and acting. A large crowd of both sexes assembled, led there by different impulses, some by mere pleasure and wonder, others for the holy purpose of exciting their religious feelings. As the crowd gathered in a thick ring, many, especially short people, went into the church; to pray or to look at the pictures, or by some form of amusement to while away the day. Some youths when they got inside, happened to find a door half open which gave access to the steps up to the top of the walls. With boyish light-heartedness they ran up and went on to the vaults and galleries [the clerestory and triforium] on the top of the church, to get, I suppose, through the lofty windows of the towers or any holes there might be

[1] Studer, *Adam*, 29; Muir's translation, 183.

in the stained glass windows, a better view of the persons and gestures of the players, and to hear the dialogue more easily, like Zaccheus when he climbed up the sycamore tree. Someone however told the sextons what the youths were doing, and as they were afraid the boys would make holes in the windows for the sake of seeing the performers, they at once gave chase, and by dint of heavy blows made them go back. But some of the boys, seeing the punishment inflicted on their companions, to avoid falling into the hands of their pursuers fled to the upper parts, and climbed beyond the great cross then placed by St Martin's altar [i.e. on the rood-loft at the entrance to the choir]. One of them, looking down, placed his foot on a block of stone which suddenly gave way, and fell with a loud crash on the stone pavement, and was broken into fragments. The boy, frightened at the noise, lost his foothold and fell to the ground and for some time lay senseless and as if dead. The bystanders wept, the parents tore their hair and screamed. But God did not suffer His church, dedicated in the honour of Him and His confessor, to be polluted by shedding of human blood; but wishing it to enjoy greater sanctity for the future, and at the same time to give testimony to the truth, which was then being shown in the representation of the Resurrection, in the sight of all those present raised up the youth supposed to be dead, whole, without the smallest injury in any part of his body. Thus it happened that those who could not through the multitude of people be present at the representation outside the church, saw a more marvellous proof of the Resurrection inside; and not only of the Resurrection, but also of the Lord's passion.[1]

(iii) The 'round': place-and-scaffold presentation

The 'rounds' or circular theatres, in which the Cornish plays and *The Castle of Perseverance* were staged, seem to belong to the tradition of the Roman amphitheatre. In France there were 'some play-houses in the form of a circus, often in the remains of a Roman amphitheatre (as at Douai and

---

[1] *Historians of the Church of York* (Rolls Series 71), I, 328; English translation by A. F. Leach, 'Some English plays and players, 1220–1548', *An English Miscellany Presented to Dr Furnivall* (Oxford, 1901), 206–7. See also R. M. Wilson, *The Lost Literature of Medieval England* (London, 1952), 216.

Bourges)';[1] and it is possible that these theatres were used for the production of secular as well as religious drama. In England, apart from the Cornish rounds which have survived at St Just and Perranzabuloe, there are the remains of similar constructions in other parts of the country. One of the most interesting of these is King Arthur's Round Table near Penrith in Cumbria (Plate 6). This earthwork is described by Stukeley (1776) as follows:

> At the conflux of the rivers Louther and Eimont there is a remarkable curiosity, that illustrates the method of the religious solemnities of the old Britons, as much as any I have seen. Upon the edge of the Louther, where the bridge now passes it, is a delicate little plain, of an oblong form, bounded on the other side by a natural declivity: this is used to this day for a country rendezvous, either for sports or military exercises, shooting with bows, &c. On this plain stands the antiquity commonly called King Arthur's Round Table, and supposed to be used for tilts and tournaments: it is a circle inclosed with a ditch, and that with a *vallum*. At first sight we may see that it was intended for sports, but not on horseback, because much too little: the *vallum* on the outside lies sloping inward with a very gradual declivity, on purpose for spectators to stand around it; and it would hold at least 10,000 people. The outside of the *vallum* is pretty steep: it was high originally, as may be seen now in some parts; but it is worn down, as being by the side of the common road; and the inhabitants carry it away to mend the highways withal. There are two entrances into the *area*, north and south, or nearly so: one end is inclosed into a neighbouring pasture: the *area* had a circle within, somewhat higher in elevation than the other. The outer verge of the *vallum* is a circle of 300 foot: the composition of it is intirely coggles and gravel, dug out of the ditch.[2]

The Round Table is similar to the Cornish rounds described a few years earlier by William Borlase (1754), although the ditch of the Cornish amphitheatre is *outside* the embankment:

> In these continued Rounds, or Amphitheatres of stone...the Britans did usually assemble to hear plays acted...these are call'd with us in

---

[1] R. S. Loomis and Gustave Cohen, 'Were there theatres in the twelfth and thirteenth centuries?', *Speculum*, xx (1945), 98.

[2] W. Stukeley, *Itinerarium Curiosum* (London, 1776), II, 43, quoted by W. Atkinson, 'On some earthworks near Eamont Bridge', *Transactions of the Cumberland and Westmorland Antiquarian and Archaeological Society*, VI (1883), 453–5.

Cornwall (where we have great numbers of them) *Plân an guare*; viz. the level place, or Plain of sport and pastime. The benches round were generally of Turf.... We have one whose benches are of Stone, and the most remarkable Monument of this kind which I have yet seen; it is near the church of St Just, Penwith; now somewhat disfigured by the injudicious repairs of late years, but by the remains it seems to have been a work of more than usual labour, and correctness.... It was an exact circle of 126 feet diameter; the perpendicular height of the bank, from the area within, now, seven feet; but the height from the bottom of the ditch without, ten feet at present, formerly more. The seats consist of six steps, fourteen inches wide, and one foot high, with one on the top of all, where the Rampart is about seven feet wide.[1]

It was in such a round that plays in the Cornish language were acted, possibly from the late fourteenth century until the sixteenth century. The Cornish biblical plays are in three parts, *The Origin of the World*, *The Passion of our Lord*, and *The Resurrection*, which form a sequence known as the *Ordinalia*, to be acted on three consecutive days. Five plans have survived, one for each day of the trilogy and two for the *Life of Meriasek*, the patron saint of Camborne.[2]

It will be seen from Plate 4 that the plan of *The Origin of the World* (*Origo Mundi*) consists of two concentric circles, between which the names of some of the principal characters and localities are written (in Latin) and distributed round the circumference roughly according to the eight principal points of the compass.

F. E. Halliday and Eleanor Prosser have both attempted to reconstruct the staging of the Cornish plays, and in doing so they have used the plans together with the stage directions, which are very full and informative.[3]

[1] William Borlase, *Observations on the Antiquities, Historical and Monumental, of the County of Cornwall* (Oxford, 1754), 195–6.

[2] See E. Norris (ed. and tr.), *The Ancient Cornish Drama*, 2 vols (Oxford, 1859) (quotations are from this edition); W. Stokes (ed. and tr.), *The Life of Saint Meriasek* (London, 1872); R. Morton Nance, 'The *Plen an Gwary* or Cornish Playing-Place', *Journal of the Royal Institution of Cornwall*, XXIV (1935), 190–211; G. E. Wellwarth, 'Methods of production in the mediaeval Cornish drama', *Speech Monographs*, XXIV (1957), 212–18; David C. Fowler, 'The date of the Cornish *Ordinalia*', *Mediaeval Studies*, XXIII (1961), 91–125; Robert Longsworth, *The Cornish Ordinalia: Religion and Dramaturgy* (Cambridge, Mass., 1967), 6; M. Harris (tr.), *The Cornish Ordinalia: A Medieval Dramatic Trilogy* (Washington, DC, 1969); N. Denny, 'Area staging and dramatic quality in the Cornish Passion Play', in N. Denny (ed.), *Medieval Drama*, Stratford-upon-Avon Studies 16 (London, 1973), 124–53.

[3] F. E. Halliday (ed. and tr.), *The Legend of the Rood* (London, 1955), 22 ff.; Eleanor Prosser, *Drama and Religion in the English Mystery Plays: A Re-evaluation* (Stanford, Calif., 1961), 47 ff.

The eight fixed stations round the *platea* or central plain were built-up stages, called *tenti* in the manuscripts. The audience stood or sat on the turf or stone steps surrounding the plain, except at the eight stations where the *tenti* or scaffolds were erected. Some scenes were played on these raised stages, but a lot of the action also took place towards the middle of the plain, so that all the spectators would have a good chance of seeing and hearing. Other scaffolds were no doubt erected in the plain: on the first day's performance, for example, the *platea* must have been used for scaffolds representing Paradise, the Ark, the Temple, and other important localities not included among the eight fixed stations round the circumference.

The stage directions indicate that the actors assigned to the fixed stages would step down into the plain whenever necessary. For example, when Solomon, seated on his throne, has made his counsellor 'bishop in the temple' (*Origin of the World*, 2601), the newly made bishop goes down from Solomon's scaffold to the plain where the temple stands:

> *hic descendit episcopus et transiet ad templum.* (2622.1)
> [Here the bishop goes down, and shall cross over to the temple.]

Later, after his meeting with Maximilla, the bishop goes up to his own scaffold:

> *hic ascendit episcopus in tentum suum.* (2660.1)
> [Here the bishop goes up to his tent.]

Then he commands the Torturers to come forth and deal with Maximilla. At this point, the Torturers presumably leave their own scaffold, where they have been waiting, go down to the *platea*, and there drag Maximilla out of the temple and beat her to death.

It will be seen that the distinction between symbols of locality (*tenti*) and neutral acting area (*platea*) – a distinction already made in the tenth-century Easter play – is still operative. Moreover, the *tenti* were all visible together, around or in the plain, so that it was possible to arrange for quick changes of action from one locality to another.

The Cornish theatre (stage and auditorium), as outlined above, is similar in general plan and in details to the theatre used for the staging of *The Castle of Perseverance*, as reconstructed by Southern.[1] Southern had the Cornish rounds very much in mind when he reconstructed the kind of theatre used for *The Castle of Perseverance* from the plan on the last page

[1] Richard Southern, *The Medieval Theatre in the Round: A Study of the Staging of 'The Castle of Perseverance' and Related Matters* (London, 1957; 2nd edn, 1975). This book has generated many articles of comment and criticism (see Bibliography, p. 309).

of the early fifteenth-century manuscript in which this moral play is preserved.

The plan for the staging of *The Castle of Perseverance* is shown in Plate 5. Like the three plans for the Cornish *Ordinalia*, the *Castle* plan consists of two concentric circles enclosing a central 'place'. The names of five of the principal characters are written outside the circles; north, south, east and west are identified respectively with Belial, Flesh, God, and World, while the north-east belongs to Coveytyse (Covetousness). (Compare the Cornish plan for the *Origo Mundi*, which has eight names written between the two circles; although the four cardinal points are not indicated in the Cornish plan, Heaven and Hell have the same positions in relation to each other as God and Belial in the *Castle* plan.) The localities assigned to the five characters are called 'scaffolds'. The words written between the two circles inform us that a ditch filled with water, or a strong fence, should surround the place, and that not too many 'stytelerys' (marshals) should be within the place. There is a picture of a castle in the centre, and the various legends grouped round the castle inform us that (1) this is the Castle of Perseverance which stands in the middle of the place, and no one shall be allowed to sit near it, in order not to obstruct the view; (2) Mankind's bed shall be under the Castle; (3) the cupboard of Coveytyse shall be at the foot of the bed.

With the Cornish rounds as a model, Southern imagines the whole central place to be surrounded by a bank with a ditch on the outside. He estimates the central place to have been possibly 110 ft across, which is something less than the 126 ft diameter of the St Just round. Further, on the analogy of the Cornish round, he believes that a large part of the audience sat in tiered rows on the bank round the *placea* or central place.

The text and stage directions of *The Castle of Perseverance* enable him to visualize the movements of the actors between the scaffolds and the place. Thus of the three references to the *placea* in the Latin stage directions, two associate *placea* with descending:

> *Tunc descendit in placeam pariter.* (490.1)
> [Then he descends together [with Folly] into the place.]
> *Tunc descendent in placeam.* (1968.1)
> [Then they will descend into the place.]

Again, there are four directions indicating ascent (614.1, 3228.1, 3585.1, 3593.1), e.g.:

> *Tunc ascendet Humanum Genus ad Mundum.* (614.1)
> [Then Humanum Genus will ascend to the World.]

As Southern points out, these directions make it safe to infer that 'a direction to *ascend* means that the player is to go up from the Place to a scaffold; and conversely, therefore, that a direction to *descend* means that the actor is to go down from a scaffold into the Place'.[1]

Southern's book is so knowledgeable and persuasive that it would be easy to forget that much of his reconstruction of the kind of theatre and staging technique used in the production of *The Castle of Perseverance* is learned conjecture based, not on the ground plan for the *Castle* or on its stage directions, but partly on the description of Cornish rounds by Borlase and partly on medieval French miniatures such as the Terence miniature of *c*.1400 (Plate 7) and Fouquet miniature of *c*.1455 (Plate 8). It is the Cornish rounds which give him the possible size of the central place and justify his assumption of a surrounding bank with a ditch outside. (But other rounds, for example, King Arthur's Round Table near Penrith, have the ditch *inside* the bank.) It is the French miniatures which give him the idea of spectators in the place itself and determine his reconstruction of the scaffold as a built-up structure with curtained sides.

One of Southern's assumptions is obviously open to criticism. This is the assumption that a round like the one he has reconstructed would have been made *ad hoc* for each performance of the *Castle* in a different place. He is probably right in believing that this dramatic spectacle was staged by travelling players, who were concerned to prevent the public from seeing the play unless they had paid the admission fee. Hence the enclosing of the acting area, whether by ditch or fence, was a necessity. But the cost of constructing a 110 ft-diameter round with surrounding bank or fence would surely have been excessive. It seems more likely that the players made use of an existing round, which could have served equally for *The Castle of Perseverance* and the Digby *Mary Magdalen* (1480–1520).[2]

(iv) The rectangular acting area

Any sizeable open space in a town could serve as a ready-made *platea* for civic ceremonies and dramatic activities. In Chester, for example, the open space at the High Cross was used as one of the fixed stations for the processional presentation of Corpus Christi pageants. And at Louth in

[1] Southern, *Medieval Theatre in the Round*, 45.
[2] For the staging of *Mary Magdalen* see Baker, *Digby Plays*, xlviii–lii.

1556–7 the corporation paid for a play 'in the Markit stede on corpus christi Day'.[1] Glynne Wickham has suggested that the early sixteenth-century Digby play *The Conversion of St Paul* was performed in a market square.[2] However, there is no English record providing detailed evidence that a market square or place was used for the presentation of a large-scale play involving several different episodes and localities. For such a record we must go to Lucerne, where a part of the text used in the performance of a Passion play in 1583, with minute stage directions added by the director, Renward Cysat, has been preserved, together with two elaborate ground plans, one for each day's performance (Plate 9). This great Passion play, with its three hundred roles, was presented in the Weinmarkt, the most important public square in Old Lucerne. Around the four sides of the quadrangle, and even within the quadrangle, were erected the 'houses' (*Höfe*), each for a specific group of actors; and of these, Heaven was in the east and Hell in the north-west corner (similar to their positions in the performance of the Cornish plays and *The Castle of Perseverance*). The houses could at times serve as stages for action and dialogue, as the stage directions show, but more often the action went on in the *theatrum* or *platea*, that is, the open space between the houses which functioned as the principal stage. The audience of about four thousand people were seated on stands erected against the buildings surrounding the square.[3]

A similar production is illustrated by a sixteenth-century plan for the staging of the Villingen Passion play between 1585 and 1600 (Plate 10).[4] The details of the Lucerne and Villingen productions may possibly provide some clue to the staging of 'the grette playe at Skynners Welle',[5] a biblical play acted by the parish clerks of London. In 1409 this play lasted four days and was watched by Henry IV and his entourage from a scaffold of timber.

---

[1] Stanley J. Kahrl, *Records of Plays and Players in Lincolnshire 1300–1585*, MSC, VIII (1969 [1974]), 84.

[2] 'The staging of saint plays in England', in S. Sticca (ed.), *The Medieval Drama* (Albany, NY, 1972), 99–119. Mary del Villar, 'The staging of *The Conversion of Saint Paul*', TN, xxv (1970–1), 64–8, has argued for performance of this play in a place-and-scaffold theatre, in the round. See the introduction to Baker, *Digby Plays*, xxv–xxx.

[3] See M. Blakemore Evans, *The Passion Play of Lucerne* (New York, 1943), esp. 138 ff. For the text of the play see H. Wyss (ed.), *Das Luzerner Osterspiel*, 3 vols (Bern, 1967).

[4] See A. M. Nagler, *The Medieval Religious Stage: Shapes and Phantoms* (New Haven and London, 1976), 36–47.

[5] Chambers, II, 380.

(v) The 'houses' arranged in a straight line or in a semicircle

The placing of both audience and houses around an oblong place is not basically different from the disposition of audience and scaffolds in the circular theatre. But a different sort of open-air theatre – with a different relationship between stage and audience – is apparently to be seen in the Valenciennes miniature, a contemporary illustration of the stage for the Passion play acted at Valenciennes in 1547 (Plate 1). In this miniature there are twelve houses, ranging from Paradise on the extreme left to Hell on the extreme right, aligned at the back of a raised platform which may have served as an acting area. If this miniature is not completely stylized and inaccurate, the audience must have stood or sat facing the stage, as they do in the modern York Festival production of the Corpus Christi play. The Valenciennes production, it will be noticed, is a late one and the design of the houses is strongly influenced by Renaissance art.

According to Gustave Cohen, a similar arrangement of houses, with Paradise on the extreme left and Hell on the extreme right, as viewed by the audience, was adopted for the eight-day performance of the Passion play acted in the Grand'place of Mons in 1501.[1] Unfortunately, although the two directors' copies (*Abregiés*) and the account-book of the Mons Passion are the most informative documents in existence for the staging of a French Passion play, no ground plan has survived for this performance.

A semicircular arrangement of houses is illustrated by the Fouquet miniature of a scene from the play *Le Martyre de Seinte Apolline* (Plate 8). Authorities such as Cohen and Southern maintain that this miniature shows a performance in a circular theate. They believe that the artist has allowed us to look into only the back half of the theatre, and that the front half, which is hidden from view, contained 'not merely spectators but a further range of actors' scaffolds'.[2] They may well be right. However, the left–right position of Heaven and Hell in the miniature recalls the theatre of Valenciennes rather than the circular theatre, in which Heaven is in the east and Hell in the north (see pp. 6–7). The positioning of Heaven and Hell in the Fouquet theatre therefore seems to weigh against the interpretation of it as a half-revealed amphitheatre.

---

[1] Gustave Cohen, *Le Livre de Conduite du Régisseur et le Compte des Dépenses pour le Mystère de la Passion joué à Mons en 1501* (Strasbourg and Paris, 1925), xliv ff.
[2] Southern, *Medieval Theatre in the Round*, 105.

(vi) Scottish plays and N-town plays

The texts of the medieval religious plays of Scotland are no longer extant, but the external evidence points to some kind of open-air, stationary presentation. It is known that there were play-fields attached to several burghs and that those at Aberdeen, Dundee, Edinburgh and Perth were used for dramatic performances. Thus Lindsay's *Ane Satyre of the Thrie Estaitis* was performed on the play-field at Edinburgh in 1554 before Marie de Lorraine, Queen Regent. On the negative side, there is no clear evidence of a processional play in Scotland, or of the word 'pageant' being used to denote a movable stage.[1]

It is now generally agreed that the N-town plays (otherwise known as the Hegge plays or *Ludus Coventriae*) were produced c.1450–75 in a fixed location on multiple stages, in the manner of the French and German Passion plays. The exact arrangements for the production of this cycle of plays are unknown, but perhaps it was staged on a number of scaffolds side by side, in a line or semicircle before the audience. If Lincoln is indeed one of the places where the N-town plays were sometimes performed, the whole production may have taken place in front of the west entrance to Lincoln Cathedral.[2]

The evidence for stationary, place-and-scaffold presentation of the N-town plays is the internal evidence of text and stage directions. Certain of the plays, including those of the Passion sequence, show a remarkable continuity from one play to another; within each play the action moves quickly from scaffold to place or from scaffold to place to scaffold, and at times there are scenes acted simultaneously on two different scaffolds. The fluidity of the action seems to demand a fixed location for its presentation, with several scaffolds arranged in close proximity to each other, the open space before or between the scaffolds serving as a general acting area.

The detailed stage directions of the first part of the Passion sequence enable us to visualize clearly the multiple staging and simultaneous action in this remarkable series of plays. Six different scaffolds were evidently required for its performance: these were structures on which scenes could be acted, and which the players could go up to from the place or down

[1] See Anna J. Mill, *Mediaeval Plays in Scotland* (Edinburgh and London, 1927), 65, 72, 349.
[2] See Hardin Craig, *English Religious Drama of the Middle Ages* (Oxford, 1955), 276 ff. In the banns of the N-town plays (399) the Secundus Vexillator refers to 'oure pleyn place'. (In this context it is difficult to decide whether 'pleyn' means 'playing' or 'plain, level'.)

from into the place. Eleanor Prosser, who has made an illuminating study of the stage directions of the N-town *Passion*, observes that the 'direction "in the meantime" becomes very significant in our attempts to visualize the play. It appears six times in the *Passion Play*, and five of the six times it undeniably indicates two or more actions which take place concurrently, often with important implications.'[1] A good example of two scaffolds in use simultaneously – with striking dramatic effect – is to be seen when Jesus and his disciples begin the Last Supper in the house of Simon the Leper, while the great ones conspiring to kill him are meeting together in the Council House in 'the myd place'. At this point there is a direction which reads:

> here Crist enteryth into the hous with his disciplis and ete the paschal lomb and *in the mene tyme* the cownsel hous befornseyd schal sodeynly onclose schewyng the buschopys, prestys and jewgys syttyng in here Astat lyche as it were a convocacyone.[2]

The contrast intended and achieved between these two tableaux is the work of an accomplished playwright who makes full use of the stage for which he is writing. It is no exaggeration to describe the N-town cycle as 'a brilliant example of late medieval drama in a highly developed form of staging'.[3]

(vii) The pageant-wagon and processional staging

Some of the most detailed records of medieval drama in England are guild documents from York, Chester, Coventry and Beverley, where the plays are thought by some scholars to have been presented processionally on pageant-wagons.[4] And yet very little is known about the theatrical potential of the wagon stage or about the stations at which the wagons stopped for a performance of the play to be given.

The word 'pageant' itself is ambiguous in medieval documents since it may refer to either the wagon stage or the play acted on it. When it means

[1] Prosser, *Drama and Religion*, 125.
[2] Block, 245.
[3] Kenneth M. Cameron, 'The Lincoln plays at Grantham', Medieval Supplement to *RORD*, x (1967), 150.
[4] Not all students of medieval drama would subscribe to this view; see pp. 58 ff.

'stage' it normally refers to a stage on wheels used in the performance of Corpus Christi plays.[1] But the origins, chronology and geographical distribution of the processional performances of plays on pageant-wagons are still obscure.

The origins could date back at least to 1318, the year when the Festival of Corpus Christi began to be generally celebrated in England, although it should be remembered that the earliest reference so far discovered to English Corpus Christi pageants is in a York document of 1376. Just as the play itself was written in honour of the Feast, so the processional method of presentation may have been suggested by the processional carrying of the Host on Corpus Christi day. At Chester and Wakefield both procession and play originally took place on Corpus Christi day, the play later being transferred to Whitsun. At York they remained together until 1426, when it was agreed to have the play on the vigil of the feast and the procession on Corpus Christi day; notwithstanding, there were many years after 1426 when procession and play were both held on the feast of Corpus Christi.[2]

The chronology of processional presentation in relation to presentation in a fixed location is still a matter for dispute. F. M. Salter has argued that the Chester cycle started life as a single long play, acted continuously in one acting area, 'for the appearance of the Doctor or Interpreter in play after play of the late series suggests an original single work. This single ancestor again suggests stationary performance. At what time this play was broken up, and when it became processional, we do not know; but we do know that individual guilds had their own plays as early as 1422.'[3] This is an interesting possibility, and yet the presence of the Doctor in several of the Chester pageants is flimsy evidence on which to base the presumption of an original single work and so, by inference, of an original stationary performance. At Lincoln, on the other hand, it has been suggested that processional staging gave way to 'staging in the round, probably on the Cathedral grounds'.[4]

The distribution in England of the processional method of staging on

[1] Anne C. Gay, 'The "stage" and staging of the N-town plays', Medieval Supplement to *RORD*, x (1967), 136, reminds us that the presence of wagons is not necessarily a proof of processional staging since there was nothing to prevent wagons from being used as scaffolds in a stationary performance.

[2] See Alexandra F. Johnston, 'The procession and play of Corpus Christi in York after 1426', *LSE*, n.s., VII (1974), 55–62. In 1569 the York city council 'aggreed that Corpus christi play shalbe played this yere on Tewisday in witsone weeke' (*REED, York*, I, 355).

[3] Salter, 45.

[4] Kenneth Cameron and Stanley J. Kahrl, 'The N-town plays at Lincoln', *TN*, xx (1965–6), 68.

pageant-wagons has been investigated by Glynne Wickham, who comes to the conclusion that during the period 1530–70 'there is no evidence that waggon-stages were used...anywhere within a radius of a hundred miles of London'. But, bearing in mind 'the glaring gaps in the records',[1] it may be misleading to base any definite conclusions on these records.

In considering the pageant-wagon stage we are bound to go back to the only contemporary description of the stage on wheels and of the processional method of presentation – that of David Rogers in the *Breviary* of Chester history (1608–9):

> they weare devided into 24 pagiantes acordinge to the companyes of the Cittie, and everye companye broughte forthe theire pagiant which was the cariage or place which they played in. And before these plays there was a man which did ride as I take it upon St Georges daye throughe the Cittie and there published the tyme and the matter of the playes in breeife. They weare played upon mondaye, tuesedaye and wensedaye in whitson weeke. And they firste beganne at the Abbaye gates, and when the firste pagiante was played at the Abbaye gates then it was wheled from thense to pentice at the highe crosse before the maior, and before that was donne the seconde came, and the firste wente into the watergate streete and from thense unto the Bridgestreete, and so one after an other till all the pagiantes weare played appoynted for the firste daye, and so likewise for the seconde and the thirde daye. These pagiantes or carige was a highe place made like a howse with 2 rowmes beinge open on the tope, the lower rowme they apparrelled and dressed them selves, and the higher rowme they played, and they stoode upon vj wheeles. And when they had donne with one cariage in one place they wheled the same from one streete to another, firste from the Abbaye gate to the pentise, then to the watergate streete, then to the bridge streete through the lanes, and so to the estegate streete. And thus they came from one streete to another, kepinge a directe order in everye streete, for before the firste carige was gone from one place the seconde came, and so before the seconde was gone the thirde came, and so till the laste was donne all in order withoute anye stayeinge in anye place, for worde beinge broughte howe everye place [play] was neere doone they came and made noe place to tarye till the laste was played.[2]

---

[1] Wickham, II, Pt 1, 181.

[2] *REED, Chester*, 238–9. (I have slightly modernized the spelling and punctuation.) For David Rogers' use of materials assembled by his father, Archdeacon Robert Rogers (died c.1595), see *Chester*, xxxii.

Several of the details of Rogers' description of the pageant-wagon have been questioned by Salter and others.[1] It is certain, for example, that the carriage was not always 'open on the tope', in the sense of having no roof, but could sometimes be covered in the manner of the Norwich Grocers' pageant (1565): 'A Pageant, that is to saye, a howse of waynskott paynted and buylded on a carte with fowre whelys. A square topp to sett over the sayde howse.'[2]

A late illustration of the pageant car is to be seen in Denis van Alsloot's paintings of the lavishly decorated wagons used in the Brussels 'Triumph' staged for the Archduchess Isabella in 1615 (Plate 11). These tableau cars help us to visualize the Corpus Christi pageant-wagons and suggest, incidentally, that Rogers' description need not be far wrong. For example, some of van Alsloot's cars are 'open on the tope', although the fact that these were cars for staging tableaux without words may explain the absence of a roof (which must have functioned as a sounding-board in the open-air performance of plays as well as housing machinery for the transportation of characters between earth and heaven). Again, the decorated cloths that hide the wheels of the cars can be regarded as making a lower room, which might be used for a variety of purposes (as a green room, or as a reception room for the damned souls after their egress through Hell-Mouth). At any rate, this detail of the curtained wheels is confirmed by the inventory of the properties belonging to the Norwich Grocers (1565), which includes '3 paynted clothes to hang abowte the Pageant'.[3]

It is probably only a matter of time before the accuracy of Rogers' description of the processional method of acting the plays is also called in question. Rogers clearly indicates that the Chester plays were acted in quick succession at different stations, with each pageant waiting in readiness for its predecessor to finish. However, he lays himself open to attack by stating first that there were four stations (Abbey Gates, Pentice, Watergate Street, Bridge Street) and, later, that there were five (with the addition of Eastgate Street). A further complication is that in a late version of the *Breviary* (1622–3) Rogers has the pageants played not at four or five stations but 'in every streete':

> The places where they played them was in every streete. They begane
> first at the Abay gates, and when the firste pagiante was played, it

---

[1] See Salter, 68; *REED, Chester*, lvi; J. Marshall, 'The Chester pageant carriage – how right was Rogers?', *METh*, 1 (1979), 49–55.
[2] N. Davis (ed.), *Non-Cycle Plays and Fragments* (EETS, 1970), xxxv.
[3] ibid.

was wheeled to the highe Crosse before the mayor, and so to every streete, and soe every streete had a pagiant playinge before them at one time till all the pagiantes for the daye appoynted weare played, and when one pagiant was neere ended worde was broughte from streete to streete that soe they might come in place thereof, excedinge orderlye and all the streetes have theire pagiantes afore them all at one time playeinge togeather, to se which playes was great resorte, and also scafoldes and stages made in the streetes in those places where they determined to playe their pagiantes.[1]

Unless we regard this as an abbreviated version, in which the words 'every streete' and 'all the streetes' are to be understood as referring to the streets named in the earlier version, it hardly makes sense; the imagination boggles at the idea of *all* the streets of Chester having their pageants playing together at one and the same time.[2]

Assuming that Rogers knew more or less what he was talking about, we have to admire the organization and careful timing required for this perambulatory method of presenting plays. Not only had the pageants to succeed each other in due order but the timing had to be such that each pageant arrived at a station just before its predecessor had finished playing. At Beverley, where there were seven different places appointed for the performance of the Corpus Christi plays, the twelve Keepers (that is, Governors of the town) were given the task of regulating the succession of pageants at North Bar, the first of the stations; and in 1460 a scaffold was erected for them so that they could sit 'at the North Bar to see and govern the pageants'.[3]

Most historians of medieval drama are bothered about the difficulty of staging a pageant involving several persons and scenes in the confined space of a pageant-wagon. Unfortunately, no one knows how confined it was. Salter has discovered that in 1574 the Tailors' carriage house (that is, the house in which the carriage was stored) was '5 royal virgates long, and $3\frac{1}{2}$ virgates wide'. If the virgate was only a yard (which is by no means certain), we have 'a building 15 feet long by $10\frac{1}{2}$ feet wide'.[4] But this may be an underestimate in view of the measurements – $70\frac{1}{2}$ ft long by $30\frac{1}{2}$ ft wide – of the parcel of land granted in 1434 for the erection of the Coventry Weavers'

[1] *REED, Chester*, 355.
[2] David Mills has suggested to me that Rogers is describing the route taken by the pageants rather than the stations where the plays were acted.
[3] Leach, 'Some English plays and players, 1220–1548', 215.
[4] Salter, 62.

'paiont hows'.[1] It is anyone's guess how big the wagon itself was. Arnold Williams guesses 18 ft long by 8 ft wide; but, remembering those narrow medieval streets, he is afraid he may be erring on the generous side.[2]

Somehow or other the medieval producer had to make an effective acting area out of the confined space at his disposal. There can be no doubt that a man like Thomas Colclow (see p. 40) managed it – but how? Arnold Williams believes that Colclow and his fellow pageant-masters created the space they needed by using the space around the pageant as an extension of the wagon stage: 'the action was not confined to, but only centered in, the pageant stage.'[3] Williams also allows for a second possibility, suggested by Glynne Wickham, that the 'scaffolds' mentioned in the Coventry records were platforms providing 'an additional acting area set adjacent to and level with the cart carrying the *loca* [that is, symbols of locality]'.[4] Yet another possibility is that more than one wagon was used in producing some of the pageants.[5]

In one way or another it was feasible to produce on a wagon stage a pageant like the Chester Painters' play of the Shepherds, which has two *loca* – a hill and a stable. Salter has shown that the Chester Coopers shared their wagon with the Painters (who used it on the first day) and the Skinners. The Coopers themselves had it on the second day to present the Scourging of Christ, while the Skinners used it at the beginning of the third day for the Resurrection. The Skinners' play also needs two *loca* – a *sedes* for Pilate and a sepulchre; the sepulchre, 'with a different exterior appearance, could be the same structure that serves for a mount or hill in the Shepherds Play'.[6] It is surely not accidental that many of the cyclic plays, in common with those of the Chester Painters and Skinners, present

[1] Craig, 108; *REED, Coventry*, 10.
[2] Arnold Williams, *The Drama of Medieval England* (Michigan State University Press, 1961), 98.
[3] ibid.
[4] Wickham, I, 171. See below, p. 45.
[5] I am indebted to Professor Martin Stevens for a reference to two wagons ('both pagyantes') in the York Mercers' records; see *REED, York*, I, 97. For the York Mercers' wagon(s) see: Alexandra F. Johnston and Margaret Dorrell, 'The Doomsday pageant of the York Mercers', *LSE*, n.s., v (1971), 9–34, and 'The York Mercers and their pageant of Doomsday', *LSE*, n.s., vi (1972), 10–35; P. Meredith, 'The development of the York Mercers' pageant waggon', *METh*, I (1979), 5–18; P. Butterworth, 'The York Mercers' pageant vehicle, 1433–1467: wheels, steering, and control', *METh*, I (1979), 72–81.
[6] Salter, 67.

two different localities; just as many, one may suppose, as could be accommodated comfortably on a wagon.[1]

The capacity of the medieval playwright for organizing his symbols of locality in a confined space should not be underestimated; nor should the willingness of a medieval audience to accept these *loca*, despite their close proximity to each other, as different localities which could be journeyed between. It should also be remembered that the open stage between the *loca* may have served as a neutral acting area which could be extended, if necessary, by the use of an adjacent platform, of a second wagon, or of the ground in front of the wagon.

In commenting on the difficulty of erecting elaborate symbols of place in the restricted area of a pageant-wagon, Anderson observes that 'any indications of buildings must have been exceedingly slight'. She finds a parallel in a panel of fifteenth-century glass in St Peter Mancroft, Norwich (Plate 12). Here Herod is seen

> enthroned beneath a canopy which is provided with a low screen, or desk, in front of him, over which the tyrant leans to take an active part in the Massacre of the Innocents. This would have been considered adequate scenery to suggest a palace and curtains could easily have been fixed to the canopy, as on a fourposter bed, which could be drawn when the King was no longer supposed to be present.[2]

Again, the Norwich roof boss showing Christ with the Doctors (Plate 2) illustrates how compactly this biblical episode could be organized, whether the compactness is enforced by the confined space of a roof boss or of a pageant-wagon.

All these devices for utilizing a confined acting area were probably employed at York and Chester. They also have to be borne in mind when discussing the mode of presentation of the Wakefield cycle, which cannot be determined from the meagre evidence of the Wakefield Burgess Court Rolls for 1556 and 1559–60,[3] or from the evidence of text and stage directions. It is doubtful, for example, whether the references in the plays to teams of oxen, journeys on horseback, and the like, can be used as

---

[1] See A. C. Cawley (ed.), *The Wakefield Pageants in the Towneley Cycle* (Manchester, 1958), xxvi.

[2] See M. D. Anderson, *Drama and Imagery in English Medieval Churches* (Cambridge, 1963), 122.

[3] For discussion of the Wakefield Burgess Court Rolls see pp. 52 ff.

evidence of presentation on multiple stages in a large circular acting area. The validity of this kind of evidence rests on the assumption that the pageant-wagon was too small to be used for multiple staging, and the medieval street too narrow and too crowded with spectators to function as an additional acting area.[1] But the truth is that nothing much is known about the 'stations' at which the processional plays were acted. In the absence of evidence to the contrary there is no reason to suppose that they were not properly organized acting areas, with sufficient space kept clear for dramatic action round the wagon or wagons on which the *loca* were placed. Richard Southern has pointed out that a mummers' play like the one belonging to Marshfield in Gloucestershire was both processional and stationary in the sense that it was presented within a circle at four different stations in the intervals of a procession.[2] Whether or not we agree with Southern that the presentation of the mummers' plays influenced the method of presenting the Corpus Christi plays, he at least reminds us that processional presentation becomes stationary during the actual performance of the play; in other words, that 'stationary' need not always be equated with performance in a 'round' or in any single fixed location.

It is sometimes argued that convenience and economy of staging, as well as unity of dramatic effect, would be better served by a performance of all the cyclic plays in one fixed location than by their performance in succession at several different acting stations. This makes good sense, especially from the point of view of a modern producer. At first glance, the processional performance of the Corpus Christi play at York, with its twenty-seven different actors playing the part of Jesus in the twenty-seven different plays in which the part occurs, does seem to be intolerably wasteful and fragmented. However, practical and artistic considerations did not necessarily decide how the plays were performed: tradition and the vested interests of the guilds were likely to be just as important. Moreover, dramatic unity, although reinforced by continuous action in one fixed acting area, does not entirely depend upon this kind of staging. A modern audience watching a processional performance of forty-eight pageants might have trouble in seeing the wood for the trees; but a medieval audience would not have had any difficulty in recognizing the separate pageants as episodes of the complete Christian story, and could not have failed to see 'in these

[1] See Martial Rose (ed.), *The Wakefield Mystery Plays* (London, 1961), 30 ff.
[2] Richard Southern, *The Seven Ages of the Theatre* (London, 1962), 55–7.

small, pageant units the grandeur of God's continuous care for man, and the progress of His plan to redeem him'.[1] An awareness that the individual pageants were not complete in themselves but were parts of the whole play is suggested by the medieval documents, which regularly distinguish between the 'pageants' and the 'Corpus Christi play'.[2]

(viii) Tournaments and royal entries

Although the tournament and royal entry are marginal to this chapter, a brief reference should perhaps be made to some of the points of contact between the staging of these spectacles and the presentation of religious drama. Robert Withington and Glynne Wickham have both stressed the theatrical elements in such entertainments; Wickham, in particular, has shown how much there is to learn from them about the staging technique of the religious plays.[3] The use of circular lists for a tournament like the 'theatre' described in the *Knight's Tale*:

> The circuit a myle was aboute,
> Walled of stoon, and dyched al withoute (1887–8)

recalls the rounds in which the Cornish plays were acted. Again, some of the pageants set up for royal entries may have been similar to the scaffolds used for religious or moral plays performed in a fixed location. In 1486, when Henry VII visited York, he was favoured with a glimpse of Heaven at the entrance to the city:

> at the entre of the Citie and first bar of the same shal be craftelyle conceyvid a place in maner of a heven of grete Joy and Anglicall

---

[1] Kolve, 271.

[2] For example, the distinction made between 'Corpus Christi plaie' and 'Pageant' in the letter sent to Wakefield by the Diocesan Court of High Commission; see p. 37. When 'play' and 'pageant' are paired together, as in 'a pageant and play called Fergus' (*REED, York*, I, 110) or as in 'plaies and pagentes' (below, p. 39), a distinction may sometimes be intended between the play itself and the pageant-wagon on which it was acted. A tendency is observable to replace 'pageant' by 'play' in the sense of a dramatic performance: thus 'pageant' and 'play' are synonymous in 'Litsters pagonn', 'lyster play' (Cawley, *Wakefield Pageants*, xv) and in 'alle the pagentes', 'all the pleys' (Craig, 74). Nevertheless, 'the play' and 'Corpus Christi Play' always refer to the whole cycle of smaller plays or pageants.

[3] Robert Withington, *English Pageantry: An Historical Outline* (Cambridge, Mass., 1918–20; reprinted New York, 1963); Wickham, I, 13–111, 174.

Armony; under the heven shal be a world desolaite, full of treys and floures, in the which shall spryng up a roiall rich rede rose convaide by viace [mechanical device, winch], unto the which rose shall appeyre another rich white rose, unto whome so being togedre all other floures shall lowte [bow] and evidently yeve suffrantie, shewing the rose to be principall of all floures.... And therupon shall come fro a cloude a crowne covering the roses.[1]

There are also parallels to the pageant-wagon of processional religious drama: at a joust held by Henry VIII at Whitehall in 1511 a 'forest' on a car, 26 ft long, 16 ft broad, and 9 ft high, was drawn by a 'lion' and an 'antelope'.[2] The dimensions of this huge car may be compared with the more modest dimensions conjectured by Arnold Williams for the pageant-wagon drawn along narrow medieval streets (see p. 28).

Further, it should be noticed that contemporary descriptions of the elaborate mechanical contrivances used in royal entries are a source of information about the devices employed in staging religious plays. On the occasion of the King's visit to York in 1486, one of the pageants which greeted him showed 'our lady commyng frome hevin and welcome the King in wordes felowing, and therupon ascend ayene into heven with angell sang, and ther schall it snaw [snow] by craft to be made of waffrons [wafers] in maner of snaw'.[3] Martin Stevens has pointed out that this 'paiaunt of thassumptoun of our Lady' (for so it is called in a contemporary account of the King's visit)[4] 'turns out to be that of the Weavers, who regularly performed an Assumption play in the cycle'.[5] As Stevens suggests, the descriptions of pageants in royal entries are especially interesting when these civic pageants are known to have been also Corpus Christi pageants.

(ix) The booth stage

The booth theatre or *théâtre de foire* is defined by Glynne Wickham as a platform 'raised on barrels or trestles for performances in market squares or other open spaces' and used by 'professional minstrels or players on

[1] *REED, York*, I, 139.
[2] *Letters and Papers, Foreign and Domestic, of the Reign of Henry VIII*, II, Pt II, ed. J. S. Brewer (London, 1864), 1494.
[3] *REED, York*, I, 142.
[4] See A. H. Smith, 'A York pageant, 1486', *London Mediaeval Studies*, I (1937–9), 394.
[5] Martin Stevens, 'The staging of the Wakefield plays', Medieval Supplement to *RORD*, XI (1968), 123.

public holidays or at other times of regular general assembly'.[1] Richard
Southern notes that the booth stage, with its raised platform and background
curtain for exits and entrances, and its provision of space behind the curtain
for the actors to change their costume, satisfies several of the requirements
of a professional theatre.[2] A sixteenth-century illustration of this kind of
stage is Pieter Balten's painting of a dramatic performance at a Dutch
village fair.

In England the booth stage was available for the acting of St George and
Robin Hood plays and other popular pieces. This kind of stage was
probably favoured by small troupes of strolling players: the Macro
Mankind (1464), acted by a troupe of six, is certainly well suited for
performance on 'a trestle stage in an innyard with a simple curtained booth
to the rear'.[3]

(x) The indoor theatre: the acting of interludes

Apart from a section on liturgical plays acted inside the church, this chapter
has so far been concerned with different kinds of dramatic entertainment
in the open. But, side by side with the open-air plays, which must have
been summer entertainments for the most part,[4] there were also short
dramatic pieces written primarily for production indoors at any season of
the year. These short pieces, most of the surviving examples of which date
from the Tudor period, are the interludes written for small companies of
professional players.[5] Early references to them include one in the fourteenth-
century *Sir Gawain and the Green Knight* ('Laykyng of enterludes', 472)
and another in the *Life of Edmund Grindal* with reference to the sixteenth
century:

But he [Grindal] thought one thing especially ought to be remedied:
to prevent great flocks of people meeting together; and likewise one

[1] Wickham, I, 51.
[2] Southern, *The Seven Ages of the Theatre*, 160–1.
[3] Bevington, *Medieval Drama*, 902. Eccles, *The Macro Plays*, xlii, suggests that *Mankind*
may have been played inside an inn. M. Fifield, *The Castle in the Circle* (Muncie, Indiana,
1967), 27, envisages this play acted in an outdoor theatre of the arena type.
[4] An exception must be made of the Hull Noah play, which was acted in the open 'early
in the year, sometimes with the snow on the ground'; see A. J. Mill, 'The Hull Noah
Play', *MLR*, XXXIII (1938), 490, 498.
[5] See T. W. Craik, *The Tudor Interlude: Stage, Costume, and Acting* (Leicester, 1958), and
D. M. Bevington, *From 'Mankind' to Marlowe: Growth of Structure in the Popular Drama
of Tudor England* (Cambridge, Mass., 1962).

thing especially, as he confessed, because he liked not the thing itself, and that was interludes. The players he called, *an idle sort of people*, which had been infamous in all good commonwealths. These men did then daily, but especially on holydays, set up bills inviting to their plays; and the youth resorted excessively to them, and there took infection.... And therefore he advised, for the remedy hereof, that Cecil would be the means of a proclamation to inhibit all plays for one whole year. And if it were for ever, he added, it were not amiss: that is, within the city, or three miles compass, upon pains, as well to the player, as to the owners of the houses where they played their lewd interludes.[1]

An early fourteenth-century interlude like *De Clerico et Puella* might well be described as 'lewd' by a puritanically-minded critic like Grindal. But all interludes were not of this kind: the later interludes could be religious or secular, grave as well as gay. *Everyman*, printed early in the sixteenth century, is an obvious example of a serious moral interlude.[2] Whether lewd or not in theme, the indoor staging of the interlude, in barn, inn, chapel, great hall, or monastic refectory, seems usually to have been a simple affair of a small acting area (not necessarily a raised platform) at one end of a room and an audience (perhaps seated at table) at the other end. The combination of small cast and small audience, in close proximity to each other and undistracted by elaborate staging, encouraged the writing of intimate dialogue in which the audience could fully participate: 'Everyone was in the play.'[3] At least one play – Sir David Lindsay's *Ane Satyre of the Thrie Estaitis* – was first performed as an indoor interlude (in 1540) and later revised for performance in the open (1552 and 1554).

(xi) The medieval heritage of the Elizabethan public theatre

Most historians of the drama are agreed that the Elizabethan public theatre, beginning with James Burbage's The Theatre (1576), was a continuation of the kind of theatre which had grown up in the Middle Ages – that is to say, it made use of an emblematic stage with symbols of locality set in a neutral acting area. This traditional stage is clearly in contrast to the

[1] John Strype, *The History of the Life and Acts of ... Edmund Grindal* (Oxford, 1821), 121–2.
[2] For its staging, see A. C. Cawley (ed.), *Everyman* (Manchester, 1961), xxix–xxxi.
[3] Craik, *The Tudor Interlude*, 26.

illusionistic stage used at court performances after 1605, the year in which Jonson's *Mask of Blackness* was performed on a proscenium-arched, landscape stage designed by Inigo Jones.

Here the agreement ends, for every literary historian has his own theory about the origins of the Elizabethan public theatre. F. E. Halliday suggests that circular playing-places (represented by the Cornish rounds) gave Burbage the shape and seating arrangement of The Theatre.[1] Southern believes that travelling companies of professional players, including Burbage's own company, probably used the booth stage 'when they played out of doors or in an inn-yard';[2] he therefore thinks it possible that the booth-stage technique influenced the design of the first permanent public theatre. Wickham, on the other hand, goes indoors in search of Burbage's prototype and argues that the 'starting point is the stage of the Tudor banqueting hall set down inside a game-house rather than a pageant-waggon or fairground booth set down in the inn-yards'.[3] All these authorities reject the pageant-wagon as a prototype of the Elizabethan stage. The principal advocate of the pageant-wagon is Leslie Hotson,[4] who imagines a pair of wagons, each with a curtained 'house' at one end, rolled together in an inn-yard surrounded by one or more galleries. In Hotson's view the medieval pageant-wagon (in duplicate) is the prototype of the Elizabethan public stage, and the galleried inn-yard the direct source of its auditorium.

Disagreements about origins are less important than the consensus of opinion that the Elizabethan public stage is in principle very similar to the medieval stage. If the historians of drama are right about this, a grasp of the potentialities of the medieval theatre – 'an actor's and a poet's theatre'[5] – must surely be a valuable aid to understanding the Elizabethan public stage and the structure of the plays written for it.

[1] Halliday, *The Legend of the Rood*, 35.
[2] Southern, *The Seven Ages of the Theatre*, 169. For the influence of the booth stage see also R. Southern, 'On reconstructing an Elizabethan playhouse', *Shakespeare Survey* 12 (Cambridge, 1959), 31 ff. Elsewhere Southern lays more emphasis on the influence of the indoor staging of interludes 'in a hall before a screen'; see 'The contribution of the interludes to Elizabethan staging', in R. Hosley (ed.), *Essays on Shakespeare and Elizabethan Drama, in Honour of Hardin Craig* (London, 1963), 14.
[3] Wickham, II, 205.
[4] Leslie Hotson, *Shakespeare's Wooden O* (London, 1959), 61 ff.
[5] Wickham, II, 155.

4 Organization of the Corpus Christi plays

Details of the administration and financing of the Corpus Christi plays can be gathered from such sources as the municipal archives, guild records, and churchwardens' accounts at Chester, York, Coventry, Beverley, Lincoln and other towns. However, the records are not always explicit and there are many difficulties of interpretation.

The guild plays, originally acted on Corpus Christi day, continued to be known as the 'Corpus Christi play' even when they were transferred to Whitsun (as at Chester, York and Wakefield) or to St Anne's day (as at Lincoln).

The traditional view that the plays were supervised by the city authorities but financed and produced by the craft guilds has been challenged for Lincolnshire, where at Lincoln and Louth it has been shown that the corporation directed 'a religious guild to assume general supervision of the cycle, with the craft guilds subordinate to the religious guild'.[1] At other towns there was also a strong measure of ecclesiastical control. At Wakefield the Burgess Court records for 1556 list payments by the churchwarden ('Cherche mester') of sums of money for the Corpus Christi play.[2] These

[1] Stanley J. Kahrl, 'Medieval drama in Louth', Medieval Supplement to *RORD*, x (1967), 133.
[2] See p. 51, below.

payments are paralleled at Louth, where the accounts of the parish church of St James record sums paid by the churchwardens in connection with the play during the early decades of the sixteenth century. Nevertheless, there is very little evidence to support the suggestion that Wakefield depended mainly on its heavily endowed religious guilds for financing the Corpus Christi play.[1] The position at Wakefield in 1556, as indicated by the Burgess Court entry for this year, is that the play was the responsibility of the Burgess Court, and that the trade guilds as well as the churchwarden had an active share in producing it. In other words, the Corpus Christi play, at least in 1556, was a community effort in which both clerics and lay people took part.

It is clear from the records that the city authorities usually had considerable supervisory powers. For example, they decided whether the play would be acted in any given year; and yet their decision to stage the play could be negated by government intervention, as it was in Wakefield at the instance of the Diocesan Court of High Commission. This is shown by the following remarkable document (Plate 13), preserved in the York Diocesan records, and dated 27 May 1576:

> This daie upon intelligence geven to the saide Commissioners that it is meant and purposed that in the towne of Wakefeld shalbe plaied this yere in Whitsonweke next or theraboutes a plaie commonlie called Corpus Christi plaie which hath bene heretofore used there / Wherein they ar done tundrestand that there be many thinges used which tende to the Derogation of the Maiestie and glorie of god the prophanation of the Sacramentes and the maunteynaunce of superstition and idolatrie / The said Commissioners Decred a lettre to be written to the Balyffe Burgesses and other the inhabitantes of the said towne of Wakefeld that in the said playe no Pageant be used or set furthe wherein the Maiestye of god the father god the sonne or god the holie ghoste or the administration of either the Sacramentes of Baptisme or of the lordes Supper be counterfeyted or represented / or any thinge plaied which tende to the maintenaunce of superstition and idolatrie or which be contrarie to the lawes of god or of the Realme.[2]

The above comprehensive tabling of objectionable matters, in a letter sent

[1] Kahrl, 'Medieval drama in Louth', 131.
[2] See Cawley, *Wakefield Pageants*, 125, and H. C. Gardiner, *Mysteries' End* (New Haven, 1946), 78. It will be noticed that this virtual prohibition of the Wakefield Corpus Christi play took place in 1576, the year in which James Burbage established The Theatre, the first permanent public theatre in England.

at such short notice to the Bailiff and Burgesses of Wakefield, amounts practically to a prohibition of the whole Corpus Christi play.

Apart from the major decision as to whether or not the play should be acted, the city authorities had the right to assign or reassign the different pageants which made up the whole cyclic performance, in order to ensure that each guild was properly represented and (in the case of an impoverished guild) not overburdened by the cost of producing a play. They issued a proclamation in the King's name to enjoin the keeping of the peace at both play and procession, to regulate the play and to ensure a satisfactory standard of acting. An example of such a proclamation has been preserved from York (1415):

Proclamacio ludi corporis christi facienda in vigilia corporis christi
We comand of the kynges behalve and the Mair and the shirefs of this Citee that no man go armed in this Citee with swerdes ne with Carlill axes [Carlisle axes, that is, battle-axes] ne none othir defences in distourbaunce of the kynges pees and the play or hynderyng of the processioun of Corpore Christi, and that thai leve thare hernas [harness, weapons] in thare Ines, saufand knyghtes and sqwyers of wirship that awe [ought to] have swerdes borne eftir thame, of payne of forfaiture of thaire wapen and inprisonment of thaire bodys. And that men that bryngnes furth pacentes that thai play at the places that is assigned therfore and nowere elles, of the payne of forfaiture...that ys to say xls....And that all maner of craftmen that bringeth furthe ther pageantez in order and course by good players well arayed and openly spekyng, vpon payn of lesying of Cs. to be paid to the chambre withoute any pardon. And that every player that shall play be redy in his pagiaunt at convenyant tyme, that is to say, at the mydhowre betwix iiijth and vth of the cloke in the mornynge, and then all other pageantes fast folowyng ilkon after other as ther course is, without tarieng, sub pena...vjs. viijd.[1]

The above reference to 'good players well arayed and openly spekyng' is recalled by a York document of 1476 which shows that the York City Council arranged in this year for the examination of would-be players, to ascertain that they were up to standard and to make sure that no one acted more than two different parts on the day of the play:

Also it is ordeinid and stablished by the ful consent and auctoritie of the Counsaile aforesaide...that yerely in the tyme of Lentyn there shall

[1] *REED, York*, I, 24.

be called afore the Maire for the tyme beyng iiij of the moste connyng, discrete and able playeres within this Citie to serche, here and examen all the plaiers and plaies and pagentes thrughoute all the artificeres belonging to Corpus Christi plaie. And all suche as they shall fynde sufficiant in personne and connyng to the honour of the Citie and worship of the saide Craftes for to admitte and able, and all other insufficiant personnes either in connyng, voice or personne to discharge, ammove and avoide.

And that no plaier that shall plaie in the saide Corpus Christi plaie be conducte and reteyned to plaie but twise on the day of the saide playe, and that he or thay so plaing plaie not overe twise the saide day, upon payne of xls. to forfet unto the Chaumbre as often tymes as he or thay shall be founden defautie in the same.[1]

The Chester Proclamation and the Wakefield Burgess Court 'paynes' (penalties) are similar in some details to the York Proclamation. The Chester Proclamation (1531–2) begins with a reminder of the serious purpose of the play:

The Proclamacion for the plaies newly made by William Newhall clarke of the Pentice...
For as much as of old tyme, not only for the augmentacion and incres of the holy and Catholick faith of our Savyour Jesu Crist and to exort the myndes of the common people to good devotion and holsome doctryne therof but also for the commenwelth and prosperitie of this Citie, a play and declaration and diverse storyes of the bible begynnyng with the creacion and fall of Lucifer and endyng with the generall jugement of the world, to be declared and plaied in the Witsonweke... at the costes and chargez of the craftes men and occupacons of the said Citie whiche hitherunto have from tyme to tyme used and performed the same....

and ends with the customary police notice:

Wherfore Maister mair in the Kyngez name straitly chargeth and commaundeth that every person and persons of what estate, degre or

---

[1] *REED, York*, I, 109. The order contained in the second paragraph may cover not only the doubling of parts in the same play but also the acting of parts in different plays. Cf. Coventry, 1444: 'shall no man of the said iiij craftes play in no pagent on Corpus Christi day save onely in the pagent of his own crafte, without he have lycens of the maiour that shalbe for the yer' (Craig, 74; *REED, Coventry*, 16).

condicion so ever he or they be resortyng to the said plaiez do use themselves pecible wthout makyny eny assault, affrey or other disturbans whereby the same playes shal be disturbed and that no manner person or persons who so ever he or they be do use or weare any unlaufull wepons within the precynct of the said Citie durying the tyme of the said play.[1]

The Wakefield 'paynes', which are included in the Wakefield Burgess Court Roll for 1556, are commented on below, pp. 55–6.

The guilds, for their part, had fairly well defined rights and responsibilities. They appointed pageant-masters and collected money from their members to defray the cost of the individual pageant they had engaged to produce. They sent out representatives to advertise the plays on holidays before the day of performance: examples of such advertisements are the banns of the Chester and N-town plays.[2] (Similar in function to these are the introductory stanzas of *The Castle of Perseverance* spoken alternately by two *vexillatores*, or banner-bearers, who give a summary of the story of the play and announce that the performance will take place 'This day sevenenyt...At ———— on the grene'.)[3] The guilds usually kept the book of their own pageant,[4] whether or not the municipal authorities held a master copy ('register' or 'original') of all the pageants, and they paid for the copying of single actors' parts. They organized the rehearsals, which could number as many as three or four. They prepared the pageant-wagon and properties, and paid the actors and the workmen whose skill or strength was needed on the day. A growing professionalism in the production of the plays is to be seen in the appointment by the Coventry Smiths in 1453 of 'Thomas Colclow, skynner', for a period of twelve years, to 'have the rewle of the pajaunt...to find the pleyers and all that longeth therto';[5] and to do this

[1] *REED, Chester*, 27–8.

[2] For the Chester banns (1539–40 and 1608–9) see *REED, Chester*, 31–9, 240–8; for the N-town banns see Block, 1–16.

[3] *The Castle of Perseverance*, 133–4. It is interesting to trace the evolution of the banns into the prologue of a later play like *Everyman*. Both banns and prologue give the purpose and matter of the play in brief; the essential difference between them is that the banns announce the time and place of the next performance, while the prologue (which is immediately followed by a performance of the play) does not.

[4] Examples of copies of individual plays which were no doubt the property of the performing crafts are the Chester Dyers' play of Antichrist (ed. W. W. Greg, Oxford, 1935) and the York Scriveners' play of the Incredulity of Thomas (ed. A. C. Cawley, *LSE*, 7 and 8 (1952), 45–80).

[5] Craig, 83; *REED, Coventry*, 27. The name of another professional producer survives: Robert Clarke, employed at Lincoln in 1488 because 'he is so ingenious in the show and play called the Ascension, given every year on St Anne's Day' (Chambers, II, 379); Kahrl, *Records of Plays and Players in Lincolnshire 1300–1585*, 38, gives the original entry in Latin.

for an annual salary of 46s 8d, which was a tidy sum at a time when the daily wage of a skilled craftsman rarely exceeded 4d. This engagement of a professional producer goes together with the possible use of professional actors to play some of the principle roles (see pp. 48–9).

5 Production of a play on a pageant-wagon

Rather than collect information about details of production from the records of several different towns and use this information to build up a composite picture which might not be true for any single town, it is proposed to take one particular play at Chester and Coventry (where processional performance on pageant-wagons is known to have been in force) and examine the documentary details of production in relation to the text and stage directions of the play.

The pageant chosen is the Purification of Mary, which was acted by the Smiths at Chester and by the Weavers and Skinners at Coventry. Both plays have early stage directions, and by good fortune the sixteenth-century guild records have survived which itemize the sums spent on properties and costumes and give details of the payments made to actors and musicians and to men for repairing and 'driving' the pageant-wagon.[1]

[1] The text of the Chester Purification play is edited by R. M. Lumiansky and David Mills, *The Chester Mystery Cycle* (London: EETS), I (1974), 204–17; the Coventry play is edited by Craig, op. cit., 39–71. The Chester Smiths' accounts (1554) are from Salter, 76–7 and from *REED, Chester*, 53; the Coventry Weavers' accounts (1525, 1563) are from Craig, 106–7. The latter have also been published in *REED, Coventry*, 124, 222.

The Chester play (Play 11) comprises the Purification (1–206) and Christ with the Doctors in the Temple (207–334); the Coventry play begins with the prophecies of Christ's birth (1–176), continues with the Purification (177–721), and concludes with the journey of Mary, Joseph and Jesus to the temple in Jerusalem (722–814) and with the episode of Christ and the Doctors (815–1192).

(i) The stage directions of the Chester play

The Chester play begins in a place representing the temple. The stage directions indicate the stage business during the first part of the play, which is concerned with the persuading of Simeon that the mother of Christ is indeed a virgin. Simeon looks at his holy book and reads Isaiah's prophecy:

> Tunc respitiens librum legat prophetiam: 'Ecce virgo concipiet et pariet filium' etc. (24.1)
> [Then consulting his book let him read the prophecy: 'Behold, a virgin shall conceive, and bear a son.']

Although he does not doubt Christ's coming, he cannot accept the word *virgo*, and so he goes through the motions of scraping it off and writing in its place 'a good woman', after which he puts the book on the altar. This unwise textual emendation brings about the first visit of the Angel, who takes up the book and makes a show of writing in it:

> tunc [Simeon] fricabit librum quasi deleret hoc verbum (virgo); et post ponit librum super altare. Et veniet Angelus et accipiet librum, faciens signum quasi scriberet; et claudet librum et vuanesset....(40.1)
> [then he shall rub at the book as if he were deleting the word (virgin); and afterwards he places the book on the altar. And the Angel shall come and take the book, making a sign as if he were writing; and he shall close the book and disappear from sight....]

When Simeon looks at the book again he marvels to find that the word *virgo* has been restored in letters of red. In order to make sure that this correction is nothing less than a miracle he again scrapes off the word he cannot believe in, and again replaces it by 'a good woman'. When

Simeon has put the book back on the altar, the Angel repeats his earlier action:

> Tunc ponit librum super altare, et faciet Angelus ut antea. (71.1)
> [Then he (Simeon) puts the book on the altar, and the Angel shall do as before.]

After Anna has expressed her faith in the truth of the original reading, Simeon again consults his book and finds the word *virgo* has reappeared, but this time in letters of gold. Simeon is at last convinced that Christ will be born of a virgin. The Angel now speaks to him and tells him he will not die until he has seen Christ. Whereupon Simeon sits down and waits for God's consolation.

At this point in the action Mary and Joseph appear, and make their way to the temple with a minimum of fuss and in the space of two stanzas. Arrived at the temple, they offer Simeon their child, three birds, and a candle of virgin wax in token of Mary's virginity. Simeon, already convinced that Christ's mother is a virgin according to the prophecy, takes the Christ-child in his arms, welcomes him as Saviour, and sings the Song of Simeon (Luke 2: 29 ff.):

> Tunc cantabit 'Nunc dimittis servum tuum, domine' etc. (166.1)
> [Then he shall sing, 'Lord, now lettest thou thy servant depart'.]

The episode of the Purification of the Blessed Virgin ends with Simeon and Anna affirming their faith in Christ's divinity.

The second episode (Christ and the Doctors) begins immediately afterwards with Mary and Joseph discovering that Christ is not with them. Christ speaks with the Doctors and demonstrates his precocious knowledge of the Mosaic law; Mary and Joseph find him seated with the Doctors, and the play ends with the Angel recapitulating the events of the first episode.[1]

It is clear from this summary of the action, as well as from the stage directions, that the Chester play was in all probability written for a confined stage. Most of the action takes place in the temple; the action outside the temple involving Mary and Joseph is limited to 119–34 and 207–26. Moreover, it is not necessary to suppose, as in the case of the corresponding Coventry play, that the action took place on two levels.

---

[1] The fact that the Angel does not also recapitulate the events of the second episode (Christ with the Doctors) may indicate that this second episode is a later insertion. It appears that the York play of Christ with the Doctors was borrowed by both Chester and Coventry; see Craig, *English Religious Drama of the Middle Ages*, 189.

(ii) The stage directions of the Coventry play

The stage directions, which are fairly detailed in this play, indicate movement up to and down from a raised structure at the back of the stage representing the temple where the infant Christ is to be presented to God. Simeon, forewarned by the two Angels, goes up to the temple with his priests in order to prepare the altar for sacrifice: 'There Semeon and his Clarks gothe up to the tempull and Gaberell cumyth to the tempull dore' (366.1). Then Mary and Joseph, instructed by Gabriel, make their way to the temple with the two white doves which are to be offered with the child. Simeon and his priests come down in procession to meet them: 'Here the[y] cum downe with pressession to mete them' (636.1), and Simeon then goes back to the altar with the child in his arms. The ceremony finished, 'There Mare and Josoff departis owt of the upper parte of the pagand' (704.1).

Later, when Mary, Joseph and Jesus (now 12 years old) go again to Jerusalem, a similar movement takes place up to and down from the altar of the temple. Mary and Joseph enter the temple and 'There the[y] all goo up to the awter and Jesus before. The[y] syng an antem' (805.1). When they leave the temple, 'There the[y] goo done [down] into the for [fore] pagond and Jesus steylyth awey' (814.1).

The Purification episode (177–721) consists of two main movements – first of Simeon and his priests and later of Mary and Joseph – from the 'for pagond', representing the world of men, to the 'upper parte of the pagand' representing the temple of God; and each movement towards the temple is brought about by an angel's command.

The temple, with its door and altar, is the focal point of the action. It must have been either (a) a raised structure at the back of the pageant-wagon, the rest of the pageant stage serving as a *platea* for worldly action, or (b) a structure taking up most of the wagon, with the *platea* at a lower level in front of it. There is more than one reference in the Coventry guild records to a 'scaffold' (as distinct from the pageant-wagon) and to the making of a 'trendell', or small wheel, for it:

> 1570   paid...for makyng an exaltre for the pagyante xijd
> paid for a trendell for the scaffold and the makyng iijd.[1]

This scaffold may have been, as Wickham suggests, a platform on wheels set adjacent to the pageant-wagon and serving as an additional acting area.

[1] Craig, 109; *REED, Coventry*, 253.

In either case the play is arranged for acting on two levels, the *locus* being at a higher level than the *platea*. The *locus* symbolizes the temple where Christ is to be offered to God, the *platea* the world of henpecked husbands, proverbial wisdom, and the comic business of Joseph's unwilling search for the two white doves demanded by Gabriel.

(iii) Costumes and make-up

There are very few references in the two plays to the costumes worn by the actors, although the same words, 'in furres fine' (Chester 314, Coventry 1040), are used in both to describe the costume worn by the Doctors. The meagre information about costume in the text can, however, be supplemented from the items listed as refurbished or renewed in the accounts of the Chester Smiths and Coventry Weavers. Thus the Smiths at Chester in 1554 paid 12*d* 'for gelldinge of Gods fase' and 5*s* 'for making of the Copes',[1] while the records of the Coventry Weavers contain the following items of expenditure on costume:

1525	payd for glovys	viij*d*.
1535	pd. for makyng of a whyt forde prelatt [white furred garment?] for Jhesus	viij*d*.
1541	payd for a amys [amice] for Symyon	ij*d*.
1542	payd for makyng of Symyons mytor [mitre]	viij*d*.
1564	paid for settynge one of Jhesus sleves	ij*d*.
	paid for payntyng of Jesus heade [mask?]	viij*d*.
	paid for solyng [soling] of Jesus hose	j*d*.
1576	payd for ij beardes and a cappe	vj*d*.
1578	payd for mendyng of the two angelis crownes	ij*d*.[2]

The 'payntyng of Jesus heade' in the Coventry records may refer to the painting of a mask worn by the actor impersonating Jesus, or it may be similar in meaning to the 'gelldinge of Gods fase' in the Chester records. In Kolve's words, 'God was played by a man, but he was distinguished from the order of men by a gilt face'.[3]

[1] Salter, 76–7; *REED, Chester*, 53.
[2] Craig, 106–7, 109; *REED, Coventry*, 124, 142, 156, 161, 226, 279.
[3] Kolve, 26. For a very full account of masks and face-painting in medieval drama, see Meg Twycross and Sarah Carpenter, 'Masks in medieval English theatre: the mystery plays', *METh*, III (1981), 7–44, 69–113.

(iv) Properties

The properties referred to in the dialogue or stage directions of the Chester play include a book (24.1), a scraping instrument (37), a pen (39), an altar (40.1), a chair (implied in 118.1), birds (132–3, 140), and a candle (144) to remind us that Candlemas is the feast of the Purification of the Virgin.[1] The Coventry text refers to the temple and temple door (366.1) and to the altar (359, 612). The Coventry accounts include:

1556	ij tapares	iij*d*.
1558	ij tapares and insenc	ij*d*.[2]

(v) Music

The Chester stage direction after 166 provides for the singing of 'Nunc dimittis'. But the Chester Smiths' accounts give a much better idea of the important part played by music in this play:

1554	to the mynstrells in mane [money]	ij*s*.
	we gave to barnes & the syngers	iij*s*. 4*d*.
	[Sir Randall Barnes, the singing master	
	of Chester Cathedral]	
	to Randle Crane in mane	ij*s*.
	[Randal Crane, a minstrel][3]	

In the Coventry play the stage direction *Cantant* appears three times (after 366, 636, 694). According to Hardin Craig, the first of these is the direction for singing the first of the two songs given at the end of the play. But the direction at 366 seems, in fact, to be an error since Simeon is there asking his priests to sing with him later, when Christ approaches the temple. Christ's coming takes place at 636, where *Cantant* occurs again; it is at this point that the first of the two songs would more appropriately

---

[1] The Chester banns (1539–40) describe the Smiths' pageant as follows:

> Semely Smythis also in Syght
> a lovely Caryage the[y] will dyght
> Candilmas day for soth it hyght
> the[y] find it with good will.
>
> (*REED*, Chester, 36)

[2] Craig, 107; *REED*, Coventry, 206, 210.
[3] *REED*, Chester, 53.

be sung, and the second at 694. The ringing of bells (624, 633) and the singing, at moments when a sense of the divine presence is to be strongly conveyed (as at 805.1), belong to a musical tradition which goes back to the tenth-century Easter play. The Coventry accounts confirm the importance of music, both singing and instrumental music, in this play:

1525	payd to the synggers	xvj*d*.
1563	paid to James Hewete for his rygoles [regals, small portable organ]	xx*d*.
	paid for syngyng	xvj*d*.[1]

(vi) Payments to actors

The following table gives the sums paid to their actors by the Chester Smiths in 1554 and by the Coventry Weavers in 1525 and 1563; the figure in square brackets is the number of lines spoken by each actor in the extant plays.

Chester		*Coventry*		
	1554		1525	1563
ould sermond [135]	3*s* 4*d*	Symyon [208][2]	2*s* 4*d*	3*s* 4*d*
————		Symyons clark [37]	10*d*	1*s* 8*d*
damane (Dame Anne) [32]	10*d*	Anne [38]	10*d*	1*s* 8*d*
Angels [15]	6*d*	Angels [30]	8*d*[3]	8*d*
Mary [48]	10*d*	Mary [174]	10*d*	1*s* 8*d*
Joseph [24]	8*d*	Joseph [260]	1*s* 2*d*	2*s* 4*d*
————		the chylde [—]		4*d*
letall God [40]	12*d*	Jesus [79]	1*s* 8*d*	1*s* 8*d*
the docters [40]	3*s* 4*d*	————		

[1] Craig, 106, 107; *REED, Coventry*, 124, 222. See J. Stevens, 'Music in medieval drama', *Proceedings of the Royal Musical Association*, LXXXIV (1958), 81–95; E. A. Bowles, 'The role of musical instruments in medieval sacred drama', *The Musical Quarterly*, XLV (1959), 67–84; JoAnna Dutka, 'Mysteries, minstrels, and music', *Comparative Drama*, VIII (1974), 112–24, and *Music in the English Mystery Plays* (Kalamazoo, Mich., 1980).

[2] R. W. Ingram, who lists the number of lines and payment for each actor in the Coventry Weavers' play, calculates Simeon's lines as 218; see *REED: Proceedings of the First Colloquium* (Toronto, 1979), 71.

[3] *REED, Coventry*, 124, has 'viij*d*'; Craig, 106, has 'xx*d*'. There is no mention in the Weavers' accounts of Gabriel, who has 22 lines to speak.

It will be noticed that Simeon received 3s 4d at both Chester and Coventry. This large fee may indicate that the actor was a professional. In any event, the Coventry actor, with 208 lines, had to work harder for his money than the Chester player with 135 lines.

The most striking difference between the two places is Coventry's payment to Joseph in 1525 of 1s 2d (which rises by an inflationary process to 2s 4d in 1563) for his important part of 260 lines, while the Chester Joseph in 1554 received only 8d for his minor part of 24 lines.

The Doctors in the Chester accounts do not appear in the Coventry Weavers' accounts, and the explanation may be that the actors who played the parts were paid, not by the Weavers but by the Skinners, who were no doubt largely responsible for staging the episode of Christ and the Doctors. On the other hand, the Coventry payment to 'the chylde' (the young boy impersonating the infant Christ in the Purification scene) is not paralleled in the Chester accounts.

One further point of interest is that the part of Anna was played by a young man or boy. This can be established at Coventry by a reference in 1550 to 'Hew [Hugh] Heyns pleyng Anne'.[1]

(vii) Total expenditure on the play

At Chester in 1554 the total cost of the play amounted to £3 4s 7d (of which 10s 6d was spent on payments to actors), while at Coventry in 1563 the total expenditure on the play was £2 4s 3d (of which 13s 4d was paid to the actors).

[1] Craig, 107; *REED, Coventry*, 186.

6 Presentation of the Wakefield plays

In this section the Wakefield plays are used to illustrate the problems of interpretation which arise when we examine different kinds of evidence, external and internal, for the purpose of learning how a medieval Corpus Christi cycle was organized and put on stage.[1]

There are two main sources of information for the organization and staging of the Wakefield plays: the external evidence of the Wakefield Burgess Court Rolls and the internal evidence of the text and original stage directions of the plays. The evidence provided by the Wakefield Burgess Court records is so meagre that it needs to be amplified and interpreted with the help of records from other towns. Again, the stage directions are few and uninformative by comparison with those of the Chester plays or the N-town plays, and it is therefore all the more important to glean from the text any scrap of information which may bear on the staging.

---

[1] It is accepted here that the plays contained in MS. HM1 in the Huntington Library, California (usually known as the 'Towneley plays'), are likely to be the Corpus Christi play of Wakefield; Cawley, *Wakefield Pageants*, xvii. See A. C. Cawley and Martin Stevens (eds), *The Towneley Cycle: A Facsimile of Huntington MS HM1* (Leeds, 1976).

(i) Organization and expenses

The relevant extracts from the Wakefield Rolls for 1556 and 1559–60 are given below:

1556

Paynes layde by the Burges Enqueste at the Courte kepte at Wakefelde nexte after the feaste of Saynte Michaell tharchanngell [29 Sept.] *in thirde and fourte yeare of the Reignes of oure Soveraigne Lorde and Ladye Kinge Philyppe and quene Marye 1556.*

Itm a payne is sett that everye crafte and occupacion doo bringe furthe theire pagyaunts of Corpus Christi daye as hathe bene heretofore used and to gyve furthe the speches of the same in after holydayes in payne of everye one not so doynge to forfett xl*s.*

Itm a payne is sett that everye player be redy in his pagyaunt at setled tyme before 5 of the clocke in the mornynge in payne of every one not so doynge to forfett vj*s.* viij*d.*

Itm a payne is sett that the players playe where setled and no where els in payne of no [*sic*] so doynge to forfett xx*s.*

Itm a payne is sett that no man goe armed to disturb the playe or hinder the procession in payne of everye one so doynge vj*s.* viij*d.*

Itm a payne is sett that everye man shall leave hys weapons att hys home or att hys ynne in payne not so doynge vj*s.* viij*d.*

The summe of the expens of the Cherche mester for the Corpus Christi playe xvij*s.* x*d.*

Item payd to the preste xij*d.*

Itm payd to the mynstrells xx*d.*

Itm payd to the mynstrells of Corpus Christi playe ij*s.* iv*d.*

Itm payd for the Corpus Christi playe & the wrytynge of the spechys for yt iij*s.* viij*d.*

Itm payd for the Baner for the mynstrells vj*s.* viij*d.*

Itm payd for the ryngyng the same day vj*d.*

Itm payd for garlonds on Corpus Christi day xij*d.*

1559–60

Itm a payn is layd that gyles Dolleffe shall brenge In or Causse to be broght the regenall [original] of Corpus Xty play before thys & wytsonday In pane....

> Itm a payn ys layde that the mesters of the Corpus Xti playe shall
> Come & mayke thayre a Count before the gentyllmen & burgessus of
> the toun before this & may day next In payn of everye on not so doynge,
> 20s.[1]

(ii) The 1559–60 record

Gyles Dolleffe, who was asked to bring in the 'regenall' (original) of the
Corpus Christi play, is twice named in the Roll for 1556 as the overseer
for Kirkgate, and at the end of this record is included among the members
of the inquest and described as 'Gyles Dollyff yoman'. It seems likely that
he is the Gyles Dolliffe named in the Rental of the Rectory Manor of
Wakefield in connection with property in Kirkgate, who died in 1569.[2] The
description 'yoman' shows that he was a man of some substance[3] – a fitting
person to take charge of the original on behalf of the Burgess Court.

The 'regenall' in his charge was no doubt the authoritative copy of the
Corpus Christi play held by the municipal authorities of Wakefield; the
corresponding master copy is referred to as the 'regenall' or 'originall
booke' at Chester and as the 'register' at York. There is reason to believe
that the Wakefield 'regenall' is none other than the Huntington manuscript
of the Towneley plays.[4]

Other documents contain orders demanding the original to be produced:
the most intriguing of these is the Chester entry of 1568:

> Randall Trever gent was called before the maior of the Citie of Chester
> and was demaunded for the originall booke of the whydson plaies of
> the said Citie who then and ther confessed that he have had the same

---

[1] The Wakefield Burgess Court Rolls for 1553, 1554, 1556 and 1579 are edited by
J. W. Walker in *Miscellanea* II (Yorkshire Archaeological Soc., Record Series, LXXIV
(1929)), 18–32. For the inaccuracies in Walker's transcript, the uncertain source of five
items grouped under 1556, and the wrong dating of the 1559–60 record under 1554, see
Jean Forrester and A. C. Cawley, 'The Corpus Christi play of Wakefield. A New Look
at the Wakefield Burgess Court Records', *LSE*, n.s., VII (1974), 108–15. The original
documents transcribed by Walker cannot now be traced, but for a photostat of items 1–30
of the original 1559–60 document see the Forrester and Cawley article.

[2] T. Taylor, *The History of Wakefield: The Rectory Manor* (Wakefield, 1886), Appendix,
x, xi, xxxvii. For further references to 'Giles Dolif [Dollyve]' see G. D. Lumb, *Testamenta
Leodiensia* (Thoresby Soc. Publ., Leeds, 1913), 240–1.

[3] See M. Campbell, *The English Yeoman under Elizabeth and the Early Stuarts* (New Haven,
Conn., 1942), 33.

[4] See Cawley, *Wakefield Pageants*, 125.

booke which book he deposeth upon the holy evangelist of God that
by comaundement he delivered the same booke againe but where the
same is now, or to whom he then delivered the same book, deposeth
likwise he knoweth not.[1]

Gyles Dolleffe seems to have been a more trustworthy custodian of the
'regenall' of the Wakefield play. We can only speculate as to why he was
ordered by the Wakefield Burgess Court to bring in the original, but
presumably the order was preparatory to a performance of the Corpus
Christi play in Wakefield in 1560.

The second item requires 'the mesters of the Corpus Xti playe' to make
their accounts tó the burgesses. These masters of the Corpus Christi play
recall the 'pageant maisters' employed by the York Marshals and Smiths,
who in 1442 were required to 'make thair rakenyng and gife accompt evere
yere fro nowe furth'.[2] The duties of the Wakefield masters were probably
similar to those assigned by the Coventry Smiths to Thomas Colclow (see
p. 40), who was given 'the rewle of the pajaunt unto the end of xij yers
next folowing', and was held responsible for returning the 'originall' of
the Smiths' play to the company after Corpus Christi day.[3] It is possible
that 'the mesters of the Corpus Xti playe' included 'the Cherche mester'
of the 1556 entry, who is commented on below.

(iii) The 1556 record

In the first item for 1556, which presumably refers to the performance of
the following year, it is made clear that the Wakefield crafts had an active
part in bringing forth the pageants of Corpus Christi day. But what were
these 'pageants', and what were 'the speches of the same' which were to
be given forth 'in after holydayes'?

'Pageant', as we have already noticed, is an ambiguous word. At least
four different meanings, or shades of meaning, are distinguishable:

1 (a) A short religious play, as in 'Thys lytyll pagent thus conclud we'
    in the last stanza of the Digby *Conversion of St Paul* (1480–1520).[4]

[1] R. H. Morris, *Chester in the Plantagenet and Tudor Reigns* (Chester, 1893), 315; also
REED, Chester, 80.
[2] *REED, York*, 1, 60.
[3] Craig, 83; *REED, Coventry*, 27.
[4] Baker, *Digby Plays*, 23.

(*b*) A dramatic performance viewed as one episode of the Corpus Christi play as a whole, as in 'bryngyng furthe of our pagent in corpus christi play' (York, 1433).[1]

(*c*) Such a performance and its attendant expenses viewed as the special charge of a particular craft or combination of crafts, as in 'they ordeyned at the lete [leet] that the chaundelers shuld pay yerely to the smythes ij*s*. towardes their paient' (Coventry, 1493).[2]

2 A special wagon or cart on which the performance took place, as in 'A Pageant, that is to saye, a howse of waynskott paynted and buylded on a carte with fowre whelys' (Norwich, 1565);[3] or as in the second Wakefield Burgess Court item for 1556 'that everye player be redy in his pagyaunt'.

Not enough is known about the origin of the word for us to be sure whether 1 or 2 is the primary sense (see *OED*, s.v.). The two senses are so closely related that the word is often used ambiguously, and it is difficult to be sure which sense is intended. In the phrase 'to bring forth a pageant' sense 2 is sometimes uppermost. It is, for example, in the following context: 'for bryngyng forth of the pagyantes into the strette' (York, 1464).[4] But, in less clear-cut contexts, the meaning 'to bring out a pageant-wagon from the place where it is housed' is possibly subordinate to the related meaning 'to perform a play in public (on a wagon made for the purpose)'. This much is certain: the two meanings are interdependent to such a degree that one frequently suggests the other.

To return to the Burgess Court item under discussion: if sense 2 of 'pageant' is uppermost, the meaning of 'bringe furthe theire pagyaunts of Corpus Christi daye' could be that the craft guilds were to bring out their pageant-wagons in order to take part in the procession on Corpus Christi day, while the 'speches'[5] or actors' parts were to be given forth, that is, the plays performed, on the holidays following ('in after holydayes'). This might imply that the Corpus Christi play at Wakefield in 1557 was performed over several days, as it was at Chester. Another possibility is that the 'speches' were the banns[6] of the entire cycle, that is, the speeches delivered by one or more *vexillatores* (banner-bearers) to declare the

[1] *REED, York*, I, 53.
[2] Craig, 75; *REED, Coventry*, 77.
[3] *NCPF*, xxxv.
[4] *REED, York*, I, 97.
[5] For a full discussion of 'speches' see Stevens, 'The staging of the Wakefield plays', 121–2.
[6] For the banns missing from the Huntington manuscript of the Towneley plays see Martin Stevens, 'The missing parts of the Towneley cycle', *Speculum*, XLV (1970), 257.

purpose of the pageants, give a short summary of them, and announce the place and time of their performance. In this case it seems that 'after holydayes' may refer to the holy days falling between the September date of the 1556 meeting of the Burgess Court and Corpus Christi day, 1557. This is plausible enough since we know that the religious plays were advertised on holidays before the day of performance: on St George's day at Chester and (with reference to the Paternoster Play at York in 1558) on St George's day and Whit Monday before the performance on Corpus Christi day.[1]

It will be noticed that 'speches' occurs again in a later item of the Burgess Court Roll for 1556: 'payd for the Corpus Christi playe & the wrytynge of the spechys for yt'. According to H. C. Schulz, the former Curator of Manuscripts at the Huntington Library, the hole in the extant opening two leaves of the manuscript of the Towneley plays may have been caused by the clasp nails of the original binding and indicate that the quire containing the banns was missing for some time before the manuscript was rebound in the seventeenth century.[2] If the banns were already missing from the manuscript in its original binding in 1556, this might explain why in that year it was necessary to pay for the writing of new 'spechys'.

The next four 'paynes' are strongly reminiscent of the wording of the York Proclamation for 1415 (see p. 38), so much so that they have the appearance of being derived from it. However, the York document is fuller and more precise: at York 'every player...shall...be redy in his pagiaunt at convenyant tyme, that is to say, at the mydhowre betwix iiijth and vth of the cloke in the mornynge', while at Wakefield 'everye player [shall] be redy in his pagyaunt at setled tyme before 5 of the clocke in the mornynge'; again at York the 'men that brynges furth pacentes...[shall] play at the places that is assigned therfore and nowere elles', whereas at Wakefield 'a payne is sett that the players playe where setled and no where els' (which leaves us in doubt as to whether the Wakefield actors acted in one place or, as at York, in several different places). One of the most interesting similarities between the York and Wakefield documents is that both refer to the play and the procession (in this order): 'that no man go armed...in distourbaunce of the kynges pees and the play or hynderyng of the processioun of Corpore Christi' (York); 'that no man goe armed to disturb the playe or hinder the procession' (Wakefield). In mentioning the

---

[1] REED, York, I, 327.
[2] See Cawley and Stevens, The Towneley Cycle: A Facsimile of Huntington MS HM1, vii, xv.

play and the procession together, the York and Wakefield documents agree with each other against the Chester proclamation (see p. 39) which, while giving a similar warning to possible disturbers of the peace, mentions only the play. The agreement of York and Wakefield in this particular may suggest that the play and the procession at Wakefield in 1566–7 took place on the same day, as we know they did at York in the year of the Proclamation (1415). The use of the general heading 'summe of the expens of the Cherche mester for the Corpus Christi playe' above what seem to be separate items for the play and the procession also points to an administrative connection between the play and the procession at Wakefield in 1556. When the brief reign of Mary, which made possible the reinstatement of the Corpus Christi festival, came to an end in 1558, the procession was no doubt discontinued and the play transferred to Whitsun, just as happened at York. That this change actually took place at Wakefield is confirmed by the Diocesan Court document of 1576 (see p. 37), where we learn that the Corpus Christi play of Wakefield was due to be played 'in Whitsonweke next or thereaboutes'.

It is suggested above (p. 53) that the 'Cherche mester' may have been one of 'the mesters of the Corpus Xti playe' who are instructed in the 1559–60 entry to 'mayke thayre a Count before the gentyllmen & burgessus of the toun'. But 'Cherche mester', it should be noticed, means 'church-warden', and so it seems that the churchwarden of Wakefield parish church was one of the officials responsible, under the general supervision of the Burgess Court, for some of the expenses of the Corpus Christi play. The churchwardens of the parish church at Louth spent similar sums on a pageant in the sixteenth century.[1] At Ludlow the authority exercised by the Guild of Palmers over the parish church was transferred to the municipal corporation, and from 1540 onwards the churchwardens' accounts are preserved among the municipal archives.[2] Some such transfer of authority from one or more religious guilds[3] to the Burgess Court may have taken place at Wakefield during the first half of the sixteenth century.

The expenses of the 'Cherche mester for the Corpus Christi playe' – the last of the Wakefield dramatic records for 1556 – apparently include sums spent both on the procession and the play. A distinction is made between

[1] Kahrl, *Records of Plays and Players in Lincolnshire 1300–1585*, 83.
[2] T. Wright, *Churchwardens' Accounts of the Town of Ludlow* (Camden Soc. Publ. 102 (1869)), iii.
[3] For the religious guilds of Wakefield see J. W. Walker, *Wakefield: Its History and People*, 2 vols, 2nd edn (Wakefield, 1939; reprinted 1967), II, 149.

the xx*d*. paid to 'the mynstrells' (in the procession?) and the iii*s*. iv*d*. paid to 'the mynstrells of Corpus Christi playe'. Again, some of the payments – to the priest, for the banner, for the ringing of bells, and for garlands – are all closely paralleled in church records which relate only to the procession. However, there can be no certain identification of all the doubtful Wakefield items as payments for the procession. In particular, the 'mynstrells' (as distinct from the 'mynstrells of Corpus Christi playe') could have been the minstrels who rode with the banns. It may be noted that the minstrels (*speculatores*) at Beverley in 1423 received 20*d* for riding with the banns.[1] Similarly, the 'Baner' is an ambiguous item, since banners were carried not only in the procession but in the riding of the banns, as we know from the use of *vexillatores* to read the banns of *The Castle of Perseverance* and the Croxton *Play of the Sacrament* (1461–1520).

But the most difficult item of all is the sum of iij*s*. viij*d*. 'payd for the Corpus Christi playe & the wrytynge of the spechys for yt'. The nearest we can get to this item in other records is the following entry from the accounts of the guild of Holy Trinity at Sleaford, Lincs. (1480):

> Item payd for the regenal of the plays for the ascencon & the wrytyng of spechys & payntyng of a garment for God, iij*s*. iiij*d*.[2]

The sum of money is similar, and 'the wrytyng of spechys' is almost the same as the Wakefield phrase 'the wrytynge of the spechys for yt'. But it is questionable whether the Sleaford 'spechys' has the same meaning as 'spechys' in the Wakefield context. In the Sleaford entry, the word 'spechys' may relate to 'God' and mean the part written for the actor playing God. It does not necessarily refer to the play as a whole, as it does in the Wakefield document. In any case, the similarities should not be allowed to obscure an essential difference – the fact that the Sleaford entry is concerned only with pageants on the Ascension, while the Wakefield entry is concerned with the complete 'Corpus Christi playe'.

It is puzzling to find such a small sum (3*s* 8*d*) spent at Wakefield on the Corpus Christi play and on what are possibly the banns ('speches') for advertising it. Indeed, the total expenditure of 17*s* 10*d* by 'the Cherche mester' on the play (or even on the procession and play together) seems trivial by comparison with the grand sum of £14 9*s* 6*d* spent on the Corpus

---

[1] Leach, 'Some English plays and players, 1220–1548', 215. The banns of *The Castle of Perseverance* end with the Secundus Vexillator saying 'Trumpe up and let us pace' (156), i.e. 'sound the trumpet, and let us go'.
[2] Kahrl, *Records of Plays and Players in Lincolnshire 1300–1585*, 86.

Christi play at Newcastle in 1561,[1] or with the sums spent at Chester and Coventry on a single pageant (see p. 49).

There has been too little comparative study by scholars of expenditure on medieval plays for any confident explanation of the Wakefield expense account to be given. One possible explanation is that the plays at Wakefield was a small-scale affair similar to the production of the Ascension play at Sleaford, and that the identification of the Huntington manuscript of the Towneley plays as the Wakefield 'regenall' is wrong. But, in view of the evidence supporting this identification, an alternative explanation is more acceptable – namely, that the 'Churche mester' was responsible for only a part of the total expenditure on the play,[2] and that he was one of several 'mesters of the Corpus Xti playe', representing 'everye crafte and occupacion' of Wakefield, who had to submit their accounts to the Burgess Court.

(iv) Staging

It is not known how the Wakefield plays were staged. They may have been performed 'in one fixed locality, on a multiple stage, and in the round',[3] in the manner of *The Castle of Perseverance*. They may have been performed processionally, that is, at several acting-stations in turn, as at Chester, York and Coventry. Or they may have been performed in each of these ways at different periods of Wakefield's history.

The evidence of the Wakefield Burgess Court records for 1556 is not very helpful in this connection. The meaning of 'pageant' is ambiguous in the words 'everye crafte and occupacion doo bringe furthe theire pagyaunts of Corpus Christi daye' (see p. 51); and even if these words imply a performance of the plays on pageant-wagons, there is still the possibility that the wagons were used as scaffolds for a performance in a single locality. Again, the order that 'the players playe where setled and no where els' may be interpreted as meaning either that the plays were acted in one place or (by analogy with the unambiguous York Proclamation – see p. 38) in several places.

Most of the arguments in support of a single-station performance of the

[1] See R. Welford, *History of Newcastle and Gateshead*, 3 vols (London, 1884–7), II, 370.
[2] Like the churchwardens at Louth who paid William Foster 4*d* 'for part of the Costs of the Pagent'; Kahrl, *Records of Plays and Players in Lincolnshire 1300–1585*, 79.
[3] Rose, *Wakefield Mystery Plays*, 26.

plays at Wakefield are unconvincing. One of these arguments hinges on 'the practical impossibility of performing the whole cycle [of 31 pageants] at a number of stations in the compass of a day'.[1] This opinion is strongly supported by Nelson with reference to the Corpus Christi cycles at Wakefield and York. He is convinced that at Wakefield the time factor 'militates against any extensive true-processional production, even one beginning early in the morning'.[2] Similarly, he believes that 'true-processional' presentation of the York plays was impossible in a single day: even if the performance began 'promptly at five o'clock in the morning... the last play cannot possibly finish at the last station before quarter past two the following morning'.[3] On the other hand, Dorrell has argued that the York cycle of forty-eight pageants could have been performed processionally 'within a reasonable time-limit'. According to her calculations, a processional performance beginning at 4.30 a.m. probably involved a sequence of all the pageants at the first station lasting 13 hours 18 minutes, with the last pageant finishing at the last station at about 29 minutes past midnight.[4] Such a marathon performance would certainly be beyond the powers of endurance of a modern audience;[5] but it should be remembered that for a medieval audience the Corpus Christi play was a prime annual attraction and that the processional mode of presentation allowed them, if they missed a pageant at one acting-station, to see it at a later station. In fact, this peculiar mode of presentation gave the audience great freedom of movement and made it possible for them to vary the plays with all kinds of other entertainments[6] during a long summer day lasting from about 4.30 a.m. to midnight.

---

[1] ibid., 24.

[2] Alan H. Nelson, *The Medieval English Stage: Corpus Christi Pageants and Plays* (Chicago and London, 1974), 86. For a useful survey of the processional/stationary controversy see Nagler, *The Medieval Religious Stage*, 55–73.

[3] Alan H. Nelson, 'Principles of processional staging: York cycle', *MP*, LXVII (1970), 315.

[4] Margaret Dorrell, 'Two studies of the York Corpus Christi play', *LSE*, n.s., VI (1972), 98–9.

[5] The York Festival performance (1980) was limited to a three-and-a-half hour production of some thirty of the forty-eight pageants. This was rightly considered long enough for a seat-bound audience.

[6] The Leeds (1975) and Toronto (1977) pageant-wagon productions of the York plays and the Wakefield production of the Towneley plays (1980) were supplemented by tumblers, musicians and morris dancers, with stalls selling food and drink, and a number of other side attractions that co-existed wonderfully well with the more serious religious entertainment. The Wakefield performance was directed by Jane Oakshott and based on a text prepared by Peter Meredith which included all the Towneley plays except the first play of the Shepherds and the Hanging of Judas. The performance was spread over two days, each play being repeated on three fixed stages near the Cathedral.

The medieval guilds were well aware of the danger of allowing too many acting-places: at York in 1399 the commons petitioned the council to limit the number of stations to twelve, claiming that the plays were not performed as they ought to be because there were too many stations.[1] And sometimes darkness fell before all the plays had been acted at the first station, as we know from the Coventry Leet Book under the year 1457:

> the quene [Margaret]...came prevely to se the play there on the morowe; and she sygh then alle the pagentes pleyde save domes-day, which myght not be pleyde for lak of day. And she was loged at Richard Wodes the grocer...and there all the pleys were furst pleyde.[2]

When darkness intervenes, it must be admitted that a theoretical possibility has become a 'practical impossibility'. But there is no evidence that the practical difficulties caused the processional mode of performance to be abandoned at York or Coventry. As for Wakefield, we cannot even be sure that all the plays were acted on the same day: one possible interpretation of the Burgess Court order 'to gyve furthe the speches of the same in after holydayes' (see p. 54) may suggest that the performance was spread over two or three days, as at Chester.

Another argument concerns the sparsity of guild-names in the Huntington manuscript of the Wakefield plays.[3] This argument may be conveniently broken down into the following parts: (1) the manuscript associates only five of thirty-two plays with craft guilds, and all the craft-names are sixteenth-century additions; (2) originally this fifteenth-century manuscript contained no reference to any craft guilds; (3) in this respect it resembles the manuscript of the N-town plays, which gives no names of performing crafts; (4) the N-town plays are likely to be the Corpus Christi play of Lincoln, where a religious guild had charge of the play; (5) the Lincoln performance was probably in a fixed locality; (6) on the analogy of N-town/Lincoln it may therefore be inferred that at Wakefield in the fifteenth century a religious guild had charge of the Corpus Christi play and that the performance took place in one locality. This seems to be an insecure as well as circuitous argument on which to base a belief that the Wakefield plays were acted in a single highly organized acting area. The reinforcing argument that the Wakefield craft guilds were too poor in

[1] *REED, York*, I, 11. See also A. J. Mill, 'The stations of the York Corpus Christi play', *Yorkshire Archaeological Journal*, XXXVII (1951), 492–502.
[2] Craig, 74; *REED, Coventry*, 37.
[3] See Rose, *Wakefield Mystery Plays*, 26 ff.

the fifteenth century to support a cycle of plays also rests on insufficient evidence. All we can be sure of is that in 1556 'everye crafte and occupacion' of Wakefield had a share in the Corpus Christi pageants, and that four of the crafts (Barkers, Glovers, Fishers, and Litsters [dyers]) are named in five pageants of the Huntington manuscript.

When we turn to the evidence to be gleaned from the stage directions and the dialogue, we soon run into difficulties of interpretation. The Huntington manuscript contains sixty-three original stage directions in Latin and three in English (in Play 14 before lines 505, 511 and 523). Eleven plays in the manuscript contain no stage directions. To show movement towards or away from a place on stage, the manuscript directions use the following words: *perget, pergent, transsiet* and *pertransient, egrediatur, vadat* and, most often, *venit, venient*. The word *intrat* is used only twice (8/88, 13/189) and *exibunt* once (1/131).[1] The sparing use of entrance–exit words and the frequent use of *venit*, even when an actor makes his first appearance, may lend some support to the notion of performance on a pageant-wagon. It would be wrong to make too much of this scrap of evidence. But on a wagon raised from the ground and in a limited acting area ringed by spectators, it must have been convenient to assemble most of the actors on the stage at the beginning of the play and to minimize their exits and entrances. The actors, it seems, may have been grouped on different parts of the stage, each part representing a different locality. Thus a stage direction such as *Tunc perget ad uxorem* (3/189) could mean that Noah simulates the journey to his home ('homward will I hast' 3/182) by crossing over the stage to where his wife is (a little later she says 'I shal not in thi det / Flyt of this flett' 3/222–3, where *flett* means 'floor' or 'house').

The text itself, it is alleged, provides evidence of practical problems of staging which cannot be solved except by assuming a performance in a large acting area provided with multiple stages or scaffolds. Two of these problems involve the use of animals and the riding of horses between *mansions* – both of which, it is claimed, exclude the possibility of performance in the limited space of a pageant-wagon. Many years ago M. H. Peacock expressed the opinion:

> It is quite clear...from the second play (*Mactacio Abel*) that no movable stage would be sufficiently substantial to accommodate, as the play seems to require, Cain with his ploughing team of four horses and

[1] Line references are to G. England and A. W. Pollard, *The Towneley Plays* (London: EETS, 1897).

Garcio, his servant, with another team of five horses or oxen. If the representations were held in Goodybower [2/367], it is even conceivable that the pretended ploughing was done in the ground adjacent to the stage in the same way as Herod in the Coventry mysteries is supposed to leave the stage and rage sword in hand amongst the spectators.[1]

Peacock both poses the problem and offers a solution – the use of the ground adjacent to the pageant-wagon. In posing the problem he misstates it somewhat, since there is only one plough-team: this is driven in by Cain and consists of four oxen and four horses. But he is surely right in believing that the ground adjacent to the stage may have been used as an additional acting area. He may also be right in guessing that the play was acted in Goodybower, although he does not concern himself with the further problem of whether this was the fixed locality for staging all the Wakefield plays, or only one of several acting-stations at which each of the plays was performed in turn.

It is also alleged that the journeys between *mansions*, especially on horseback, 'would seem to dispose of the possibility that the mansions were placed on the same pageant':

> To suggest that the Wakefield Plays, which contain references to two or more mansions, could nevertheless be staged on the same pageant is to turn a blind eye to the stage directions, whether implicit in the dialogue or explicit in the rubrics, which, for instance, indicate that the three kings (in *The Offering of the Magi*) make separate entries from different directions on horseback.[2]

In the Magi play there is only one stage direction concerned with riding; this is the direction preceding the First King's entrance: *Tunc venit primus rex equitans* (14/84). But the Third King's words 'I rede we ryde togeder' (14/164) show that all three kings were mounted. While there can be no doubt that entrances on horseback necessitate an extension of the pageant-wagon at ground level, it remains uncertain whether more than one pageant was used. It is also uncertain whether the additional acting area needed could be provided only in a single fixed locality or whether it would also have been available at several different acting-stations organized for this purpose. At Chester, where processional performance at different stations seems to have been the rule, there was apparently no difficulty in arranging

[1] M. H. Peacock, 'The Wakefield Mysteries. The place of representation', *Anglia*, XXIV (1901), 518.
[2] Rose, *Wakefield Mystery Plays*, 30–1.

for Abraham to give Melchisedech a horse (Chester plays, 4/88) or for the Expositor (4/112) to enter on horseback.

Another practical problem is the accommodation of large-scale properties. First, it must be emphasized that it is not always possible to be sure whether a property, large or small, is real or just make-believe. It may be thought, for instance, that the richer foods consumed by the shepherds in the *Prima Pastorum* (Wakefield Play 12) are necessarily make-believe; that, apart from the prohibitive expense of providing so many aristocratic dishes, the make-believe character of the feast is an essential part of the total meaning of the play.[1] On the other hand, there is no reason for not accepting Cain's plough and plough animals as real enough, or for not believing that Noah put the finishing touches to an ark resembling a medieval ship. As far as the Noah play is concerned, it is arguable that a single pageant-wagon could have accommodated most of the *loca* needed, including the ark. If this method of production is rejected as impracticable, it is necessary to postulate at least three separate scaffolds representing Heaven, the ark, and the hill on which Noah's wife does her spinning.

Production on a pageant-wagon is difficult to visualize because of our ignorance of the theatrical potential of a cart mounted on wheels. However, the Norwich description and the van Alsloot paintings (see p. 26) are reminders that the pageant-wagon was a substantial structure which could have been used to accommodate at least two of the *loca* required for the Noah play – the balcony for God and the superstructure of a ship. We know that God spoke to Noah from a high place representing Heaven: Noah's words to God, 'bryng [me] to thi hall / In heven' (3/67–8), suggest this. The English alabaster carvings of the Middle Ages give us reason to believe that Heaven was sometimes symbolized on the stage by a 'gallery in which sat an actor representing the Heavenly Father';[2] and this gallery or balcony may have been part of the structure of the pageant-wagon. The ark, as we know from the dialogue, had many of the features of a medieval ship. We are free to suppose that the wagon itself was fashioned like a ship (as in the van Alsloot painting),[3] or that the ship was a sizeable affair carried on the wagon (as in the case of the Hull Plough Ship).[4]

If the above premises are accepted, an examination of the dialogue may

[1] See A. C. Cawley, 'The "grotesque" feast in the *Prima Pastorum*', *Speculum*, XXX (1955), 213–17.
[2] Hildburgh, 'English alabaster carvings', 67–8.
[3] The van Alsloot painting (1615) of 'The ship of Charles V' is reproduced in colour by James Laver, *Isabella's Triumph* (London, 1947), Plate 12.
[4] See A. J. Mill, 'The Hull Noah play', *MLR*, XXXIII (1938), 489–505.

support the idea that the action could all have taken place on a single pageant-wagon, except for the scene where Noah hurries off to summon his family to go on board the ark (3/289–324). This scene must obviously have taken place outside the ark, and 'this hill' (3/338) is apparently a raised place provided for Uxor so that she could more easily be seen by the spectators.

To sum up: it is possible to imagine a medieval production of the Wakefield Noah play on two or more scaffolds in a fixed acting area or, alternatively, on a single pageant-wagon at several stations. But the second method of production implies certain extensions of the wagon stage: a balcony for God, the use of adjacent ground for the scene outside the ark, and a raised place ('hill') for Noah's wife.

So far we have looked at practical problems of staging which can be tackled, if not always solved, by more than one method of production. But there is another sort of evidence yet to be considered, which may point to the multiple staging on different scaffolds of at least some of the Wakefield plays. This evidence has been found in the Passion sequence, which 'sweeps on in continuous action from play to play and from stage to stage':[1]

> there is very strong evidence, especially in the *Passion* sequence, of continuity of playing: *The Conspiracy* runs straight into *The Buffeting*, *The Buffeting* into *The Scourging*, *The Scourging* into *The Crucifixion*, and *The Crucifixion* into *The Talents*. It is significant, too, that in this sequence which so clearly suggests a multiple stage, set in a circle round 'the place', none of the plays has any close association with those of York.[2]

This is a pretty strong argument of the kind generally accepted as establishing the multiple staging of the N-town *Passion*. There is no denying that if enough convincing examples can be assembled of multiple staging, including simultaneous staging, and of frequent movement from scaffold to place, it becomes tolerably certain that the plays concerned were written to be performed in a theatre of the type associated with the N-town *Passion* and *The Castle of Perseverance*. Having conceded this much, we may ask how significant it is that the Wakefield Passion sequence has little or no connection with York. The reason could be that these plays were written by the same playwright specially for Wakefield, that they were conceived

[1] Rose, *Wakefield Mystery Plays*, 32.
[2] ibid., 38–9.

as a Passion group and designed to be performed as a group, with multiple staging and continuity of action. But it is doubtful whether we can go on to argue that *all* the Wakefield plays were staged in a similar fashion. We need a good deal more investigation of the text of the plays from the point of view of their staging before it can be affirmed that the Wakefield cycle as a whole was performed on several scaffolds in one fixed locality.

Apart from this particular problem of fixed locality versus processional staging, there is much other business of theatrical interest in the Wakefield plays. In the Noah play, for example, the words are continually being reinforced by actions – Noah's carpentry, his wife's spinning, and their exchange of blows; Noah's sounding of the water at intervals, to see how far it has gone down; and his wife's suggestion that the gluttonous raven should be cast forth (a nice non-biblical touch), followed by Noah's release of the trustworthy doves. There is no way of knowing what sort of attempt was made to represent the animals; perhaps it was done by means of painted boards, as in the production of the Chester *Deluge*, one of the stage directions of which reads: 'the arke muste bee borded rownde about. And one [on] the bordes all the beastes and fowles hereafter reahersed muste bee paynted, that ther wordes may agree with the pictures.'[1] The Wakefield equivalent of Thomas Colclow or Robert Clarke no doubt hit on some ingenious solution of this problem, as well as arranging for appropriate light and sound effects to lend terror to such words as

> Thise thoners and levyn [lightning] downe gar fall
> Full stout
> Both halles and bowers,
> Castels and towres. (3/346–9)

Future studies will no doubt add to our knowledge of English medieval staging. But they are unlikely to invalidate Wickham's observation that the basic conventions of medieval drama – especially the use of *platea* and *loca* – are common to all the different methods of staging, and that 'the use of pageant waggons and the repetition of performances at several "stations" is only a particular manifestation of a universal stagecraft'.[2] Further study of medieval staging with reference to later forms of theatre may also confirm that the staging of plays in the Elizabethan public theatre is more closely

---

[1] Lumiansky and Mills, *The Chester Mystery Cycle*, 48.
[2] Wickham, I, 168.

related to the compact performance of a pageant on a wagon in a limited acting area than it is to the multitudinous action of a play like *The Castle of Perseverance*, which requires 'an "epic" form of theatre'[1] with multiple scaffolds.

[1] Southern, *Medieval Theatre in the Round*, xvi.

11 The drama of religious ceremonial

David Mills and Peter F. McDonald

1 Preliminary note: the language of medieval drama

David Mills

The plays discussed in this volume survive in handwritten manuscripts and printed books from the tenth to the seventeenth centuries, with vernacular English plays clustering at the end of the period, from the early fifteenth century onwards. These vernacular plays were copied during and just after a major period of change in the English language which marks the transition from the form of English known to philologists as 'Middle English' in the fourteenth century to the 'Modern English' of the sixteenth century. Thus, in some of the plays the language-forms seem reassuringly familiar, being contemporary with sixteenth-century Tudor drama, while in texts of the fifteenth century the language-forms seem dauntingly unfamiliar and difficult. This prefatory note is intended to account for the existence of these problems and to remove some of the feeling of alienation which unfamiliar language-forms induce in readers.

(i) Languages and registers

After the Norman Conquest, three languages – Latin, French and English – were in use in England. Latin was the language of the Church and scholarship, an international language which was also the key to the writings and culture of the classical past. As the language of the Bible and liturgy, it was inevitably the language of the liturgical drama and of other forms also – a number of long religious plays evidently not written for performance within the liturgy, and some medieval imitations of classical drama, including the plays of a Belgian nun called Hrotswitha, comedies from the Loire district, and similar plays from England.[1] Latin survived in its religious function until the English Reformation, and in its scholarly and classical functions for much longer. In English vernacular drama it is a ready-made register, a shorthand way of suggesting the ecclesiastical *milieu*, particularly when allied to liturgical hymn or chant, or delivered in the incantatory tones of a clerical reader. A Chester devil self-consciously claims:

> Yea, this thou [i.e. God] sayd, verament,
> that when thou came to judgment
> thy angelles from thee should be sent
> to put the evyll from the good
> and put them into great torment,
> there reemynge and grennynge [wailing and gnashing the teeth]
> verey fervent;
> which wordes to clearkes here present
> I wyll rehearse:

> '*Sic erit in consummatione seculi: exibunt angeli et seperabunt malos de medio justorum, et mittent eos in caminum ignis, ubi erit fletus et stridor dentium.*'
>
> (Chester mystery cycle, 24/573–80 + Latin)[2]

The majority of the audience here, and presumably elsewhere in the cycles, is not assumed to understand the Latin – only 'clearkes' (clerics) will be able to do that, and in any case the preceding lines virtually translate the Latin text. But they would surely recognize the religious and learned connotations of an authorized Latin text. Such Latin forms the upper limit of that stylistic continuum in the Wakefield cycle which E. Catherine Dunn calls 'the Church voice',[3] for Latin influences also the vernacular

---

[1] See, further, Richard Axton, *European Drama of the Early Middle Ages* (London, 1974), 26–32.

[2] Hereafter, Chester. Plays are referred to by number: see Appendix, pp. 292–302.

[3] 'The literary style of the Towneley plays', *American Benedictine Review*, 20 (1969), 481–504.

'high style' discussed below and clearly exemplified by the 'Englysch Laten' (124) of Mercy's speeches in *Mankind*.

The language of the ruling class after the Conquest, French, remained a 'high status' language throughout the Middle Ages. But political events of the thirteenth century weakened the ties binding England to France and prepared the way for the re-establishment of English as the language of the court and government in the following century. Noblemen's children no longer acquired French as their first language but had to be taught it later, preferably in France and in the form of Central French, the language of Paris, rather than of Norman French, the form used by the Norman Conquerors, which had in any case developed so many unique features in England through its separation from its parent form in Normandy that the French of England was virtually a distinct dialect – Anglo-Norman French. Anglo-Norman was the original language of the *Ordo representationis Ade* (twelfth century) and *La Seinte Resureccion* (*c.*1175), both plays probably performed in England before French-speaking – and hence perhaps educated, upper-class – audiences. Although English vernacular plays date from a period when French was no longer a living language and were written for a different kind of audience, playwrights still found French on occasion a useful linguistic indicator of upper-class status, as in the dialogue between King Herod and the Magi in the Chester cycle:

PRIMUS REX.   Syr roy, ryall and reverent,
   Deu vous gard, omnipotent.
SECUNDUS REX.   Nos summes veneus comoplent,
   novelis de enquire.
HERODES.   Bien soies venues, royes gent.
   Me detes tout vetere entent.
TERTIUS REX.   Infant querenues de grand parent,
   et roy de celi et terre.

                       (Chester, 8/153–60)

[FIRST KING.   Sir king, royal and revered,
   May God preserve you, all powerful one.
SECOND KING.   We have come together
   to seek tidings.
HEROD.   Welcome, noble kings.
   Tell me all that you intend.
THIRD KING.   We seek a child of high parentage
   and king of heaven and earth.]

Although the words have been corrupted by the copying of uncomprehending scribes, the dialogue is meaningful; but the Magi have already explained the reason for their visit to Herod's messenger (126–32) and the French is more important as an indicator of social *milieu* than for its specific meaning.

Though many 'middle-class' men – administrators, traders, etc. – would need to be bilingual or even trilingual during the Middle Ages, and the knowledge of Latin and French was the mark of the educated and well-born man or woman, the majority of the population would speak only their local variety of the English language. Although a 'low prestige' language in the centuries after the Conquest, English slowly gained ground and cultural respectability as French ceased to be the first language of court and government. But throughout our period there was no prestigious variety of English which served as a norm or standard against which linguistic change could be measured. The considerable regional variety of English and the marked divergences between dialects are a major feature of the period. The diversity of regional usage is the counterpart to the diversity of regional culture within which the vernacular drama must be evaluated.

English playwrights at this time were influenced by a general concern for compatibility between subject and style which became particularly formalized in the fifteenth century. High themes and subjects demand a 'high style', low themes and base subjects a 'low style'. The high style is characterized, particularly, by a vocabulary containing many words and word-elements borrowed from Latin and the Romance languages, poly-syllabic in form and 'abstract' rather than 'concrete' in meaning. These words are woven into elaborate, rhetorically ordered structures in which tautology, repetition and circumlocution serve as embellishments and in which rhymes exploit the sounds and rhythms of Romance word-endings. Conversely, in a low style the vocabulary consists of familiar words in general use with strong, concrete associations – often sexual or scatological, and making frequent use of oaths. This language forms the basis for wittily inventive imagery, particularly in abuse. The style suggests a more colloquial kind of language in its syntax and rhythms. The antithesis of the two styles is exploited in *Mankind* in the speeches of Mercy and the Vices, and underlies the different speech-forms in Wakefield's *Mactacio Abel*.

For a playwright, the styles could provide an immediate way of identifying a character since a 'noble style' befitting a 'noble subject' would characterize a 'noble (that is, spiritually enlightened) mind' while the reverse held true of the 'low style'. In a figure such as God, the compatibility would be complete:

> I ame greate God gracious,
> which never had begyninge.
> The wholl foode of parente [the entire progeny of parents/our first parents] is sett
> in my essention [essence].
> I ame the tryall of the Trenitye
> which never shalbe twyninge [separating],
> pearles patron ymperiall,
> and Patris sapiencia [wisdom of the Father].

> (Chester, 1/5–12)

Though meaningful, the speech is unlikely to have been readily intelligible delivered from a wagon in a Chester street on a Monday morning. But the Latinate diction, which yields directly to Latin at times, marks the speaker as 'noble'. Sometimes, however, figures who hold high status lack nobility of mind and will reveal their true natures by a process of stylistic degeneration from high to low style, as Chester's Herod does (8/161–212).[1] And sometimes characters of low social station but noble mind may, non-naturalistically, move from low to high style when confronted with a 'high' subject, as do the shepherds of Wakefield or Chester at the news of Christ's birth (see below, pp. 172–9).

Decorative alliteration tends also to be a feature of the high style, but its origins are diverse. Although compatible with rhetorical concern for rhythm and sound, alliteration in English also served more important structural purposes at times. Poetry in which a set number of stressed and alliterating syllables marked the metrical structure of each line was the usual form before the Conquest and an 'alliterative long line' survives after the Conquest in modified form, to provide the medium for a number of important fourteenth-century poems of the so-called 'alliterative revival'. This form was particularly characteristic of the West Midlands and North, and permeates the cycles of York and Wakefield. Beside it stand the syllabic forms favoured by French poets with their regular alternations of strongly and weakly stressed syllables, the familiar modern forms. There alliteration is used, not structurally, but as a stylistic embellishment. But the alliterative

---

[1] See David Mills, 'Some possible implications of Herod's speech: Chester Plays VIII, 153–204', *Neuphilologische Mitteilungen* 74 (1973), 131–43.

tradition not only accustomed hearers to the use of alliteration; it also, by its constraints, ensured the survival of words such as *capel* (horse) or *gome* (man) as elements in a special alliterative poetic vocabulary, and encouraged formulaic collocations such as *cares colde*.

Any specialist skill is likely to acquire its own vocabulary and even its own pronunciation, morphology and syntax. The York playwright, for example, who wrote the *Building of the Ark* (Play 8) for the Shipwrights' Guild employs technical vocabulary for the display of shipwright's tools and techniques (65–111). The Chester Painters dazzle their audience with lists of sheep-diseases and their remedies (7/9–40, 77–80) to characterize the shepherds. The trial scenes in York's Passion-sequence (see below, pp. 190–2) provide ample scope for legal terminology, which can be taken up also in the Doomsday plays. Such technical terms are often unfamiliar and puzzling today, and would not necessarily be widely understood by the contemporary audiences of the plays. If their specific meaning is important, it is usually indicated by the context both of the text and the action; if such indications are absent, the terms may well be used rather for their connotations and associations.

(ii) Dialectal variety and linguistic change

Although playwrights are conscious of the artistic possibilities of register, their staple is the current speech of their local audience, and in the absence of a culturally prestigious form of English, all current forms were equally suitable as literary and dramatic media. And there were many regional varieties, for only the necessity of communication between neighbouring communities limited the in-built tendencies of language to change. Moreover, in the north and east, the former Danelaw, the structure and vocabulary of regional dialects were markedly different from those in other parts of the country because of the influence of Norse. Philologists distinguish five large dialect-areas in Middle English – the south-east and south-west, the east and west Midlands, and the north; but each area contained a considerable variety of sub-dialects and some areas, notably London (which was to be influential in the rise of a standard form), fell between major dialect areas.

Many regional forms, particularly in syntax and vocabulary, did not gain acceptance in the standard dialect of English and hence seem unfamiliar

and strange to us today. Hence, while a medieval audience could presumably
distinguish a register, with its unusual but strongly connotative terms, from
the local speech-forms which they used in daily discourse, it is difficult for
us to make that distinction. We might share with them the problems of
understanding God's opening speech at Chester, but would have difficulties
which they did not share with the York Joseph's lines:

> Þat reproffe dose me pyne,
> And gars me fle fra hame.

> (York mystery cycle, 13/56–7)[1]

Yet this is acceptable northern speech. *Gars* derives from Norse *gøra*, 'to
cause', corresponding to our standard 'makes'; *fra* is a northern form of
from, influenced again by Norse; and *hame* corresponds to modern *home*,
where the northern dialect has retained the pre-Conquest *a* (sound as in
car) while other areas have modified the sound to *o*. Multiplied over long
sequences of lines, such regional forms create difficulties for the modern
reader, who can resolve the difficulties only through notes and glossaries.
But they are an inevitable result of rooting the action in the daily language
and experience of the audience. The local speech-form, like local topo-
graphical and contemporary allusions, is a major link between the drama
and its community.

So strong was this link that the Wakefield Master could exploit the speech
of a 'furriner' for comic ends. When Mak demands reverence as a king's
yeoman in lordly manner (Wakefield mystery cycle, 13/201–7, 211–13), he
is abruptly told:

> Now take outt that sothren tothe
> And sett in a torde.

> (13/215–16)

Not only does Mak act in the domineering manner of a southerner in the
north; he also, as A. C. Cawley has shown,[2] incorporates some southern
usages into his usual northern speech, saying, for example *Ich be* for the
northern *I am*. Chaucer had used dialect earlier to characterize the northern
clerks in his *Reeve's Tale*[3] but the Wakefield Master is the first dramatist
in English to exploit dialect differences for dramatic ends. In so doing, he

[1] For the use of Þ and other forms, see p. 77.
[2] A. C. Cawley, *The Wakefield Pageants in the Towneley Cycle* (Manchester, 1958),
Appendix IV.
[3] See, for example, J. R. R. Tolkien, 'Chaucer as a philologist', *Transactions of the
Philological Society* (1934), 1–70; N. F. Blake, 'The northernisms in *The Reeve's Tale*',
Lore and Language 3 (1979), 1–8.

can assume that the audience is aware of such differences and their possible social implications.

Yet this emphasis upon 'living speech' in the plays demands some qualification. Between the fourteenth and sixteenth centuries the English language continued to change markedly. In phonology, the first effects of the Great Vowel Shift on the pronunciation of long vowels were being seen. The process of shifting the main means of marking grammatical function from the forms of words (morphology) to their position within a sentence (syntax) was being completed. The vocabulary was changing. Neighbouring dialects continued to modify each other, producing new regional varieties. And concern was being expressed about lack of a standard form, the supposed inadequacies of English as a cultural medium, and the possible debasement of the language by loan-words. Texts of medieval drama were at once traditional and also subject to frequent revision, and it is probable that their language became a mixture of older and newer usages. The post-Reformation banns of Chester's mystery cycle, apologizing with doubtful sincerity for the rusticity of the plays, draw attention to archaic features of their language:

> Condemne not oure matter where groosse wordes you heare
> which importe at this daye smale sence or vnderstandinge
> As sometimes postye [power], bewtye, in good manner or in feare [together]
> with suchlike wilbe vttered in theare speaches speakeinge.
> At this tyme those speeches caried good lykinge
> Thoe if at this tyme you take them spoken at that tyme
> As well matter as wordes, then all is well. fyne.[1]

If current local speech linked the text with the contemporary community, archaic forms were evidence of a long and continuing tradition. A conservative quaintness might evidently check the modernizing tendencies, at least in minor details of style. The Chester banns may indicate that audiences could have shared some of our difficulties about words no longer in use. They also bear out what may be inferred from the variant readings for the same line in Chester manuscripts, that there were, at different periods, different ways of stressing words and calculating the number of syllables in a line.

---

[1] The last two lines might be paraphrased: 'If you, living at this present time, understand these speeches as taking the form of speech used in the past – and do so for the content as well as the words – then all will be well'. *REED, Chester*, 241, ll. 25–31.

(iii) The extant texts

The scribes who copied out our manuscripts were trained in the use of an alphabet and certain spelling conventions, but as yet there was no nationally agreed written standard form and no dictionary to help the scribe. So a scribe took into account several factors in deciding how to spell a word – the form he was copying; the forms he had copied before; the way he usually wrote the word; the conventions of his own spelling system; the pronunciation of the word. Though these considerations might all lead to the same conclusion, they might equally prove contradictory and the scribe might resolve the contradictions in different ways on different occasions. Printed texts, being later than most manuscripts, show less variation; but variation is still possible and may be exploited or deliberately introduced to 'justify the line' – to ensure that each line ends at the same point on the page to give a straight right-hand margin.

To a modern reader a text in which familiar words appear in unfamiliar spellings tends to be particularly disturbing. Compare the form of Anna's speech in N-town 8/53–6 on p. 65 of Block's edition:

> For dred and ffor swem of ȝour wourdys I qwake
> thryes I kysse ȝow with syghys ful sad
> and to þe mercy of god · mekely I ȝow betake
> and þo þat departe in sorwe god make þer metyng glad.

with the far less daunting appearance of the same speech with modern spelling substituted:

> For dread and for swem of your words I quake.
> Thrice I kiss you with sighs full sad
> And to the mercy of God meekly I you betake.
> And tho that depart in sorrow, God make their meeting glad.

Some of the difficulties here lie in the use of unfamiliar letters – þ for *th*, ȝ for *y*; we will also find elsewhere *æ* for *a*, ȝ for our *gh* (for example, *bouȝt* for *bought*). Many more result from the use of familiar letters in unfamiliar positions or combinations: *y* used medially where we use *i* (*metyng*); similarly N-town uses *x* for *sh* in *xal*, *qw* for *qu*, *ff* for *F*. Many scribes interchange *u* and *v*, writing *vs* for *us* and *hauing* for *having*. A major group of unfamiliar forms results from the absence of any consistent indication of vowel length in the spelling convention. We are today not consistent in such indications but we do have only one spelling for each word, whereas the medieval scribe often had a variety of possibilities. Thus we write *full* for N-town's *ful*, *meekly* for *mekely*, *meeting* for *metyng*. Final *-e* today usually indicates something about the preceding vowel or consonant, as it does not in *kysse*. A major difficulty arises from the absence of punctuation and systematic capitalization in the text and, in the passage cited, as often in N-town, from the use of a dot, placed at mid-height in the line, to indicate the position of a caesura.

Editors vary in their practice with such spelling problems. Block, the editor of N-town, is extremely conservative; most editors will punctuate and many will resolve the *v/u* interchange by substituting modern practice. But few wish to remove the original inconsistencies entirely. First, these may be a useful guide to language and pronunciation – in *syghys* and *wourdys*, the N-town scribe's *y* suggests that the words are disyllabic, as regular metre would require, while *sorwe*, unlike *sorrow*, suggests an acceptable monosyllable. Secondly, the substitution of modern forms might misleadingly suggest that the words also necessarily had their modern meanings, an error we readily fall into in dealing with Tudor texts. The variations are too numerous to attempt to classify comprehensively and cumulatively they add to the daunting appearance of a play text. But a modern reader would do well to remember that many strange-looking words are modern forms in disguise and that when the text is read aloud many of the ostensible difficulties will disappear. In the chapters which follow, we have used standard editions of the various texts and have accepted the particular conventions of each edition. But we have added glosses of particularly difficult words in English texts and have supplied translations of texts in other languages to help the reader. Some changes in punctuation have also occasionally been made.

2 Medieval and modern views of drama

David Mills

(i) Approaches to medieval drama

The people living in England before the sixteenth century would not have known the key-word of this series of volumes, *drama*. Drama came into existence and flourished for a considerable time before it was distinctively named, and it is clear that what we nowadays unhesitatingly label *drama* amongst the works of the Middle Ages was not always and regularly distinguished from other activities. The *Oxford English Dictionary* (hereafter, *OED*) records the word first in 1515, when it is used as an apparent alternative to *a play*. It is not until 1661 that the word is evidenced in the sense of a genre – 'the dramatic branch of literature, the dramatic art' – and not until 1714 that it appears referring to an action not textually controlled: 'a series of actions or course of events having a unity like that of a drama, and leading to a final catastrophe or consummation.' The introduction and semantic development of *drama* focuses the problems of a modern critic in talking about 'medieval drama', for this Renaissance loan-word, from late Latin *drama* (Gr. *drama*, from *dran*, 'to do, act'), arises from a general consciousness of classical drama and its forms by scholars and comes to express the idea of *drama* as a distinctive art-form, characterized by its own attributes and potential and capable of being appreciated by its own aesthetic. The word today evokes a range of standards and assumptions shared by those who write and present plays and those who read and watch them, but there is no evidence to suggest that the Middle Ages had similar standards and assumptions, still less that they were conscious of 'drama' as a genre apart. The most that can be said is that there are indications of unformulated intuitions that activities we would now label dramatic were different from other activities with which they happened to be associated.

'Medieval drama' thus presents two major problems for the modern critic. The first is to determine the limits implied by the use of the term, to establish criteria which will define the corpus of material to be studied. The second is to establish the critical standards by which the corpus is to be assessed. In many ways these problems are those of any modern critic approaching any area of English medieval literature. As Arthur K. Moore has aptly put it:

> While the works of Dante and Chaucer, after more than five centuries of steady approval, were regarded as proper subjects of critical scrutiny, medieval literature was for the most part secured from objective evaluation by suspicions and reservations engendered by the *Liedertheorie*, literary evolutionism, and the Romantic concept of *das dichtende Volk*.[1]

But the serious criticism of medieval literature by professional scholars according to formal criteria – as opposed to the amateur critic seeing in works of any period the reflections of his own contemporary interests and outlook – is now well established. Moore sees it as a development since the Second World War, but D. S. Brewer, dealing with Chaucer criticism, finds it beginning in *c*. 1933.[2] At any rate, we can now find a variety of critical approaches to medieval literature and the emergence of a study of theories of criticism in the medieval field. Against this background of general critical activity, the criticism of medieval drama did not become the province of the professional scholar until about the mid-1960s, and it is still in a fluid and somewhat experimental stage.

It is difficult to establish why medieval drama was neglected by critics for so long. Two possible reasons are, first, that medieval drama seemed a less amenable genre for study than the works of 'pure literature' such as the works of Chaucer or the *Gawain*-poet towards which medievalists

---

[1] 'Medieval English literature and the question of unity', *MP*, 65 (1968), 285.
[2] D. S. Brewer (ed.), *Chaucer, The Critical Heritage*, 2 vols (London, 1978), I, 1–2.

largely directed their attention; and, secondly, that for those interested in drama, the achievements of the Elizabethan stage, culminating in Shakespeare, seemed to offer more accessible and exciting material. A third reason was the overriding influence of one man, Sir Edmund K. Chambers, with whose two-volume work, *The Mediaeval Stage*, published in 1903, scholarly interest in medieval drama may be said to begin. His book can be confidently recommended to the modern reader as an example of scholarly thoroughness and also for its projection of its author's interest and delight in his subject, a combination of qualities rarely found in the work of modern critics.

Perhaps paradoxically, the subject was too well served by the well-researched, wide-ranging, and readable work of this erudite gentleman scholar. Chambers's great survey came to be regarded as definitive and hence inhibited further exploration of its subject. It also proved an unfortunate influence in other ways. Chambers's view of literature was conditioned by a Darwinian biology; as life evolved through simple forms to more complex forms, so genres evolved from simple to more complex forms, both acting in response to external stimuli. Chambers expressly denies the literary autonomy of the dramatic genre, arguing that any literary history must start from 'the social and economic facts upon which the mediaeval drama rested' (I.v), and hence provides a wide-ranging and entertainingly idiosyncratic account of a number of 'dramatic' activities which provide the context for the main line of dramatic evolution. He disarmingly apologizes for the length of the work, 'unduly swelled by the inclusion of new interests as, from time to time, they took hold upon me' (ibid.). But he also regarded 'mediaeval drama' as the simple ancestor of the 'complex' forms of Elizabethan drama. The work began in the desire for a short preface to what was to be his *William Shakespeare* and this aim remained: 'It endeavours to state and explain the pre-existing conditions which, by the latter half of the sixteenth century, made the great Shakespearean stage possible' (I. v–vi). It was these sociological and evolutionary views of drama which were to influence subsequent studies and to equate 'medieval' with 'pre-Shakespearean' in the scholarly and popular mind.

The reaction against Chambers' viewpoint which was to align the criticism of medieval drama with established trends in medieval literary criticism had three aspects. In his *Christian Rite and Christian Drama in the Middle Ages*, published in 1965, O. B. Hardison, Jr, convincingly isolated the underlying theses of Chambers and indicated their deficiencies. In so doing, he pointed the way to a new and independent status for the Latin drama of the Church, often treated merely as the simple historical precursor of vernacular drama. Meanwhile, in the first volume of his *Early English Stages, 1330–1660*, published in 1959, Glynne Wickham had provided the catalyst for a series of studies which related 'medieval drama' to the wider context of ceremonial and celebration – procession, tournament, triumphal entry, the festivities of the nobility, etc. – and focused attention upon the conditions under which 'plays' were produced and performed. The mere unearthing of isolated facts of medieval staging would not of itself be particularly valuable, but studies in production have challenged generic notions and proposed a new taxonomy of medieval drama. Thus Alan H. Nelson, in *The Medieval English Stage: Corpus Christi Pageants and Plays*, has queried whether the extant York mystery cycle, and other plays in English towns, were capable of being performed in a single day on pageant-wagons; and Stanley J. Kahrl has argued that staging-criteria are more valuable in the criticism of drama than theories of genre:

> Determining the relative excellence of a particular medieval play requires...consideration of the adaptation made to the theatre for which the play was written. In such a study, generic terms, 'Corpus Christi cycle play', or 'morality play', are of little or no help. Rather than comparing the play under scrutiny with plays of similar theme or content, we must compare them with other plays written for place-and-scaffold, station-to-station, or booth stage theatres.[1]

Thirdly, a mode of generic criticism owing much to the parallel concerns in literary criticism also appeared. Its most influential product is V. A. Kolve's *The Play Called Corpus Christi*, published in 1966. Setting up a proto-cycle for all possible cycle-plays containing 'the formally significant material', he poses the specifically generic questions of 'how the Corpus Christi play is constructed, why its essential episodes are essential, and in what manner form in this drama governs and expresses meaning' (p. 55). Less explicitly 'literary' concepts of drama underlie the 'medieval' aesthetic of drama in Rosemary Woolf's *The English Mystery Plays* (London, 1972), which looks to art-iconography and eschews modern concepts of nationalism for the English play-cycles while insisting that 'a play had obviously to be self-sufficient in narrative terms' (p. 54), and Robert Potter's view, in *The English Morality Play*, of the mythologically satisfying pattern which characterizes the morality form:

> A concept – what it means to be human – is represented on the stage by a central dramatic figure or series of figures. Subsidiary characters,

[1] Stanley J. Kahrl, *Traditions of Medieval English Drama* (London, 1974), 70.

defined by their function, stand at the service of the plot, which is ritualized, dialectical, and inevitable. (pp. 6–7)

In seeking a generic description of medieval drama, modern critics are investing the concept of genre with a permanence which places it outside historical circumstances. By so doing, they gain the freedom to discuss its manifestations in terms of the range of aesthetics which it implies. They also break down the chronological restrictions of the term 'medieval', so that, for example, Potter can find the apotheosis of the morality play in Marlowe, Shakespeare and Jonson. And, in seeking to classify the variety of medieval forms generically, they replace the older hierarchy of simple–complex forms with a synchronic variety of genres among which an individual dramatist or 'choreographer' might choose. As with studies of other aspects of medieval literature, however, the new professionalism emphasizes the need for the publication of more primary material in more scholarly forms than previously. Taxonomies based on staging and production founder at the moment because too few of the records of early drama have been edited and too much speculation about the circumstances of a particular performance is involved. Taxonomies based on literary criteria are dependent upon the availability of new, more accurate editions of the material with full scholarly apparatus. And, as yet, the two approaches, of dramatic and literary emphasis, remain disturbingly distinct, while all critics feel the need at least to postulate the non-literary circumstances which might give rise to dramatic genres, if not also the non-literary artistic contexts against which the plays should be evaluated. A critic entering the field of medieval drama is uneasily aware of the absence even of agreed terminology, the considerable variety of critical attitude and the rapidly changing state of scholarship.

(ii) A medieval view: *A Tretise of Miraclis Pleyinge*

But the twentieth-century search for an appropriate context within which to assess medieval drama is not a new phenomenon. The Middle Ages themselves were similarly concerned with the functions and paradigms of drama, then an emergent genre, but by the end of the fourteenth century some people at least were conscious that a new and potentially subversive art-form had been born, for which existing justifications and critical standards were inadequate. Central to our understanding of this development is a late fourteenth-century Lollard work, *A Tretise of Miraclis Pleyinge*.[1] *Miracle* is a word which today is often used beside the un-medieval 'dramatic' terms *mystery* (*OED* 1744) and *morality* (Potter records as 1741) as if it meant 'a play on a saint's life', but, as the *Middle English Dictionary* (hereafter, *MED*) defines it – '2b. a dramatization of any Scriptural event or legend of a saint, martyr, etc., also, a performance of such a play' – it is a term applicable to any play on a religious subject, and hence to the kind of play with which this chapter is concerned. The *Tretise* author objects to such plays, but in so doing demonstrates his awareness of the usual connotations of the term *play*, suggests that the issue was one of contemporary controversy by voicing arguments in defence of the plays, and provides us with valuable evidence of the circumstances of performance. Above all, however, he indicates his awareness that drama has outstripped its religious function to become an art-form in its own right.

At the centre of his and our discussion is the word *play*, a term of wide semantic range first instanced with dramatic reference in Middle English by the *OED* in 1325. With it we should follow Kolve in linking *game*, well attested in dramatic application by the *MED*, since the two words present similar semantic problems.[2] The *Tretise* author's attitude to religious plays is conditioned by his consciousness of a primary antithesis between the trivialities connoted by the word *play* and the spiritual truths inherent in the religious subject-matter. His main objection to religious plays is that they represent a breach of the second commandment: 'No man shulde usen in bourde and pleye the miraclis and werkis that Crist so ernystfully wroughte to oure helthe.' The opposition of *bourde and pleye* to *ernystfully* takes up a common antithesis of 'joke, jest' (cf. *MED* 4a, *OED* 7) and what is serious or in earnest, an antithesis conveniently reflected in Chaucer's line: 'And eek men shal nat maken ernest of game' (*Canterbury Tales*, I.3186).

In developing his attack, the author counters a number of arguments in defence of religious plays, notably that they are an effective mode of religious instruction and an aid to devotion. Evidence from other sources confirms that such defences were used; a Wycliffite tract commends the York Paternoster play in 1378 for teaching the Lord's Prayer in English,[3] and Friar William Melton commended the York Corpus Christi play for

---

[1] Clifford Davidson, *A Middle English Treatise on the Playing of Miracles* (Washington, 1981).

[2] Kolve, chapter 2.

[3] *De Officio Pastorali*, cap. 15.

its content in 1426.[1] The arguments here, however, raise interesting issues. The plays are defended as a medium particularly suited to the needs of a section of the contemporary populace:

> Also prophitable to men and to the worschipe of God it is to fulfillun and sechen alle the menes by the whiche men mowen leeve synne and drawen hem to vertues and sithen as ther ben men that only by ernestful doinge wilen be convertid to God, so ther been othere men that wilen not be convertid to God but by gamen and pley.

They are also defended as a vivid extension of religious painting:

> betere thei ben holden in mennus mynde and oftere rehersid in the pleyinge of hem than in the peyntynge, for this [the painting] is a deed bok ['dead' book], the tother [the play] a quick.

To such arguments the *Tretise* author responds by denying that the plays can convert men, for compared with the word and sacraments of God, they are false; unlike pictures, which are neutral records of the truth which clerks can interpret, they are 'made more to deliten men bodily than to ben bokis to lewid men'; and they work upon the bodily senses and desires of men to produce the illusion of repentance: 'and, therfore, hauyng more compassion of peine than of sinne, they falsly wepyn for lakkinge of bodily prosperite more than for lakking of gostly.' Despite the similarities, plays differ from true worship and instruction in their basic conception, in the nature of their appeal, and in the kind of response which they produce in their audiences.

This dichotomy leads the *Tretise* author ultimately to a position in which he can separate drama from its subject and function and suggest its existence as an autonomous genre. Religious plays, he claims, are not concerned to present religious truths – that is, to give prominence to content. Rather, they assimilate religious material for their own ends – to create effective drama:

> Thes miraclis pleyeris and the fawtours [supporters] of hem ben verre apostaas, bothe for they puttun God bihinde and ther owne lustis biforn, as they han minde of God onely for sake of ther pley and also for they deliten hem more in the pley than in the miraclis silf.

Thus, the pernicious nature of drama lies in its neutrality as an art form.

---

[1] *REED, York*, 1, 42–4.

Though it superficially resembles and even expressly alludes to the subjects and modes of religious expression, its presuppositions and aims are different from those associated with such expression. The result is dangerously misleading for the audience since it confuses important distinctions of meaning and response, and the play becomes an act of deception – 'a plan, project; scheme, trick, plot' (*MED* 5(c)) 'an act or proceeding, esp. of a crafty or underhand kind; a trick, dodge, "game"' (*OED* 9), as *play* may also be defined.

The actor typifies this deceit, for the author of the *Tretise* is conscious of the discrepancy between the actors' performances and their lives:

> Siche miraclis pleyinge ne the sighte of hem is no verrey recreasion, but fals and worldly, as provyn the dedis of the fautours of siche pleyis that yit nevere tastiden verely swetnesse in God, traveilinge so myche therinne that their body wolde not sofisen to beren siche a traveile of the spirite.

But the actor is like the apostate who goes through the outward signs of devotion without the substance and who preaches of God while thinking of profit in the same way that the actor enacts God's deeds while thinking of his play. The author implies a link between the drama and the sermon, the main medium of lay instruction, which he uses to make a familiar point about the preacher and his text. The subjects of plays and sermons were often the same and sermons could be heard where drama could be seen – in churches, churchyards, market-places. Both were oral. And the sermon could be regarded as a dramatic monologue with the preacher as actor, except that the true Christian preacher meant and practised what he preached. But a false preacher, like Chaucer's Pardoner, was indeed an actor. The prologue to his story explains that he learned the lines of his sermon by heart, that he had a set pattern of delivery on all occasions, and that his preaching was for his own profit, in direct contradiction of the theme of his address. Moreover, Chaucer's Pardoner decides to enter his famous sermon-exemplum in the Host's story-telling contest as an example of his professional skill, detaching it entirely from its usual spiritual contexts and functions and inviting evaluation of it as effective narrative. The reader is, however, directed to a reaction similar to the *Tretise* author's attitude towards religious drama and its actors when the Pardoner angers the Host by cynically evoking the appropriate spiritual response to a sermon at the conclusion of his tale.

The techniques of oral publication underlie medieval drama, sermon and literature and may obscure some of the distinctions between them. The *Canterbury Tales* purport to be a series of dramatic monologues which derive from a variety of genres; saint's life, exemplum and sermon stand beside fabliau and romance, levelled as examples of narrative. They remind us of the possibility of divorcing art from function. They also remind us that literary publication may well have been oral in many cases and that, whatever the reality, many medieval texts affect an oral form, with an intrusive 'narrator-figure' whom the text serves partially to characterize. Actor, preacher and 'poet-*persona*' share a common ethos and can be distinguished only in so far as the relationship of performer to performance is clearly specified.

The deceit of drama, according to the *Tretise*, is also exemplified by the production itself, at once blasphemously inadequate in its depiction of the divine and dangerously misleading in its mixture of truth and falsehood. The presumption of imitating God has been a recurring objection to religious drama. The medieval concern is clearly exemplified in the poem 'On the Minorites':

> First þai gabben [tell lies about] on god þat all men may se,
> When þai hangen him on hegh on a grene tre,
> with leues and with blossemes þat bright are of ble [colour],
> þat was neuer goddes son by my leutè [by my faith]....
> Þei haue done him on a croys fer up in þe skye,
> And festned in hym wyenges, as he shul flie,
> Þis fals feyned byleue shal þai soure bye
> On þat louelych lord, so forto lye.[1]

It is the blatant inadequacy of the representation which seems to offend the author here as he describes what is apparently a dramatic presentation. But, the *Tretise* author also complains, the texts of religious plays inextricably fuse 'lies' (presumably material which lacks the authority of the Church or of texts approved by the Church) with truth, so that the audiences are led into false belief: 'For now the puple giveth credence to many mengid leesingis [interspersed lies], for othere mengid trewthis and maken wenen to been gode that is ful yvel.' It is the presence of recognizably true, authorized material in the plays which makes them dangerous, because it lends spurious authority to 'unauthorized' material. Above all, drama encourages men to acknowledge a distinction between illusion and

---

[1] Cited by Kolve, 29.

reality without indicating the exact location of the dividing-line, so that belief in God's serious purpose may be diminished. To those who say 'Pley we a pley of Anticrist and of the Day of Dome / that sum man may be convertid therby', the *Tretise* author replies: 'Many men wenen that ther is no helle of everelastinge peine, but that God doth but thretith us, not to do it in dede, as ben pleyinge of miraclis in signe and not in dede.'

The most serious aspect of drama's deceitfulness for the *Tretise* author lies in the audience's response to religious plays. A powerfully convincing performance evidently stirred the audience's emotions, but the author believes that it leads to the confusion of an emotional response to dramatic art and the emotional accompaniment proper to spiritual introspection and to the action prompted by true religious meditation. Drama appeals to earthly, not spiritual, sight. The tears of an audience at plays of the Passion are tears of compassion at the sight of the suffering player-Christ, not tears of remorse arising from a consciousness of their own sin, which is what the Passion should call to mind:

> Siche miraclis pleyinge giveth noon occasioun of werrey wepinge and medeful, but the weping that fallith to men and wymmen by the sighte of siche miraclis pleyinge, as they ben not principaly for theire oune sinnes ne of theire gode feith withinne forthe, but more of theire sight withoute forth.

Such a comment indicates the considerable emotive power of religious plays, and also the *Tretise* author's recurring awareness of a distinction between response to art and response to spiritual edification which is threatened by what he sees as the use of religious material for dramatic ends.

The dangers in this new art-form are intensified by its popularity. Drama, the *Tretise* indicates, has been brought into existence by the need to communicate to contemporary men; it is a product of cultural and social circumstances. It has come to be regarded as an appropriate form of entertainment on 'holidays' after people have been to church. And it reaches – and thus perverts – not just individuals or small groups but a whole community: 'As it is sinne it is fer more occasion of perverting of men, not onely of oon singuler persone but an hool comynte.' And its production is supported by two distinct groups, equally reprehensible. The first group, against whom the *Tretise* is mainly directed, is the clergy, who are forbidden to act in plays or to watch them, but who seem nevertheless to be considered as their instigators. The severest criticisms are directed against religious evangelists who see the plays as a new, modern medium for communicating religious truths and are blind to the dangers.

But the *Tretise* also attacks a second group of play-sponsors, the traders in the community, who have their own interests at heart. The author makes three specific criticisms against such people. First, he objects to the lavish sums of money spent unhesitatingly upon the plays by them, arguing that it would be better if these patrons spent their money on settling debts or paying rents, or in giving donations to the poor. Secondly, he objects to the occasions of the plays, because inducements are given to the people to spend money, to indulge in gluttony and lechery. Thirdly, these inducements to sin result from the avarice of the people who will profit by such expenditure. So, he claims, in advance of the play-days 'thei bisien hem beforn to more gredily bygilen ther neghbors, in byinge and in selling' and on the days themselves they grossly inflate prices for the crowds who have come for the performance. The background of unscrupulous commercialism thus serves to complement the false belief which finds expression in the plays. Friar Melton, on his visit to York, found the Corpus Christi play itself commendable, but was much concerned at the activities of the crowds:

> Ludum predictum populo commendavit affirmando quod bonus erat in se et laudabilis valde dicebat tamen quod cives predicte civitatis et alii forinseci in dicto festo confluentes ad eandem non solum ipsi ludo in eodem festo verum eciam comessacionibus ebrietatibus clamoribus cantilenis et aliis insolenciis multum intendunt servicio divino officii ipsius diei minime intendentes.[1]
>
> [He commended the aforesaid play to the people, affirming that it was good in itself and highly laudable. But he said that the citizens of the city and other 'outsiders' gathering there were much intent, at the said feast, not only upon the play itself but also upon acts of gluttony and drunkenness, shouting, vulgar songs and other enormities, paying little attention to the divine service of the Office of the day itself.]

Such accounts may to some extent modify the comfortable compatibility of religious edification and commerce envisaged in such descriptions as William Newhall's 1532 Proclamation to the Chester plays:

> Not only for the Augmentacion and incres of the holy and Catholick faith of our sauyour Iesu Crist and to exort the myndes of the common people to good deuotion and holsome doctryne therof, but also for the commonwelth and prosperitie of this Citie.[2]

[1] *REED, York*, I, 43.

[2] *REED, Chester*, 27. The text here has been amplified from BL Harley 2012 and slightly edited.

Divorced from its religious context, religious drama could serve other functions.

Towards the end of the *Tretise*, the author explores some further implications of the word *play* which suggest at once the entertaining and the serious aspects of drama. First, *play* is characteristically the activity of the child, absorbing him without consciousness of wider and more serious issues, as the participants are absorbed in their plays. In the fourteenth-century alliterative poem *Sir Gawain and the Green Knight*, an insolent green challenger rejects the sport of tourneying, arguing that because the courtiers around the hall are only 'berdles childer', a Christmas game would be more fitting, implying a mere functionless and empty entertainment. The *Tretise* author raises the notion of art as play, only to counter it with the criticism of the detached religious observer. Like actors in their plays, children in their games reveal their own folly, the sins of their forefathers, and original sin, and bring down chastisement upon themselves.

But, secondly, there can be serious implications in play, for, as Kolve notes, the limits of *play* and *game* are hard to determine. If a game is a finite, rule-governed action, then much of normal social behaviour could be comprehended under that heading. The game in *Gawain* proves to be one of beheading, translating the mimetic beheading of folk-play into a gruesome reality. The poet thus dissolves the boundary between game and reality and is able to use game as a paradigm for the activities of social man and indeed of all creation, and conversely to imply that in 'games' we have the microcosm of 'real' and 'serious' action. Similarly, the *Tretise* author reapplies the play-image to reality when he finally urges man to act out the three parts assigned to him by God – of meditation and thanksgiving, of steadfast faith and of humility – asking for grace, 'the whiche thre perselis wel to pleyn heere'. One is reminded that game also has the sense (*MED* 5(a)) of 'an action, proceeding; happening, occurrence; course of events'. Certainly, the notion that man acts out roles in society underlies a work such as the *Canterbury Tales*, and the whole issue of the relationship of illusion to reality is not merely a problem of dramatic aesthetics but one of general concern to medieval writers of literature. Ultimately it corresponds to the distance between the audience and the work which, for drama, is both a physical and a textual problem.

The *Tretise* suggests that before the end of the fourteenth century there was already an awareness that drama was a distinct art-form. On the one hand it had affinities with a number of other activities broadly subsumed under the terms *play* and *game*; but on the other it had begun to develop its own *raison d'être* and could equally be regarded as an autonomous genre. Its danger as an art-form lay not only in its concern for effect and in the immediacy of the response which it evinced, or in its inadequacies as mimesis of sacred history. It lay in its still ambivalent status, its dangerous resemblance to functional forms of religious worship and instruction, and in its widespread appeal to a community, with all the dangers that the community would redirect it to serve its own self-interest. The *Tretise* undertakes the difficult task of defining the issues involved. In so doing, it separates drama from its possible functions and attests an awareness of genre and its implications. It implies a truism of generic criticism, that, since genres are permanent, new genres are called into being by new social and cultural circumstances. It is with this in mind that we shall consider the generic diversity comprehended under the title of 'The drama of religious ceremonial'.

3 Drama in the Church

Peter F. McDonald

(i) Introduction: liturgy and drama

All during the Middle Ages and throughout western Europe parts of the liturgy, the public communal worship of the Church,[1] were, from time to time, 'dramatized'. That is to say, an event recorded in a passage of Scripture used in the liturgy, or commemorated by a Feast celebrated on that day, was acted out in the church as an intrinsic part of that day's celebration. Sometimes only a fragment of history was re-enacted, sometimes a whole sequence of events. Nor were these re-enactments only of events in scriptural history, for the liturgy, especially the Office, the daily prayer of priests and monks, incorporated very many legendary as well as scriptural narratives. These re-enactments are often too fragmentary and embodied too deeply in the celebration to be 'plays': frequently a liturgical service will combine, simultaneously, liturgy and mimesis. Sometimes a text of what is undeniably a play will specify the time of performance as being a saint's day, and the place a church, without the play being liturgical in any way. Older histories of drama have presented the relationship between the

[1] For a general introduction to liturgy and liturgical history see Cheslyn Jones, Geoffrey Wainwright and Edward Yarnold (eds), *The Study of Liturgy* (London, 1978).

liturgy and drama as one that developed – and progressed, as far as drama is concerned – systematically in the course of the Middle Ages: such a view is no longer tenable. Liturgy and drama co-existed throughout the Middle Ages as distinct activities, albeit related in many respects. Both the celebration of the liturgy, and the performance of a play, depend upon the existence of an organized, relatively stable, community; they simultaneously depend upon the existence of that community, affirm it to itself and to outsiders, and in so doing ensure its continuation into the future. The monastic chapel, the cathedral and the parish church were established and sustained by the Church for the celebration of the liturgy, but the official liturgy became remote from the peoples of Europe and lost its capacity to sustain, as an act of worship, the sense of corporate identity a community needs in order to survive. The institutional Church did not respond to the alienation of the peoples from the liturgy by encouraging or endorsing the dramatization of parts of the liturgy; individual men and women – possibly encouraged or merely tolerated by their ecclesiastical superiors, and in some cases doubtless unknown to them – recognized and exploited the possibilities of drama.

The event most frequently chosen for re-enactment in the liturgy was the way in which Christ's followers first heard of His resurrection from the dead. The events of the first Easter Sunday (the anachronistic term is convenient and should not be misleading) as recounted in Scripture[1] are inherently dramatic, as the grief of the Apostles and the other followers of Christ after His suffering and death gives way to joy on hearing of His resurrection, and then on seeing Him in His glorified state. The way in which one of these ceremonies was performed has been discussed above (pp. 8–11): although none of these additions to the liturgy ever received the full endorsement of the Church, the *Regularis Concordia* had the institutional authority of the Synod of Winchester, and the personal authority of St Æthelwold. As befits such an authoritative and definitive document, it is not original.[2] Of this version Glynne Wickham says: 'It was clearly intended that the congregation should be confronted with a double image... Thus the event of Christ's resurrection is commemorated by re-enactment in the most artificial and formal manner imaginable: yet what is patently a highly ornate ritual from one standpoint is just as patently a

[1] Matthew 28: 1–15; Mark 16: 1–11; Luke 24: 1–12; John 20: 1–10: the different accounts vary.

[1] *Regularis Concordia. The Monastic Agreement*, ed. and trans. Thomas Symons (London, 1953), xlv–lii.

dramatic representation of a turning point in Christian history when viewed from another.'[1] This 'double image' is the result of combining methods and patterns of movement, dress, speech and singing drawn from two different activities – liturgy and drama. The use of vestments is, for example, liturgical, but albs and copes (see Plate 16) are not usually worn at Matins, the liturgical service to which this *Visit to the Sepulchre* is attached. They are worn here by the monks representing the angel and the women, and as Professor Cawley notes above (pp. 9–10), they are worn to 'distinguish' – not to deceive. They are not quasi-naturalistic costuming, but serve to distinguish the monks who are playing the parts of historical characters – in Scripture history angels are characters – from the anonymous and undifferentiated monks celebrating the liturgy in choir. The use of thuribles and incense at Matins is liturgical; that the women should carry thuribles with them to the sepulchre is a reminder to those who knew the story that the women carried ointment to embalm the body. Finally, although Latin in a tenth-century Benedictine service book cannot be called a dead language, it is not naturalistic either; the dialogue is sung, not spoken, and by the three women in unison, not individually. These details alone indicate that naturalistic illusionism was not the aim of the compiler of this ceremony, yet by the individualizing and particularizing of four members of the choir a past event is re-presented, made to live again in its essential: the joy felt by the followers of Christ at His resurrection. The other members of the choir remain in their normal, liturgically determined place in the church, but for a few minutes during the celebration of the liturgy they cease to be participants in the celebration of the liturgy and become an audience. When they revert to being a congregation participating in the liturgy they can, having witnessed this vivid re-enactment of the joyful event of Christ's resurrection, carry out with renewed fervour and commitment the command which is repeated again and again in the Easter liturgy: 'This is the day which the Lord hath made: let us rejoice and be glad in it' (Psalm 118: 24).

The events of the first Easter Sunday were the most popular subjects for dramatization all through the Middle Ages. These dramatizations drew upon the same fund of material, but combined it and other material in what often seems a bewildering variety of subtly different ways. The very popularity of these dramatizations is daunting, confusing and possibly misleading. It is not known, for example, if there was one 'original' version,

[1] Glynne Wickham, *The Medieval Theatre* (London, 1974; repr. 1977), 41.

or several independently arrived at; it is not known whether it, or they, came into existence as a *trope*, a variation on liturgical music and words, as an adaptation of an existing liturgical service the function of which had lapsed, or as a partly didactic stimulus to increase and intensify devotion.[1] Possibly at some time in the future if all the manuscripts in which versions are found are liturgically and musically edited, and located in their geographical, historical and social context, patterns of derivation and influence will emerge. The wealth of versions can be misleading because it has often been suggested in modern times that 'similar' plays on other subjects were attached to the liturgy in similar numbers.[2] This is certainly not so. What is certain, and not least from modern performances, is that these ceremonies in which liturgical and mimetic methods were fused to create a distinctive kind of activity are to be experienced and assessed in their own terms and not as imperfect harbingers of later dramatic styles.

Even if it is agreed that the *Visit to the Sepulchre* in the *Regularis Concordia* is a successful fusion in a double image of methods borrowed from liturgy and drama, it does not follow that all such efforts as recorded in extant texts succeeded. There was no recipe for writing good plays in the Middle Ages any more than there is one now. In some texts liturgical methods predominate and in others dramatic, in such a way that the use of one set of methods is inhibited without the other being fully exploited; in some cases the compilers of ceremonies did achieve a successful fusion, in others merely a mixture, and in others a hotch-potch of unresolved and conflicting presentational methods. The attempt to assign texts to discrete categories: dramatic, half-dramatic, liturgical-drama, etc. is as mis-directed as it is sterile. Both the celebration of the liturgy and the performance of plays[3] depend upon written or printed texts, but those texts are only an aid to performance, they are not the liturgy and they are not the play. Our concern is with performance in so far as we are dealing with plays. Furthermore, an important differentiating criterion between drama and liturgy is the difference between audience and congregation. The congregation has an active part to play in the celebration of the liturgy, they are participants in the action, not spectators of it. In a play, the audience

---

[1] The alternatives are not, of course, exclusive. See Chambers, II, 2–28; Hardison, 178–219; Richard Axton, *European Drama of the Early Middle Ages* (London, 1974), 61–74, 209.

[2] Hardin Craig, *English Religious Drama of the Middle Ages* (Oxford, 1955; repr. 1964), 31.

[3] It is essential to remember that most of the liturgy was sung, not spoken, and that the plays were music-drama. See W. L. Smolden, *The Music of the Medieval Church Dramas*, ed. C. Bourgeault (Oxford, 1981), and his article on 'Liturgical music-drama' in *Grove's Dictionary of Music and Musicians*, ed. Eric Blom, 5th edn (London, 1954), V, 317–43.

assumes a more passive role: they are called upon to respond intellectually and emotionally, but rarely physically. Sometimes it is impossible to tell from the text what was intended, to what extent liturgical material has been adapted in a particular service, and re-enactment, principally by impersonation, has replaced recitation, reading and singing as the dominant methods of celebration.

To summarize: in a performance of the *Quem Quaeritis*, or in performances of similar texts, no single, settled set of conventions, still less a dramatic or theatrical set of conventions, would have dominated. What was done, and how it was done, was determined in part by conventions drawn from the well-established, conservative, yet ever-changing set of conventions which constitutes the liturgy, and in part by conventions, at this time not well-established but in the process of formulation, which eventually coalesce to form drama as we know it at historically later periods. And what has subsequently become an almost wholly independent third set of conventions – music – was also drawn upon the more freely, its distinctiveness not being recognized. Any part of any text, and, it is reasonable to infer, any part of any performance, may have been over-determined, following simultaneously both liturgical and dramatic conventions, and the degree of relative determination may similarly vary. Likewise, the response of the congregation (so-called if a liturgical convention dominates) or the audience (if a dramatic convention dominates) to what it sees, hears, smells, and what it is requested to do and to refrain from doing, may vary. Dramatists, actors and musicians, and audiences, could, given that both the set of dramatic conventions and the set of performance conventions were fluid, incomplete and innovative, combine and synthesize to produce a performance of great polysemic power or a dreadful confusion of unresolved and conflicting elements.

(ii) Dramatizations in the liturgy: the Emmaus play

Although it is a commonplace that originality as such was not prized, conflicts between fidelity to the scriptural narrative and fidelity to the liturgical mood were not always resolved in favour of scriptural authenticity, and fidelity to the liturgical mood could demand of the dramatist a re-shaping of the narrative: the creation, in effect, of a new event. Re-enactments of Christ's appearances on the road to Emmaus, to the Apostles, with and without St Thomas, and immediately prior to the ascension, were never as popular as those based on the events of Easter Sunday. The Emmaus story has, according to the Middle Ages, practical moral implications: in so far as we are charitable to the poor we are demonstrating our love for Christ himself.[1] The liturgy is, however, affective rather than overtly didactic. The text which follows, one of the few on this subject, comes from a Sicilian manuscript, probably reflecting Norman practice. A dramatization which resembles this one in some respects was certainly current in England some time later (see p. 104).

Christ at Emmaus[2]

De Peregrino in Die Lune Pasche

Hoc dicat chorus:	Iesu, nostra redemptio,	1
	amor et desiderium,	2
	Deus, creator omnium,	3
	homo in fine temporum,	4
	Que te uicit clemencia,	5
	ut ferres nostra crimina,	6
	crudelem mortem patiens,	7
	ut nos a morte tolleres?	8

Duo clerici induti cappis dicant: Tercia dies est quod hec facta sunt. 9, 10

PEREGRINVS: Qui sunt hii sermones quos comfertis ad inuicem ambulantes, et estis tristes? Alleluia! Alleluia! 11, 12

DISCIPVLI: Tu solus peregrinus es in Jerusalem, et non cognouisti que facta sunt in illa his diebus? Alleluia! 13, 14

PEREGRINVS: Que? 15

DISCIPVLI: De Iesu Nazareno, qui fuit uir propheta, potens in opere et sermone coram Deo et omni populo, alleluia, alleluia. Et quomodo tradiderunt eum summi sacerdotes in damnatione mortis, alleluia. 16, 17, 18, 19

[1] *The Monastic Breviary of Hyde Abbey, Winchester*, ed. J. B. L. Tolhurst, 6 vols (London, for the Henry Bradshaw Society, 1932–42), II (1933), F. 102, 102v. *Breviarium ad usum insignis ecclesiae Sarum*, ed. Francis Procter and Christopher Wordsworth, 3 vols (Cambridge, 1879–86), I (1882), columns dcccxxiii–dcccxxv. See also F. C. Gardiner, *The Pilgrimage of Desire. A Study of Theme and Genre in Medieval Literature* (Leiden, 1971).

[2] Text adapted from Karl Young, *The Drama of the Medieval Church*, I, 459–60. There are extracts from other dramatizations, with musical quotations, in modern notation, in W. L. Smoldon, 'Liturgical drama', in Anselm Hughes (ed.), *New Oxford History of Music*, vol. II: *Early Medieval Music up to 1300* (London, 1954; repr. 1976), 190–2.

PEREGRINVS: O Stulti et tardi corde ad credendum in omnibus   20
his que locuti sunt prophete, alleluia! Nonne sic   21
oportuit pati Christum, et ita intrare in gloriam suam?   22
Alleluia!   23

CHORVS: Cum autem appropinquaret castello quo ibant, ipse   24
se finxit longius ire, et coegerunt illum ut remaneret   25
cum eis.   26

DISCIPVLI: Mane nobiscum, quoniam aduesperascit et inclinata   27
est iam dies, alleluia.   28

PEREGRINVS: Michi longum iter restat, alleluia.   29

DISCIPVLI: Sol uergens ad occasum suadet ut nostrum uelis   30
hospicium; placent enim nobis sermones tui, quos   31
refers de resurrectione magistri nostri, alleluia.   32

CHORVS: Et intrauit cum illis, et factum est dum recumberet   33
cum eis, accepit panem, benedixit ac fregit et porrigebat   34
illis, et cognouerunt illum in fractione panis, et   35
ipse euanuit ab oculis eorum, alleluia.   36

Et ita, tenendo in medio eorum Peregrinum ueniat usque ad altare;   37
ac ibi sit parata mensa cum pane et uino; et discumbant; et   38
frangat panem eisque det; ac postea ab oculis eorum euanescat.   39

Tunc dicant Discipuli: Nonne cor nostrum ardens erat in nobis de   40
Ihesu, dum loqueretur nobis in uia, et aperiret nobis   41
scripturas? Heu! miseri, ubi erat sensus noster? Quo   42
intellectus abierat? Alleluia!   43

Et iterum eis se ostendens dicat: Pax uobis. Ego sum. Nolite   44
timere. Uidete manus meas et pedes meos, quia ego   45
ipse sum. Palpate et uidete quia spiritus carnem et ossa   46
non habet sicut me uidetis habere, alleluia, alleluia.   47

Discipvli versvs chorvm dicant: Surrexit Dominus de sepulchro,   48
qui pro nobis pependit in ligno, alleluia, alleluia,   49
alleluia.   50

CHORVS: Deo gracias, alleluia, alleluia, alleluia.   51

The performance opens with the first two verses of a hymn[1] sung by the choir: the later verses of the hymn refer to Christ's glorified state after the resurrection, reigning with the Father in Heaven. It is not possible to tell whether there would be a congregation or audience other than the

[1] Translation in *The English Hymnal*, No. 144.

choir – non-choral monks, novices, laity. The choir is performing its normal liturgical function of praying, in words and music, and if others are praying also they would have a normal role, praying as prompted by the hymn. For choir and congregation alike the physical activity of singing is a way of directing the mind to the contemplation of God's actions.

The extent to which the differentiated singing by two members of the choir in unison of the line 'It is the third day since these things happened' (line 9), would surprise a member of the congregation–audience would depend very much on their familiarity with the celebration of the liturgy. One can reasonably assume that a non-choral member of the congregation would not have had an extensive and detailed knowledge of the complex liturgy of this, the Easter season. The choir itself would, of course, be quite aware of what was happening. The impersonation involved for the two singers is minimal – their copes suggest the cloaks of travellers, but they do not carry staffs. They sing in unison and do not simulate dialogue between themselves. It is not at all apparent whom, if anyone, they are addressing. They may not be addressing anyone, for their function is to evoke a vivid recollection of the historical event, not to re-present it. At this point the text is open to widely varying interpretations: all of the principal material is liturgical, including the words given to the pilgrim: 'What talk is this that you are having, as you walk along sad-faced?' (11–12) It would be quite possible for the singer to address himself clearly by movement and gesture to the two disciples if the dramatic potentialities of the text were being brought out in a particular performance. If they were not, however, it would not be incongruous if no one were obviously and explicitly addressed, since the same material is sung by the choir in other services in which there is no question at all of re-enactment.

The next lines do seem to be dialogue:

> What, are you the only pilgrim in Jerusalem who has not heard of what has happened there in the last few days?
> What?
> To Jesus of Nazareth, a prophet whose words and acts had power with God, and with all the people, and how the chief priests delivered Him up to be condemned to death. (13–19)

But the fundamental scriptural source itself is very close to dialogue, as are the liturgical adaptations of it, and very little alteration of it is required to produce what is in this text. The crucial difference between this version and the scriptural one is, of course, that this is sung. (This can produce a different kind of incongruity: the two lengthy 'recitatives' of the disciples are separated only by the pilgrim's one word – 'What?' – and this can produce the same effect as a single word or short phrase interjection in a nineteenth-century opera.)

The isolation of the pilgrim, standing and singing alone, the only individualized character, and the spectators' knowledge, not shared by the disciples, that He is in fact Christ, influence the spectators to identify with the disciples, with other men rather than with Christ. The audience therefore ranges itself with those who, in their daily lives, refuse to recognize Christ even when He is present before them – as an object of charity in the poor and oppressed. Such a response, in which all of those participating in the performance save for the man playing Christ are feeble and falter in their faith, would justify reading 'Too slow of faith, too dull of heart, to believe all those sayings of the prophets! Was it not to be expected that the Christ should undergo these sufferings, and enter so into His glory?' (20–2) as a generalized reproof to all who refuse to respond to the clear meaning of Scripture. Scripturally and liturgically there is justification for regarding the remark as being addressed to the disciples, who later profess to have been moved by His words: 'Were not our hearts burning within us for Jesus when He spoke to us on the road, and when He made the Scriptures plain to us?' (41–2). Textually, including musically, there is nothing to indicate that they did respond in that way. Such a moment would have been potentially 'dramatic' as the hitherto somewhat laconic pilgrim rebukes the unwitting pair, but it is not exploited. Expressions of joy would have been premature.

The narrative intervention by the choir at this point (24–6) should not be taken as cover for action, allowing the pilgrim to walk towards and possibly slightly beyond the table, and the disciples to catch up with Him and detain Him. No church is so big that such a long choral passage would have been needed: such movement, no matter how slowly carried out, could not be sufficiently stretched to occupy that length of time. The action must be completed, then all movement cease whilst the choir sings, or the action must take place after the choir has finished. There is nothing either undramatic or unliturgical in people standing still. In almost every service at some point some of the celebrants have nothing (physical) to do, and their business is to do nothing. They stand, sit or kneel in the correct liturgical posture, and avoid distracting the other participants or the congregation by fidgeting or indulging in non-productive, because insignificant action. In performance an actor, even in character, can 'disappear' whilst remaining fully visible in the acting space or on the stage by remaining still and not calling attention to himself.

Although the disciples were lacking in faith in their sorrow they were not lacking in charity. Having reached their destination (*castello quo ibant*) where supper awaited them, common courtesy demanded that as night fell they extend hospitality to any traveller, especially to a pilgrim. The readings from St Gregory in the Office at this time draw the moral clearly. In this story, however, the disciples receive part of the reward for charity in this world, without having to wait for it in the next, for the stranger they have entertained reveals Himself to them as Christ.

Again one can respond to, and interpret, the text in at least two ways. The Scripture is no more explicit than is this text in explaining exactly how the disciples recognized Christ. The episode could be performed naturalistically, the breaking of bread being akin to a mannerism we suddenly recognize, enabling us to identify someone we had hitherto failed to recognize. Or, it can be argued, no explanation need be presented: that they knew Him in the breaking of bread is the fact as it is reported in Scripture, and that is what we are shown in re-presentation. (Other medieval versions account for their recognition by saying that Christ broke the bread cleanly, without crumbling it, as if it had been cut by a knife.)[1] Immediately following their recognition of Christ the fact that the disciples have always sung in unison and that the distinctions between actors, choir, audience and congregation have always been indistinct facilitates the fulfilment of the didactic function. The disciples have responded adequately in charity but not in faith, and we too can and should be aware that we can fail in both faith and charity: in neither have we been tested in this performance, but we should identify sufficiently with the unwitting disciples to draw the moral for ourselves.

As the charity shown by the disciples is rewarded more immediately than can usually be expected, so too is their faith, for their remorse and self-reproach are banished by the reappearance of Christ. This reappearance of Christ at Emmaus is not scripturally sanctioned, but seems to have been an invention of the compiler. His words used here are, in Scripture, those He spoke to all of the Apostles at a later appearance in Jerusalem and the liturgical use of the material is later in Easter week. The reappearance of Christ provides a climax to a sequence of events that would, otherwise, have ended with the disciples reproaching themselves – and the audience – for

[1] As in *The Shrewsbury Fragments*, ed. Young, II, 520.

their failure to recognize Christ, and such sorrow would not be appropriate at Easter. Fidelity to the emotional mood of the liturgy demands that the re-presentation go beyond what is scripturally and liturgically sanctioned in the creation of event.

When Christ first appeared after His resurrection to Mary Magdalen He told her not to touch Him; when, later, He appears to St Thomas (John 20: 24–31) the sceptical Apostle is told by Christ to place his hands in Christ's wounds, so that he may be convinced of the truth of the resurrection. Christ's words to the disciples here are a similar invitation: 'Peace be with you. It is myself, do not be afraid. Look at My hands and My feet to be assured that it is Myself. Touch Me and look; a spirit has not flesh and bones as you see I have' (46–7). The disciples verify, on behalf of the audience, the proof of Christ's resurrection and confirm it: 'The Lord has risen from the sepulchre, who for us hung upon the Cross. Alleluia, alleluia, alleluia' (48–9). The triple Alleluia, confined to the Easter season as an indication of rejoicing, concludes the ceremony.

This relatively brief ceremony – it should not be forgotten that these ceremonies are sung, not spoken – uses many of the mimetic methods of the better known *Visit to the Sepulchre* plays. There are clearly differentiated choral and individual parts; there is clear, although restrained, impersonation. There is costuming and the use of properties: there are copes which would not normally be worn at Vespers and there is a table set with bread and wine at which part of the action takes place. Words and music are generally an adaptation of liturgical material. The text is found in a *troper*, a collection of material not strictly part of the liturgy, but intimately related to it, between material obviously associated with Easter and material obviously associated with the Feast of the Ascension. No precise liturgical time of performance is specified, but the liturgical season is clear, and the ceremony has many liturgical characteristics. The performance is to take place in church, not in some convenient open place or space, vestments are used, and the liturgically appropriate *alleluia* is found at points in the text which are, naturalistically, inappropriate (for example, lines 14, 19). Clearest of all the liturgical characteristics is the ambivalent function of the choir. As this is probably a monastic service (because it is in a *troper*), either there is no congregation, or the congregation is of secondary importance: but the choir comment on the action (lines 24–6) and anticipate it in narrative (lines 33–6). Even so, they are the recipients from the disciples of the confirmation of Christ's resurrection (line 48). It could be that this merely indicates that the disciples should sing 'publicly', that is, to the body of the church rather than to the altar. Similarly it could be argued that the passage beginning *Et intrauit cum illis...* (line 33), was an attempt to convey to those in the church whose view of the action was obscured some idea of what was happening, although no such justification could be argued for the earlier passage, *Cum autem appropinquaret...* (line 24). To argue such conclusions would be, however, to continue a sterile debate which attempts to separate out liturgical and dramatic elements. Placing this short ceremony in its liturgical context, in amongst the many different Masses and parts of the Office sung at this season, would soon make it abundantly clear that no stable, unchanging role for the choir is possible, given the diversity of scriptural material the liturgy draws on.

There is in this text fusion or, arguably, confusion, of liturgical and dramatic methods, especially in the location of the second part of the action at the altar. There are three possible motives for locating the most spectacular part at the altar. In older churches and chapels the altar would still have been in the part of the church most clearly visible to all present, and so dramatic, or more specifically, performing, considerations would lead to the location of the action there. Secondly, even when the design of churches had changed, and the altar was no longer as clearly visible to all in the church, it remained the liturgical focus, so that liturgically the altar is appropriately the place where the action culminates. Thirdly, there are symbolic considerations which illustrate well both the theological and pastoral advantages and dangers of dramatizing the liturgy. In this ceremony the simple supper of bread and wine at Emmaus stands in an obvious relationship to Christ's Last Supper with His Apostles, and both are no less obviously related to the Mass, the sacrifice of the altar, in which Christ is really and physically present in the form of bread and wine. In very close proximity to the altar table itself, at which every Sunday, or even daily, Mass is celebrated by a priest and Christ made present in the form of consecrated bread and wine, in this ceremony an actor–priest playing the part of Christ reveals himself as Christ in the blessing and breaking of bread to the disciples, and to the congregation–audience. Mimetic and sacramental realizations of Christ are powerfully and dangerously linked.

Whatever the intention of the compiler was in assigning parts of the material to individuals who impersonate, to some degree, the historical characters who originally spoke the words, the effect produced in this addition to the liturgy proper is an immediacy in presentation achieved by non-liturgical methods. In time, however, what was once new and striking becomes familiar and remote, and in a manuscript some two to three hundred years later[1] there is evidence of further re-working of an extra-liturgical dramatic version of *Christ at Emmaus* which must have been very similar to the one above. The *Shrewsbury Fragments* are an actor's parts in three plays, including one of Christ's appearance at Emmaus. What is distinctive about these plays is that they are in both Latin and English. The Latin speeches are very close in wording to those in dramatizations associated with the liturgy, and are followed by versions in English:

> CLEOPHAS: Et quomodo tradiderunt eum summi sacerdotes
> et principes nostri in dampnacionem mortis, et
> crucifixerunt eum.
> Right is þat we reherce by raw
>   þe materes þat we may on mene
> How prestis and princes of our lawe
>   Ful tenely toke him hom betwen,
> And dampned him, withouten awe,
>   For to be dede with dole bedene.
> Þai crucified him, wele we knaw,
>   At Caluary with caris kene.[2]

For an early fifteenth-century English audience—congregation represen-tational methods alone were no longer enough to enliven liturgical celebration, and English as well as Latin had to be used.

(iii) Devotional drama: the Digby *Burial and Resurrection*

In order to maintain the liturgically appropriate mood of rejoicing the compiler of the Latin *Christ at Emmaus* had to draw upon scriptural and liturgical material from different historical and liturgical times in the enactment of the reappearance of Christ. A much later play, the Digby *Burial and Resurrection*,[3] is radically determined by the playwright's desire to inculcate in the audience a liturgically appropriate emotional and

---

[1] On the date, see *NCPF*, xiv.
[2] Young, II, 519.
[3] Baker, *Digby Plays*, 141–93. (*The Burial and Resurrection* are also sometimes known as the *Bodley Burial and Resurrection*, after the MS – Bodley e Museo 160. The dramatic status of these texts has been disputed: the most recent study is Peter Meredith's 'The Bodley "Burial and Resurrection" plays: late English liturgical drama?' in *Proceedings of the Third Colloquium of the International Society for the study of Medieval Drama* (Dublin, 1980), forthcoming.

intellectual sequence of responses, responses appropriate to Good Friday and Easter Sunday rather than one which might have arisen from an autonomous re-presentation of historical or imagined events, as in the Digby *Mary Magdalen* (see pp. 195–7). In both plays the human aspect of Mary's love for Christ finds expression in physical terms, but this is all they have in common in the characterization of Mary Magdalen. In the *Burial and Resurrection* the dramatist brings out the essentially and universally human reaction of Christ's mother and His followers to His death, as well as placing these events in their context in Salvation-history. The play dramatizes the taking down of Christ from the cross, His burial and, in the second part, the visit of the women to the tomb, the appearance of Christ to Mary Magdalen and to the other followers of Christ. The characters are sharply individualized, consistently with their function in Scripture, not primarily as early Christians, but as any, and all, sorrowing relatives and friends who have suffered the death of a loved one. The Virgin Mary is any mother who has lost a son by an early and cruel death:

> O sisters, Mawdleyn, Cleophe, and Jacobye!
> Ye see how pitefulle my son doth lye
> Here in myn armys, dede. (*Burial*, 612–14)

Her desire to suffer the same death as her son (761–6) is psychologically convincing as is her reliving in recollection the events of His life (624–37). There is even a hint of reproach in her words to Mary Magdalen:

> A! A, Mawdleyn, why devise ye nothinge
> To this blessid body for to gif praysinge?
> Sum dolorose ditee express now yee,
> In þe dew honour of þis ymage of pitee! (*Burial*, 793–6)

No one, however, is allowed to encroach upon the prominence given to the Virgin Mary in the first part of the play. But ordinary human beings, members of a congregation–audience, can identify with the Virgin Mary only to a limited extent: she was born without sin, and lived without sinning – in that she was unique as a human being, and she was unique, too, in being the Mother of God. What members of an audience can share with her is her suffering at the death of Christ, and this they are invited to do in the Digby play. With Mary Magdalen, however, they can identify much more completely, for Mary Magdalen is the great example of the sinner who repents and whose repentance and devotion are complete and unquestioned. As sinners we are all in the situation that Mary Magdalen

was in, and because we should repent our sins and devote ourselves to Christ
we should put ourselves in Mary Magdalen's later situation – as a penitent
and a devoted follower. Mary Magdalen dominates the second, Resurrection,
part of the Digby play as the Virgin Mary dominates the first. Her
prominence is scripturally justified, since although she was accompanied
by the other two women to the sepulchre and heard the news of Christ's
resurrection with them, it was Mary Magdalen alone, after the other two
had left her, who had had the honour of being the first living person to
see the glorified Christ. Mary Magdalen mourns both for Christ, the
Incarnate Son of God, and for Jesus, the man. She requires for consolation
both the angel's announcement that Christ has risen from the dead, and
also the reassurance of seeing again the man who had been compassionate
to her.

When Mary finds the tomb empty she reproaches herself for not having
kept watch, not for the traditional reason that she might thereby have
prevented the body of Christ from being stolen, but because she has lost
an opportunity of seeing her beloved Christ again:

> A! A, sisters! My slewth and my necligence!
> I haue not don my dewty ne my diligence,
> > Ose vnto me did falle!
> At my masters sepulcre if I hade gifen attendance,
> And waytid wisely with humble affiance,
> > Os I was bound most of alle,
>
> I shuld haue seyn his vprisinge gloriose
> Of my swete Lorde....
> O, wold to God I had made more haste!   (*Resurrection*, 203–10, 229)

Mary Magdalen's lines almost lapse into naturalism in the evocation of her
grief, and there is a vivid, strikingly physical reference to the nature of her
sins and the quality of Christ's compassion:

> Notwithstandinge the gret abhomynation
> Of my grete synnes fulle of execration,
> > Yit of his benignite,
> As with alle mercy he was replete,
> He sufferte me with teris to wesh his fete!
> > Loo, his mercyfulle pitee!
> My synfulle lippes, which I did abuse,
> To towch his blessit fleshe he wald not refuse.
> > And ther right oppenlye. (*Resurrection*, 238–46)

Rosemary Woolf has pointed out 'the freedom and frequency with which' Mary Magdalen expresses her love for Christ 'in the erotic language of the Song of Songs or in variations on it':[1]

O, I, writchit creature, what shalle I doo?
O, I, a wofulle woman, whidere salle I goo?
　My Lorde, wher shalle I find?
When shalle I se that desirid face,
Which was so fulle of bewty and grace,
　To me, the most vnkind?

I haue sought and besely inquerid
Hym whom my harte alleway has desired,
　And so desiries stille.
'*Quem diligit anima mea, quesiui;*
Quesiui illum, et non inueni!'
　When shalle I haue my wille?

I haue sought hym desirusly,
I haue sought hym affectuosly,
　With besines of my mynd.
I haue sought hym with mynd hartely,
The tresure wherin my hart dose lye....

Filie Jerusalem, wheros ye goo,
Nunciate dilecto meo
　Quia amore langueo!

Of Jerusalem, ye virgyns clere,
Schew my best loue that I was here,
　Telle hym, os he may prove,
That I am dedly seke,
　And alle is for his loue.   (*Resurrection*, 570–86, 594–601)

Christ does appear to Mary and she eventually recognizes Him, having mistaken Him at first for a gardener; after He has left her again her words are

O, myn harte, wher hast thou bee?
Com hom agayn, and leve with mee!   (629–30)

This emphasis on her human grief and this aspect of her relationship with Christ, although it establishes her as a living being, could border on the

[1] Rosemary Woolf, *The English Mystery Plays* (London, 1972), 334.

self-indulgent, on a colossal concern with her happiness at the expense of Christ's mission to all of humanity, indeed it could be 'maudlin'. But Mary Magdalen is given a long, and because of its position at the beginning of the second part of the play, a crucial speech. In it she has compared the cruelty of those who crucified Christ with that of Cain, Joseph's brothers, and Herod – conspicuous examples of cruelty against the innocent, the trusting, the loyal and the vulnerable. The death of Christ is seen as the likely fate of gentleness:

> O rygore vnright! O crueltee!
> O wikkit wylfullnese! O peruersitee!
> O hartes harde os stone,
>
> To put to deth a lamb so meke!   (177–80)

She responds to the sight of the risen Christ almost as to a human lover, but He charges her, as in Scripture (Matthew 28: 10), with the task of telling the Apostles that He has risen, and so she has her unique part to play in the history of the first Christian community: she is both penitent sinner and missionary. The dramatist can explore fully the emotions of Mary Magdalen as a human being, whilst remaining within the narrative framework sanctioned by Scripture, and without evoking liturgically incongruous reactions.

The manuscript of the play is very clear about when it is to be performed: 'This is a play to be played, on part on Gud Friday afternone, and þe other part opon Ester Day after the resurrection.'[1] It would be inappropriate, indeed it might very well have been impossible, to stage a full-scale reconstruction of the Passion and Crucifixion; moreover, whilst a congregation as audience may very fittingly be invited to express its joy at the news that Christ has risen from the dead, a congregation that witnesses as audience a re-enactment of the Crucifixion can have no role other than that of the hostile crowd. In this play, as in other dramatic traditions, spectacular events occur off-stage and are reported to us (lines 16–55) and the dramatist is more concerned with the reactions to those events than with an accurate reconstruction and imitation of them. This play is not 'liturgical' in drawing upon liturgical material, verbal or non-verbal (although this is done): it is liturgical in so far as it seeks to stimulate and intensify in the audience emotions that will enable them to respond fully and appropriately to the liturgical mood of the time – hence the precise instructions for the

---

[1] Baker, *Digby Plays*, 142.

time of performance. In using dramatic methods to serve liturgical aims in this way the Digby *Burial and Resurrection* is less akin to contemporary drama than to contemporary quasi-liturgical practices that seek to stimulate a similar devotional, rather passive, spirituality. It was through lyrical, personal, artistic forms utilized for devotional purposes that the Church and its ministers sought to re-animate worship.

In the *Stabat Mater*[1] the poet asks of the Virgin Mary to be allowed to share in the sufferings of Christ:

> Sancta Mater, istud agas,
> Crucifixi fige plagas
>   Cordi meo valide.
> Tui Nati vulnerati,
> Tam dignati pro me pati,
>   Poenas mecum divide.
>
> Fac me tecum pie flere,
> Crucifixo condolere
>   Donec ego vixero;
> Juxta crucem tecum stare
> Et me tibi sociare
>   In planctu desidero. (31–42)

[Holy mother do this for me. Pierce my heart once and for ever with the wounds of your crucified Son. Let me share with you the pain of your Son's wounds, for He thought it right to bear such sufferings for me. Grant that my tears of love may mingle with yours and that, as long as I live, I may feel the pains of my crucified Lord. To stand with you beside the cross and be your companion in grief is my one wish.]

The poem is so intense a plea to share the sufferings of Christ that it was at one time thought of as a prayer for the *stigmata*, marks on the body corresponding to Christ's five wounds, and granted by God for devotion to the suffering of Christ. The hymn dates from the second half of the thirteenth century and although popular in the Middle Ages did not secure a place in the liturgy proper until the eighteenth century: it has also, of course, been detached from its liturgical context and enjoyed considerable popularity as a secular concert piece.

[1] Text and translation in Joseph Connelly, *Hymns of the Roman Liturgy* (London, 1957), 186–91; the reference to the stigmata is on 187.

The most popular, and the longest-lasting, of all such additions to the liturgy of the Easter season in the later Middle Ages was dependent upon a variety of re-enactment from which all drama was eradicated. The *Way of the Cross*, or *Stations of the Cross*, is a sequence of prayers and meditations based upon events in the Passion and Crucifixion. There are traditionally fourteen stations, or places within the church or along a processional way, at each of which a plaque, painting, or group of statuary, depicts a scene from the Passion and death. The priest and assistants – or, when space permits, the whole congregation – move from station to station and are led in prayer and meditation by the priest. The *Hours of the Cross*[1] are similar attempts to structure a sequence of prayers according to the chronology of the Passion. The *Stations of the Cross* were originally associated with Good Friday, but they have never been part of the liturgy proper and soon became detached from a specified liturgical locus, and celebrated on any day except a Sunday or a major feast, although Friday was always the preferred day. Such practices as *The Stations of the Cross*, and *The Rosary of the Blessed Virgin Mary*, although the latter is not processional and not representational, proved more enduring ways, until the Second Vatican Council (1963–5), of providing communal worship in the Roman Church than did re-enactments of scriptural history. The Church did not draw exclusively, or even principally, on drama to re-invigorate worship, but dramatists did draw upon liturgical methods and material. The borrowings and dependencies can easily be confused as most of the dramatists were churchmen and churchwomen, not professional playwrights. It would have been difficult for any dramatist who wanted to dramatize, for whatever purpose, the annunciation to Mary, to avoid using the words of Scripture, adapted for use as the *Hail Mary*. Anyone in the Middle Ages in a position to produce a play would have been thoroughly familiar with a store of liturgical materials, prayers, hymns and passages from Scripture, memorized without much conscious effort through constant repetition.[2] And any audience would have been more or less accustomed to liturgical methods of presentation. At its most tenuous the use of liturgical material may be no more than the singing of the *Te Deum* at the end of a play, a practice analogous to the singing of a national anthem at a public ceremony in modern times. But liturgical presentation methods could be used structurally

[1] As in *The Lay Folks Mass Book*, ed. Thomas Frederick Simmons (London, 1879; repr. 1968: EETS 71) 'York Hours of the Cross', 81–7.

[2] Paul Edward Kretzmann, *The Liturgical Elements in the Earliest Forms of the Medieval Drama* (Minneapolis, 1916), lists liturgical material but does not take into account how it was assimilated; see Peter F. McDonald, *The Chester Corpus Christi Play* (unpublished MA thesis, University of Liverpool, 1967).

and thematically in plays otherwise unconnected to the liturgy, and not necessarily staged in church.

(iv) Religious drama: the *Ordo Representacionis Ade*

Whilst the Winchester *Visit to the Sepulchre*, and other re-enactments within the celebration of the liturgy, fuse liturgical and mimetic methods, in the Anglo-Norman *Ordo Representacionis Ade [Adam]*[1] the dramatist combines liturgical and other methods to present the story of God's relationship with man.

Adam tells the story of the Creation, the temptation of Adam and Eve by the Devil, and the murder of Cain. The final part, unfinished in the unique manuscript, is a series of speeches by some of the outstanding figures from Old Testament history: Abraham, Moses, Aaron, David, Solomon, Balaam, Daniel, Habakkuk, Jeremiah, Isaiah and Nebuchadnezzar. Dr Lynette Muir, in her study of the play,[2] draws attention to how the tripartite division by content, into an Adam and Eve play, a Cain and Abel play, and a Prophet play, 'has obscured the threefold "horizontal" division into a Latin play, a mime play and a French play' (p. 2). The stylistic quality of the French play, its transcendent realism, was identified and described by Erich Auerbach[3] and Dr Muir shows how the gestures, based upon the ritual gestures of the liturgy, constitute the 'mime play' (p. 45). The very strength and effectiveness of these parts contribute to the problems associated with the Latin parts. Latin is used by a choir, who sing a series of partly narrative verses interspersed in the action and the Norman-French dialogue in the first two parts, the Adam and Eve and Cain and Abel scenes, and also by the Old Testament figures, who speak in Latin and Norman-French. The following extract is from the Adam and Eve part, and begins with the end of Adam's speech in which he regrets having sinned:

> ADAM.   Ne sai de nus prendre conroi,
> Quant a Deu ne portames foi.
> Or en soit tot a Deu plaisir:
> N'i ad conseil que del morir.

[1] Text and translation in Bevington, *Medieval Drama*, 80–121. Translation in Richard Axton and John Stevens (trs), *Medieval French Plays* (Oxford, 1971), 7–44.
[2] Lynette R. Muir, *Liturgy and Drama in the Anglo-Norman Adam*, Medium AEvum Monographs, n.s., III (Oxford, 1973).
[3] Erich Auerbach, *Mimesis. The Representation of Reality in Western Literature*, tr. Willard Trask (New York, 1953), chapter 7, 'Adam and Eve'.

Tunc incipiat chorus: ℞ Dum deambularet. [Dominus in paradyso ad auram post meridiem, clamavit et dixit: 'Adam ubi es?' 'Audivi Domine vocem tuam. Et abscondi me. Vocem tuam Domine audivi in paradyso et timui, eo quo nudus essem. Et abscondi me'.]

Quo dicto, veniet Figura stola[m] habens et ingredietur paradisum circumspiciens, quasi quaereret ubi esset Adam. Adam vero et Eva latebunt in angulo paradisi, quasi suam cognoscentes miser[i]am, et dicet Figura:

Adam, ubi es?

Tunc ambo surgent, stantes contra Figuram, non tamen omnino erecti, sed ob verecundiam sui peccati aliquantulum curvati et multum tristes, et respondeat

ADAM. Ci sui jo, beal Sire.

Repost me sui ja por ta ire;

E por ço que sui tut nuz

Me sui jo ici si embatuz.

[ADAM. I don't know whom to ask for help

When we've not kept our faith with God.

Now in God's keeping all must be:

There's nothing left for me but death.

Then let the choir begin: 'While God walked in the garden in the cool of the evening, He called out saying: "Adam, where art thou?" "I heard Thy voice and I hid myself. I heard Thy voice in the garden and I was afraid, because of my nakedness, so I hid myself."'

After which God shall come, wearing a stole, and he shall enter Paradise and look around him, as if searching for Adam. But Adam and Eve shall hide in a corner of Paradise, as if acknowledging their wretched state, and God shall say:

GOD. Adam, where are you?

Then they shall both get up and stand before God, not, however, completely upright, but stooping a little because of the shame of their sin, and very sorrowful; and Adam shall reply:

ADAM. I'm here, my Lord.

I've hidden to avoid your anger.

My nakedness makes me ashamed –

And so I've shut myself away.][1]

---

[1] Anglo-Norman and Latin text from Bevington, *Medieval Drama*, 97–8; translation of Anglo-Norman and expansion of Latin *incipit* from Axton and Stevens, *Medieval French Plays*, 26–7; translation of Latin antiphon adapted from Ronald Knox's translation of the Vulgate Bible.

The choral part resembles the choral parts of the *Christ at Emmaus*, and the editors of this version say that whilst the choir is singing the dramatic action should be 'frozen', producing a tableau effect: 'Experience shows that this can be strikingly effective in performance' (p. 5). The effectiveness of the final part of the play, in which the Old Testament figures deliver their prophecies has been generally questioned. It is, however, possible that the lengthy final section is not quite as undramatic as it might appear, if, as is possible, liturgical methods of presentation were used in this part, as they are in other parts, of the play.

Adam opens in fact with a lengthy 'reading'. Medieval manuscripts abbreviate liturgical material if familiar, providing only the *incipit* or first few words, and modern editions that do the same can be, superficially, misleading. The play begins: '*Tunc incipiat lectio*: In principio creavit Deus caelum et terram.' [Then let the lesson begin: God, at the beginning of time, created heaven and earth.] This is, of course, the beginning of the Book of Genesis, and no indication is given as to how long the reading should be. It is, however, reasonable to suppose that it would extend as far in the narrative as the creation of Adam (verse 27) for that is the point after which the narrative is re-enacted in the play. The normal liturgical method of recollecting scriptural history is by such reading, and this lesson from Genesis, along with others, has always[1] formed part of the Easter Vigil service during which 'the whole history of salvation is rehearsed in readings and song'.[2] It can be assumed that the audience for a play such as *Adam* was familiar with the passage and with the way in which it was usually delivered. There was no sharp distinction in liturgical practice between speaking and singing: it is more than probable that the way in which that lesson was read was in cantillation, rather than in anything resembling the modern 'reading aloud'. Cantillation, used especially in the reading of the Bible, is a form of 'rhythmo-musical recitation.... The word being proclaimed remains in the foreground. Such elements of rhythm and melody as are introduced do not constitute a musical form independent of the words. The rhythm is that of ordinary speech, stylized .... It is a type of recitative....'[3] If, in a performance of *Adam*, this lengthy opening lesson from Genesis were delivered in this fashion, as also the Latin parts of the

---

[1] See S. J. P. van Dijk, *Sources of the Modern Roman Liturgy*, 2 vols (Leiden, 1963), I, 246; and cf. Josef A. Jungmann, *The Early Liturgy* (London, 1959; repr. 1966), 263.

[2] Peter G. Cobb, 'The history of the Christian Year', in Jones, *et al.*, *The Study of Liturgy*, 410.

[3] J. Gelineau, 'Music and singing in the liturgy', in ibid., 451.

speeches of the prophets in the final part, there would be a stylistic consistency in the play as a whole, and a satisfying aesthetic integrity in the final part's return to the presentation techniques of the opening. The Latin speeches of the final part are followed by Norman-French speeches:[1] this Latin material would not have been as familiar as the opening chapters of Genesis, and the audience must grasp its import for a full understanding of the play, so translation, paraphrase and addition were all required. The manuscript is incomplete, but all of the conjectural endings of the play include choral singing, either with or without the participation of the audience, and nothing suggested here is incompatible with such endings.

Even if the play did not depend as heavily as is suggested here on liturgical methods – and the choral singing at least is indisputable – the playwright did draw upon them to tell part of the story and to locate stylistically that part of the action in which God actively participates, for the choral music is associated only with those parts of the action in which God participates. Having found such strikingly appropriate discourse for Adam and Eve, only by associating God with an equally distinctive one could the playwright avoid drawing God wholly within the earthly world of Adam and Eve and making of Him a grumpy old man. Similarly, as the playwright's intention included the dramatization of some of the preaching and prophecies in the Old Testament, a distinctive dramatic mode had to be found for Abraham and the other patriarchs and prophets, and its acceptability established from the beginning of the play, in order to avoid an awkward stylistic transition towards the end. The consensus of modern commentary on the text, for the full version is rarely performed, is that the playwright failed. Such judgements must always be provisional, for they are validated only by performances.

(v) Liturgy as spectacle: the Feast of Corpus Christi

Incorporating re-enactments of events in history, sacred or legendary, and staging performances of plays in church on Feast days, were entertaining and possibly even spiritually edifying ways of enriching and embellishing the public worship of the Church; but although the liturgy was enormously enlarged and extended in the course of the Middle Ages this was done

[1] Muir, *Liturgy and Drama in the Anglo-Norman Adam*, 93–112, analyses the speeches.

principally through the multiplication of existing forms. New Feasts were added, and new Offices for them, but patterned on existing ones; new prayers and hymns were added, but in accordance with precedents. Historians of the drama have not unnaturally concentrated on the use of dramatic methods within the liturgy, and the performance of plays as part of the Church's celebration of Feasts, without always making it clear what a tiny fraction of the worship of the Church as a whole these were. There are many and not incompatible possible reasons why drama did not replace liturgy to any significant extent: the general overloading of the liturgy through the addition of Feast days, the physical limitations imposed by the size and design of churches and the size of congregations, the growth of vernaculars which entailed that new things would be done in new languages, rather than in an old one. And although as we have seen there was not a fully articulated concept of what drama was, there was a realization, however incoherent, that it was incompatible with liturgy. It is, however, only in histories of drama that one finds the question posed in the form − why is there not more drama associated with the public worship of the Church? It would seem more natural to ask: why did the Church associate itself and its public worship with drama at all, however reluctantly and with whatever misgivings?

In the course of the Middle Ages the principal service of the Church, the Mass, became less and less of a communal activity in which priests and laity alike had an active part to play, and more and more a private devotion which the priest conducted and the congregation overheard.[1] The fact that the liturgy continued to be celebrated in Latin long after most of the people and many of the clergy no longer spoke any form of the language has sometimes been over-emphasized − that was only part of, and in part the result not the cause of, a wider alienation. The practice of infant rather than adult baptism, universal in western Europe from shortly after the beginning of the Middle Ages, the mass conversions of uninstructed and uneducated peoples to Christianity, the increasing number of priests, many of whom viewed the celebration of the liturgy as their private concern, the Church's changed status from a minority sect to a universal public religion, and with that the interdependence of the ecclesiastical and civil powers − all of these are amongst the factors which brought about a historical situation in which the officially sanctioned public worship of the Church was something which paid professionals carried out, and which the laity simply attended.

[1] J. D. Crichton, 'Mass...', in J. G. Davies (ed.), *A Dictionary of Liturgy and Worship* (London, 1972), 254–6.

Discussion of the relationship between liturgy and drama in the Middle Ages should always recognize that despite all that worship and drama have in common – in all societies – two different things at different periods in their history are being compared. First, the Middle Ages had, as we have seen, no dramatic theory and, it follows from that, no dramatic criticism and no dramatic history. People did, on the other hand, know what liturgy was, investigate the history of the liturgy, and devote considerable efforts to explaining it and commenting on it, so that it could be appreciated by all to the best of their abilities. That their methods were deficient and their conclusions wrong is not, here, pertinent.[1] Secondly, although a distinctive form of the liturgy did emerge in western Europe, much of it was derived from earlier Christian liturgies and those, in turn, owed much to Jewish liturgical practices, whereas if there was any continuity at all between the drama of late Antiquity and that of medieval Europe it was vestigial and tenuous. Thirdly, the celebration of the liturgy was universal throughout settled and civilized Europe: communities secured for themselves or were provided with priests and bishops, and the establishment of a monastic community, dedicated in principle above all else to the celebration of the liturgy, led often to the growth of a secular community. It is certain that dramatic activity was much more sporadic and localized. The celebration of the liturgy was – or at least should have been – the principal task of the Church and enjoyed its authoritative support, and the means at its disposal for the preservation, copying and supplying of texts. The Church was at best tolerant of dramatic activities, no matter how enthusiastically individual churchmen and women participated in them. Twentieth-century historians have radically different views of the Middle Ages depending on whether their preoccupation is with liturgy or drama: historians of drama have been enthusiastic students of medieval drama even if only because it was pre-Shakespearean; historians of the liturgy have become increasingly unsympathetic towards the Middle Ages, seeing it as a period of decline during which the liturgy lost its authenticity as a communal act of worship. It should, additionally, be borne in mind that there was never uniformity in either liturgical principle or practice in the Middle Ages, even though this was often the protested aim of reformers. Indeed, given the universality of the Church, and the conditions of a scribal culture in which the printed

---

[1] Ludwig Eisenhofer, *The Liturgy of the Roman Rite* (London, 1961), 44–6. Later historians and critics have often failed to distinguish between the liturgy and medieval commentaries on it, accepting the latter as definitive descriptions; see also Axton, *European Drama of the Early Middle Ages*, 65.

book as an instrument of centralized regulation and control did not exist,[1] it is difficult to see how uniformity could ever have been achieved.

Despite reservations, generalizations about the history of liturgy and worship in the Middle Ages must be risked, not least because of the importance in the history of drama of the establishment of the Feast of Corpus Christi. The form of the Mass as it had been introduced by Pepin and Charlemagne in their liturgical reform was derived from Rome, and was a communal service. But the community it had served in Rome had been the papal court, and not the country or town parish church of the European Middle Ages. During the period from the Carolingian reform until about the end of the eleventh century, the Mass changed, not so much in its essential form, but in the way in which it was celebrated and perceived generally. It ceased to be a communal service and became the means by which the priest, exercising the power given him by God through the Church, made God really and truly present, in the consecrated bread and wine, so that the faithful could adore and worship Him. At the Fourth Lateran Council in 1215 the theology of this aspect of the Mass was definitively formulated in the doctrine of transubstantiation. According to this doctrine, although the outer forms (accidents) of bread and wine remained unchanged at the consecration, their inner, invisible natures (substances) were transformed into the real body and blood of Christ. This authoritative promulgation of the doctrine had many consequences.

Thus the Mass acquired a new center, a new focal point, and the devotion of the people acquired an object which corresponded to their understanding [of the nature of the Mass] and to which they henceforth clung tenaciously. To see the celestial mystery – that is the climax of the Grail-legend in which, at this same period, the religious longing of the Middle Ages found its poetic expression. And as in the Grail-legend many grace-filled results were expected from seeing the mystery, so too at Mass. Esteem for this opportunity to look upon the Host went to such lengths that it was placed side by side with Holy Communion.... To look at the Sacred Host at the elevation became for many in the later Middle Ages the be-all and end-all of Mass devotion. See the Body of Christ at the consecration and be satisfied! In the cities people ran from church to church, to see the elevated Host as often as possible....

---

[1] Cf. Elizabeth Eisenstein, *The Printing Press as an Agent of Change*, 2 vols (Cambridge, 1979), I, 16.

People even started law-suits to ensure their getting a favourable view of the altar.[1]

Plates 19 and 20 reflect different responses to this new mystery. The change profoundly affected the whole liturgy, determining eventually the design of churches, and in them, of the altar or altars.[2] Every other consideration had to be subordinated to the display and enthronement of the Host, revered as an earthly ruler, but greater than any earthly ruler:

Welcome, Lord, In fourme of Bred!
. . .
Heil kyng, heil kniht,
heil mon of most miht,
    Prince in þi Trone,
Heil Duyk, heil Emperour,
Heil beo þou gouernour
    Of al þis worldus wone.[3]

There could no longer be any doubt that the consecrated bread and wine were changed irreversibly into Christ's body and blood, so that the reservation[4] of consecrated Hosts after the Mass had ended was no longer canonically dubious but positively meritorious. Christ's continuing presence in the community was thereby guaranteed, and His saving power made readily available (see the Croxton *Sacrament*, below, pp. 146–51).

The liturgical distinctiveness and uniqueness of the priests of the Church was given full doctrinal validation, for they alone of all the faithful had the power to effect this transubstantiation, and also the grace to hold the body of Christ in their hands. The Mass was a miracle capable of releasing special grace, and as guardians of this transforming power the priesthood gained a new and important status; it became a sacrificial priesthood. Such a view is central to the morality play *Everyman*:[5]

For preesthode excedeth all other thinge.
To us holy Scripture they do teche,

[1] Joseph A. Jungmann, *The Mass of the Roman Rite*, 2 vols (New York, 1951, 1956), I, 120–1.
[2] ibid., 83–4.
[3] From 'Sixe salutacions to þe trinite in tyme of þe eleuacioun of godis body'; *The Minor Poems of the Vernon Ms. Part I*, ed. Carl Horstmann (London, 1892; EETS 98), 24–5.
[4] A. A. King, *Eucharistic Reservation in the Western Church* (London, 1965). Many of the liturgical ceremonies associated with the dramatizations at Easter are provisions for the solemn transfer of the Host from the High Altar.
[5] Bevington, *Medieval Drama*, 939–63.

And converteth man fro sinne, heven to reche.
God hath to them more power given
Than to ony aungell that is in heven.
With five wordes he may consecrate
Goddes body in flesshe and blode to make
And handeleth his Maker bitwene his handes.
The preest bindeth and unbindeth all bandes
Bothe in erthe and in heuen.   (732–41)

The definition of transubstantiation both reflected and stimulated devotion to the Blessed Sacrament, but there were limits as to how far the thirteenth-century liturgy could be restructured to accommodate this increased devotion. In the course of the early Middle Ages the Feasts of the Christmas and Easter season had been reinterpreted as commemorations of the events that occurred on those days, and so Holy Thursday, the historically appropriate Feast of the Institution of the Blessed Sacrament, occurred at a time of sorrow and mourning. A new Feast, detached from the emotionally inappropriate atmosphere of Holy Week, was required so that the institution of the Sacrament could be celebrated with lavish and joyful ceremony. The immediate impulse leading to the institution of the Feast of Corpus Christi[1] was a vision enjoyed by the Blessed Juliana, prioress of Mount Cornillon, near Liège (1222–58). She persuaded the Bishop of Liège to order a festival in honour of the Sacrament in the diocese in 1246. It was a former archdeacon of Liège, Jacques Pantaléon, who, as Urban IV, issued a bull in 1264 ordering the whole Church to observe the Feast, the office for which has been attributed to St Thomas Aquinas. Because Urban died later in 1264 his order was not implemented until Pope Clement V confirmed it at the Council of Vienne in 1311. It was widely accepted by the mid-fourteenth century – an oft-quoted entry from Gloucester in 1318 says that the Feast was then generally celebrated throughout the whole English Church.

A Procession of the Blessed Sacrament soon became the dominant feature of the Feast, although it is not mentioned in the papal decrees of 1264 and 1311. Processions were, of course, common, either within services, as at the Gospel and offertory in the Mass, or as independent acts of worship – soliciting God's blessing on the crops, transferring relics, or in the dedication of a church. Nor was a Procession of the Blessed Sacrament anything new in itself, for from at least the eleventh century onwards the

[1] 'Corpus Christi', in *The Oxford Dictionary of the Christian Church* (Oxford, 1974), 349.

Sacrament was being carried in the Palm Sunday procession. This was one of the many customs that had been introduced to the west from Jerusalem by Egeria, a member of a religious community somewhere near the Atlantic, who wrote an account of her travels in the Holy Land:

> And now when it will begin to be the eleventh hour, that passage from the Gospels is read where the children, with branches and palms, ran to meet the Lord, saying: Blessed is he who comes in the name of the Lord. And at once the bishop rises, together with all the people; all go forward on foot from the top of the Mount of Olives; all the people go before him with hymns and antiphons, answering repeatedly, Blessed is he who comes in the name of the Lord; and as many children as there are in those places...all carrying branches, some of palms, some of olives; and thus the bishop will be escorted in the same figure as formerly the Lord was escorted. And from the top of the mount to the city, and thence through the whole city...all of them on foot the whole distance...thus they escort the bishop with their responses.[1]

This spectacular re-enactment, which had the authority of age and its place of origin, Jerusalem, to justify it, was universally adopted into western Christianity as a commemoration of Christ's triumphal entry into Jerusalem. At Jerusalem itself, as we see from Egeria's account, the bishop took the most important position at the end of the procession. At Rome the practice was to carry a Gospel Book, but in England from the eleventh century onwards it became usual for the Blessed Sacrament to be carried.[2] The Blessed Sacrament was always, however, carried in a portable shrine or a pyx; it was never carried exposed to public view in a monstrance. It is clear that the Palm Sunday procession did not originate as a procession of the Blessed Sacrament, and although technically Sundays are not part of Lent, Palm Sunday at the beginning of Holy Week is inevitably overshadowed by an anticipation of the events of the following week, so that the Palm Sunday procession was inhibited from developing into an elaborate and joyful triumphant procession of the Host, just as Holy Thursday could not be joyfully celebrated. The institution of the Feast of Corpus Christi provided an opportunity for a procession that could be designed *ab initio*

---

[1] Egeria is the preferred modern form of her name. See *The Study of Liturgy*, 65. The translation of her account is from the extract in Bevington, *Medieval Drama*, 10, 11; the most recent comprehensive translation is included in John Wilkinson, *Abbess Etheria. Travels: newly translated with supporting documents and notes* (London, 1971).

[2] King, *Eucharistic Reservation in the Western Church*, 142–3. See Plates 21 and 22.

to honour the Sacrament. The Church paraded in triumph the supreme king and magistrate, Christ, and the lesser kings and magistrates could confirm their allegiance and so demonstrate the legitimacy of their authority. In a ceremony sacramentally linked to the Mass, the preserve of the clergy, but independent of it, the whole community, lay and clerical, could honour the myth by which the community was sustained.

4 Drama and folk-ritual

David Mills

(i) The village and its rituals

The settlement of England from $c.450$ by the Anglo-Saxons marks the start of village life in the country. Although other forms – the hamlet or the single farmstead – are found, the village becomes the predominant form of settlement.

The beginnings of village life in England are significant for drama, for they suggest the large-scale sense of community which is essential to this most socially dependent of art forms. There is no evidence to suggest that any earlier tradition of drama, deriving from Celtic culture or the dramatic traditions of the Romans, existed in the British Isles. Medieval drama is the generic expression of the new communities, deriving from the awareness of the community as an economic, social and 'religious' unit. The consequences of economic pressures upon the village in the development of social order and autonomy have been described by Walter Ullmann:

> The village communities regulated their own affairs without any direction 'from above': times of ploughing, harvesting, and fallowing were fixed by the village community itself, which also arranged for the

policing of the fields. Water supply, utilization of pastoral lands, the use to be made of rivers, wells, brooks, etc., compensation for damage to crops by cattle or fire, for damage to woods by unlicensed timbering, and so on, were subjects of regulations made by the community itself. The same applied to quarries, smithies, tileries, potteries, where working conditions were fixed. The mechanics by which the 'officers' of the village community came to be created were simple enough, and yet, incontrovertibly, proved the ever-active urge to self-government. The mayor no less than the other 'functionaries' were elected by a community small enough to dispense with any idea of representation.[1]

This autonomy was the consequence of the primary purpose of a village, to produce enough food to survive, for the community was constantly threatened by natural disasters such as flood, drought, blight, cattle-disease or plague, as well as the man-made disasters of warring armies. The village was therefore organized as a food-producing co-operative in which people were expected to undertake the same communal tasks of ploughing, sowing, harvesting, herding, clearing wasteland, etc. Later, in an age when land was being enclosed for sheep-raising and the town represented a new, alternative community, the fourteenth-century poet William Langland could use the image of the open village field farmed on the strip-system by the community as his emblem of the ideal society. The annual pattern of work and the survival of the community were determined by the cycles of cultivation and their determinants, the seasons and the local features of climate and geography, and their rituals expressed a mythology which arose from and explained these factors and hence accounted for the existence of the village-community. The rituals associated with these myths were performed by or on behalf of the village-community as an act of worship which both acknowledged the continuity from the past and was efficacious in ensuring the future continuity of the cycle of cultivation.

With the coming of Christianity, conveniently dated from the arrival in England of Augustine in 597, these rituals were deliberately 're-mythologized' to accord with Christian belief, but their communal functions remained and even acquired new forms. The transition is seen in Bede's account of advice given in 601 to Augustine by Pope Gregory:

> He [Augustine] is to destroy the idols, but the temples themselves are to be aspersed with holy water, altars set up, and relics enclosed in them.

[1] Walter Ullmann, *A History of Political Thought: The Middle Ages* (Harmondsworth, 1965), 160–1.

For if these temples are well built, they are to be purified from devil-worship, and dedicated to the service of the true God.... And since they have a custom of sacrificing many oxen to devils, let some other solemnity be substituted in its place, such as a day of Dedication or the Festivals of the holy martyrs whose relics are enshrined there. On such occasions they might well construct shelters of boughs for themselves around the churches that were once temples, and celebrate the solemnity with devout feasting.[1]

Gregory was concerned to divorce practice from its underlying myth, replacing the latter by Christian myth and its ritual, but he allowed communal celebration to continue, giving it a focus upon church and churchyard and, where necessary, introducing new practices. A comparatively late result of this functional change and its attendant generic developments was the folk-play.

Before continuing, it is advisable to keep a number of considerations in mind. First, there is little detailed description of folk-customs in the Middle Ages, although much may be inferred from the disapproving references of clerics objecting to the importance attached by the populace to such occasions and also to the licence and riot which accompanied them. Typical of such complaints are the series of prohibitions issued by Robert Grosseteste, Bishop of Lincoln, between 1236 and 1244; that of c.1244 is interestingly explicit:

> Faciunt etiam, ut audivimus, clerici ludos quos vocant miracula: et alios ludos quos vocant Inductionem Maii sive Autumni; et laici scotales...miracula etiam et ludos supra nominatos et scotales, quod est in vestra potestate facili, omnino exterminetis.[2]
> [The clerics also, as we have heard, put on plays (ludos) which they call miracles (miracula); and other plays which they call the Bringing-in of May or of Autumn; and the lay people put on scotales.... You should stamp out entirely the miracles and plays named above and the scotales, which is easily within your power.]

Similar practices are evidenced in the 1240 prohibitions of the Bishop of Worcester:

> Prohibemus clericis...nec sustineant ludos fieri de Rege et Regina, nec arietas levari, nec palaestras publicas fieri, nec gildales inhonestas.[3]

[1] Bede: A History of the English Church and People, tr. Leo Sherley-Price (Harmondsworth, 1955), 86–7.
[2] Chambers, I, 91, fn. 2.
[3] Chambers, I, 91, fn. 3.

[We prohibit clerics supporting the production of plays (*ludos*) about King and Queen, or ram-raisings, or the holding of public wrestling-matches, or dishonest guild-ales.]

The prohibitions pose the usual problems of semantics – what precisely is meant by *ludus* and *miraculum* here? – and tantalize by their throwaway references to the induction of May and Autumn, scotales and dishonest guild-ales, ram-raisings and public wrestling. But they attest the thriving traditions of folk-activity in the Middle Ages. Occasionally a clearer picture of the custom emerges, as in the prohibition by the University of Oxford in *c.*1250 on students participating in a folk-custom:

> Ne quis choreas cum larvis seu strepitu aliquo in ecclesiis vel plateis ducat, vel sertatus, vel coronatus corona ex foliis arborum, vel florum vel aliunde composita alicubi incedat...prohibemus.[1]
> [We prohibit anyone leading ring-dances with masks (*larvis*) or any rhythmic sound (*strepitu*) in churches or streets, or going anywhere garlanded or crowned with a crown made from the leaves of trees, or of flowers or from elsewhere.]

Again, in *Handlyng Synne*, an early fourteenth-century poem, Robert Mannyng of Brunne tells of the twelve dancers of Colbek (see Plate 23) who danced in the churchyard one Christmas in defiance of the priest and were condemned to dance there for the whole year.[2] But such detail is rare and presented from a hostile viewpoint.

Hence, the evidence of medieval records has often been supplemented by reference to modern folk-custom, to cognate practices in other countries and appeal to mythology. Traces of primitive ritual are undoubtedly shared by medieval and modern folk-customs. An example is the practice of animal-disguise, condemned in a late fifth- or early sixth-century prohibition ascribed to Cæsarius of Arles:

> Alii vestiuntur pellibus pecudum; alii assumunt capita bestiarum, gaudentes et exsultantes, si taliter se in ferinas species transformaverint, ut homines non esse videantur.[3]
> [Some are clothed in the skins of cattle; others put on the heads of wild beasts, rejoicing and leaping, as if they had thus transformed themselves into a species of wild beast, so that they should not seem to be human.]

[1] Chambers, I, 92, fn. 2.
[2] Robert Mannyng of Brunne, *Handlyng Synne*, ed. F. J. Furnivall, 2 vols (London: EETS, 1901 and 1903).
[3] Chambers, II, 297–8.

Such guises are adopted in many parts of Britain today; an example is the Christmas Bull of Dorset, Gloucestershire and Wiltshire:

> A man wearing, or supporting on a pole above his own head so that he seemed to be wearing, a hollowed-out bull's head, complete with horns and glaring eyes of bottle-glass. His human body was concealed in some cases by the animal's hide, with the tail hanging down behind, and in others by rough sacking, or a long white sheet. Thus disguised, the Bull went round the parish at Christmas-time, usually at dusk, with a man who acted as his keeper, and an attendant band of men and boys.[1]

The Bull would arrive unexpectedly at a Christmas party and had the freedom of the house, driving the revellers before him. The same practice of animal-disguise is found in the Hodening or Hooden Horse which appears at Christmastide in Kent and the Yorkshire area around Doncaster; the White Horse of the Cheshire Soulers; the *Mari Lwyd* of Wales; or the Abbot's Bromley Horn Dance in Staffordshire, once a Christmas celebration; or the May Hobby Horse.

Several features link modern and medieval practices. First, the 'guise' is the remains of a real animal (*capita bestiarum/a hollowed-out bull's head*); but, secondly, there is no attempt at verisimilitude, no attempt at imitating animal stance. The celebrant stands, wearing perhaps an animal skin (*pellibus pecudum/the animal's hide, with the tail hanging down behind*) or merely a concealment of the human form (*rough sacking or a long white sheet*). The effect is not to disguise the celebrant but to remove his human identity, for he has in his new role become possessed by another power and in this form has powers which a mere human cannot have; the medieval prohibition rightly says, 'si taliter se in ferinas species transformaverint, ut homines non esse videantur'. Thirdly, this transformed being can now transmit his power to the faithful, for the purpose of his visitation to the faithful is to confer fertility, prosperity or good fortune. The Bull, the Hodening Horse, the Horn Dancers, are generally welcomed in the community, despite their fearsome appearance and unruly conduct, for the good fortune that they bring. Fourthly, the celebration follows a set pattern. It occurs only at a certain time of year, its ritual is fixed and familiar, and the traditional properties are produced like a saint's relics. The Abbot's Bromley horns have been used since the seventeenth century, though no one knows their origins, and the head of the Wild Horse of Antrobus,

---

[1] Christina Hole, *A Dictionary of British Folk Customs* (London, 1979, reprint), 65.

Cheshire, is always said to be two hundred years old. Women are not among the celebrants, though they may be among the recipients of 'grace'. But what is not known is where the power will be released, for the route is not fixed.

It is easy to abstract the mythology underlying these rituals, for they are fertility myths, centring usually on the shortest day of the year, the winter solstice, or the point of equal day and night, the spring equinox, heralding summer. A source or spirit of fecundity and regeneration is to be released. The ritual can be seen as an act of appeasement by sacrifice, from which perhaps the 'relic' of the victim, annually produced, derives. But the ceremonial is magical, locating the spirit in the relic itself so that the resurrection of the properties is not merely commemorative but also efficacious, carrying with it the power of fecundity. If the ritual was not performed, that power would depart from the community. Thus the ritual is a way by which a village community controls the factors which determine its survival.

Finally divorced from its validating mythology by the domination of the Christian myth, pagan ritual lost this primary function. If it was to continue, the pagan ritual demanded an explanation of its function in a community of non-believers who needed to justify the labour, time, cost and disruption of an occasion outside Christian ritual. Gregory had already foreseen a second function for such rituals, as acts of communal celebration which linked present to past as an emblem of continuity. For the surviving community, the recurring celebration linked them with past generations who had celebrated in the same way, and hence gave the promise of future continuity by succeeding generations. As Susan Pattison says of the Antrobus Soul-caking play today:

> The behaviour which the Soulcakers value, and which they are trying to perpetuate in the community, is that condoned by their 'fore-fathers'.... By turning out every year as their fathers and grandfathers did before them, wearing the clothes they wore and performing their play, the Soulcakers are resurrecting their ancestors' values.[1]

This sense of communal continuity is unlikely to be a new function, since it must have been latent in pagan times, but it readily becomes primary. But only members of the community will fully understand and value this function. An 'outsider', such as a sceptical cleric, is less able to appreciate

[1] Susan Pattison, 'The Antrobus Soulcaking play: an alternative approach to the Mummers' play', *Folk-life*, 15 (1977), 10.

it, and may indeed demand functional justification in terms which he *can* understand and accept.

(ii) Rationalizations of ritual

Beside the communal function, therefore, another justification may arise, that the ritual commemorates an event in the history of the community. Such explanations are the community's response to the disbelieving outsider who might challenge the continuity of the practice, and they therefore constitute evidence both of the objection and also of the community's determination to preserve a ceremony which affirms its independence. On 1 November the Celtic year began, and among the rituals 'fires were kindled upon hill-tops and open spaces for the purification of the people and the land, and the defeat of the powers of evil, which were then at their strongest'. After the coming of Christianity, the fires were lit on 31 October, All Hallows Eve. On 5 November 1605, a band of men was arrested while preparing to blow up the Palace of Westminster, and Parliament ordered that the day be henceforth a holiday. The Hallowe'en fires were often moved to this date and a figure, held to be an effigy of Guy Fawkes, the plotter who was to have lit the fuse, was burned. Hence the national occasion afforded a rational defence of a folk-custom threatened by Puritan critics. Its communal and participatory aspects can be seen today in Lewes, Sussex, where the occasion is marked by torchlight processions through the streets of the town and six different bonfire societies are responsible for various effigies and fires. But other national foes have been substituted on occasion to provide a rational explanation – the Pope, Napoleon, the Kaiser, Hitler, etc.[1]

The loss of the underlying mythology, however, did allow greater freedom of practice, and modern celebrations are a mixture of features from different periods. The Abbot's Bromley Horn Dance, for example, is today performed on the first Monday after 4 September, but was once a Christmas ritual. Its costumes were specially designed in the last century – previously the dancers wore workaday clothes decorated with ribbons and patches of coloured cloth. The first reference to it is in 1686, yet it was not then being performed and so performance must have been revived later. As the original

---

[1] Hole, *Dictionary*, 123–7.

impulse dies, so possibilities of 'natural' change and antiquarian 're-touching' grow. Despite the widespread practice of well-dressing in Derbyshire, no village has an unbroken tradition of a custom apparently originating in the veneration of springs and wells as sources of life. Buxton seems to have begun in 1840 in imitation of surrounding villages, and at Wirksworth it is the waterless sites of the public taps, installed in 1840, which are adorned. The use of pictures, often religious in character, is a nineteenth-century addition to the older garlands. And the practice may be further rationalized, as at Tissington where it is said to commemorate the town's escape from the Black Death in 1350 and from a great drought in 1615.[1] Records of customs tend to belong to a period of scepticism and rationalization, and the customs themselves undergo modification. Our modern view of the 'Men's Morris' is inevitably conditioned by its co-existence with schoolgirls' Morris teams, a specialist form of precision dancing unrelated to community or custom, and with modern ballroom formation dance teams. As 'non-believers', we perceive all as forms of dance and assign the older ritual to a new genre.

As communal customs these rituals seem to have required no texts; Alex Helm has drawn attention to mummers' plays which survive as mimetic action only; he regards text as a late addition to ritual action.[2] The text may be an extension of the need to explain the activity and justify it to the 'non-believer'. But no text of a mummers' play survives from the Middle Ages and it is possible that such plays develop in response to a model of drama already established elsewhere. Certainly at later stages the folk-play looks to 'non-folk' culture; R. J. E. Tiddy sees the play changing particularly after the Puritan attacks, both incorporating popular heroes and villains into the action and also directly borrowing from eighteenth-century professional theatre.[3] The famous *Revesby Sword-Play*, though often included in discussions of medieval drama, was supposedly:

> Acted by a set of Plow Boys or Morris Dancers in riband dresses, with swords, on October 20th., 1779, at Revesby Abbey in Lincolnshire, the seat of the Right Hon. Sir Joseph Banks, Bart, P.R.S.

J. Q. Adams, introducing it thus in his *Chief Pre-Shakespearean Dramas*, recognized the play as a compilation of three separate plays which he called 'The Morris Dance of the Hobby Horse' with prologue and epilogue

---

[1] ibid., 322–5.
[2] Alex Helm, 'In Comes I, St George', *Folk-lore*, 76 (1965), 118–36.
[3] R. J. E. Tiddy, *The Mummers' Play* (Chicheley, 1972 reprint), 81.

(1–65); 'The Killing of the Fool' (66–258); and 'The Sword-play' (259–569). He also realized that the reference to 'this good time of Christmas' (179) meant that the play was not originally intended for October performance.[1] But Alex Helm has plausibly argued that the play was compiled for, or even by, Sir Joseph Banks, and that, since he was married in 1779, it might have been composed for the occasion of the first joint meeting of himself and his new wife with the tenantry.[2] The importance of such social allegiances for folk-drama will be considered below (p. 139); sufficient here to say that the Revesby play in its present form is unlikely to antedate 1779, and that, although its constituent elements are probably older, they cannot be dated nor their texts unquestioningly accepted as unmodified. This eighteenth-century text may be a misleading guide to medieval folk-drama.

On the other hand, it is possible to find useful indications of the new genre of folk-drama and the circumstances in which it developed. Although no text of the Coventry Hock Tuesday Show survives, we are fortunate in that the show was performed for Queen Elizabeth at Kenilworth in July 1575 and the performance was described by Robert Laneham, a courtier, in a letter to a friend in London.[3] His account falls into four parts. First, Laneham explains what the play is about and why it is performed. Secondly, he says that the play, despite its age and the historicity of its contents, has been suppressed by certain preachers and the citizens would like it to be reinstated. Thirdly, he describes the action as performed. Finally, he comments on its favourable reception, noting that a second performance had to be arranged because the Queen could not be present for the full performance on the first occasion.

Laneham says that the play was a historical commemoration:

> Of argument, how the Danez whylom heere in a troubloous seazon wear for quietness born withall, *and* suffeard in peas, that anon, by outrage *and* importabl insolency, abuzing both Ethelred, the King then, and all estates euerie whear beside: at the greuoous complaint *and* coounsell of Huna, the King's chieftain in warz, on Saint Brices night, Ann. Dom. 1012 (Az the book sayz) that falleth yeerely on the thirteenth of November, wear all dispatcht, and the Ream rid.

More detail is given in Sir Richard Morison's *Discourse Touchinge the*

---

[1] J. Q. Adams, *Chief Pre-Shakespearean Dramas* (Cambridge, Mass., 1924), 357.
[2] Helm, 'In Comes I, St George', 124–5.
[3] Chambers, II, 264–6; *REED, Coventry*, 272–4.

Reformation of the Lawes of England, written in the reign of Henry VIII,[1] in which he describes the folk-custom marking the occasion:

> Women for the noble acte that they did in the distruction of the Danes, whych so cruelly reigned in this realme, have a daie of memorye therof called hoptide, wherin it is leaful for them to take men, bynde, wasshe them, if they will give them nothing to bankett.

The full custom is still more explicit in the 1450 prohibition of the Bishop of Worcester:

> Uno certo die heu usitato hoc solempni festo paschatis transacto, mulieres homines, alioque die homines mulieres ligare, ac cetera media utinam non inhonesta vel deteriora facere moliantur et exercere, lucrum ecclesiae fingentes, set dampnum animæ sub fucato colore lucrantes.[2] [On one certain day by custom, alas, in this solemn feast of Easter past, the women bind the men, and on another day the men bind the women, and would that they might not be busy to devise and practise the other methods, dishonest or worse, bringing profit to the church, but earning damnation for the soul under a feigned colour.]

The custom was of capture and ransom – one day of women by men, the next of men by women. Hock Monday and Tuesday are the days following Low Sunday, and the practice was justified to the Church because the ransom-money went to church funds; in 1497 the women contributed 13s 4d to St Mary-on-the-Hill, London, on 'Hob Monday', but next day the men raised only 5s.[3] But it was a riotous celebration apparently deriving from the need for a sacrificial victim. Its separation from its mythological substructure left its communal function intact, but under pressure from critical 'non-believers' it found a new and spurious justification as a commemoration of a historic victory, thereby setting the community not within the recurring cycle of nature but in the developing pattern of national identity.

The Kenilworth production was both an offering to the Queen and a 'political' act. It was appropriate because it enacted a historical event ('grounded on story') in which women had acted with heroism. But it was

---

[1] Quoted in Sydney Anglo, 'An early Tudor programme for plays and other demonstrations against the Pope', *Journal of the Warburg and Courtauld Institutes*, 20 (1957), 176–9. Hereafter, Morison.

[2] Chambers, I, 155–6, fn. 3.

[3] Hole, *Dictionary*, 145.

also an ancient custom and harmless fun – 'for pastime woont too be plaid in oour Citee yeerely'.[1] Consequently it contained no immorality, 'papistry or ony superstition', but kept a number of people out of mischief. So, 'politically', the production aimed to outflank the religious opponents of the play. This justification, evidently set out in a petition to the Earl of Leicester, suggests the pressures which led to the rationalizing of folk-custom, culminating in drama.

Thus, the folk-custom described by Morison had in Coventry become a play. It had speeches as well as actions – 'expressed in actionz *and* rymez after their maner'. Its action was a battle, in three conflicts: 'twise the Danes had the better; but at the last conflict, beaten doun, ouercom, and many led captiue for triumph by our English weemen.' Participants led by one Captain Cox, a stonemason, wore battle-gear. Laneham relished the exuberant violence of the mock battles:

> First by speare and shield, outragious in their racez az ramz at their rut, with furious encoounterz that togyther they tumbl too the dust, sumtime hors and man: and after fall too with sworde *and* target, good bangz a both sidez.

The battles were obviously the focus of the play, and one can only assume that the speeches explained the occasion and identified the participants. Yet this play seems to have stood beside other historical actions in a 1591 Coventry resolution:

> That the distrucion of Ierusalem, the Conquest of the Danes, or the historie of K[ing] Ed[ward] the 4, at the request of the Comons of this Cittie, shal be plaid on the pagens on Midsomer daye *and* St. Peter's daye next in this Cittie *and* non other playes.[2]

Elizabeth responded to the play as a satisfied patron – she paid the performers. Her presence and response suggests how the old folk-ritual was transformed. With new cause and new occasion it became a spectacle for a 'non-believer' whose attention had to be engaged and support secured.

---

[1] Cf. *REED, Coventry*, 7, for the first reference to the play, in 1416: 'The Pageants and Hox tuesday invented, wherein the King and Nobles took great delight.'
[2] Chambers, II, 361–2; *REED, Coventry*, 332.

(iii) Robin Hood plays

While Morison approved of the nationalistic theme of such actions, he objected strongly to another folk-play, *Robin Hood*:

> In somer comenly upon the holy daies in most places of your realm, ther be playes of Robyn hoode, mayde Marian, freer Tuck, wherin besides the lewdenes and ribawdry that ther is opened to the people, disobedience also to your officers, is tought, whilest these good bloodes [exuberant youths] go about to take from the shiref of Notyngham one that for offendyng the lawes shulde have suffered execution.[1]

Such actions are doubly subversive, extolling criminality and corrupting public morals. The hero of such plays, Robin Hood, belongs both to the reality of the medieval outlaw and to the literary tradition of the outlaw-hero. His historicity matters here less than his recurring literary role as a figure of licensed anarchy, rebelling against a social order which, by its injustices, sets him on the side of justice. Yet it seems that stories of him emphasized him as a figure of anarchy rather than of justice, for references constantly place Robin Hood in contexts of idle and dissolute conduct. Sloth, in William Langland's *Piers Plowman* (*c*.1377), provides the earliest known reference:

> I kan [know] noʒt parfitly my paternoster · as þe preest it syngeþ,
> But I kan rymes of Robyn Hood · and Randolf Erl of Chestre.
>   (B-text, Passus V, 394–5)[2]

and *Dives and Pauper* (*c*.1405–10) is similarly critical:

> þey han leuer [rather] gon to þe tauerne þan to holy chirche, leuer to hereyn a tale or a song of Robyn Hood or of som rybaudye þan to heryn messe or matynys or onyþing of Goddis seruise or ony word of God.[3]

Such references both confirm Morison's disapproval and attest the currency of such tales from the late fourteenth century, antedating the first extant ballad text, *Robin Hood and the Monk*, of *c*.1450.

Yet Robin Hood can also be seen socially as the hero of the yeoman class, midway between the unfree peasant and the gently born noble. R. B. Dobson and J. Taylor claim that 'the greenwood legend can and

---

[1] Morison, 179.
[2] George Kane and E. Talbot Donaldson, *Piers Plowman: the B Version* (London, 1975).
[3] Priscilla Heath Barnum, *Dives and Pauper* (London, 1976: EETS 275), 189.

should be seen as an expression of social aspiration based on the real economic progress achieved by many Englishmen before and after 1400',[1] and against his anarchic role is the argument that Robin Hood became the acceptable embodiment of social authority and natural gentility. J. C. Holt has argued:

> It is highly probable that Robin's earliest audience thought of him as an outlawed forester, who had been an established and in no way menial member of a lord's or gentleman's household. As such, he was on the landlord's side, not the peasant's.[2]

And it is from a landlord in a family which had risen socially that we have the first reference to Robin in drama. Sir John Paston, writing to his brother on 16 April 1473, laments the departure of his servant, W. Woode:

> I have kepyd hym thys iij yere to pleye Seynt Jorge *and* Robynhod *and* Shryff off Notyngham, and now when I wolde have good horse he is goon into Bernysdale, and I wythowt a kepere.[3]

The letter may, as has been suggested,[4] be an ironic allusion to Woode's unauthorized dramatic activities, but it indicates a jovial familiarity with Robin Hood plays and kindred drama on the part of Sir John. Some distinction should therefore be maintained between the 'moral' and 'social' implications of the Robin Hood tales.

Such a distinction may help to explain the association of Robin Hood with May rituals. May was the occasion of folk-rituals deriving from fertility myths, in which natural emblems invested with the power of fertility were gathered by villagers in the countryside and borne round the village with processional song and dance. The emblems were often garlands of flowers and leaves; equally frequently they were stylized trees or Maypoles, cut from forest trees and having ritual power. On such occasions it was usual to choose a young girl and young man to preside over the occasion, a practice yielding to the modern May Queen, with its nineteenth-century crowning-ceremonies. This Lord and Lady of May, or May King and Queen, seemingly typifying sexual regeneration and fecundity, are

[1] R. B. Dobson and J. Taylor, *Rymes of Robyn Hood: an Introduction to the English Outlaw* (London, 1976), 35.

[2] J. C. Holt, 'The origins and audience of the Ballads of Robin Hood', *Past and Present*, 18 (1960), 101.

[3] N. Davis (ed.), *The Paston Letters, and Papers of the Fifteenth Century*, Part I (Oxford, 1971), no. 275, 460–1.

[4] See David Wiles, *The Early Plays of Robin Hood* (Cambridge and Totowa, N.J., 1981), 36.

evidently the *ludos...de Rege et Regina* of the 1240 Worcester Prohibitions above (p. 124) and feature in many similar prohibitions. Their titles vary. Aberdeen had its Abbot and Prior of Bonacord, Edinburgh an Abbot of Narent, and Shrewsbury an Abbot of Marham. But in many places the presiding figures are called Robin Hood and Maid Marian, and their followers include Friar Tuck and the outlaws. *Robertus Hod* is first recorded in Edinburgh in 1492, and the title ousts other titles in most places in Scotland in the sixteenth century; at Shrewsbury, Robin Hood is the title from 1553. The change was very deliberate, as an Aberdeen order of 17 November 1508 suggests:

> all personis burges nichbouris and Inhabitaris burges sonnys habill to Rid to decor and honour þe towne in þar array conveniant þarto sall Rid with Robert huyd and litile Iohne quhilk was callit in ʒeris bipast Abbot and priour of Bonacord one euery Sanct Nicholas day throw the towne as wse and wont has bene quhen þai war warnit be þe said Robert huyd or litile Iohnne or ony ane of thame.[1]

The ballad hero evidently provided an acceptable rationalization for a ritual associated with nature and the forest.

Consequently, the ritual itself changed. Dobson and Taylor quote from the churchwardens' accounts of Kingston-on-Thames, 1507–29, which reveal 'regular expenditure on the costumes and appurtenances ("banner", "cote", gloves and shoes)' of 'Robyn Hode', indicating that identification by costume was essential. The same accounts indicate the extension of the legend to explain the May Queen as Maid Marian and to accommodate a friar among the Morris dancers.[2] In *Albion's England* (1586) a simple northern man is made to say:

> At Paske began our Morris, and ere Penticost our May:
> Tho Robin Hood, Liell John, Frier Tucke and Marian deftly play,
> And Lard and Ladie gang till kirk, with lads and lasses gay.[3]

The name Marian, first mentioned by Barclay in 1500, is that of the shepherdess in French pastourelles – exemplified in Adam de la Halle's courtly adaptation, *Le Jeu de Robin et Marion* (*c*.1283) – and suggests a separate literary explanation for the May Queen, perhaps aided by the use

[1] Anna J. Mill, *Medieval Plays in Scotland*, 137.
[2] Dobson and Taylor, *Rymes of Robin Hood*, 39.
[3] F. J. Child, *The English and Scottish Popular Ballads*, 5 vols (New York, 1965, reprint of 1885 edition), III, 44–5.

of Robin as the traditional shepherd's name. Dobson and Taylor claim that in the May games Marian, 'played by a boy, developed into a by-word for sexual impropriety'.[1] The friar seems to have been a figure in the Morris who acquired his name even later than the principal figures. Text was probably the final explanatory element, completing the generic substitution.

Three early texts of Robin Hood plays are extant. The earliest, a fragment of *c*.1475 (Dobson–Taylor No. 19), was probably once part of the Paston Papers and hence may be the play referred to in Sir John Paston's letter of 1473.[2] The play, which has no rubrics, is a dramatization of the ballad of *Robin Hood and Guy of Gisborne*. The knight Guy vows to capture Robin and competes with him at shooting, stone-throwing, throwing the axle-tree, and wrestling. When the knight blows his horn to call help, Robin fights and kills him, cuts off his head and changes clothes with him. A dialogue between two observers then seems to describe a fight between the sheriff's men and the outlaws, using bows, which ends in the capture of the outlaws. It is reasonable to suppose that the rest of the play showed their rescue by the disguised Robin, with further violent actions.[3]

This early fragment supports the implication of violence in Morison's allusion (above, p. 133) to 'these good bloodes'. But it contains two different kinds of violence. The episode of Robin and the knight culminates in a hero-combat which is akin to the hero-combats of the St George folk-plays; Sir John's letter suggests that the same actor excelled in both plays, perhaps by his prowess and exuberance. But this combat is the climax of a series of competitive games indicative of village-sports and mostly inappropriate to the knight who suggests them. One, wrestling, is expressly comprehended in the 1240 Worcester prohibitions. The text is a justification for traditional activities, but part of its effect derives from the comic social inversion of the knight's defeat, and a further part from the recognition and dramatic frustration of the 'death-resurrection-triumph' pattern of hero-combat plays. The knight's death here is final, followed by his functional beheading (to prevent identification?). The ensuing communal conflict, on the other hand, recalls the mass battles of the Hock Tuesday

---

[1] Dobson and Taylor, *Rymes of Robin Hood*, 42.

[2] Wiles, p. 36, argues: 'I would suggest that Wood – or someone similar – noted down the text in the course of the travels in which his duties involved him and circulated it among the servants of one of the Paston households. The copy that has survived belonged to a servant who had no further use for it after Whitsun 1475. The game was imported to the area and quickly died out.'

[3] For a different view of the action, see Wiles, 33–5.

play and seems to have been similarly inclusive. A comment of 1553 by Richard Robinson almost justifies the plays on military grounds:

> Myself remembreth of a childe, in contreye native mine
> A May game was of Robyn Hood, and of his traine, that time,
> To traine up young men, stripplings, and eche other younger childe
> In shooting; yearely this with solempne feast was by the guylde
> Or brotherhoode of townsmen don.[1]

The fragment offers no support for Morison's major objection, 'ribaudrye', and has no reference to Maid Marian. Greater justification is to be found at the end of a later play, *Robin Hood and the Friar*, where a 'maid' is present and is the object of low-style bawdry by the friar, who himself thereby becomes the butt of anti-clerical satire. His lewd speculations that the 'maid' is

> A prycker, a prauncer, a terer of shetses,
> A wagger of ballockes when other men slepes

give an indecent twist to Robin's

> And her chapplayn I the make
> To serve her for my sake.

But this indecency is only one aspect of a general sense of burlesque more appropriate to a comic interlude. The violence in this play, and in its companion-piece, *Robin Hood and the Potter*, is motivated by a comic irreverence for Robin by his opponents. The friar and Robin engage in a *flyting* before the friar agrees to carry Robin across the stream – and tips him into the water. A fight ensues which ends in Robin bribing the friar to enter his service. Similarly, the potter refuses to pay Robin 'passage' and to provoke him Robin accosts his servant and breaks his pots. In the subsequent sword-play Robin meets his match and must appeal for help.

These two later plays are an appendix to William Copland's edition of *A Mery Geste of Robyn Hoode* (Dobson–Taylor Nos. 20 and 21), published sometime between 1548 and 1569; they are usually identified with the play of Robin Hood entered in the Stationers' Register on 30 October 1560. They are therefore some eighty-five years later than the Paston fragment. Since Copland claimed they were 'to be played in May games', they may well contain features typical of the genre by the mid-sixteenth century; but their

[1] Child, III, 45, fn.

tone, their stress on the verbal as well as the visual, their appearance in printed form, all suggest an awareness of the plays in the context of Tudor theatre and drama, and of an audience rather different from that of Sir John Paston.

(iv) Plough plays and hero combats

Two important forms of village-ritual seem to have developed into distinct primary and secondary rationalizations. The transporting of a fertility deity around the fields on a plough pulled by men seems to have been the starting-point for the custom of the Fool Plough, decorated and pulled round the houses of a village by young men on Plough Monday, the Monday following Epiphany (6 January). The young men, beribboned and otherwise adorned, are variously called plough stots, bullocks, jacks or jays, and are accompanied by a man dressed as a woman who is known as a Bessy and who takes a collection at the various houses visited.[1] It is said that the plough is used to dig up the gardens of non-contributors. But evidently the plough came to acquire itself the supernatural powers of the deity it once transported and, adorned, the Fool Plough could dispense that power to those it visited. The money collected was used in part by the Ploughmen's Guilds to maintain a 'plough light' perpetually burning in the parish church, and the custom of blessing the plough as an emblem of labour is scornfully described by John Bale in his *Image of Both Churches*.[2] Hence a folk ritual first recorded from Durham in 1377–8 ('Dona...hominibus del Maudelans...in educcione caruce post Natale')[3] is assimilated into the ritual and mythology of the Church.

In seaport communities of the East Midlands, the ship replaced the plough as the emblem carried in effigy round the town. This is presumably the function of the ship mentioned in an order of 10 January 1508, as built by the Grimsby mariners and associated with the plough-light:

> le maryners do Grymesby faciant unam naven stantem
> in ecclesia beate marie pertinentem lumen aratri.[4]

[1] Hole, *Dictionary*, 238–9; see also Chambers, II, 207–10.
[2] H. Christmas (ed.), *John Bale, Selected Works* (Parker Society, Cambridge, 1849), 528.
[3] *Durham Account Rolls* I (London, 1898: Surtees Society 99), 212.
[4] Stanley J. Kahrl, *Records of Plays and Players in Lincolnshire, 1300–1585*, MSC, VIII, 1969 (1974), 11.

In some towns such celebration was associated with the performance of an appropriate religious play. At Hull, the accounts of 1483 indicate that Trinity House, the mariners' guild, presented a play of Noah.[1] But perhaps because there was no obviously appropriate subject, the ploughmen do not seem to have included drama in their celebrations. The 'wooing-plays' of the East Midlands, associated with such occasions, seem to have been a modern creation.[2]

One text, a Scottish *Pleugh Song* of *c.*1500, has attracted particular attention as an example of the adaptation of the Fool Plough custom as a dramatic offering to the lord of the manor.[3] As entertainment for a 'non-believer', the custom acquires an explanatory text, and a new genre emerges. The focus of the action is now the loyalty of tenant to lord, seen in the professed concern at the impending death of the lord's old plough-ox:

> And I am wo your pleugh suld lie
> and I might come and be nearby
> to yoke another in his steid.

and the summoning of the lord's servants to help with the despatch of the beast and the provision of a replacement. The old ox is evidently played by a member of the team and is apparently to be beaten to death ('suppose ye brod him whil he die'). After his 'death', the parts of the plough are listed and the replacement 'ox' harnessed. Richard Axton notes: 'There is one ox (or ox-man) and yet it is composed of the whole team of men. Nine traditional names are used to hail the ox.'[4] The leader of the team doubles as presenter of an action which combines ritual death with symbolic resurrection and then dissolves into the folk-dance associated with the plough-festival. But the action now has a new context in the hierarchy of local society, divorced from the purely economic and mythological concerns of the village, and it is to the concept of tenant-service that the text finally reverts:

> And if ye please this pleugh of mine,
> tell me shortly into time
> or I contract or hired be
> with others that desires me.

---

[1] Chambers, II, 370–1.
[2] C. R. Baskervill, 'Dramatic aspects of medieval folk festivals in England', *SP*, 17 (1920), 38.
[3] Text in *Music of Scotland* (Musica Britannia 15), no. 30.
[4] Axton, *European Drama of the Early Middle Ages*, 41.

using 'hiring' to suggest the *quête*, the payment expected of the lord for entertainment.

This text in itself seems to be 'occasional' and specific. It is fairly late; the text is dated *c.*1500 and *OED* does not evidence the legally precise *contract* before 1548. It is doubtful whether it could be regarded as a 'typical' form. But it reveals the dramatic potential which can readily be exploited in folk-custom when translated to a new context.

The second village ritual with two rationalizations seems to be that of hero-combat. This men's ritual in modern mumming-plays has been characterized by Alan Brody in *The English Mummers and their Plays* as an action containing never fewer than three people – the hero, his opponent and a healer.[1] In the battle following the opening vaunts, the hero is killed, but is then restored to life by the healer and goes on to victory. This modern play, seen for example in the Lutterworth Mummers' Christmas play,[2] evidently developed from a ritual of death and rebirth at the time of the winter solstice, probably associated with sacrifice. Though no medieval texts survive, a similar action may underlie the Christmas game at King Arthur's court in *Sir Gawain and the Green Knight*, where a green stranger, huge and bearing axe and holly-branch, is beheaded by Gawain at his own request, but then retrieves his head and rides off, challenging Gawain to receive a similar blow the next year. King Arthur places this violent action in the context of celebrations appropriate to the season:

> Wel bycommes such craft vpon Cristmasse,
> Laykyng of enterludez, to laȝe and to syng,
> Among þise kynde caroles [dances] of knyȝtez and ladyez.　(471–3)

It is an 'interlude' among the more courtly and 'natural' (*kynde*) activities of the nobility.

Such ritualized action, divorced from its mythology, demands explanation. Arthur regards it as entertainment, and so it seems to be in modern mummers' plays, which add new comic characters and actions to the ritual base. Even so, one is inclined to accept, for the fictional court and the modern audience, the sense of communal solidarity generated by the presence of alien beings which Susan Pattison finds in the Antrobus Soul-caking play:

> What the characters do have in common, which makes them at once amusing and frightening, is their peripherality.... In laughing at

[1] Alan Brody, *The English Mummers and their Plays: Traces of Ancient Mystery* (London [1971]), chap. 3.
[2] Chambers, II, 276–9.

characters who would normally generate some degree of fear, the audience is coming to terms with its fear and suspicion, and in doing so is coping with feelings which might produce conflict destructive to the community.... Exaggeration and ridicule condemns [*sic*] their ways of life and so the central community and its norms are reinforced.[1]

Such a view has a number of consequences. First, the champion represents the norm of communal conduct and it is his battle with the abnormal and rather sinister figures that matters; his death and resurrection cease to be the mythical focus of the play and merely indicate the fragile and vulnerable character of the community which he defends. Secondly, an expansion of the play by the addition of such figures then becomes appropriate; after the battle at Antrobus, figures such as Dainty Dout (a man in schoolboy's cap, blazer and shorts), Beelzebub (with dripping-pan) and the Wild Horse enter; a corrupt text from Malvern includes old Father Christmas and 'little man Dick with my big big head and little wit', while old Belsey Bob ('on my Soulder I carry a nob, in my hand I carry a can') puts in an earlier appearance.[2] Thirdly, the healer is assimilated to the pattern, being half within the acknowledged community, in his passing allusions to medical practice, and half outside it, in his nonsensical claims and magical success in raising the dead hero. Typical is the claim from Pillerton, Warwickshire:[3]

> I am a doctor, a noble doctor,
> A doctor of high degree,
> Travelled thro' all hospitals
> In England, France and Wales:
> And I can cure all sorts of complaints:
> Rheumatics, itch, stitch, palsy and gout,
> Pains in the belly, pains out.

Any old man or woman being dead three score years and ten
who takes one of my pills can rise and come to life again.

where the boast of a not impossible skill practised in medical institutions yields to the absurdity of magical powers.

With the focus upon conflict rather than upon death and resurrection, however, there is opportunity for further rationalization by reference to national heroes and foes. Classical heroes such as Alexander and Hector, romance figures such as Sir Guy, and particularly notable 'Englishmen'

[1] Pattison, 'The Antrobus Soulcaking Play', 8–9.
[2] Tiddy, *The Mummers' Play*, 232–3.
[3] ibid., 224.

such as King Alfred, Lord Nelson or Wellington, lend their names to the champions, although the text makes little use of the allusion.[1] Sometimes figures from May games, such as General Valentine and Colonel Spring (Dorset) or Robin Hood (Shipton-under-Wychwood, Oxfordshire) appear. And, occasionally, the hero is St George, the patron saint of England and patron also of the Order of the Garter. It is perhaps a result of the Hanoverian period that the hero appears today as George, Prince George or King George – possibly St George was more common at an earlier period.

Although St George, as national saint and hero, seems to provide a most convenient justification for hero–combat ritual, his most famous exploit, the subjugation of the dragon and the rescue of the daughter of the King of Libya, described in *Legenda Aurea*, is not hero-combat. It builds upon the biblical image of the subjugation of the dragon of the devil by the archangel Michael to suggest the symbolic defeat of evil by Christian strength and courage. Its mythic focus is not the natural cycle of death and rebirth but the Christian consciousness of the need to combat evil. And the story effectively combines the symbolic Christian struggle with the chivalric obligations of a knight to protect the helpless, defend his realm and his Christian faith; religious and chivalric concerns fuse. Hero-combats, even where they include St George, are not usually on 23 April, his day, and his name is only one of many rationalizations of ritual action.

(v) Christian myth in the village

With St George we approach the Christian myth represented in the village by the Church. St George's celebrations in the Middle Ages seem often to be a result of co-operation between a community and its church, not a development of an existing folk-custom. The fullest records of such celebrations concern the guild of St George at Norwich, founded in 1385 and dissolved in 1732. They indicate that in Norwich, as in other towns, there was a ceremonial riding of the guild on the saint's day to the chapel of St George in a wood near the city where interludes were played. The 1408 records suggest St George's costume ('coat armour beaten with silver'), require a train of attendants, and demand a mimetic conflict: 'The

[1] Chambers, I, 212.

George shall go in procession and make a conflict with the Dragon and keep his estate both days.'[1] The princess is represented by a person variously called 'the Lady' or 'St Margaret' (another saint associated with a dragon). Although organized by a religious guild with a chapel in the cathedral, the Norwich celebrations of St George are not totally distinct from folk-custom in its processional form, its movement from city to woodland and the action of combat. St George and the princess recall the King and Queen of May. At Dublin, the link is suggested rather by the supernumerary figures of the emperor and empress:

> The Mayor of the yeare before to finde the Emperoure and Empress with their followers, well apparelled, that is to say, the Emperor with two Doctors, and the Empress, with two knightes, and two maydens to beare the traynes of their gownes, well apparelled, and St. George to pay their wages.[2]

At Norwich, by the eighteenth century, the Dragon had become the centre of activities usually associated with folk-custom, being accompanied by 'whifflers' who juggled with swords, and 'fools' in motley with cats' tails and bells. Sir John Paston's servant, Woode, acted in both Robin Hood and St George plays – indeed, since Sir John's younger brother, Sir John Paston III, was a member of the Norwich guild of St George in 1496, it is possible that Woode performed in the Norwich play, presumably with the same 'acting-style' as in Robin Hood.[3]

Yet recognition of the possible compatibility in dramatic appeal between the St George plays of folk-ritual and those of Christian celebration involves awareness of the different functions and significance to which the common dramatic elements were directed in the different mythologies. The saint's play manifested the officially sanctioned mythology guarded and transmitted by the Christian Church, an international organization. As such it differed from folk-custom in some important respects. First, its mythology, though having features analogous to the natural cycle of death and rebirth, did not directly derive from the agricultural activities on which the social and economic existence of the village depended. Rather, it proposed a pattern of spiritual destruction by sin and spiritual redemption through divine grace for all men, confirmed by the myth of the incarnate God who, motivated by love, offered Himself as an atoning sacrifice and rose again from the dead.

[1] Chambers, I, 223.
[2] Chambers, II, 365.
[3] But see also Wiles, 36, and above, p. 136, fn. 2.

Secondly, this myth was incorporated in authorized texts written in the Church's official language, Latin, and was therefore fixed by textual authority, unlike the folk-customs, which were fixed by traditional and repeated practice. Thirdly, the interpretations and enactments of the myth were controlled by a class of trained, literate clergy, ensuring that no essential feature of enactment or detail of interpretation was lost or distorted. Fourthly, the organization was officially recognized; its influence emanated from the parish church and its priest, supported by the dues of the parishioners, and its mythology alone had official legal support. The drama which this myth generated is not the exclusive property of a village-community, and some of its forms seem uniquely urban. Its juxtaposition with village folk-celebration permitted a clearer assessment of the limits of the two forms and also suggested a possibility of interaction within the new genre, drama, which produced new and interesting forms.

The accounts of a play of 'the holy martyr St George', published in abridged form by Chambers,[1] indicate some of the major features of the Church's drama in the village. The play was performed on the feast of St Margaret, 20 July, in 1511 in the village of Bassingbourne in Cambridgeshire. The play seems to have been a life of the saint, presumably based upon the authorized legend of St George. It was written by 'John Hobarde, Brotherhood Priest', and hence by a member of the clergy, a trained and literate man. The production was on a lavish scale, with expensive costumes and properties ('First paid to the garnement man for garnements and propyrts and playbooks, xx$^{s.}$') and painted sets ('Item to John Beecher for painting of three Fanchoms and four Tormentors') and music ('To a minstrel and three waits of Cambridge...'). One assumes that the attention to production, like the requirement of an official text, reflects the need to present the action faithfully so that its reference and significance may be clear. Here St George's specific identity is important; it is not just one of many possible names to explain the hero. And the action is too lavish for its cost to be sustained by one village; twenty-seven neighbouring villages contributed to the expenses of the production and presumably were represented among the audience.

Beside this example of village drama, a saint's play, may be set the play performed at the Corpus Christi celebrations in Sherborne, Dorset, beginning in 1543.[2] The town had a Corpus Christi procession, and in

---

[1] Chambers, II, 338.
[2] A. D. Mills, 'A Corpus Christi play and other dramatic activities in sixteenth-century Sherborne, Dorset', *MSC*, IX (London, 1977), 1–15.

1543–9 introduced a play to mark the occasion. No performance is recorded after 1549 until the tradition was briefly revived in 1572–6 with detailed accounts of expenditure. This later play seems to have dealt specifically with the destruction of Sodom and Gomorrah, for there are references to 'Sodom clothes' and 'a peacke of wheatten meale for to macke louttes wyfe'. This action also seems to have been textually controlled and there are references to masks and costumes which attest the lavish scale of production. The costumes were a major item of expenditure, and were carefully stored in a specially secured place. Two large tents were set up and other smaller ones, including a tiring-house, together with scaffolds; spectators also stood 'vppon the churche Leaddes', evidently the roof, for which they paid – the main source of recorded revenue (xj^s x^d in 1574). Others rented ground in the churchyard, presumably for stalls. Although Sherborne, unlike Bassingbourne, seems to have borne the production costs itself, costumes were hired out between 1557 and 1559 to neighbouring villages – Wincanton, Castle Cary, Bishops Caundle and Beer Hackett – as well as to various individuals, and there are references in 1551 and 1553 to the brushing of costumes, presumably before re-storage. The implication may be that Sherborne's play was imitated or directly borrowed from time to time by other villages in the area. There is good evidence for such borrowing. In 1490 the chaplain of the guild of St George, New Romney, visited Lydd to see a play there with a view to reproducing it in his home-town and this may be the play mentioned in the New Romney accounts of 1497.[1]

The sharing of costumes and texts between neighbouring communities, the combination of villages to support productions, the overall sponsorship of Church and local authorities are an important reminder that, although most evidence relates to urban drama, religious drama thrived in rural areas on quite a lavish scale. Saints' plays and plays on biblical subjects put on by religious guilds and parishes were a widespread genre – see the discussions of *Mary Magdalen* and the *Brome Abraham and Isaac* below (pp. 193–7); and, though cycle-drama is an urban form, the evidence of both the Digby *Killing* and the N-town cycle suggests that this too could be broken into convenient units and toured. Cycles, too, borrowed from each other (see p. 170). The evidence is that a medieval playwright was conscious of a wide range of dramatic modes available to him.

It is difficult to make similar postulations for folk-drama because the texts on which comparisons might be made do not survive. But as Chambers

---

[1] Chambers, II, 386.

says, it is likely that when one village took its May-game to another, this was not just a procession with a garland and a *quête* but also a mimetic action.[1] The co-operation of Lydd and New Romney in the St George play extends to the May celebration of *c.*1422 when the men of Lydd visited New Romney 'with their May and ours'. Different celebrations might originate in the different mythologies of nature and of Christianity, but as a new genre of communal celebration, they could co-exist and interact and medieval people could witness both forms in their community. The 1527 petition of Norwich's guild of St Luke says that Pentecost was celebrated with a procession of

> many and diuers disgisinges and pageauntes as well of the lieffes and marterdams of diuers and many hooly Sayntes as also many other light and feyned figures and pictures of other persones and bestes.[2]

Thus the two forms of celebration stood together – one the product of international Christianity, the other, less well represented by texts, deriving from a desire to justify the folk-customs now detached from their original mythology. The folk-play suggests contact with the 'non-believer', whether the local lord, the national nobility or the Christian clergy.

(vi) Drama incorporating folk-motifs: the Croxton Sacrament play

Folk-drama is not 'literary' drama, its text being mainly a pretext for traditional action, and in so far as it fulfils its communal function in a village, it is not generically significant. Its importance for the development of drama lies in its distinctive and connotative mode to which literary dramatists, whether writing for Church or professional troupe, could allude. Discussing *Mankind*, Richard Axton aptly comments: 'Structural motifs from the Christmas mummers' drama have long been recognised in the bizarre medley of the action.'[3] In 1510, Halle relates, Henry VIII and courtiers visited the Queen and her attendants 'like outlawes or Robyn Hodes men', and the greenwood setting remained a strong symbol; Robin gained a new aristocratic lineage, and Shakespeare exploited the forest-setting

[1] Chambers, II, 177; also Baskervill, 'Dramatic aspects of medieval folk festivals', 84–7.
[2] Nelson, *The Medieval English Stage*, 119.
[3] Axton, *European Drama of the Early Middle Ages*, 200.

in *As You Like It*. In *c*.1539 John Redford could adapt the hero–combat form to humanist ends in *Wit and Science*. The shearers' feast of *The Winter's Tale* is a literary re-creation of folk-celebration with its telling connotations of joyous regeneration and fertility. Examples could be multiplied.

But this distinctive mode was exploited by authors of Christian drama which might be performed in town or village. A good example of this adaptation is the late fifteenth-century *Play of the Sacrament* of which the banns state: 'At Croxston on Monday it shall be sen[e]' (74).[1] A further reference to Babwell Mill (621) suggests that the venue was the village of Croxton, Suffolk, although the banns indicate that the play could be toured from village to village; hence the preliminary announcement, accompanied by minstrel and tableau. At the centre of the play is the central Church doctrine of transubstantiation (see pp. 117–19), described by the disbelieving Jews at 197–216 and validated by the historical events of the Last Supper and Christ's death and resurrection which the Jews also recount at 393–440. The story of the play is allegedly authentic; it is said to have happened in Aragon (11) and to have been witnessed recently in Rome, suggesting authentication from the very centre of Christianity (56–60).

The historical and sacramental features of the play's mythology contribute to a structure which is based on a dual consciousness of time. First, the action of the play is itself a mimetic Passion and Resurrection. The Host is sold to the Jews by a Christian merchant who regards it as a mere commodity and sells it as Judas sold Christ. The Jews mock and stab the wafer and it bleeds, in imitation of the buffeting and flagellation; they nail it to a pillar as Jesus was nailed to a cross, then take it down, wrapped in a cloth, and toss it into a cauldron, suggesting deposition and burial. Finally, to destroy it, they throw it into an oven. Here, it is transformed into the image of Christ who breaks out of the burning oven and rebukes the Jews, suggesting the Harrowing of Hell and the Resurrection. Hence the banns fairly claim that the Jews 'put him to a new Passion' (38).

Simultaneously, the contemporary ritual of the Mass, which recreates the Passion, allows the Host to act as symbolic link between past and present. The local church at Croxton is an important focus of events and its rituals contribute to the climax. The Host seems to be stolen from the church and is ceremonially restored there by the bishop. When he learns

---

[1] Text in Bevington, *Medieval Drama*, 754–88.

from the penitent Jews what has happened, he raises the Host on high and leads the audience in procession, singing 'O sacrum convivium' (834–41), blending mimesis with ritual and engaging the audience as worshippers. As such, they enter the church for the final action (865 + SD–7). Hence the Sacrament brings together the Passion of Christ, the miracle of fifteenth-century Aragon, and the daily worship and faith of the community at Croxton. It at once demonstrates and affirms the power of the Sacrament and also, in its incorporation of religious ceremonial in its dramatic structure, demands an act of fideistic affirmation from its audience. The boundaries of mimesis and sacramental rite, of 'illusion' and 'reality', are thereby dissolved.

But the concluding ritual and affirmation proceed from different dramatic modes established earlier in the play, for the play, apparently a defence against doctrinal disbelief in the community, incorporates such disbelief within its structure. There are two kinds of unbeliever. One is the worldly-minded man who professes Christianity without being aware of its implications for his own existence. The major example is the Christian merchant, Aristorius, who steals the Host for his own status and gain; but he is aided by the negligent priest who dines and drinks with him and whose drunken slumbers allow Aristorius to take the church keys and steal the Host. These two figures are not involved in the central action, the abuse of the Sacrament, but they return at the end of the action, confess, and are sternly rebuked by the Bishop. Aristorius' worldly-mindedness is reflected in his introductory speech in which he thanks God for his wealth and power (81–124). Its major feature is the boasting rhetorical catalogue of places with which he trades, a comically overweighted vaunt. The heavy satire of his worldly vanity stresses his limited values and essential stupidity. The priest is similarly a comic figure of self-satisfaction, accepting Aristorius' hospitality and then staggering off to bed. Neither is wilfully evil, but their comic realization does not diminish the enormity of their deeds.

The second group of unbelievers are the Jews. Here there is progressive and comic degeneration. The Jew Jonathas is at first the dignified equal of Aristorius, a merchant whose vaunt of wealth is rhetorically complementary to Aristorius' catalogue in its extended list. As Aristorius thanks God for his wealth, so Jonathas thanks *Machomet* for his. Jonathas's opening invocation nevertheless expresses a commendable, if misdirected, concern with the salvation of his soul and a desire to obey his god which is not only ironically answered by his final conversion to Christianity but implicitly condemns Aristorius' worldly-mindedness. Divided in faith, the two men are socially and economically equal, and Aristorius greets his Jewish counterpart with display 'as owith for a marchant of the banke' (260). But while it is Aristorius' economic concern which directs his actions and our response, Jonathas is placed by a comic descent from this 'norm' of social dignity.

In criticizing the absurdity of Christian belief, Jonathas and his men instigate an absurd demonstration of its fallacy; they attack a wafer. This self-conscious absurdity, reflected in Jonathas's mock-martial image 'Now am I bold with bataile him to bleyke' (477), yields to his comic stylistic descent:

> Ah owt, owt harrow! What devill is this?
> Of this wirk I am on were!
> It bled as it were woode, iwis!
> But if [unless] ye help, I shall dispaire!   (481–4)

The descent from confidence and dignity to panic is mirrored in the loss of stylistic decorum when he turns to his colleagues with a plea for help which should appropriately be addressed to Christ. The ascription of madness to the Host (*as it were woode*) is now almost immediately redirected towards Jonathas as he seizes the Host to cast it into the boiling cauldron and it sticks to his hand: 'Here he renneth wood, with the ost in his hand' (503 + SD). Events build to their comic climax in the Jews' frantic pursuit of Jonathas round the stage, the nailing of the Sacrament to the pillar, and tug-of-war in which Jonathas's hand comes away from his arm and hangs fixed to the Host (515 + SD) – an 'amputation' found also in the York play of *Fergus* whose producing guild complained of the laughter it roused (see p. 205).[1] Malchus provides some hilariously inadequate observations, saying in effect: 'Oh dear! Now he's only got one hand! What a pity!' (516–19) and Jonathas subsides into stoical forbearance (520–4). The Jews attempt a dignified exit.

At this point the Aragon miracle is intersected by the episode of 'the

---

[1] Cf. *REED, York*, I, 47–8: 'quod materia pagine illius in sacra non continetur scriptura et magis risum et clamorem causabat quam deuocionem' ['because the matter of that pageant is not contained in Holy Scripture and was causing more laughter and din than devotion']. Kolve comments (131): 'Its literalness would make it ludicrous and attention would be focused far more on the costuming and the trick, and on Fergus' humiliation, than on the serious miracle it was supposedly enacting.' There is, of course, a considerable gulf between the apparently misplaced comedy of *Fergus* and the purposively directed comedy of the *Sacrament*.

Doctor'. His servant Colle enters to address the audience (525–72) in a manner very different from Aristorius and Jonathas at the start of the play. They admit the audience to participation in the action, but Colle sees them as a crowd to be swayed to support him in mocking his master:

> I trowe, best we make a crye:
> If any man can him aspye,
> Led him to the pillery.   (561–3)

while his master regards them as potential customers:

> Here is a grete congregacion
> And all be not [w]hole, without negacion.   (601–2)

This acknowledgement is more striking because Jonathas's final injunctions were to keep the Jews' dealings secret (523–4), yet although Jonathas lost his hand 'privately' a minute before, Colle already knows of it. He and the Doctor belong with the audience in the contemporary world. Colle has an English name, and though Master Brundiche is from Braban (533), he lives close by near Babwell Mill (621), far from the forest of Aragon. The doctor is comically undercut by Colle's picture of him as a drunkard, a debtor, a lecher and a quack and he thus appears as a travelling con-man, outside the historical action. Yet he is within the play; he and Colle take their skills to the Jews, offer to heal Jonathas's hand, and are driven away with blows.

This intrusive anachronistic action represents a major structural division. It continues the comic line away from the Jews and the Sacrament, trivializing the comedy while presenting new butts for our entertainment. In driving them away, the Jews perform an action acceptable to the audience, but also expel from the play a particular kind of comedy. The historical action resumes with the episodes of the cauldron and oven, leading to a ceremonial formality which replaces the earlier grotesque mythological parodies. Christ argues that, with the soul washed in contrition, Jonathas's hand can be healed in the cauldron which had seemed to run with blood. Healing becomes a sign of salvation (775–7). Jesus also establishes a new decorum of style, formally invocatory, looking towards biblical and liturgical language and authority and employing imagery which Jonathas takes up, abandoning his earlier literal outlook:

> O thow my Lord God and Saviowr, osanna,
> Thow king of Jewes and of Jerusalem!
> O thow mighty, strong Lion of Juda,
> Blissyd be the time that thou were in Bedlem!   (778–81)

It is now that the focus of the action shifts to bishop and church, and the audience is again directly addressed and involved, but this time in an appropriate religious celebration.

The 'doctor' episode is however highly significant. In moving between an audience witnessing the play of a miracle and a congregation involved in a contemporary act of devotion to the Host, the dramatist risks a confusion of the kind that concerned the *Tretise* author. Is it possible to distinguish the audience's amazement at a miracle, a sign of spiritual import, from their amazement at the ingenuity of stage-effects – the bleeding Host, the detachable hand, the cauldron of blood, the transformation of Host into image, the disintegrating oven? The sense of dramatic spectacle may well outweigh the sense of religious wonder, and a suspension of disbelief when in the grip of a well-structured and carefully graduated play may not lead to positive spiritual faith. Above all, the analogy of audience and congregation may reduce rather than enhance, leaving the priest as actor and the Mass as dramatic illusion. Confronted with this problem, the dramatist offers a further perspective – that the audience is also a crowd whose attention can be seized by any calculating opportunist for fraud and self-profit. If the play is like ritual, so also is it like deceit, and the village-audience is thus compelled to locate the dramatic illusion more accurately between the contemporary allusion of the doctor-episode and the formality of the concluding ritual.

Thus the dramatist evokes three dramatic modes – the liturgical, the mimetic, and the folk-mode. It is not that the Doctor and his boy are folk-figures as such, but that in the modern mummers' play there are figures of comic healers who effect resurrections. A comparison here with such figures not only indicates a compatibility of tone and mode; it also reveals the elements deriving from nature-myth which are excluded, notably the healing and the resurrection which are here thematically abandoned to focus attention upon the central mythology and rituals of the Christian Church.

Croxton's play is generally agreed to represent a response to a challenge, a growing scepticism, seen in Lollard accounts of the doctrine of transubstantiation. Arguably, we can see it as a Christian equivalent to the situation which produced folk-drama, namely a response to changing social and cultural circumstances which leads to the need to explain rituals to 'non-believers'. Yet, compared with *Everyman*, the Croxton play is much more one of affirmation than explanation. It engages the audience's emotions as a means of leading them through dramatic involvement to worshipful reverence, and at the same time incorporates a range of dramatic modes into a single coherent dramatic structure.

5 Religious drama and civic ceremonial

David Mills

(i) Mythology and the urban community

The drama of religious ceremonial in a town may be considered as the product of two impulses. On the one hand, the towns of the Middle Ages, in so far as they were felt to be distinct from the villages, required a mythology to explain the origins and purpose of their communities. On the other hand the Church, from the thirteenth century onwards, embarked on a definition of its mythology and rituals which placed the doctrine of transubstantiation and its administration by a sacrificial priesthood at its centre, and simultaneously initiated a wide-ranging programme of clerical and lay education to enable the mythology and rituals to be better understood. This chapter will examine ways in which these two impulses contribute to the creation of new dramatic forms and the resulting relationship between those artistically autonomous forms and the ceremonial and celebratory functions which they were alleged to serve.

Although there had been towns and an urban economy in Anglo-Saxon England, most English medieval towns originated under the Normans and their successors.[1] The twelfth and thirteenth centuries saw a significant

[1] For a convenient account of the subject see Colin Platt, *The English Medieval Town* (London, 1979 reprint), from which a number of details here derive.

increase in England in the creation of new boroughs, both through the extension of market rights to existing communities and also through the establishment of boroughs on new sites. These new foundations were usually speculative acts by the local landowner or the king who believed, often correctly, that such communities would, in the settled conditions of the period, yield greater returns in rents and dues than could be gained from agriculture. The towns were thus a response to the by-products of stability – rising population, growing consumer-demand and expanding international trade.

But the distinction between town and village was not usually sharp. London was always exceptional; with an estimated population of *c*.50,000 by the later Middle Ages, it had faced problems of size and large-scale organization earlier than other places and could therefore provide a model for other parts of the country as they developed. Most towns, however, would have populations of 1000 or fewer; 3–4000 was unusual and York, with *c*.8000 in the later Middle Ages, was very large. Many towns remained little more than expanded villages whose inhabitants continued to engage in agriculture and whose function as a market-centre remained primary, with the result that their economies, like those of the villages, remained dependent upon agriculture and the natural cycle. The nature-mythology and its ceremonial retained their significance in the towns.

Although medieval England was urbanized to a very limited extent compared with mainland Europe, the English town could still be regarded as economically, legally and socially distinct from the village. Its legal distinction lay in its charter, which conferred a high measure of freedom and autonomy upon the town, although the exact terms of charters varied with place and time. The town and its inhabitants were free, exempt from the local tolls and dues and from the jurisdiction of the local sheriff. The town was free to regulate its own trading and social conditions by passing its own regulations and enforcing them through its own courts. Its burgesses could freely own and transmit property and land. Like a modern business corporation, the town itself could own money, property and land. And its administration was vested in a group of its citizens, initially probably people who had taken a leading part in local administration before incorporation.

Socially the urban community was more complex than the village-community, with more difficult problems of group-definition and group-relationships. Most towns were strategically located on major routes which improved and extended as trade expanded. The fairs and markets confirmed by charter were symptomatic of the town's *raison d'être*, and those who shaped the government of many towns were the merchants, the long-distance traders, who were united by their common enterprise and commercial interest against their competitors and the demands of the local lord. Joining together in trading organizations, the merchants constituted a prosperous and influential pressure-group at the head of urban society:

> In the guilds people cultivated common interests, even when they threatened to come into conflict with the sphere of economic and political power of the episcopal authorities. Thus the guild of respected merchants became of itself an organ in which the whole urban population had an interest.[1]

But in addition to its trading function, the medieval town was also a centre of production, for its strategic location meant that raw materials could be readily brought together and assembled, while the local fairs and the long-distance connections of the merchants provided convenient sales outlets. Growing towns attracted artisans who set up workshops and who shared the merchants' interest in winning independence from a local overlord.

The guild system typifies this society. A guild was, simply, a group of people united by a common interest. In the towns a major interest was commercial self-protection and the guilds of merchants tend to be among the earliest associations, with manufacturing or craft guilds, each representing an individual skill, emerging later. The guilds were monopolistic organizations seeking to regulate the number and conduct of people engaging in trade or manufacture in the town. Specifically, they sought to protect their members from such evils as 'unfair' outside competition, malpractices by suppliers of raw materials, poor workmanship and the enticement of employees by fellow craftsmen. The emergent craft guilds often gained official recognition by the governing bodies of the town as a useful tier of administration by which the town authorities could regulate trade and standards; many eventually obtained a legally secured stake in town government:

> It was the power to vet admissions to the freedom of the city, granted to the London crafts by the royal charter of 1319, that confirmed these emergent associations in their place in the civic constitution. The crafts, in fourteenth-century London, were to come to play a dominant role in city politics, and though it remains true that it was only the greater

[1] Fritz Rörig, *The Medieval Town*, trans. Don Bryant (London, 1967), 20.

misteries – the fishmongers, the skinners, the corders and others, prospering in the Hanseatic trade – who penetrated the aldermanic class, the organisation of craft associations generally spread rapidly downwards through the trades, bringing the possibility of effective collective action for the first time to many who had no knowledge of it before.[1]

The picture of a large medieval urban society thus becomes one of uneasy interactions between economically based groups whose influence varied with their economic power and changing fortunes. York presents a useful example of a society sustaining a diversity of urban drama.[2] It had three 'merchant' guilds in the sixteenth century – the Mercers, the Drapers and Tailors, and the Haberdashers, Feltmakers and Cappers – all prosperous, influential and relatively stable. Below these was a shifting mass of craft-companies in textiles, leather, victualling, building and furnishing, and some specialist crafts such as metal-working – which, though large in total membership, were individually small, more vulnerable to changes in local economic conditions and trading practices, and less influential in town government. The decline of the Weavers' Guild from being the most influential of the craft guilds in the later Middle Ages to having only ten impoverished members in the mid-sixteenth century – with the migration of the textile industry to the West Midlands – typifies their vulnerability. As trade techniques changed, so guild rivalries intensified and guild regulations became more restrictive:

> The carpenters, who built almost all private houses, and the plasterers and tilers, who covered and roofed them, were large and important gilds throughout the [sixteenth] century. The carpenters were involved in some ineffective unions with the joiners and others, which led to much squabbling, and they were clearly trying to gain a privileged position over all the woodworking crafts. They were perhaps spurred on as timber ceased to be the only available building material, for the use of brick was increasing, and it is symptomatic that by 1592 the brickmakers were trying to break away from the tilers' gild.[3]

Hence, unlike the village, the larger towns suggest an uneasy co-existence of different specialist groups striving for economic independence, stability

[1] Platt, 137.
[2] Details from D. M. Palliser, 'The trade gilds of Tudor York', in P. Clark and P. Slack (eds), *Crisis and Order in English Towns 1500–1700* (London, 1972), 86–117.
[3] Palliser, 94.

and influence and, in their vulnerability, acutely conscious of restrictions imposed by superiors, kindred trades and changing technology. The underlying tensions of such a society are exemplified from York's 1419 Corpus Christi procession, when members of the Carpenters' and Cobblers' guilds set upon members of the Skinners' guild with clubs and Carlisle axes.[1]

Such a disparate society required a mythology which would confer upon it a sense of origin, order and purpose, and also a ceremonial to give expression to the mythology. To the Christian mythology the town brought the tradition of the secular city state, and for its expression it adopted the genre of civic procession. Hence the procession included not only religious leaders, but also the mayor and aldermen of the town and the craft-masters of the companies in livery who processed in a pre-arranged order. The procession was thus multi-functional. It affirmed corporate entity; it manifested the complexity and ideal stability of urban society; it displayed the wealth on which the town's existence and the influence of each company depended. When Richard II returned to London in 1392, thereby tacitly acknowledging his dependence upon the wealth of the London merchants, the civic ceremonial was a political statement.

> Arrange a procession of the clergy of every church and let each order carry its crosses before it. Let every Craft ensure that it rides out across the river in its own ceremonial livery more grandly than usual. Let the honour of the City be shown in your bearing.... The Mayor is at the head accompanied by twenty-four Aldermen whom the city elects as its governors: for this City is ruled by them as Rome was ruled by its Senate, while they are themselves responsible to the Mayor, elected by the citizens.... First, then, rides the Mayor, bearing the keys and the sword of the City, followed by the City Fathers in whose wake come the gaily caparisoned representatives of the Crafts. Each Guild manifestly keeps its own ranks. Here go the silversmiths; there the fishmongers; with them the mercers and vintners.[2]

The clergy represent both an order within the civic hierarchy and also the Christian mythology which that hierarchy serves. But the civic community has its own secular traditions, looking back to the model of Rome; the procession thus displays a hierarchy of elective and responsible power. Civic autonomy is given classical sanction, hence historical depth and the

[1] *REED, York*, I, 32.
[2] Wickham, I, 66–7.

corresponding affirmation of continuity. Within the procession lavish display ('more grandly', 'gaily caparisoned') and self-conscious order ('each Guild manifestly keeps its own ranks') affirm the corporate entity to which all the processors subscribe ('the honour of the City'). If more grand 'than usual', the procession is otherwise typical in general order and organization. It was repeatable, and each repetition proclaimed the continuity of the ideals and wealth of the independent town and its ordered society.

The recurring features of civic ceremonial could be given specific reference. In 1392, as the King and Queen returned with the civic procession through the streets, they encountered a number of scenes. At the Great Conduit at Cheapside a youth dressed as an angel and a girl with a crown were lowered from a specially constructed tower, 'without the aid of any visible steps or ladder'; they offered the King a cup of wine and a crown and made a speech. The initial tableau was a sort of riddle, for 'the King and Queen draw near and spend much time speculating what this high tower or these youths might signify';[1] the ensuing action and speech serve to resolve the riddle. A new form has been created to explain the ceremonial. The same riddling appropriateness without textual explanation is evident in the displays which companies might carry with them in civic procession. At Edward I's entry to London in 1298, among the many 'shews' displayed by the citizens, the Fishmongers bore gold sturgeon and silver salmon, escorted by armed knights 'made like luces of the sea', followed by 'one representing Saint Magnes, because it was upon S. Magnes day'.[2] The honour of the company is sustained by the lavishness of its display, but it is an appropriate display, wittily linking the craft, through its fish-emblems – the royal sturgeon and salmon – with the King, both having their escort of knights, all magnificently displayed; and also linking craft and King with the religious occasion of St Magnes' Day. Hence the act of group aggrandizement functions within the image of an ordered civic community, and display becomes itself a mark of social assertion and competition.

The link of Church and town in ceremonials reflected a link at guild level also. Guild regulations generally insisted upon the moral integrity of the members and their aims included acts of practical charity such as caring for the sick, burying the dead and providing chantry masses. A guild might well be connected with a local church, have a chapel for its use, employ a mass-priest and participate in religious rituals on important occasions in

[1] Wickham, I, 69–70.
[2] Wickham, I, 53–4.

the guild calendar. Moreover, the Church had its own guilds, religious confraternities united to honour the Trinity, the Holy Spirit, the Blessed Virgin, the various saints, the Creed or the Blessed Sacrament, etc. Membership of such guilds was nominally open to all subscribers, unlike the craft guilds where the membership was occupationally restricted, and they therefore provided a second kind of grouping within urban society.

The situation in Coventry has been examined by Charles Phythian-Adams and serves as an example of the function of religious guilds in a city which produced a famous play-cycle.[1] There, those members of upper-status crafts who were groomed for roles of administrative importance would join the religious guild of Corpus Christi, four years after their oath-taking for their craft guilds, and in mid-career would transfer to the guild of Holy Trinity. The meeting in mid-January to elect mayor and junior officers was attended by the ex-mayors, preceded by the master of the Trinity guild, and a number of civic junior officers, headed by the master of the Corpus Christi guild. The Church presented opportunities for prominent citizens to join organizations of religious aims as well as their occupational guilds, and thereby facilitated social interactions which cut across occupational interests and served to establish social and administrative continuity in the ruling hierarchy. Meanwhile, the town acknowledged the Church as the guardian of the mythology which validated its existence and accepted the continuing centrality of established religious institutions in the new social structure. For example, civic oath-taking and elections were associated with acts of worship; the mayor and his retinue were required to attend church daily up to the Reformation.

Hence, until the Reformation public civic and religious ceremonial are interconnected. They also focus on the first six months of the year. The Church then commemorates the major events in the life of Christ – Christmas, Epiphany, Candlemas, Lent, Palm Sunday, Maundy Thursday, Good Friday, Easter Day, Ascension Day and Whit Sunday. In the same period public civic ceremonies occur. Coventry burlesqued retiring mayors at Christmas and elected their successors and officers in mid-January, inaugurating them at Candlemas; the parishes celebrated Lent and Easter; and the religious guilds processed on St George's Day, Whit Sunday and Ascension. As the public liturgical year culminated in Corpus Christi day, so the civic ceremonial reached its climax with processions on Corpus Christi, Fair Friday, Midsummer Eve and St Peter's Eve. Thus, in

---

[1] Charles Phythian-Adams, 'Ceremony and the citizen: the communal year at Coventry, 1450–1550', in Clark and Slack (eds), *Crisis and Order*, 57–85.

conjunction with surviving folk festivals, the liturgical feasts and civic ceremonials came together in a cycle of celebration which formalized in display the relationships between different sections of urban society. The genre of procession becomes multi-functional.

The celebration of Candlemas provides a useful illustration of the connections and distinctions between religious mythology, procession and drama. The commemoration of the purification of the Virgin Mary and the presentation of the infant Christ in the temple (Luke 2: 22–39) on 2 February takes its name from the ceremonial of the day:

> The blessing of candles is now the distinctive rite on this day in the West. Beeswax candles, which are blessed, distributed, and lit whilst the Nunc Dimittis is sung, are carried in a procession commemorating the entrance of Christ, the 'True Light' (cf. Jn 1:9), into the temple.[1]

The rite is a symbolic interpretation of the historical event and an act of communal celebration in which each member of the congregation, by processing, affirms faith in the underlying myth and, re-enacting the event, becomes the bearer of divine truth into the darkness of ignorance. The provision of candles for this celebration seems to have been the main function of medieval religious guilds of Candlemas or St Mary.

In Beverley, where the feast was celebrated by the guild of St Mary (founded 25 January 1355), ceremonial was strikingly elaborated:

> Every year, on the feast of the Purification of the blessed Mary, all the bretheren and sisteren shall meet together in a fit and appointed place away from the church; and there, one of the gild shall be clad in comely fashion as a queen, like to the glorious Virgin Mary, having what may seem a son in her arms; and two other shall be clad like to Joseph and Simeon; and two shall go as angels, carrying a candle-bearer, on which shall be twenty-four thick wax lights. With these and other great lights borne before them, and with much music and gladness, the pageant Virgin with her son, and Joseph and Simeon, shall go in procession to the church. And all the sisteren of the gild shall follow the Virgin; and afterwards all the bretheren; and each of them shall carry a wax light weighing half a pound. And they shall go two and two, slowly pacing to the church; and when they have got there, the pageant Virgin shall offer her son to Simeon at the high altar; and all the sisteren and bretheren shall offer their wax lights, together with a penny each. All

---

[1] 'Candlemas', in *The Oxford Dictionary of the Christian Church* (Oxford, 1957), 226.

this having been solemnly done, they shall go home again with gladness.[1]

The activities focused upon the church, the rite and the feast, but they began and ended outside, in the contemporary world in which the members assembled and to which they finally returned with renewed joy. Their celebration not only honoured the feast; it demonstrated the participants' faith to the world, the observers, and gave them renewed joy, the better to sustain their mundane existence. The celebration had two elements – the liturgical procession of lights and the historical-mimetic representation of the purification. The latter glossed the former, explaining the occasion, but also demanded visual identification of the historical figures impersonated, whose disguise set them apart from the other members in the procession. Inside the church the link was made clearer by the mimed enactment; but, simultaneously, the contemporary liturgical celebration went on, with candles borne in procession, carried round the church and deposited at the altar with a donation. Each guild-member has, as it were, brought his share of Christian truth to the church as Mary brought her Son, and each member sustains the mythology (by rite) and (by donation) its institution, the Church, within which that mythology is transmitted and celebrated. Religious ceremonial and mimetic action interweave in a procession that links the streets of the town with the altar of the church and the historical Holy Family with the people of fourteenth-century Beverley.

Beside this ceremonial may be set part of a play found in Bodley MS Digby 133 and headed 'Candlemes Day and the Kyllynge of þe Children of Israelle. MDxij. Anno Domini 1512. the vij booke.'[2] The action of 'Candlemes day' is the second part of the play (389–566). At its centre is the figure of Simeon, teacher of God's laws to the people (393–6), for whose obedience he prays to God (389–92). He institutes the historical action by affirming his knowledge of Christ's miraculous birth and asking to see the Child before he dies. The ensuing stage directions suggest an action similar to that at Beverley:

> *Here shalle Oure Lady come forth, holdyng Jhesu in hir armys, and sey this language foluyng to Joseph* (412 + SD)
> *Here Maria and Joseph go toward the temple with Jhesu and too dowes, and Oure Lady seith vnto Symeon* (428 + SD)
> *Her shalle Symeon receyve of Maria Jhesu and too dowis [doves], and*

[1] L. Toulmin Smith, *English Gilds* (London, 1870; EETS 40), 149–50.
[2] Baker, *Digby Plays*, 96–115.

holde Jhesu in his armys, expownyng 'Nunc dimittis', et cetera, seyng thus. (436 + SD)

But the accompanying text up to 436 not only identifies characters and actions, but interprets the action in terms of obedience to the law ('the lawe commaundith so', 415; 'the lawe to obeye', 432), and obedience directed by divine grace ('toward this temple grace list me conveye', 433). Beverley's mimetic action now finds logical motivation both in Mary's obedience and also in divine grace – the former developing Simeon's emphasis upon the law, and the latter released by Simeon's prayer. The Nunc Dimittis follows logically as the expression of Simeon's joy, intensifying the sense of universal deliverance which looks to the Harrowing of Hell:

Of the derk dungeon · let the gates brest [burst]
Before the face of thyn people alle!   (449–50)

and extending the image of light with which the Nunc Dimittis ends; compare:

Lumen ad revelationem gentium, et gloriam plebis tuæ Isræl.

Thu art the light and the hevynly skye!
To the relevyng of folk most cruelle,
Thu hast brought gladnesse to oure oratorye,
And enlumyned thy people of Israelle.   (457–60)

At this point a second, ceremonial action begins. Anna summons a group of virgins with tapers of wax to worship Christ. The reference 'come forth' (462) suggests an appeal to a body of people in the audience or congregation, and 464 + SD: '*Her virgynes, as many as a man wylle, shalle holde tapers in ther handes*' seems to suggest that the circumstances are variable. With the liturgical procession assembled, the three principal figures abandon their historical roles to join it:

SYMEON.   Now, Mary, I shalle telle you how I am purposed.
  To worshippe þis Lord I wil go procession,
  For I se Anna with virgynes disposed,
  Mekly as nowe to youre sonys laudacion.
MARIA.   Blissed Symeon, with hertly affeccion,
  As ye han seyd, I concent therto.
JOSEPH.   In worshippe of oure child with gret devossion,
  Abought þe tempille in ordire let vs go.   (469–76)

Simeon assumes his representative role as teacher, directing the participants to sing Nunc Dimittis and explaining the symbolism of the taper – wax as humanity, wick as soul, light as godhead. As he kneels he recreates Simeon's historical homage to the Christ-child as Man's contemporary homage to the invisible and living God.

The two actions finally separate. Mary and Joseph leave with dignified courtesies, Mary assured by Simeon of her exemplary obedience: 'The lawes, Mary, ful welle ye han obbeyed' (519). Then Simeon, with pre-vision, links the particular action with the total Christian mythology by meditating upon the Crucifixion and Mary's sorrow. In completing the mythological celebration, Simeon also moves out of historical time and can appropriately acknowledge the participants in the ceremonial, instructing Anna to lead them away in procession and 'teche hem to plese God, of most honoure' (544).

The play looks directly to liturgical ceremonial and combines it with mimesis in a way reminiscent of the Beverley procession. But although the play utilizes and explains religious ceremonial, its allusiveness and explanations serve also to underline its achievement as a dramatic structure. In writing it, the playwright was conscious of four groups – the minstrels, the actors in the principal parts, the virgins and the audience:

> Besechyng you to geve *vs* [the players] peseable audiens!
> And *ye menstrallis*, doth youre diligens!
> And *ye virgynes*, shewe summe sport and plesure,
> *These people* to solas, and to do God reuerens!
> As ye be appoynted, doth your besy cure!   (52–6)

He distinguishes between the *solas* which observing the play will bring to the audience, and devotional function which its performance serves. The structural patterns of the action are heavily underlined, the transition from the historical action of the purification to the liturgical ceremonial of the procession being accompanied by the abandonment of historical role by the principal actors and the accompanying introduction of the second group, the virgins, who stand in closer relationship to the audience. Simeon is pivotal to this structure, being initially a historical figure but, in the processional action, the representative of the priesthood who, having initially composed the Nunc Dimittis, now transmits it to succeeding generations through the Church. This heavily marked structure with its accompanying stylistic formality is the dramatic counterpart to the procession and liturgical chant. The audience is distanced from this formal drama as from religious ceremonial, but it is a distance created by the language as well as the ceremonial and the reverential distance of the observer of sacred ritual has a counterpart in the aesthetic distance from which the audience observes and appraises the dramatic artefact.

The structure does not involve characterization. The figures are agents of the plot and speak in a single mode. But the action is thematically unified as liturgical celebration need not be. Faithful obedience releases God's joy-giving grace. Simeon, obedient to God's law, receives the sight of Christ while Mary, obedient to the Church's law, is the vehicle of God's grace to him. In the ceremonial commemoration the historical action is also exemplary, enjoining upon the people obedience to the teachers of the Church who, from their faithful observance of ceremonial, will themselves receive and transmit grace. The causative sequence which is explicit in the historical action is continued in the ceremonial commemoration. The structure serves thematic ends.

The 'Candelmes' play is already a self-contained and thematically coherent work. In fact, it was not performed on Candlemas day but in honour of St Anne's day, 26 July, and hence did not rely on the context of the specific feast for its meaning. Moreover, it was one of an annual sequence of plays presented by a particular company which apparently had no explicit connexion with St Anne but presented scenes from the life of Christ; the previous year they had performed the visits of shepherds and Magi (25–8); this year it was the innocents and purification (29–48); next year it would be Christ before the doctors (561–2). While it incorporates and explains the ceremonials of the Church, it also alludes to other events in the life of Christ, looking outwards to the extra-dramatic context of the liturgy and also onwards to the wider dramatic cycle of which it is a part.

The effect of the play is further determined by its relationship to the preceding action, 'The Killing of the Children', in lines 57–388 + SD, an action very different in tone and dramatic mode. It centres upon two figures, King Herod and his messenger Watkin. Herod trusts in Fortune and the pagan gods (cf. 60, 65, 67) and has an illusion of self-sufficiency which is destroyed when he seeks to control an action directed by God. Since the Magi have not returned, he orders the slaughter of all babies in Bethlehem. But the Holy Family flee before the soldiers arrive, the pagan idols symbolically falling as they enter Egypt. After the massacre, Herod recognizes that he has still no assurance of Christ's death and that he has destroyed his own friends. In despair he dies, commending his soul to Mahound.

Watkin, the messenger, plays an important role as a comically reductive figure who makes Herod and his knights the butt of the audience's laughter. Hearing Herod's commission to the knights and the rewards which he promises, he decides that killing children is a safe and profitable occupation and requests knighthood. In his dialogue with Herod the comic perversion of the chivalric ideal is dominant; Watkin is brave enough against babies but terrified of angry women with distaffs:

> And this I promyse you, that I shalle neuer slepe,
>   But euermore wayte to fynde the children alone,
> And if the moder come in, vnder the benche I wille crepe,
>   And lye stille ther tylle she be goon!   (185–8)

and begs the other knights to stay close to him. In the massacre, Watkin is caught by the women and beaten with distaffs until the soldiers rescue him. This incongruous reversal of the ideals of knighthood overwhelms the potentially tragic action of the massacre, which is brief and unelaborated ('*Hic occident pueros*', 314 + SD) and accompanied less by anguish than by angry cries for vengeance upon the soldiers and Herod. Watkin becomes the immediate object of the women's anger and his beating translates their demands for justice into a comic mode. But he is indignant at the insult voiced against his master (326–8) and this resentment remains when he returns with the soldiers to make their report to Herod. Watkin then supplements their account of carnage by reporting the absence of men in Bethlehem ('alle the men out of the cuntre be goon', 359) and the women's hostility towards Herod (360–4). Hearing this, Herod despairs. Paradoxically, it is the comic coward Watkin who brings Herod to his death.

In itself the 'Killing' is not about the innocents, as it might appropriately be if it had been conceived as an extension of the ceremonial of Holy Innocents Day (28 December). Instead, it is a play of *solas* in two senses – the 'consolation' of the operation of divine justice in the escape of Christ and the death of Herod; and the 'entertainment' arising from the absurd pretensions of Watkin. A causative sequence is established, whereby Watkin's pretensions arise from the cynical perversion of chivalry by Herod, while Herod's despair is motivated by Watkin's report. The structure of the play connects and to an extent equates two different kinds of comic action. Conversely, its comic mode excludes on the one hand the pathos apparently inherent in the subject, and on the other the formal allusiveness of the 'Candelmes' action.

Yet by playing the 'Killing' and 'Candelmes' as a single continuous performance, Digby forces into juxtaposition the modes of comic irony and ceremonial formality and so compels the audience to recognize and respond to their contrasting effects and implications. The liturgical allusions of 'Candelmes' can be seen as one of several elements in a dramatic structure, invested with particular effects by the associations and contrasts which that structure generates. The play has a function as an act of worship on St Anne's day, but that function does not seem to extend beyond the realization of aspects of the same Christian mythology which, through different aspects, gives rise to the feast. The occasion does not determine the play's form or content in any narrow limits, and the play would be effective on any occasion. As drama it is pleasingly competent, but unsophisticated. Its significance in the present discussion lies in the wider aspects of medieval ceremonial drama which it raises.

(ii) Processional drama and cycle form

The specific circumstances in which the Digby play was produced are unknown, but a religious feast could as readily be the occasion of civic ceremonial as it could of the observances of a religious guild, if the two could indeed be separated. Aberdeen, for example, celebrated Candlemas with an annual guild-procession of nine companies, each providing historical personages; in 1442, for example:

> þe littistarez [dyers] sal fynd þe emprioure and twa doctourez
> and alsmony honeste squiarez as þai may.
> þe smythez and hammirmen sal fynd þe three kingis of
> Culane and alsmony honeste squiarez as þai may.
> þe talȝourez sal fynd oure lady Sancte bride Sancte helene
> Ioseph & alsmony squiarez as þai may.[1]

The procession was 'in þe offerand of oure lady' and may have been an extended civic version of the 'Beverley' ceremonial; mimetic action may be implied by a register entry for 1505–6: 'þai sale in ordire to þe Offering *in þe play* pass tua & ij togidder socialie'.[2] But the occasion now became one for civic display. Lincoln's day of civic display was St Anne's day, when the guilds processed annually from the chapel of St Thomas on the bridge

[1] Mill, *Medieval Plays in Scotland*, 116.
[2] ibid., 120 – italics added.

to the cathedral on the hill to make an offering, taking with them elaborate sets mounted on carts. Although the event was organized by the religious guild of St Anne, founded in 1344, the guild was merely the organizing body acting on behalf of the town. All citizens had to contribute to the guild and the companies had to submit to its organization, as the 1519 entries indicate:

> Agreid that euery man and woman within this citie beyng able schall be broder and syster in scaynt anne gyld and to pay yerly iiijd man and wyf at the lest.... Also that euery occupacion schall bryng furth ther pageantes that be longyng to scaynt anne gyld sufficiently.[1]

As befitted the occasion, the tableaux were evidently religious in character – we know of a Noah's ship and a Bethlehem pageant, and 'The Coronation of the Virgin' was displayed in the cathedral. But the hierarchy and wealth of the city were simultaneously on display in the service of the Christian mythology. It is against a background of ceremonial of this kind that the Digby play should perhaps be assessed.

But the most widespread occasion for civic ceremonial was the feast of Corpus Christi, standing at the culminating period of the public civic year and at the end of the liturgical year. Unlike the other feasts, Corpus Christi did not commemorate a historical event in the life of Christ but the central sacrament of the Church whose underlying theology was formulated by the Fourth Lateran Council of 1215 (see above, pp. 117–21). But during the fourteenth century, when English towns were developing and expressing their social ideal in public ceremonial, Corpus Christi became a major focal point, and often the climax, for civic ceremonial.

The feast came at the end of the ritualistic half of the year, on the Thursday after Trinity Sunday (23 May to 24 June, depending upon the date of Easter). Its detachment from the commemoration of the Sacrament's historical institution, Maundy Thursday, was deliberate, for the intention had been to honour the Sacrament with a lavish and joyful ceremonial which the liturgically crowded and emotionally sombre period before Easter Day would not permit. Hence its position at the end of the public liturgical year was both distinctive and climactic, a celebration of God's grace to Man through the Church which perpetuated His Sacraments. Inevitably, given the interaction of liturgical and civic years, the Feast provided the occasion for civic display; its main feature was a communal procession in which the consecrated Host was borne round the town via the major churches and

[1] Nelson, *The Medieval English Stage*, 105.

holy places. Whether organized by the civic authorities or a religious guild of Corpus Christi, this procession was a traditional display of civic hierarchy in which the crafts, carrying torches and wearing their liveries, went in fixed order, led by Christ Himself in His real presence in the consecrated Host. Displaying their wealth and their ideal of social order, the community honoured indivisibly the God who led it, the Sacrament in which He was realized, and the institution of the Church, whose ritual effected His presence. The town affirmed the myth on which its existence rested.

It often seems convenient to regard the Corpus Christi Feast in England as a catalyst for the coalescence of three compatible celebratory forms – procession; display of appropriate symbols, emblems, tableaux or mimes; production of religious plays. Such seems often to have been the case, with guilds processing in order, each escorting its wagon with stage-set and performing a play-sequence to which each guild contributed an episode at an appointed place or places. Beverley's Corpus Christi guild, founded in 1352, organized a procession for the Feast in which the craft guilds in order marched between the religious guilds who headed and concluded the procession. By 1377 Beverley also had a *pagine ludi Corporis Christi*, and an ordinance of 1390 requires every craft guild to appear with *suos ludos et pagentes* at Corpus Christi. A 1411 order makes it clear that the wagons were stages for a play ('honestam et honorabilem pagendam fabricari faciant, et honestum ludum ludi in eadem').[1]

But the three celebratory forms seem always to have been in uneasy tension and could remain separate. At Lincoln the civic display of St Anne's day remained distinct from the play on Corpus Christi until the two combined as a St Anne's day celebration in 1554. At York by 1468, after Friar Melton's advice that the *ludus* interfered with the procession and should be separated from it, the procession had been moved to the day after the Feast.[2] In Chester the civic display was separated from the Corpus Christi procession and moved to Whitsun some time after 1471–2;[3] but the pre-Reformation banns to the cycle indicate the continuing association of Feast, procession and drama:

Also maister Maire of this Citie
withall his bretheryn accordingly

[1] ibid., 91–3.
[2] *REED, York*, I, 42–4, shows the cycle in 1426 on the vigil of the Feast.
[3] See Lawrence M. Clopper, 'The history and development of the Chester cycle', *MP*, 75 (1978), 219–46.

> A Solemnpne procession ordent hath he
> to be done to the best
> Appon the day of corpus christi
> The blessed sacrament caried shalbe
> And A play sett forth by the clergye
> In honour of the fest
> Many torches there may you see
> Marchaunty and craftys of this Citie
> By order passing in theire degree
> A goodly sight that day.[1]

Chester not only separated its civic drama from the communal procession for the Feast; it also transferred features of its cycle to the major secular civic display, the Midsummer Show, where they co-existed with other sights and entertainments:

> Many guilds rode with characters from the cycle plays; thus, the Painters rode with their angels on stilts, the Smiths with Simeon, the Shoemakers with Mary Magdalene and occasionally Judas, the Innkeepers with the alewife and her devils.[2]

Finally, Chester transferred its cycle to Midsummer in 1575 and later defended the play as a venerable civic custom, not a religious celebration.

The possibility of divorcing drama from its specific festal occasion exists because at its most extensive civic drama is a comprehensive and self-contained account of the principal elements of Christian mythology. Its meaning does not depend upon the context of the Feast, nor are specific allusions made to a Feast by the text. But Corpus Christi nevertheless provided the obvious occasion for such productions, since the significance of the Sacrament could most clearly be explained by the representation of the total historical Christian myth, while the civic procession provided the resources for such representations and the season afforded an extended period of daylight for the production. Being mythological rather than commemorative, the Feast did not specify a particular historical event. But the centrality of its Sacrament seemed to require at least some account of the historical act of Christ's Passion and the ritual act of the establishment of the Sacrament at the Last Supper. For example, in the extant cycles the

---

[1] *REED, Chester*, 38–9.
[2] *REED, Chester*, liii.

discourses at the supper provide the opportunity for establishing the significance of the Sacrament, while in Chester and Wakefield the risen Christ links the historical fact of resurrection with the continuing act of sacrifice in the Mass. Both aspects, however, require wider contexts. The historical Passion is set in the wider context of the history of Man from the Fall to Doomsday, while the ritual act of sacrifice is seen as the culmination of God's plan for the redemption of all men. Whatever the final occasion, the starting point for this drama therefore lies in the myths, theology and rituals of the Christian Church.

Formally, however, the character of the drama seems to have been defined by its social function. Beginning from the fact that its content is subdivided and individual episodes are performed by different guilds, each playwright's problem was to define the interconnections between the episodes, thereby creating an over-all structure which could even imply connections to episodes as yet undramatized. What Benson says of cycle-form in romance is also valid for cycle-form in drama:

> These cyclic romances...are not distinct and independent tales...each is part of a larger and coherent 'history' that comprehends all stories of Arthur and his knights.... Yet a medieval reader did not have to read all the parts of a cycle to know that a cycle existed.... The authors of the prose romances lost no opportunity to establish the 'cyclic' character of their works and to specify the exact relation between their individual romances and the whole works of which they were parts.[1]

Read 'drama' for 'romance' and 'God and His servants' for 'Arthur and his knights' and the quotation effectively isolates the central characteristics of cycle-form in the drama. And it is satisfyingly logical that the feast which celebrated the central mythology of the Church, the climax of the ritualistic year, and which was also an occasion for great civic display, the climax of the ceremonial year, should simultaneously be the time for the production of the most extensive structure of dramatic episodes, the most complex form of civic drama. On such an occasion, a sophisticated literary structure was invested with multiple extra-literary significance. But nevertheless, as a literary structure, the play-cycle, like other forms, was always potentially detachable from a specific feast and would remain dramatically effective and mythologically edifying.

Although there is considerable diversity within the small corpus of extant

[1] L. D. Benson, *Malory's Morte Darthur* (Cambridge, Mass., 1976), 5, 8.

civic cycles,[1] the various playwrights start from the same structural problem. Like romance-writers they explore the effect of a 'marvel' in a norm of human experience and expectation.[2] Their 'marvel' is the direct intervention of God in human affairs, and the effect of this intervention is explored in a mimesis of human experience which links the 'historical' action of the 'marvel' with the contemporary world of the audience. In cycle-forms, the playwrights have a further task, to establish the place of the 'marvel' and its consequences in a wider pattern of human history through which God is progressively revealing Himself to Man and working out His purpose in creation. In the resulting cyclic structure the recurring norm of human expectation and experience throughout time is intersected by a progressively revelatory series of divine 'marvels', producing a structure which is both cumulatively repetitive and also thematically informed and progressive. The structure imposes a dual perspective – a 'synchronic' response to the individual marvel and its effect, and a 'diachronic' response to the wider cyclic perspective; and in so far as the audience retains this dual awareness, the form has a potential for irony, setting the limited perspectives of particular characters against the wider context known to the audience.

The play-cycle is a structure of structures, a form of functional flexibility. Although its mythological subject inevitably meant that different cycles presented the same material, the power of the myth to generate new interpretations and the requirements of the form that the episodes should be structurally coherent meant that cycles had different thematic centres. As towns followed each other's ceremonial forms, so they borrowed each other's play-episodes, but, in so doing, gave them new significance in a different cyclic structure. Thus the play of 'Christ Before the Doctors' is essentially the same text in Chester, Coventry, Wakefield and York; Wakefield and York also share substantial parts of plays on 'Pharaoh', the 'Harrowing of Hell', 'Resurrection' and 'Doomsday'; Chester's 'Sacrifice of Isaac' is substantially the same as the Brome text. Textual borrowing of this kind indicates that those responsible for the texts of the cycles were aware of what happened in other centres and had access to their texts. But this re-adaptation of material has its counterpart in the processes of revision which are well attested in the history of most cycles. One may instance the two play lists of the York cycle by the town clerk Roger Burton, one of

---

[1] See Appendix, pp. 292–301, for a complete list of extant civic cycles and cycle fragments.
[2] On *merveille* in romance, see Douglas Kelly, '*Matière* and *genera dicendi* in Medieval Romance', *Yale French Studies* (1974), 147–59.

fifty-one plays in 1415 and another of fifty-seven at an unspecified date, which show a somewhat different cycle from the extant form;[1] or the amalgamation of four plays at York in 1432 to produce 'The Condemnation of Christ', still evidently different from the play in the extant text.[2] The factors behind such changes were many: changes in the fortunes of the companies; problems in administration; concern at the doctrinal implications of the material; or perhaps simply a desire for a more effective dramatic celebration. Cyclic form had the flexibility to sustain such changes.

But this functional flexibility also means that cycles had no fixed and definitive form. A Chester document states:

> it is at the libertie and pleasure of the mair with the counsell of his bretheryn to Alter or Assigne any of the occupacons Aboue writen to any play or pageant as they shall think necessary or conuenyent.[3]

And when the town-crier rode through Chester on St George's day with representatives of the guild in play-costumes he 'there published the tyme and the matter of the playes in breeife'.[4] The citizens were told not only of a performance, but of the cyclic form for that occasion. And the Chester text shows evidence of the alternatives from which the authorities might choose, including two versions of the Cappers' play of 'Balaam and Balak', one with prophet-sequence and the other, expressly to end a first day's performance, without.[5] The Chester Smiths' record of 1574–5, 'Spent at Tyes [a proper name] to hear 2 plays before the Aldermen to take the best xviij d',[6] suggests that possibly aesthetic considerations played a part in the choice. Wakefield's two Shepherds' plays suggest a similar area of choice. V. A. Kolve's claim that 'the Corpus Christi cycle was repeated at frequent intervals, and a citizen of Chester or York could easily have seen the plays performed ten times in his lifetime'[7] implies a degree of continuity which the texts and records do not support.

If cycle-form was responsive to demands for flexibility, it was to some extent also conditioned by those demands. The effect of witnessing a cycle

---

[1] *REED, York*, I, 16–26.
[2] *REED, York*, I, 48–50.
[3] *REED, Chester*, 33.
[4] *REED, Chester*, 239.
[5] David Mills, 'The two versions of Chester Play V: Balaam and Balak', in Beryl Rowland (ed.), *Chaucer and Middle English Studies* (London, 1973), 366–71.
[6] *REED, Chester*, 105.
[7] Kolve, 4.

in a single performance, as at York, must obviously have imposed a different notion of structure from that of witnessing it over three successive days, as at Chester, or piecemeal over a series of years, as in the Digby St Anne's day series. Such factors impose upon the playwrights different concepts of the relationships between episodes. Moreover, the structural and thematic linkages involved in playing the Fall of Man and Cain and Abel as a single episode in Chester are different from those in York, where the same material is covered in six episodes. Coventry's wide-ranging, multi-subject plays require a different concept of drama from the more narrowly focused plays of York or Wakefield. Between the guild-play and cycle-form lies an intermediate pattern of sub-groups of plays whose limits are defined by a variety of criteria. A causative narrative sequence involving recurring figures, for example, marks out the sequences 'Annunciation–Innocents' and 'Last Supper–Resurrection' as potential sub-groups which may be dramatically defined by character-consistency or recurring motifs and themes. The Old Testament plays, structurally distinct from the following 'Annunciation', have the potential to form a sub-group which may be exploited by emphasizing their figural significance. The functions of the drama determined the choice of form and also certain aspects of structure. But the problem for the playwrights was to establish a thematically and structurally coherent form, and a wide range of possibilities was open to them.

(iii) Cycle-structure and dramatic mode in Chester and Wakefield

The Shepherds' plays of Chester and Wakefield indicate how two cycle-dramatists approached these problems. The Chester play opens with a wandering shepherd:

> On wouldes have I walked wylde
> under buskes [bushes] my bowre to bylde,
> from styffe stormes my sheepe to shilde,
> my seemely wedders to save.
> From comlye Conwaye unto Clyde
> under tyldes [coverings] them to hyde,
> a better shepperd on no syde
> noe yearthlye man maye have. (7/1–8)

The lines explain the shepherd's presence. The breeding rams ('my taytfull tuppes', 11) have been released to the ewes which have then scattered and got lost in the wild storms. The shepherd has followed his flock across the Welsh hills from Conway to the River Clwyd, the sheep-raising area of east Wales. The long hard search establishes his professional diligence, a trait further revealed in the knowledge of sheep-ailments and their treatments which he displays. The explanation and outlook are local and familiar, with as yet no sense of the historical shepherds of Bethlehem (Luke 2: 8–16). Joined by two companions, they eat local produce – Blacon butter, Halton ale, Lancashire jannock – and perhaps share some of their food with the audience. This cheerfully self-satisfied gathering is overthrown literally by Trowle, their malcontented and disrespectful boy, who defeats them in wrestling and bears off the remains of the feast.

Here the 'contemporary' action yields to the historical biblical 'wonder' as a star blazes in the sky and an angel sings the 'Gloria'. The shepherds respond with fear at the star – though Trowle is both fascinated and puzzled by it – then with bewilderment at the song, yielding to admiration at its performance. Man's comic inadequacy in the face of the divine is seen in their attempts to assimilate what has happened to their own experience; they suspect the angel:

> By my fayth, hee was some spye,
> our sheepe for to steale.
> Or elles hee was a man of our crafte,
> for seemely hee was and [wounder] defte.   (394–7)

The audience is invited to appreciate the shepherds' self-conscious professionalism, their 'deftness'; and also their unconscious absurdities of conduct and response, their 'daftness' (*craft – defte*). Simultaneously, however, they must be aware that the craft of shepherding is here enacted by the craftsmen of the Painters, the performing guild, a fact that adds a further comic level to the reference. Yet, with their professional pride, the shepherds nevertheless recognize the miraculous nature of their experience, and mingle with their colloquialisms a new dignified formality of diction and conduct:

> Fellowes, will wee
> kneele downe on our knee
> after comford

to the trewe Trinitee,
for to lead us for to see
our elders lord?   (334–9)

The resulting stylistic tension continues in the debate about the meaning
of the song, towards which they all grope intuitively:

For hee sange 'bonæ voluntatis';
that is a cropp [a thing of value] that passeth all other   (426–7)

until, having understood its consolation, they parallel it in a loud popular
song:

Singe wee nowe, I rede us, shryll,
a mery songe, us to solace.   (442–3)

With the arrival at Bethlehem, the play enters its final phase. The
shepherds' initial sniggers at the sight of the aged Joseph are checked by
Mary's assurance that they come through the grace of God and by the
explanation by both Mary and Joseph of the divine endorsement of lawful
marriage which their apparently unequal match signifies. Thereafter, the
shepherds speak with dignified formality:

Great God, syttynge in thy troone,
that made all thinge of nought,
nowe wee may thanke thee eychone:
this is hee that wee have sought.   (540–3)

The shepherds make offerings to the child, debating on the appropriate
order of presentation ('Hayle, kynge, borne in a maydens bowre', 556), and
are followed by Trowle and other boys. The simple offerings provide a
humorously touching anticlimax to the dignified addresses, and the
shepherds show a consciousness of the inadequacy:

My deare, with dryrie [a token of love] unto thee I mee dresse
[turn],
my state on felloweshippe that I doe not lose;
and for to save mee from all yll sycknesse,
I offer unto thee a payre of my wyves ould hose.
For other jewells, my sonne,
have I none thee for to give
that is worthe anythinge at all,
but my good harte whyle I lyve
and my prayers tyll death doth mee call.   (588–96)

On their departure the shepherds complete the abandonment of the 'contemporary' opening mode by pledging to abandon their occupation for preaching vocations at home and overseas, or for service as an anchorite and hermit. All say farewell to their colleagues and to their audience and depart for their new vocations.

The 'marvel' of the play serves to mark a transition from the opening mode of contemporary allusion and comic disorder to the more formal mode of the presentations and new vocations. As the shepherds change function, so they change style; the self-indulgence and the disorderly contest of the feast and wrestling give way to a concern with order and decorum and vocational selflessness. While the opening acknowledges the reality of Chester, the play goes on to suggest that diligent labour is the emblem of spiritual devotion. Through its final formality, its exemplary offering and change of vocation, it proclaims the power of the Christian myth and its institution to inform and direct the lives of men. For beneath the action one can see the force of commentaries such as that of Bede (*Homilia* 45 and *In Lucæ Evangelia* 1/2), according to which the grace sent to the literal pastors figures the special grace and responsibility of the spiritual pastorate, later confirmed in Christ's image of the Good Shepherd (John 10: 14) which Chester uses in its Play 13. While showing the exemplary response of those who rightly interpret God's signs to Man, the shepherds, in their change of vocation, transform the action into a specific sign of pastoral charity and devotion. This widened interpretation admits a retrospective revaluation of the opening, whereby the professional devotion of the literal shepherd transforms him into a 'Good Shepherd' and implies an appropriateness in God's choice of these shepherds to receive the first news of Christ's birth.

Wakefield's famous *Secunda Pastorum* is dramatically more complex and thematically more ambivalent. It opens with a series of complaining soliloquies by three shepherds. The first endures physical discomfort on the moor, but is mainly concerned at the oppression of the tenant-farmer by the landlord and his men who have effectively destroyed agriculture:

> These men that ar lordfest [in the service of a lord] thay cause the ploghe tary.
> That men say is for the best we fynde it contrary;
> Thus ar husbandys [husbandmen] opprest in pointe to myscary [to the point of being destroyed],
>   On lyfe. (20–3)

The second, while also complaining of cold, comically voices the *mal marié* theme of oppression in marriage, typified in his gross caricature of his own wife:

> She is as greatt as a whall [whale],
> She has a galon of gall:
> By hym that dyed for vs all,
>   I wald I had ryn to I had lost hir.   (105–8)

The switch from serious social to comic marital complaint quickly disorientates the audience; it is not yet clear how the action can develop, what kind of drama this will be. The third shepherd speaks in ambivalent tone. He sees the world dominated by an unstable fortune, and with a widely resonant hyperbole links the hostile weather to the Flood with its terrible destruction and the promise of succeeding grace:

> Was never syn Noe floode sich floodys seyn;
> Wyndys and ranys so rude and stormes so keyn;
> Som stamerd, som stod in dowte, as I weyn [understand];
> Now god turne all to good, I say as I mene,
>   ffor ponder [for something to ponder on].   (127–31)

In the ensuing dialogue it emerges that this third shepherd is the servant of the other two. They accuse him of idleness ('thou art a ledyr hyne [worthless servant]', 147) and he accuses them of mean and tardy payment which merits his idleness:

> Bot here my trouth, master, for the fayr that ye make,
> I shall do therafter, wyrk as I take.   (163–4)

Hence a world is realized which negates moral responsibility and manifests instead the effects of conflicting self-interest and the consciousness of grievance when such interests are not satisfied. The products of this society are serious enough – landlessness, poverty, physical suffering, domestic misery; but the allusions to contemporary ills are made in speeches of tonal ambivalence – even the third shepherd's accusations seem without malice and are received in good humour. All are content – the sheep graze the cornfield!

The 'sheep-stealing episode' is a particular manifestation of amoral pragmatism and its accompanying dramatic method, typified by the values of the trickster and illusionist Mak:

> I am worthy my mete,
> ffor in a strate [straitened circumstances] can I gett

More then thay that swynke [toil] and swette
All the long day.   (310–13)

Mak proclaims his intention to avoid the curse of Adam: 'In the sweat of
thy brow shalt thou eat bread' (Genesis 3: 19) and inverts Christ's advice
to His disciples to trust divine charity, not material provision, in their
missionary journeyings, 'for the workman is worthy of his meat' (Matthew
10: 10). Mak's 'mission' to the shepherds is anti-pastoral, as he wrily
acknowledges:

Was I never a shepard, bot now wyll I lere.
If the flok be skard yit shall I nyp nere [seize tightly].   (288–9)

and in their image of Mak:

IIJUS PASTOR   Me thoght he was lapt [enfolded] in a wolfe skyn.
PRIMUS PASTOR   So are many hapt [clothed] now namely within.
    (368–9)

the shepherds recall Matthew 7: 15: 'Beware of false prophets, which come
to you in sheep's clothing, but inwardly they are ravening wolves.'

But this underlying moral condemnation of Mak is offset by a number
of considerations. First, the shepherds are not innocent victims; they know
of Mak:

TERTIUS PASTOR   Is he commen? then ylkon take hede to his thyng.
    (200)

SECUNDUS PASTOR   And thou has an yll noys
    of stelyng of shepe.   (224–5)

They know that Mak has somehow deceived them and there is comedy in
their inability to uncover his deception. Secondly, Mak is an illusionist,
seeking to confuse his victims and exulting in his skill. He is an actor who
demands an audience, who defies the shepherds and us to penetrate his true
nature ('why, who be ich?', 207), brazenly invites them to search him ('I
pray you, looke my slefe that I steyll noght', 396), and when his victims
are asleep will acknowledge the real audience in seeking appreciation: 'lord!
what thay slepe hard! that may ye all here' (287). It is the operation of
Mak's nimble mind that we are invited to observe and acclaim on its own
amoral terms:

Bot he nedys good counsell
That fayn wold fare weyll,
    And has bot lytyll spendyng.   (275–7)

Mak acts a series of contradictory and disorientating roles – an oppressive king's yeoman (201) and an oppressed husband (236–7); a maligned man of good character (226); a sickly individual (227–8) who may even be mentally unbalanced (192); a cunning thief (269–77), and one endowed with magical power (278–86).

But all these roles are further undercut by Mak's relations with his wife Gill who emerges as the practical side of the partnership. She is the one who copes with the details of running a home (415–21) and she is concerned less with the display of criminal skill than with its consequences. She it is who cuts across Mak's self-indulgent glee with the harsh reality of criminal justice: 'By the nakyd nek art thou lyke for to hyng' (308). Her practicality both belies Mak's earlier complaints of her and also puts his irresponsible trickery into perspective. At the same time her practical concern takes us back to the harsh reality of their urban poverty. Mak can cynically exploit this aspect to win the shepherds' sympathy:

> Wo is hym has many barnes,
>   And therto lytyll brede.   (393–4)

and confusingly contradict it in offering hospitality to the visiting shepherds. But he is hungry, and the house-search reveals no meat 'but two tome [empty] platers' (547). Mak and Gill seem to share with the shepherds a common experience of need and suffering. Mak is no more oppressive yeoman than oppressed husband and, though agent of the shepherds' misfortune, he nevertheless shares their basic need.

These serious overtones are, however, only a means of distancing the absurd illusion, the transformation of sheep into child, which Mak and Gill successfully effect. Ironically, Fortune turns against Mak; as an afterthought the shepherds return to give gifts to the newborn infant and thus discover the deception. No moral condemnation is offered or, given the ambivalence of the opening, appropriate. For a brief moment Gill's practical vision of civil justice is revived – 'A fals skawde [scurvy fellow] hang at the last' (596) – but only to be swept away by an 'aesthetic' appreciation of the illusion in Mak's terms and by the shepherds' substitution of an appropriate 'mock' punishment, tossing in a canvas. Illusion, role-playing, pretence and deception triumph in their own terms, divorced from the functions of enforcing morality or legal observation.

As the shepherds return and the play proceeds swiftly to the angel's song, the visit to the stable and the offering of gifts, a tension is created between the 'sheep-stealing' and the 'visit' which is exploited in the stylistic contradictions of the latter:

> hayll, comly and clene! hayll, yong child!
> hayll, maker, as I meyne, of a madyn so mylde!
> Thou hast waryd [cursed], I weyne, the warlo [warlock, devil] so wylde;
> The fals gyler of teyn [deceiver of malice] now goys he begylde.
>   lo, he merys [is happy];
> lo, he laghys, my swetyng,
> A welfare metyng,
> I have holden my hetyng [kept my promise];
>   haue a bob of cherys.   (710–18)

The inspired and formal praise of the Christ-child recognizes the purpose of the Incarnation but dissolves into a human response to a laughing infant. The final speech recognizes that he like them suffers cold: 'bot he lygys full cold' (747). Accepting the wonder of the Incarnation, the shepherds respond still with the human sympathy that took them back to Mak's 'child'. Son of God or of sheep-stealer, the basic response is the same. As the shepherds appreciated the deception of the deceiver Mak, so they now appreciate God's deception of the arch-deceiver, the Devil. A sheep can only acquire the 'essence' of a child by Mak's deceit, but God's miracle allows a child to be invested with the essence of the divine. The structural equation set up between 'sheep-stealing' and 'visit' must be evaluated in terms of the historic reality of the Incarnation. The wildly comic absurdities of the disguised sheep emphasize the incredible and yet true fact of Incarnation. Though the shepherds voice our reductively sympathetic response to all new life, here it is their 'out-of-character' formal praises of divinity which point out of this episode into the wider context of the cycle. Meantime the shepherds, unchanged in their humanity, return to their flocks and the situation of which they complained at the outset, and Mak lives to prove the truth of his unconvincing plea that he will never 'trespas' again.

The same subject here yields two very different dramatic structures. And the two plays are symptomatic of, and actually predicate, very different cyclic structures. Chester's shepherds are one manifestation of dramatic action as sign, itself part of a wider concept of sign which gives coherence to the cycle.[1] All history conforms to the will of God from the start:

> It is my will it shoulde be soe;
> hit is, yt was, it shalbe thus.   (1/3–4)

He has repeatedly announced His purpose in prophecies and visions; indeed, before the Fall, in an ecstasy while the rib was removed for the creation of Eve, Adam saw the consequences to follow from the as yet unaccomplished Fall (2/449–52 ff.). Man must recognize and act on these prophecies – yet, despite Adam's revelation, Cain still kills Abel; despite his awareness of the power of God, Balaam still tries to resist, though compelled to attest Christ's coming (5/320–27). Herod hears the prophecies of the Jews but, though well-versed in Scripture himself, rejects them (8/268 + Latin–345), whereas the Magi, having initially only their one prophet Balaam, accept his prophecy (8/1–48) and learn of the Jews (9/140–3). Christ prophesies and fulfils his own mission, and those in Hell acknowledge the fulfilment of their own words as He approaches. Antichrist is prophesied (22/1–260). Doomsday alone awaits fulfilment for contemporary Man, but at the end of the cycle the four Evangelists remind us that this too is prophesied (24/677–708); God is fulfilling His intent (24/8–9) and is the agent of His promises even to the devils (24/549–68).

Events not only confirm the truth of prophecies; they serve as signs in themselves. They may be understood by or explained to their participants, like the rainbow (3/309–24), circumcision (4/185–92), the Nativity star (8/77–84) or the Magi's gifts (Play 9). Miracles and wonders confirm truths – the withered hand of the doubting midwife (6/548–63), the blind man (13/1–35, 51–66), the raising of Lazarus (13/337–56, 385–93). Sometimes the function is identification, like Jesus' consumption of food (19/190–9, 20/33–40), His wounds (19/176–87) which are also tokens of His right to judge (20/129–52, 24/381–412), together with other instruments of the Passion (24/17–24). But on other occasions the event is explained to the audience by an 'Expositor' – the offerings of Abraham and Melchisedech (4/113–44), the figural significance of circumcision (4/193–208), the sacrifice of Isaac (4/460–75), the Temptation (12/169–216), the woman taken in adultery (12/281–312), as well as the wonders attendant upon Christ's birth (6/564–643, 699–722) and the various prophecies in Plays 5 and 22.

[1] See further, J. J. McGavin, 'Sign and transition: the *Purification* play in Chester', *LSE*, 11 (1980), 90–104.

But while looking to and extending a Johannine concept of sign in relating event to mythology, the Chester cycle itself becomes a sign. God, initiating history, also initiates a significant dramatic action. Mimesis becomes the imitation of sign, and speeches of prophecy or explanation serve to establish the essentially symbolic nature of this drama as they establish the connection of each episode with God's revelatory purpose. The cycle explores the compatibility of God's promises and Man's experience throughout history so that an action initially complete in the mind of God can be seen complete in the memory of Man. The cycle proclaims its authorities, quoting directly from the Bible – often in Latin and with book, chapter and verse; or citing specific authorities ('freere Bartholemewe', 6/565; 'Gregorye', 12/170; 'Augustine', 12/285); or by directly utilizing familiar aspects of the liturgy – the Gloria, the Nunc Dimittis, the Creed (Play 21); or alluding to the Sacraments. The cycle thus has the force of a logical and causative argument. God's existence and purpose can be demonstrated to rational Man who is willing to read the signs aright. Herod, given both prophecies and signs, rejects them for illusory self-sufficiency; but the emperor Octavian knows that supreme power cannot be a sign of divinity:

> And godhead askes in all thinge
> tyme that hath noe begininge
> ne never shall have endinge;
> and none of this have I. (6/329–32)

God sends His sign to the rational pagan, who understands it.

Chester's cycle, thematically unified and showing a remarkable consistency of stanza-form and tonality, was clearly the product of a single impulse, if not a single author/editor. Its cross-references, its recurring emphasis upon sign, provide a logical structure which operates across the three days – God utters a preface to the action on Monday (1/1–32), and this is balanced by the coda of the Evangelists on the Wednesday (24/676 + SD–708). It remains the conscious demonstration of a thesis, an intellectual construct which, by its expository speeches, invites the audience to stand back from the action and think about its extra-dramatic significance. To create this distance it acknowledges the community. At the end of Play 4 Abraham – apparently without freeing Isaac – sacrifices a lamb while God reiterates His covenant to end the 'historical' action (4/436–59). The Expositor interposes himself as teacher, explaining the historical action as figure of the Passion (4/460–75); but then, as a contemporary observer, he kneels in prayer for Abraham's exemplary obedience to be followed by himself and the audience (4/476–83). But during his prayer a messenger bursts in, demanding that the next play be given space and whirls away again (4/489–91). The action ends in a significant tableau, which is immediately set first in the context of cyclic structure, a distancing of perspective emphasized by the physical intervention of the Expositor; then cyclic significance yields to exemplum and the Expositor joins the audience in prayer before the tableau; and finally interpretation and meditation yield before the urgency of the guild-ceremonial whose demands for schedules and order sweep away illusion and return us to the streets of Chester. Progressively, an action which had held its audience by its dramatic immediacy is now robbed of that immediacy and restored to its place in the mind and memory, to be held there and reflected upon amid the hurly-burly of contemporary life. Chester's constant allusion to the urban community – the gossips outside the ark, the overtaxed wright Joseph, the Welsh shepherds, the ale-wife who enters Hell after the Harrowing, etc. – are means of objectifying the historical action. The drama works not by catharsis but by rational demonstration.

Wakefield was not the product of a single revision, and clearly shows constituent elements:

> The plays fall distinctively into groups: five plays borrowed outright, though sometimes with additions, from York; . . . five plays indisputably by the Wakefield Master, all written in his characteristic stanza-form [$\frac{aaaa^2}{bbbb^2}c^1ddd^2c^2$], namely Noah, the two Shepherds' plays, the Massacre of the Innocents, and the *Coliphizacio*; a group of plays, all of which have some striking dramatic individuality, which may be partly the work of the Wakefield Master, namely Cain and Abel, Lazarus, the *Fflagellacio*, and the *Processus Talentorum*, and Thomas of India (the Last Judgement could also be included in this group); two plays about Jacob and Esau and Jacob's Ladder, which in their brevity and simplicity suggest some quite different origin; and, finally, the remaining fourteen plays, associated together largely for negative reasons, though many of them reveal very markedly the influence of York.[1]

Moreover, a number of plays are incomplete, and the cycle lacks a Fall of Man and a Nativity.[2]

---

[1] Woolf, *The English Mystery Plays*, 310.
[2] See also Martin Stevens, 'The missing parts of the Towneley cycle', *Speculum*, 45 (1970), 254–65.

But Wakefield still has overall structure deriving from the polarization of the forces of good and evil and their unremitting struggle for the souls of men. The Devil's success establishes sin's dominion in the world; with God's grace to His servants – Noah, Abraham, Moses, the Prophets – goes an awareness of the Fall in the openings of Plays 3 and 4, with pictures of Man's terrible sin and God's fearful retribution:

> Sithen Noe, that was trew and good,
> his and his chyldre thre,
> was saued when all was flood:
> That was a wonder thyng to se,
> And loth fro sodome when he yode [went],
> Thre cytees brent [burned], yit eschapyd he;
> Thus, for thai menged my lordis mode [remembered His will],
> he vengid syn thurgh his pauste [power].   (4/25–33)

The Devil and his servants are so powerful that only God can save the true believer and in so doing reassert the power on earth that the Devil usurped. Man's rescue is God's triumph, to be set against the perspective of the Fall (cf. 12/332–403, 17/1–16, 19/1–8, 33–40, 23/447–79, 25/1–24 ff., 27/166–81, 202–33, etc.). At two key points there are important expositions. God initiates the Annunciation by figurally rather than causatively linking past with present, indicating that He will use to restore harmony the very means the Devil used to destroy it:

> ffor reson wyll that ther be thre,
> A man, a madyn and a tree:
> Man for man, tre for tre,
> Madyn for madyn; thus shal it be.   (10/31–4)

And in Gethsemane *Trinitas* explains to Christ the strategy of deception, whereby Christ's humanity will take Him to Hell but His divinity will secure His release, and with Him all the Devil's prisoners (20/548–54).

In establishing this purposive movement, Wakefield asserts that Man, as heir to sin in this continuing conflict of good and evil, is in constant need of Christian mythology. It makes this assertion in a formal mode which evokes Christian mythology, theology and celebration. E. Catherine Dunn has identified a basic lyric voice in the cycle which she terms 'the voice of the Church', and Martin Stevens has effectively suggested that this voice is also heard in prophetic speeches, associated with the use of hymns and chants, and with certain characteristic stanza-forms.[1] An extreme example is provided by the play of the Baptism (Matthew 3: 13–17, Mark 1: 9–11, Luke 3: 21–2), which deals both with the historical baptism of Christ and the Sacrament of baptism which it inaugurates. Yet the significance of the Sacrament – the expunging of Adam's original sin – was not the significance of the historical event, for Christ was immaculately conceived and sinless. These theological complexities are resolved in a structure focusing on John, not Christ, and in a mode which repeatedly moves to symbolic and ritualistic action.

John is at the outset conscious of Man's need and God's purpose and, in foreseeing the Passion, links the baptism to it as a means to redemption. Christ's divinity is suggested, by John's reluctance, dramatically; in the supplementing of baptism by coronation with oil and cream, ritualistically; and, in the two angels representing Christ's dual nature of God and Man (146), symbolically. Both Jesus and John are agents of God's will, enacting a rite for others to follow; John acknowledges baptism as a sacrament (130) and sets it beside the other six (193–200), and is, as it were, ordained by Christ to undertake it (159–60). The baptizing looks to the contemporary ritual in action and Latin formulae (185–92). The play reverts to Christ's sacrifice in the gift to John of a symbolic lamb and Jesus' prophecy of His death (241–8). The formal language rises to high lyric praise as Jesus leaves (249–72). Finally, John reminds the audience of the significance of the action for them in the rituals of the Church:

> Thynk how in baptym ye ar sworne
>> To be godis seruandis, withoutten nay;
> let neuer his luf from you be lorne,
>> God bryng you to his blys for ay. Amen.   (285–8)

This dominant and allusive 'Church voice' provides the wider contextual emphasis for the 'cradle-scene' of *Secunda Pastorum*. But with the assertion of necessary mythology runs the complementary realization of Man's inevitable destiny of sin and damnation without it. John looks back to the Fall (57–64). Jesus, promising grace, chillingly depicts eternal damnation:

> ffor at the day of dome I shall thaym peche [accuse]
>> That herys not the nor trowys not this.   (239–40)

---

[1] E. Catherine Dunn, 'The literary style of the Towneley plays', *American Benedictine Review*, 20 (1969), 481–504; and Martin Stevens, 'Language as theme in the Wakefield plays', *Speculum*, LII (1977), 100–17.

and enjoins John to preach against sin (241–2), which he does (273–84), warning of the seven sins and mortality while directing them to the Church, custodian of the saving myth:

> here gods seruice, more and lesse;
> Pleas god with prayng, thus red [advise] I. (277–8)

The warning references to an a-mythological world here are enforced dramatically in figures such as Cain, Pharaoh, Herod or Pilate. God's figural preface to the Annunciation structurally complements Caesar Augustus' worldly vaunt at the start of the previous play. A-mythological Man is the subject of the Wakefield Master, best typified in Cain's rejection of God to His face:

> Whi, who is that hob-ouer-the-wall?
> we! who was that that piped so small?
> Come, go we hens, for perels all;
> God is out of hys wit. (2/297–300)

The logical impossibility of the final line has a counterpart in the inadequate sneer of 'hob-ouer-the-wall' and 'piped so small'. Cain reveals his limited perception and his wilful determination to reshape reality into an acceptable a-mythological form, whereby God becomes another form of Cain, with comparable human limitations. Simultaneously, Cain suggests to the audience the diminution inherent in mimesis – that compared with the real God, the actor-God is like a squeaking hobgoblin – but the comic appropriateness of the allusion remains a measure of the literal mind which produces it.

This reshaping of reality results in a self-contained and self-validating structure which finds coherence as the expression of a particular character's mind. Tithing for Cain is merely a convenient formalization of commercial transaction; spiritual contemplation for Noah's wife is an excuse to escape practical responsibilities; Christ's divine kingship, for Herod or the tormentors, is a cloak for worldly ambition. Trapped in a world without mythology, such figures move in comically predictable patterns, with a paranoiac fixity of purpose and total lack of self-knowledge. They are set in the wider purposive cyclic pattern, where their self-constructed illusions, closed and self-validating, are challenged by God's revelations. Their 'play' is established against the mode of formal drama, of 'Church voice', being characterized by the violence of language and action with which they seek to coerce reality and the sustainers of myth to their own viewpoint. Cain constantly mouths blasphemies, obscenities and oaths, and for him violence has also become a natural mode of self-expression, divorced from concepts of pain. The formal discourses of Noah with God stand against the angry exchanges and physical battles of Noah and his wife. Human beings are reduced to objects for the expression of an individual viewpoint, a move reaching its climax in the tormentors' games in which their violence is contained, denying Christ's humanity by assigning Him the role of victim.

Compared with Chester, which alludes to the community in the course of objectifying its actions, Wakefield narrows its focus and, in so far as it does allude to contemporary circumstances (as in the complaints of *Secunda Pastorum*), does so as a prelude to an action which belongs to a world of the absurd. There, normal expectations of conduct are no longer applicable and our usual standards of evaluation are not shared by its inhabitants. We can only observe the actions and derive from them the underlying rationale created by the playwright. While Chester's 'Flood' play acknowledges the community and focuses upon the family as unit, Wakefield's 'Flood' virtually ignores the wider issue, concentrating on the struggle for domestic *maistrie* which becomes microcosmically extended. Moreover, Wakefield's a-mythological mode is sharply separated from its ritualistic mode, leaving some characters eternally imprisoned within their actions. The stylistic divide is symptomatic of a failure of communication between the mythologically orientated characters and their 'a-mythological' opposites which contributes to a strong sense of predestination in the cycle and leads some critics to see the 'figures of evil' as ultimately manifestations of a single 'Antichrist'.[1] In Chester, the divide is not absolute. Finally, these structures deny to characters of the Wakefield cycle the possibility of self-awareness and hence of change. Even where change is promised – as with Noah's wife's new co-operation or Mak's penitence – it is against the dramatic weight of the play. In contrast, disregard of mythology in Chester must be a wilful act of irrationality and carry with it the alternative possibility – Herod, ordering the Massacre, knows he does wrong (10/21–4) and can acknowledge his suffering, death and damnation as just (10/417–34).

---

[1] See especially, Walter E. Meyers, *A Figure Given: Typology in the Wakefield Plays* (Pittsburgh, Penn., n.d.).

(iv) Character and structure: York, Coventry and the Digby *Mary Magdalen*

From what has been said already, it follows that medieval drama, like other forms of medieval literature, saw 'character' as a function of 'structure'. The style and conduct of Wakefield's Noah, when addressing God on the one hand and his wife on the other, are determined not by a concept of Noah's 'inner life' but by the situations in which he stands, each requiring a different stylistic level. Psychologically, Noah is two people; but such evaluation is inappropriate in the context of this kind of drama. The stylistic contradictions of the figure focus our awareness of the wider contradictions in the play and their thematic implications. Even where figures do not change situations, they remain vehicles of predetermined patterns, figures with no past or future, fixed in the forms in which we see them. It is their lack of 'inner life', their lack of verisimilar complexity, which makes them comic rather than tragic. They accept the logic of their own conduct and cannot envisage alternatives to it. Nothing in the ensuing discussion will radically contradict this thesis, but it seems important to demonstrate that some dramatists could combine structural coherence with an illusion of psychological consistency in the same manner as their counterparts, the authors of romance.

A comparison of York with Wakefield indicates the extent to which the former considers with sympathetic humour the effect of divine 'wonder' upon normal human consciousness. In Wakefield, *Joseph's Doubt* is a formally ordered play. Joseph, in lyric stanzas, sadly reviews his position, logically confronting Mary's explanation:

A heuenly thyng, for sothe, is he,
And she is erthly; this may not be.   (10/296–7)

and concludes that he must leave her since she is either, as adulteress, unworthy of him, or, as God's elect, far above him (299–314). This logic does not diminish his regard for Mary; he feels responsible for her fate ('And then am I cause of her dede', 311) and is delighted at her exoneration. He formally seeks her forgiveness in a scene reminiscent of the Prodigal Son's return (Luke 15/21):

IOSEPH.   Bot I wote well, my lemman fre,
I haue trespast to god and the;
        fforgyf me, I the pray.

MARIA.   Now all that euer ye sayde me to,
   God forgyf you, and I do,
      With all the myght I may.   (10/356–61)

But in York the doubt, separated from the formal Annunciation, stresses Joseph's self-regarding response of injured pride:

I dare loke no man in þe face,
Derfely for dole why ne were I dede / ... [why were I not dead of grief straightaway]

Allas! why wrought þou swa,
   Marie! my weddid wiffe?   (13/147–8, 154–5)

Joseph's earthbound incomprehension and bewilderment set the comic mode for this action. Wakened by the angel, he complains of being disturbed and responds doubtfully ('And is this soth, aungell, þou saise?'). He awkwardly kneels to Mary to 'aske forgifnesse nowe, Wist I þou wolde me here' (295–6) and, when she brushes aside such penitence, he moves swiftly on with evident relief to prepare for the journey to Bethlehem:

MARIA.   Forgiffnesse sir! late be! for shame,
   Slike [such] wordis suld all gud women lakke.
JOSEPH.   Yha, Marie, I am to blame,
   For wordis lang are I to þe spak.
   But gadir same [together] now all our gere....   (13/297–301)

Although the stock figure of the comic doting cuckold underlies the York play, its true comedy lies in Joseph's resistance to the role which, he believes, has been unjustly thrust upon him in place of the role of dignified old man which has been his former part. His 'character' is a product of a structural tension, absent in the Wakefield play.

   The extent to which York exploits the comedy of 'the externally imposed role' can be seen particularly in the Passion sequences, and its consequences emerge in the divergent treatments of the resurrection in York and Wakefield, recognizably still the same basic text. The action covers the centurion's report and the setting of the watch, the resurrection, the coming of the Marys with the lament of Mary Magdalen, and the soldiers' report. Wakefield, however, gives Christ an extended audience-address, 26/226–333, in which He reviews the Passion, displays His wounds and explains His sacrifice, finally proclaiming His abiding grace and the sacrament of the Eucharist which continues to transmit it. The speech thus links the action to contemporary ceremonial, and specifically to the central doctrines of Corpus Christi. Moreover, the play ends not with the soldiers' report but with a subsequent scene in which Christ comforts the sorrowing Magdalen, giving the play a joyful ending.

York's mythological statements are implicit in the act of resurrection and the empty tomb. The resurrection is purely visual, with no explanatory address ('*Tunc Iesu resurgente*', 38/186 + SD). Similarly, the comfort of Mary is postponed to the following play and joy is not released dramatically. But York does not open with the vaunting speech of Wakefield's evil Pilate proclaiming his triumph over Christ, but with the image of a duly convened and orderly council (38/1–6 ff.) whose members affirm, in formal and dignified language, the legality of their previous deed ('By lawe it was done all be-dene', 14). Stylistic formality and ordered conduct desert the leaders only momentarily, in the shocked reaction to the news of the resurrection (38/363–6), in contrast to the coarse colloquialisms which habitually punctuate Wakefield ('Harlot, wherto commys thou vs emang With sich lesyngys vs to fang?', 26/140–1). In York Pilate recognizes that the news threatens the system within which they hold authority:

If we amisse haue tane oure merke
    I trowe same faile (38/397–8)
[If we have set our target wrong, I believe we shall all miss together.]

The soldiers are bribed and the play ends, not with Mary's comfort – her lament forms a sorrowful conclusion to the *Visitatio* section – but with the cynical assertion that order can be sustained without regard for mythological truth:

Thus schall þe sothe be bought and solde,
And treasoune schall for trewthe be tolde,
Þerfore ay in youre hartis ʒe holde
    Þis counsaile clene. (38/449–52)

Wakefield sets Pilate's deluded attempts to make reality conform to his vision against a formal and allusive action which points out into the wider patterns of Christ's comfort to Mary and, through the Mass, to all men; York sets up an opposition between Christian mythology and the order of state. While the power of the former is implicit, the latter dominates the action to the final assertion that a falsely based order can, and always will be, sustained – this is merely one example of how the social élite maintain their power. That the hierarchy survives, however, depends upon the willingness of all members to accept their appointed role, formalized by law. Pilate reminds the centurion of his position and duties:

> Þou arte a lered [educated] man in þe lawe,
> And if we schulde any witnes drawe
>   Vs to excuse,
> To mayntayne vs euermore þe awe [ought],
>   And noȝt reffuse.   (38/68–72)

and, terrifyingly, the soldiers do as they are told, despite their earlier concern for the truth.

The unwillingness of men to question their given role in an established social order forms the basis for the figure of the York Pilate, a creation primarily of the so-called York Realist who is credited with the composition of plays 26, 28–33 and 36.[1] Rome is the source of the system which endows him with authority (compare the claim, above, p. 156, for the government of Rome as the model for the government of medieval London), but it is a secular power, transmitted by heredity through an established élite:

> { For sir Sesar was my sier
> { And I sothely his sonne,
>   That exelent Emperoure exaltid in hight,
>   Whylk all this wilde worlde with wytes [pains] had wone.
>   (30/10–12)

His power has been duly delegated, and has given him authority over the Jews to administer the laws which determine their order:

> And sithen Sesar hym selffe with exynatores [senators] be his side,
> Remytte me to þe remys, þe renkes [people] to redresse.
> And yitte am I graunted on grounde, as I gesse
> To justifie and juge all þe Iewes.   (30/21–4)

This system maintains an individual who is broadly characterized as lecherously uxorious, tender of constitution ('but loke þat þou tene me not with þi tastyng, but tendirly me touche', 135), a lover of wine. In turn, this weak and hedonistic leader respects the system and its laws which

---

[1] On the York Realist, see Jesse Byers Reese, 'Alliterative verse in the York cycle', *SP*, 48 (1951), 639–66; and J. W. Robinson, 'The Art of the York Realist', *MP*, 60 (1962–3), 241–51.

maintain him and which he sustains. Though he would like to dally with his nobly born and equally sensuous wife, he accepts his Beadle's advice that she must leave since her presence is against the law (30/82–5). Ironically, it is the Devil who voices to her what Pilate himself later accepts, that Jesus's condemnation will destroy their power (30/168–76); and, though Pilate dismisses her dream, a suspicion of the High Priests' motives seems to impel him to make the trial scene an affirmation of their relative positions in the hierarchy.

The formality of trials and legal procedures becomes the major image of the action. Pilate insists on a properly convened court (30/364–77), calls Jesus to the bar, calls for accusations (400–4) and finally ridicules the Priests, not only for their false arguments, but for the absurdity of the law to which they appeal as Jews and upon which their power rests:

Yha, for he dose wele his deth for to deme?
Go, layke [play] you, sir, lightly,
{ Wher lerned ye such lawe?
{ This touches no tresoune, I telle you.
Yhe prelatis þat proued are for price,
Yhe schulde be boþe witty and wise,
And legge [appeal to] oure lawe wher it lyse,
Oure materes ye meve þus emel [among] you.   (30/450–6)

Beneath the dignified formality of legal proceedings, a battle for control of the play's central action is being waged between Pilate and the Priests. Even in sending Jesus to Herod, Pilate continues to affirm his own authority – Herod is to be reminded that he owes tribute to the Romans (30/538–9).

Yet this need to assert authority implies an underlying insecurity which focuses upon Pilate's hedonistic nature. He and the Priests have common self-interest in sustaining the ordered system from which their power descends. They all expect obedience, as do their underlings – the Priests' soldiers are shocked at Christ's 'disrespect' for their 'bishop' (29/326–9) as the Priests and soldiers are by the Beadle's disrespect for Pilate in bowing to Jesus (30/306–25). Pilate's son is shocked at Jesus' disrespect for his father (30/387–95), and Herod is offended by His disrespectful silence (31/226–41). The disruptive threat posed by Christ is typified by Judas who seeks to cancel his bargain and, in return for his breach of contract, proffers lifelong service (32/211–21). A man who betrays his superior and

seeks to cancel legal contracts represents the most contemptible figure to
Pilate, Priests and soldiers, all of whom have profited by Judas's disloyalty
but pour scathing contempt upon him:

> PILAT.   Ʒaa, and for a false faitoure,
>   Thy selffe fully gon selle hym,
>   O! þat was a trante [despicable trick] of a traytour,
>   So sone þou schulde goo to begile hym.   (32/250-3)

Having closed ranks, the leaders combine to purchase the Field of Blood
by fraud, and the stage is set for the return of Jesus.

Unfortunately, the York trial play contains a lacuna at the key moment
of condemnation, but its motivation lies in the dramatic demonstration of
the power of Christian myth over secular power by the 'perversion' of legal
formality. As Christ enters, the banners bow, and Pilate and Priests
are compelled to worship Him. Pilate remains concerned at the absence
of indictable offence, but he finally seizes on Caiaphas's charge of
political ambition and condemnation speedily follows (33/329-40). The
play ends in a grim parody of secular ceremonial as the soldiers crown
Jesus with thorns and do Him homage in violence, mocking stylistic
and dramatic formality.

Pilate acts with apparent dramatic logic throughout. All his later actions
find their source in the tension between his own weak, pleasure-loving
nature and the role of responsibility which the social system has conferred
upon him. He is the focus of an action of ceremonial which alludes to
administrative institutions of council and law-courts and which expresses
itself in a formal, impersonal language. Pilate acts the role and wears the
costume of leader. But the order is divorced from mythology and exists only
to sustain the authority of the weak and corrupt; its forms have become
ends in themselves, both mimetic and parodic of true forms of order as the
drama's incorporation of those forms is itself mimetic and parodic. The
empty forms are revealed in their true functions by the coming of Christ,
who during much of the busy formality says nothing but remains a silent
and challenging representative of the mythology needed to give purpose
and meaning to the ceremonial. It is for the audience to assess this implicit
criticism and make the necessary links.

The links are further suggested by two other considerations. First, in
the procession to Calvary and the Crucifixion, the soldiers continue to
pursue their busy duty, doing their task of conveying two objects up a hill,
'þis traitoure and þis tree' (34/219). On Calvary, as they argue

and complain, Christ provides a second focus of attention for the audience.
As they squabble, He prays for their forgiveness (35/49–60); amidst
their busy-ness He calmly lays Himself upon the Cross (75–6); and
finally, as a living wayside crucifix, He looks over them, out of the
historical frame, and speaks down the centuries to contemporary Man
(253–64). Echoing Lamentations 1:12, He points the moral of the
preceding action by seeking to arrest a world of bustling indifference, to
call to all men entrapped by their daily concerns, that they remember the
Christ who still suffers for their sin and prays for their forgiveness:

> Al men þat walkis by waye or strete,
> Takes tente ʒe schalle no trauayle tyne.   (35/253–4)

That pathetic contrast of caring God and indifferent Man will recur with
the image of trial at Doomsday:

> All þis I suffered for þi sake,
> Say man, what suffered þou for me?   (48/275–6)

As contemporary Man is challenged to deny his alliance with the
uncaring persecutors of Christ, so also he is edified by the circumstances
of performance. If the historical action points the divorce of civil ceremony
from Christian mythology, the occasion of Corpus Christi presents the
spectacle of the York community honouring that mythology, following the
Real Presence of Christ. Pilate, for all the apparent individuality of his
presentation, becomes more important for what he represents than for what
he is, product and agent of an ordered but flawed secularity which presents
a continuing threat to the just society and the spiritual aspirations of
mankind.

To some extent the thematic concern with the individual as type or
representative is the inevitable counterpart of his function as structural
device. But the resulting focus upon predetermined patterns of action is
also most readily compatible with comic action. The recurrent use of stock
comic types – the wilful woman, the aged dotard or cuckold, the ranting
tyrant, the *miles gloriosus* – belongs to the same concern, and may be seen,
not as a failure to rise to the heroic grandeur of the vast cyclic theme, but
rather as a refusal to introduce notes of pathos or tragedy which are at times
latent in the material. A cycle's action is inevitably 'comic' in that it realizes
an ultimate divine justice which precludes tragedy. To introduce a
verisimilar complexity and self-awareness in characters may be to threaten
this perspective, at least in dramatic terms. Arguably this is the effect of

Brome's *Abraham and Isaac*, where God's intention of testing Abraham as an example to all (33–46), concealed from Abraham but revealed to the audience, is set against the play's concluding stress on Isaac's response. As we see Isaac's disbelief at his reprieve (343–5, 348–9), his suspicion that his father may change his mind (377–8), his determination never to revisit the spot 'but it be aȝens my wyll' (418) and never again to leave his home (429–34), we are conscious of the traumatic effect of the experience on the young boy, of the destruction of his trusting innocence for nothing more than a divine experiment of questionable necessity. By retaining a verisimilar mode, the Brome dramatist has invited an identification of audience with Isaac, losing the distance necessary to permit the action to be viewed as example. The play was evidently non-cyclic; the Chester dramatist, as we have seen, insists upon a concluding dramatic distance through the figure of the Expositor, and hence successfully integrates the action into his cyclic form.

What sometimes appears a retreat into comedy proves rather to be an attempt to avoid the difficulties raised by a concentration upon verisimilar emotional response. Nowhere is this more pronounced than in the Massacre of the Innocents, where cycle-dramatists share with the author of the Digby 'Killing' the avoidance of tragic potential by employing the stock comic figures of the ranting Herod and *miles gloriosus*, and by reducing the Massacre to a comic belabouring of soldiers by mothers in the manner of Coventry's Hocktide play. The farcical action is, in Chester and N-town, strengthened by the exemplary assertion of divine justice in the death of Herod – in Chester he is further punished by the death of his son among the slaughtered children.

The dangers of the alternative approach are evident in the Coventry Shearmen and Tailors' pageant which, like the Weavers' pageant, was revised in 1534 by the Capper, Robert Croo.[1] Croo is a competent dramatist, capable of accommodating a diversity of events in a firmly structured action. His Shearmen and Tailors' play is divided into two parts by a dialogue of two 'Prophets' (332–474), separating the events from the Annunciation to the Gifts of the Shepherds from the Coming of the Magi, their presentation and departure, with the Massacre concluding the play. The first action sets the formal style of the Holy Family and Gabriel beside the homely colloquialisms of the shepherds, the second the formality of the

---

[1] On Croo, see R. W. Ingram, '"To find the players and all that longeth therto": Notes on the production of medieval drama in Coventry', in G. R. Hibbard (ed.), *The Elizabethan Theatre V* (Waterloo, Canada, 1975), 25–9.

Magi against the comically inflated bombast of a Herod required to rage on the pageant and in the street also. Both actions focus upon the Holy Family and have the recurring motif of the presentation of gifts.

To some extent, however, this parallelism with its focus on the Holy Family serves to isolate the Massacre as a coda to the play; Herod's comic rage is the prelude to his terrible command to the knights, who are presented as shocked by his words and have to be compelled to the deed on pain of death for rebellion (801–5). With swift brevity the Holy Family, focus for the main actions, now flee (818–29). The mothers immediately enter, singing the poignantly simple Coventry carol as lullaby. They know that the soldiers are coming to kill their children and are helpless. Their care for the sleep of their doomed infants carries with it a prayer:

> Thatt babe thatt ys borne in Bedlem, so meke,
> He saue my chyld and me from velany!   (833–4)

But the audience has seen the departure of that babe – the divine perspective is lost. The soldiers carry out their order with a brutality of language and action which contrasts with the women's quiet lullabies, but they too are helpless victims, conscious of the horror they create:

> Who hard eyuer soche a cry
> Of wemen thatt there chyldur haue lost.   (870–1)

The soldiers fear some future vengeance; Herod finally learns that the Holy Family has escaped. But the deed remains unnecessary, futile, a powerful evocation of destructive violence and divine indifference. The naturalistic mode obscures the cyclic form, the sense of divine justice is sacrificed to the dramatic power of human suffering and helplessness, and the play concludes by dramatically questioning rather than endorsing the will of God.

Brome and Coventry suggest that a naturalistic drama which focused upon complex emotions and responses was a mode available to the dramatists but one hardly appropriate to their themes. It is particularly unfortunate that only two examples of 'biographical religious drama', the saint's life, survive, since the emphasis upon the individual might suggest greater scope for psychological drama. Even so, the Digby *Mary Magdalen*, for example, still uses character as the agent of structure. In dealing with the legend of the converted harlot who becomes the beloved follower of Christ, the play offers an explanation of her youthful sins which goes some way towards diminishing Mary's responsibility. She is set against a background of worldly power as the great leaders of the Roman empire – Emperor, Herod, Pilate – make their vaunts. Among these is set the wealthy Cyrus, her father, whose death brings for Mary both a deep sorrow and also a purposeless life of wealthy idleness. To this environmental conditioning is added the hostility of the World, Flesh and Devil, who recognize Mary's spiritual potential and mount a campaign to corrupt her. Hence Mary is at the centre of an ironic structure, the victim of forces of whose existence she is ignorant. In her bower, in a state of relaxed happiness, Mary manifests an innocent sensual delight quite free from all sense of subjective sin.

Mary falls asleep in a state of sin, but is warned by an angel of her plight and awakes in remorse, determined to seek Christ. Her sleep marks a transition in her life, a death to sin and an awakening to a new life, which picks up a recurring motif of death in the play. Cyrus' death is the starting-point for Mary's fall. Later, her brother Lazarus' death and resurrection points to the life beyond physical death, prefiguring Christ's own death and resurrection which brings eternal life for all. After her own spiritual awakening and Christ's ascension, Mary becomes the vessel of Christ, coming to the King of Marseilles in his sleep to convert him as an angel once converted her, and being inexplicably associated with the death and resurrection of the Queen and her child during the King's pilgrimage to Jerusalem. Finally, she too dies and is received into the eternal joy of Heaven. Conversely, the powers of the world and the foes of Man are comically discomfited and reduced – the sins flee squealing from Mary, the Devil rushes in terror from the harrowed Hell, and the priest and boy of the pagan temple are figures of crude fun, cast down by Mary. The great leaders are also thrown into disarray by Christ's resurrection, and Mary herself takes over the governorship of the realm during the king's absence. From being victim, Mary assumes a new positive role as the instigator of action, beginning from her resolve to seek out Christ as He feasts, just as once she was sought as she drank in a tavern.

Mary gains consistency as a dependent being, offering and receiving love. Her delight in the attentions of Luxuria and her pleasure in her admirers:

> A! god be with my valentynes,
> My byrd swetyng [my sweet young man], my lovys so dere!
> (564–5)

give way on conversion to a constant desire to be directed and dominated by Christ, whom she addresses with a lyric formality which often carries erotic overtones:

O þou rythewys regent, reynyng in equite,
Þou gracyows lord, þou swete Iesus! (889–90)

with the movement towards personalized reference and sensory overtone in 'swete Iesus'. In her strong desire to kiss the risen Lord:

Lord! long hast þou hyd þe from my spece [from me],
Butt now wyll I kesse þou, for my hartes bote. (1072–3)

her devotion is conveyed with an emotional intensity which suggests that it is to be considered almost as a feminine sublimation of worldly love. To that extent the play presents a continuity of character as well as a contrast of sin and virtue.

(v) Ritual distancing: the N-town cycle

Of the extant cycles it is N-town which most effectively succeeds in creating a dramatic counterpart to the formal modes of religious ceremonial. Despite the composite nature of its extant form, the cycle has an overall thematic concern, the grace of God available to penitent Man. Set against this is a stern justice evoked as a second divine attribute which is to be tempered until Doomsday by the primary attribute of love. Even at the height of God's anger, at the expulsion from Eden, Man is promised that grace will be restored through the Crucifixion (p. 27, 365–77). The cycle expresses this theme in an almost unbroken formal manner, which suggests Wakefield's 'Church voice', and in the relationships and lyric expressions of love which evoke God's own loving concern.

The play about 'The Parliament of Heaven; the Salutation and Conception' (pp. 97–108)[1] shows this mode at its best. Just before Joseph departs at the end of the preceding episode, Mary sits to read the psalter and turns to Psalm 85 (AV). The context of the psalm is not given, but it provides the starting-point for the ensuing action, for it is a plea and a confident affirmation of God's mercy and forgiveness: 'Thou hast forgiven

---

[1] Because of the peculiar composition of the manuscript, it is helpful to give references for N-town not only by play and line-number, but also by the page in Block's edition.

the iniquity of thy people...show us thy mercy, O Lord, and grant us thy salvation.' Mary evidently remains studying her psalter, but across the stage the allegorical figure of Contemplacio interposes himself to initiate 'Play 11'. The presence of this figure is one of several devices which marks Plays 8–13 as a separate sub-group. Hitherto he has been the actors' spokesman, silencing the audience (8/1–25, pp. 62–3) and abridging the action (p. 71, 9/1–17). Now, however, he serves new and important functions. In one sense he is the externalization of Mary's own contemplation as she reads and meditates upon the psalm, and it is her plea for mercy which prompts the ensuing action. But he is also the representative of the collective contemplation of mankind, brooding upon its plight and pleading with God for grace, and as such a spokesman for the audience. He also serves to break the historical action, to shift audience attention from the historical action of Joseph and Mary to the wider debates and actions which will focus upon Mary. He cries to God for recognition of the contrition which Man has shown for sin since the Fall: 'As gret as þe se lord · was Adamys contryssyon ryght' (p. 98, 11/29); and lyrically begs for the Incarnation: 'Gracyous lord. Gracyous lord. Gracyous lord come downe' (p. 98, 11/32).

Contemplacio's cry is taken up in heaven by Virtutes, who present Man's prayers to God ('Mercy. mercy. mercy we crye'; p. 98, 11/40), and God is moved to declare 'tyme is come of reconsyliacion' (p. 99, 11/52). As Contemplacio voices Mary's inner pleas, so the ensuing action dramatizes the fulfilment of the pledge made in her psalm, 85/10: 'Mercy and truth are met together: righteousness and peace have kissed each other.' The allegorical mode changes in the debate of the four daughters of God, where the formally rehearsed arguments of the figures focus attention upon the central issue of justice versus mercy and display the workings of the divine mind for the audience in the fulfilment of Man's penitent aspirations. Mary remains between audience and Heaven as the action goes on above and around her. The daughters search Heaven and Earth to find one able to undertake Man's salvation, but are unsuccessful. In a second brief consultation Filius is agreed to be the person of the Trinity most appropriate for the task.

At this point the action reverts to its historical course as Gabriel is despatched to Mary to explain God's purpose. Mary is not a random choice and is no ordinary woman. She has already been shown as miraculously conceived, spiritually elect, a child prodigy in the Temple. She is accustomed to angelic messengers and is not daunted by Gabriel who explains that she will regain what Eve lost, that *Eva* is changed to *Ave*.

But the play stresses that Mary has free choice and is not a helpless agent of divine authority. Gabriel pictures Heaven awaiting her decision: 'they thynkyth longe to here what ȝe wyl seyn' (p. 106, 260) and evidently one must picture the anxious expectation of Heaven and the dramatic tension of an uncertain audience ('Has she forgotten her lines?') as the playwright boldly risks stillness and silence to enforce his point: 'here þe Aungel makyth a lytyl restynge and mary beholdyth hym and þe Aungel seyth: "Mary come of and haste the"' (p. 106, 260 + SD–61). With her voluntary acceptance Gabriel rejoices and a confirmatory and climactic action occurs:

> here þe holy gost discendit with iij bemys to our lady · þe sone of þe godhede nest with iij bemys · to þe holy gost · the fadyr godly with iij bemys to þe sone · And so entre All thre to here bosom. (p. 107, 292 + SD)[1]

However interpreted, the action somehow visually links Heaven and Earth, the Godhead with Mary, realizing the start of an action of reconciliation born in the thoughts of each. The episode closes joyfully as Gabriel returns to Heaven, affirming a harmony between Heaven and Earth which the angelic host endorses by singing the Ave:

> And as I began I ende with An Ave new
> Enjoynyd hefne and erth. with þat I Ascende.
> Ave maria gratia plena ⎫   Angeli cantando istam
> Dominus tecum. uirgo sesena ⎭   sequenciam.

With the Annunciation we recognize the centrality of the Virgin Mary to a carefully worked out divine plan manifested in the causative sequence of dramatized events from her life. The plan requires Mary's election from the moment of her conception, her special grace which sets her apart from all others. But the dramatist affects complementary dramatic remoteness by removing all but the most formal dramatic modes. The action includes allegorical figures who serve as vehicles of scholarly debate, such as the daughters of God, and often moves into emblematic gestures, such as the ascent by the child Mary of the fifteen steps to the Temple reciting the fifteen psalms (pp. 74–7, 9/84–144 + Latin). Whether in scholarly exposition or lyric praise, characters speak formally and their voices move from the formal style easily into the sacred texts of Bible and liturgy, as when Mary declaims the Magnificat in Latin while Elizabeth translates each

---

[1] See David Mills, 'Concerning a stage-direction in the *Ludus Coventriae*', *ELN* 11 (1974), 162–4.

section into English (pp. 118–20, 13/81–104). Dialogue is replaced mainly by formal speeches – prayers, debates, formal commissions of master to servant. Actions are important confirmations of significant moments and, as with the silence of Mary or the descent of the Godhead, must be carefully specified and executed. Nothing breaks this tonal consistency. The formal action is the counterpart of the ritual action of church ceremonial, to which it alludes and which it may explain:

> lystenyth sovereynys here is conclusyon
> how þe Aue was mad · here is lernyd vs...
> they mad Benedictus · them beforn
> And so Magnificat · And · Benedictus
> ffyrst in þat place þer made worn. (p. 121, 13/153–4; p. 122, 13/22–4)

And appropriately, at the end of the complete sub-group, Contemplacio apologizes for any offence and leads the company away still singing:

> With Aue we begunne · and Aue is oure conclusyon
> Ave regina celorum · to oure lady we synge. (p. 122, 35–6)

Yet the distance which separates audience from dramatic action is only analogous to that which separates worshipper from the object of worship. The distancing of the action serves to invite contemplation of and wonder at the special role of the Virgin Mary in the Christian myth; but it also invites an aesthetic appreciation of the play as artefact. These two responses become inseparable as the cycle progresses, for the pleasing logic of its central thesis is complemented by a unified artistic structure which reconciles the diverse elements of drama in a complete and emotionally satisfying action. The first Passion play, for example, demonstrates in slowly unfolding ceremonial the assembly of the civil powers, guardians of justice, under the High Priests, and then the triumphal processional entry of Christ, the agent of mercy, into Jerusalem, an event explained by the sermons of Peter and John. The two actions are juxtaposed; each has processional character and strong visual appeal and each is invested with symbolic force. Later, this opposition will crystallize into the two parallel assemblies: the Last Supper, where Christ affirms that He will offer Himself for Man and institutes the Eucharist, and the Council of the Jews, who purchase His betrayal. Judas, angered by Christ's previous mercy to Mary Magdalen, moves between the assemblies, selling the God who offered His life freely and then damning himself by receiving the Sacrament in a state of sin. The assembly of the Priests breaks up and while Christ institutes the Eucharist, pointing the link to the rituals of the Church and using a consecrated Host, the audience can see the preparations for His capture in progress to complete the myth validating the Sacrament (p. 254, 26/668 + SD). The preparations continue as Christ and the disciples move to Olivet, where He is comforted by an angel affirming God's mercy and displaying the Sacrament:

> þis chalys ys þi blood þis bred is þi body
> ffor mannys synne evyr offeryd xal be
> To þe fadyr of heffne þat is al-mythty
> Þi dyscipulis and all presthood xal offere fore thee.   (p. 264, 953–6)

until finally the two groups meet in *þe place* (p. 264, 27/972 + SD) for the capture. This finely choreographed action ends with the constituent elements again separating. Christ is borne out in unruly procession, the dramatic decorum totally destroyed ('with gret cry and noyse some drawyng cryst forward and some bakwarde', p. 267, 1040 + SD), while simultaneously Mary Magdalen takes the news to the Virgin who laments in formal lyrics and finds comfort in the fulfilment of divine intent. The play concludes with the assertion of the 'Church voice' and the renewed focus upon the Virgin.

The functional formality of the play, in actions and language, has a counterpart in its satisfying structural integrity, in the slow but relentless unfolding of the two actions of earthly 'justice' and divine grace to their inevitable congruence in the capture. There the steady order is momentarily disturbed in the perturbation of the Jews and Peter's angry wounding of Malchus. In Jesus's restrained rebuke:

> Ffrendys take hede ʒe don vn-ryth [wrong]
> so vn-kendely [unnaturally, unkindly] with cordys to bynd me here
> And þus to falle on me be nyth [night]...   (p. 267, 27/1025–7)

we hear, beyond the gentle *ffrendys* and the understated *vn-ryth*, a sense that the *vn-ryth* is inseparable from the breach of dramatic formality – *so vn-kendely...to falle on me*. The carefully scripted din and disorder of the exit, an unceremonial procession, gives dramatic contrast with symbolic import.

Although N-town is a play-cycle, its techniques in the plays just discussed cannot be directly compared with those in the other English cycles, for N-town has been detached from whatever civic ceremonial it may have been associated with and adapted for performance in sections – possibly sections divorced from the wider cyclic context – by travelling performers. Whereas the authors of civic cycles were constrained, *inter alia*, by the need to accommodate play-division to the number of performing guilds, the N-town writer(s) can create more comprehensive structures out of originally distinct plays, allowing considerations of dramatic effect and unity to determine the scope and nature of their action to a greater extent. Moreover, writing for 'place-and-scaffold' production, the writer(s) could exploit the possibilities for multiple and simultaneous action, for large-scale grouping and crowd movement, and for visual spectacle, to a greater extent than wagon-based production might allow. They also seem to have specified effects requiring considerable control and expertise on the part of the performers. Finally, it may be only coincidental that N-town does not consistently evoke any alternative dramatic mode to its formal style, has nothing quite comparable with the communal reference of Chester, the a-mythological mode of Wakefield or the formal secular procedures of York. Written for different theatre and different circumstances from those of our 'occasional' cycles – perhaps more akin to the professional stages and companies of the sixteenth century – it may not be surprising that N-town has unique qualities.

Yet, given its uneven pattern of revision, it is also not surprising that the cycle contains other, more directly allusive, modes of drama. In *The Baptism* the emphasis rests on the explanatory speeches and the action is denied its full dramatic weight. The distance between audience and historical action is created by the direct didactic addresses to the audience by John which open and conclude the play and intrude before the moment of baptism (79–91). The glossing apparatus is insistently heavy (116 lines out of 182) and somewhat awkwardly managed – the baptism of Christ exemplifies humble obedience, but the whole play is wrenched into the cyclic theme of penance by the opening and closing speeches. At the other extreme, *The Trial of Joseph and Mary* threatens the formal mode by its contemporary allusion to the corrupt procedures of the ecclesiastical courts. A Summoner threatens the audience, identifying members, in the Prologue, and the detractors engage in smutty sexual speculations:

> A ȝonge man may do more chere in bedde
> to A ȝonge wench than may An olde   (p. 126, 14/69–70)

The dramaturgy of 'The Salutation and Conception' (plays 8–13) or 'Passion Play I' (plays 25–7) may, then, be the product of deliberate restraint.

Even in other modes, however, N-town can still on occasion display its characteristic control to build up suspense and release it through dramatically appropriate gestures. An outstanding short example is *The Woman Taken in Adultery*, where Christ's opening exhortation to mercy is followed by the plotting of the Scribe, the Pharisee and the Accusator to sustain their law. This plot leads into the indecorous action of the taking of the adulteress, an action characterized by a low-style speech ('com forth þou hore and stynkynge bych clowte [dog-turd]', 147) and by the disordered appearance of a young man fleeing from the house and threatening violence to his pursuers: '*hic juuenis quidam extra currit indeploydo calligis non ligatis et braccas in manu tenens*' [at this point a certain young man runs out in his doublet, his boots untied and holding up his breeches with his hand] (p. 204, 24/124 + SD). Characteristically, the woman is not an innocent victim but evidently a known harlot who tries to bribe her captors to protect her reputation. This indecorous action yields to the concluding debate with Jesus where the issue is reduced to cold principle, justice versus mercy. It unfolds through a dialogue which is evidently punctuated by silence and expectation ('In a colde stodye me thynkyth ȝe sytt/good sere awake telle us ȝour thought', 225–6), finally releasing the sudden, violent, visual gesture: '*hic ihesus iterum se inclinans scribet in terra et omnes accusatores quasi confusi separatim in tribus locis se disiungent*' [at this point Jesus, bending again, shall write in the earth and all the accusers, as if thrown into confusion, shall move apart from each other to three places] (p. 207, 232 + SD) – an action explained in the succeeding speeches, leaving Jesus to release the now truly penitent woman and point the moral of the action to the audience. In its use of low-style language and violent action, the play recalls the Wakefield Master rather than the large-scale actions already considered. But it shows the same careful development of intersecting actions, the ability to create and release suspense within a dramatic structure, the attention to significant visual detail, which make the play both effective exemplum and effective drama, in contrast to *The Baptism*.

The N-town 'Nativity' and 'Passion' playwright recognizes that his drama has as its function the presentation of Christian mythology in a selected aspect and the explanation of the continuing rites of the Church which commemorate and recreate that mythology. But simultaneously he is conscious of the potential of the genre through which he approaches those functions and, while constantly alluding to the rituals and their meanings and expression, uses the devices of drama to direct the audience's responses. The multiplicity of means and the consciousness of what drama can achieve have been summarized by K. S. Block in the claim that, compared with the other cycles, N-town has

> more singing, more 'devices', more processions, more harangues, and, above all, in some cases, more acting.... In several of the plays the writer or writers show command of stage effect, and understanding of the impressiveness of significant gesture and movement.[1]

If functionally his text explains ritual action, dramatically it generates and releases significant dramatic tension.

We do not know in what circumstances N-town was originally composed, nor do we know the kind of places for which independent units such as the two Passion plays were intended. It is, however, clear that the play-cycles could be broken up and toured, and in this respect the circumstances of N-town's production were probably similar to those of the Digby St Anne's day play. What is lost is the single experience of the complete cycle possible perhaps at, for example, Coventry or York, and particularly the sense of corporate involvement which guild-production in association with civic procession conveyed. The result is not necessarily a different kind of drama, as the Digby 'Candlemes and Killing' demonstrates; but in their different ways Brome and N-town do suggest that divorce from a civic and cyclic context may lead to the emergence of new modes of artistic completeness, to an emphasis upon genre as well as, or even above, function.

It would be misleading to distinguish sharply between the drama of the towns and that of the village. Villagers visited the towns and saw the cycles, and evidently cycles could be toured piecemeal round the villages. It is similarly misleading to overestimate the currency of cyclic drama. The most recent opinions, based on current research by John Wasson, suggest:

> (1) folk plays outnumbered all other types of religious drama in the Middle Ages...; (2) of the religious plays, miracles were the most popular, followed by single Christmas and Easter mysteries; (3) very few cycle plays existed, and very few were acted from pageant wagons.[2]

These generalizations are almost in inverse proportion to the surviving evidence of texts. Moreover, it is clearly impossible to claim cycle-drama as the sole dramatic form of civic ceremonial where there is strong evidence

---

[1] Block, lv–lvi.
[2] Sheila Lindenbaum, 'Report of the MLA 1978 Special Session on medieval drama', *RORD*, 22 (1979), 99.

to suggest that other forms, such as the York Creed play or the Paternoster plays of York, Beverley and Lincoln, were similarly performed processionally by guilds, and, in times of opposition to the cycle, could be substituted for it.[1] Our picture of medieval drama is sadly limited, and despite the obvious borrowing of texts and awareness of other activities elsewhere, there is no means by which we can establish the typicality of any part of our small corpus of texts.

It is thus easy to exaggerate the possible significance of the English cycles as ceremonial drama. But against this caveat is the undeniable fact that statistical frequency is no necessary guide to dramatic influence. The majority of the population in the Middle Ages lived in villages or in towns not markedly dissimilar in economy and society from villages, and it is therefore not surprising that the folk-play should be the most widespread dramatic form. But just as those who lived in towns exerted a disproportionate influence upon the economic, political and social life of the nation, so it is probable that their culture was also significantly more influential than that of the village. Royalty and nobility visited towns such as Coventry specifically to see the cycles, and towns might stage a particular cycle-play specially for the visit of an important personage. The cycles were important manifestations of urban society, the products of a new urban culture and, in their multifarious demands of theme, subject, episodic division and cyclic structure, posed considerable problems of organization to both pageant-masters and playwrights. In many respects the cycles of drama may be compared with the cycles of romance in their resolutions of formal problems. But their authors were working in a new genre with few models to guide them and understandably allude primarily to the mythology and rituals of Christianity which are not only celebrated in the circumstances of performance but are known to be the familiar and shared experience of playwright and audience. Yet the playwrights seem simultaneously to have been conscious of their role as creators of illusion and in their different ways to have been exploring the potential of the genre to move the audience emotionally. There is even, as with the York Masons' play of *Fergus* (see above, p. 149 and n.), or the Chester Smiths' play (*The Purification and Christ before the Doctors*: see p. 171), evidence of a conscious concern for appropriate dramatic effect, and possibly revisions of the cycle were made as much with the intention of improving the effectiveness of the drama as of meeting practical requirements of organization. If figures

[1] See Alexandra F. Johnston, 'The plays of the religious gilds of York: the Creed play and the Pater Noster play', *Speculum*, L (1975), 55–90.

such as the 'Wakefield Master' or the 'York Realist' did exist, it seems likely that their commissions resulted from the awareness that they could produce effective drama. In time, their achievements condition the expectations of urban audiences, not only about the mode and content of a particular cycle, but also about the potential of drama itself, and these expectations transfer readily to the professional stage of the sixteenth century.

6 Conclusion: new kinds of drama

David Mills and Peter F. McDonald

The drama discussed in this section was an adjunct of ritual; consequently the distinction between drama and ritual, which can be clearly established in the abstract, is difficult to establish in some of the activities described. This is not the only distinction which is uncertain. Other modern distinctions are neither clear nor obviously relevant: between action and celebration, art and worship, theme and mythology, audience and congregation. For example, a congregation has a continuing identity as the members of a parish or a religious house; an audience comes together once only for a particular performance. That is obviously over-simplified: in villages and small towns – and most towns were small – the distinction is formal as the people involved would be the same in both cases; what would differ would be their expectations and assumptions, dependent upon whether they had assembled as a congregation or an audience. On the one hand, the geographically defined parish may be too large, too populous, or too socially, economically and occupationally diverse to form a community and a congregation, and other social groupings may emerge and dominate. On the other, audiences may have a continuing existence, associating themselves by regular attendance with a group of players or a place of playing, thus preserving a continuity of experience from performance to performance. As an increasingly experienced and self-conscious society established and sharpened these distinctions, so the emergent genre of drama became recognized as an autonomous art-form, capable of divorce from its religious function and of being adapted to other functions, or simply as a self-sustaining art-form with no other justification.

In so far as the drama is an adjunct of religious ritual, it cannot survive. Its existence, we suggest, arises from the need to explain the ritual and hence presupposes a 'non-believer' who readily becomes a hostile sceptic. In affirming, the plays also defend and in defending they attest hostility. For all the ritual forms, the main 'enemy' is the form of Christian mythology which finds its most extreme expression in Puritanism but which seems to have been a tendency within the Church in England particularly from the later fourteenth century. For drama inextricably interwoven with Catholic liturgy there could be no defence against the liturgical changes of the post-Reformation prayer-books. For drama celebrating the saints, the suspicions of reformers towards the cult of saints proved decisive. For folk-drama, seeking a 'non-mythological' justification for folk-rituals, the process of decline was somewhat slower. Hostility towards it focused, rather, on its unedifying nature and on the riotous behaviour of its performers and spectators.

The mystery cycles, being multi-functional, still retained popularity as civic occasions and often required determined suppression by the authorities after the Reformation. At Chester, for example, in 1575 the council voted to stage the plays despite the fact that a performance in 1572 had been prohibited by the Archbishop of York and had proceeded with the claim that the prohibition had arrived too late to stop the performance. The cycle was transferred from the religious feast of Whitsun to Midsummer, the occasion of Chester's Midsummer Show, a great secular civic event, and seems to have been staged on a single site, not processionally. This attempt to claim the cycle as a civic occasion finds expression in the letter from Henry Hardware, mayor in the following year, to the Privy Council at the request of Sir John Savage, the mayor at the time of the production, who was called to London to explain his act in authorizing the plays against the wishes of the citizens, as it was claimed. The letter states that the production was

> acordinge to an order concluded and agried vpon for dyuers good and great consideracons redounding to the Comen wealthe benefite and profitte of the saide Citie in assemblie there holden according to the

1 Design for the Valenciennes Passion play, by Hubert Cailleau and Jacques de Moëlles (1547)

2 Christ with the Doctors, a roof boss from Norwich Cathedral (sixteenth century)

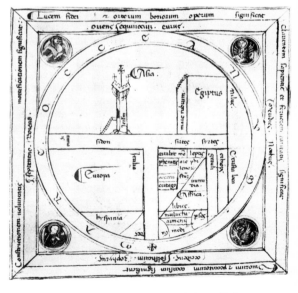

3 *Mappa mundi* (a world map) from *Bellum Jugurthinum*, Sallust (fourteenth century)

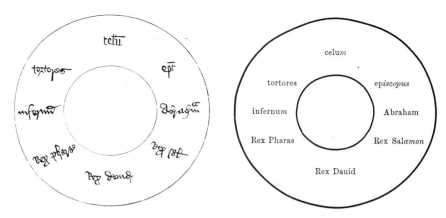

4 Stage plan (and translation) of Cornish *Origo Mundi* (fifteenth century)

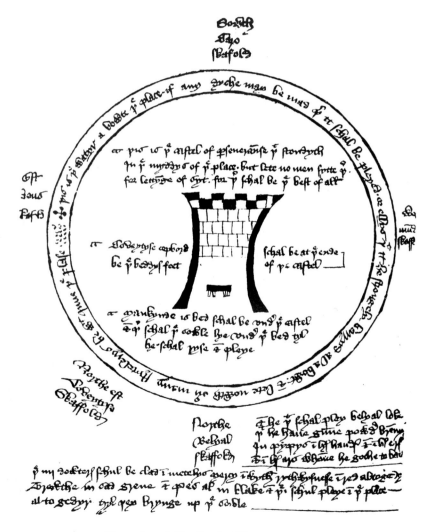

5 Stage plan of *The Castle of Perseverance* (c. 1400–25)

View of the Circus of the Britons on y.e Bank of y.e Louther near Perith. Aug. 15. 1725.

Stukeley delin.

6 King Arthur's Round Table, an engraving from *Itinerarium Curiosum* by W. Stukeley (1776)

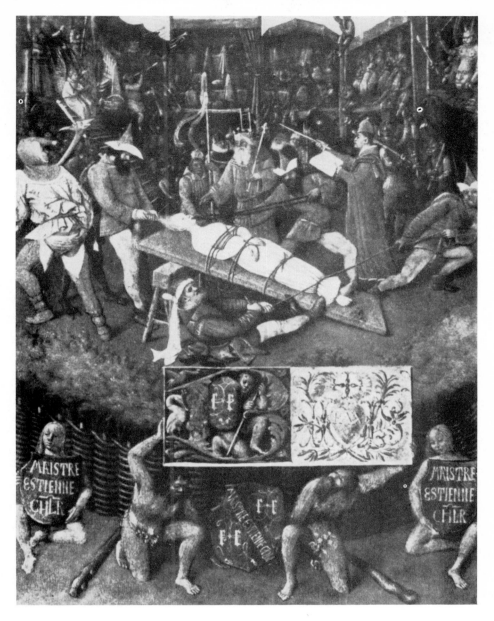

8 The martyrdom of St Apollonia, a miniature by Jean Fouquet
in the *Livre d'Heures d'Etienne Chevalier* (*c.* 1452–6)

7 Calliopus reading from Terence while actors
mime to his words, by the 'Josephus Master',
from a Terence MS of the Duc de Berry (1407)

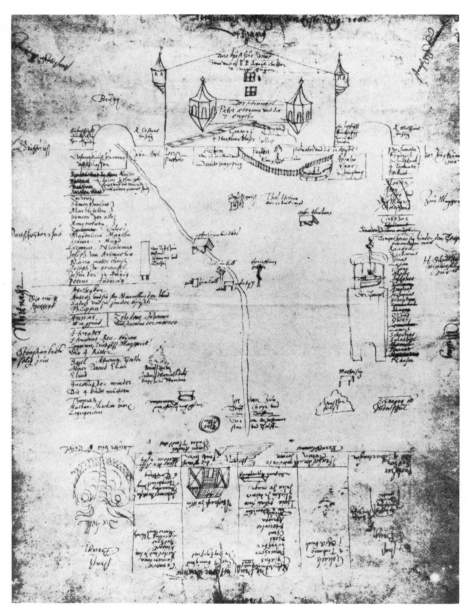

9 Stage plan for the Lucerne Passion play, by Renward Cysat (1583)

12 Herod and the massacre of the Innocents, from a window of the
Church of St Peter Mancroft, Norwich (mid-fifteenth century)

13 Document of the Diocesan Court of High Commission forbidding the playing of parts of the Wakefield cycle tending to 'superstition and idolatrie' (1576)

14 Vigil Raber's stage plan for
the Palm Sunday play of the
Bozen Passion cycle (1514)

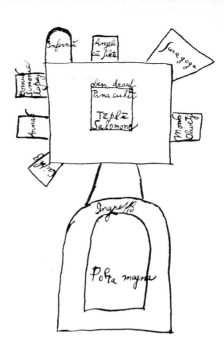

15 A medieval artist's design for a
tapestry showing the production of
La Vengeance de Notre Seigneur
(Rheims, 1531), from a nineteenth-
century engraving in *Toiles Peintes*
by Louis Paris (1893)

16 The Syon Cope (1300–20)

17 The Erpingham Chasuble (early fifteenth century)

18 Christ at Emmaus, a
detail of a leaf from an
English psalter (*c.* 1130–50)

19 The Eucharist, a central panel of
a triptych, *The Seven Sacraments*, by
Rogier van der Weyden (1452–5)

20 St Anthony of Padua refuting a denial of the Real Presence, by Jean Colombe (c. 1485), from *Les Très Riches Heures du Duc de Berry*

21 Corpus Christi procession
from the *Hours of Cardinal
Alessandro Farnese*
(mid-sixteenth century)

22 A modern Corpus Christi procession, Barcelona, Spain

23 The dancers of Colbek condemned to dance all year for
interrupting Divine Service (*c.* 1410), from *Trésor des Histoires* (*c.* 1410)

25 The immoral effect of theatre on the Romans, by the 'Valerius Maximus Master', (*c.* 1425), from a French version of Augustine's *City of God*

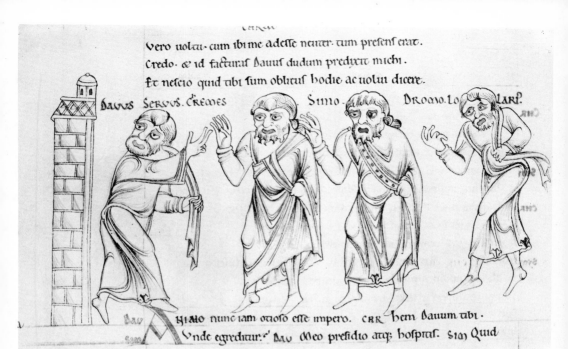

26 Scene from a Terence play as shown in a book probably
made at St Albans in the mid-twelfth century

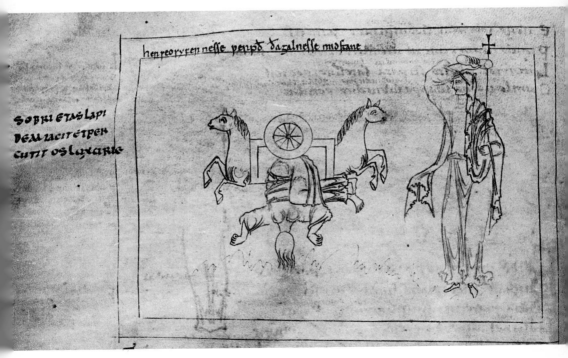

27 The defeat of Luxuria, from an early eleventh-century MS of Prudentius, *Psychomachia*

28 Siege of an allegorical castle, *La Fortresse de la Foy* (fifteenth century)

29 A medieval feast with performance of artificial siege,
and stage ship, from *Les Grandes Chroniques* (1375–80)

30 Death wounding Man with his dart, illustration to Act v
of *Liber Apologeticus*, by Thomas Chaundler (*c.* 1460)

auncyente and lawdable vsages and customes there hadd and vsed fur
above remembraunce.[1]

The letter seems to have exonerated Savage, but its attempt to find new
function and justification for a cycle that its banns falsely claimed to have
been written by the most famous monk of Chester Abbey, Ranulf Higden,
and first played in the mayoralty of Sir John Arneway, allegedly Chester's
first mayor, does not seem to have convinced the Council. Yet the affection
with which the cycle was held as an ancient custom of Chester is attested
in the lengthy account of productions by the antipapal archdeacon Robert
Rogers, and by the survival of eight manuscripts, including all five cycle
manuscripts, copied out by or for people of antiquarian taste between 1591
and 1607. Although finally its established function as the affirmation of
Catholic doctrine meant that cycle-drama also died, its death was more
protracted because of its civic functions, and can be seen as typifying not
only the power of Protestant mythology but also the growing centrality of
Tudor government against local communal autonomy.[2]

For long the study of medieval drama was dominated by an evolutionary
approach, and in discussing the significance of these plays for English drama
we are anxious to deny the validity of any such approach. The potentialities
of various dramatic forms were exhausted and other forms took their place.
But what replaced them was nevertheless dependent upon them. The drama
had proved itself as a vehicle for religious mythology, and was to remain
an important vehicle for religious polemic and propaganda in the sixteenth
century, albeit detached from its ritual links. It could be further readapted
to serve political and philosophical ends. As the play as offering to God
was suppressed, the play as offering to patron or king proliferated, such
offerings being common at court at the times of religious feasts. If the drama
of liturgy ended, music-drama at court of a non-liturgical kind continued
to be provided by the Children of the Royal Chapel or the Children of St
Paul's. A view of history looking to Christ the King yielded to a view of
national history looking to the King of England, the English chronicle-play;
the victories of Christian hero-saints and the deaths of martyr-saints are
replaced by the triumphs and tragedies of noble men.

Above all, the idea of drama as genre had been established and

---

[1] *REED, Chester*, 112–17.
[2] See, further, Harold C. Gardiner, *Mysteries' End: An Investigation of the Last Days of the Medieval Religious Stage* (Yale, 1946).

subsequent playwrights could turn to a common experience of drama which they shared with their audiences in a way which the early medieval dramatists could not. This genre no longer needs the justification of function, nor the allusions to non-dramatic ritual or ceremonial. The autonomy of the drama allows emotional response and aesthetic appreciation to be the primary purposes of a play, and with this development comes new status for the playwright as creator, the actor as mimetic artist, and the audience as responsive critics whose attention must be held.

III Early moral plays and the earliest secular drama

Marion Jones

1 Introduction

The initial and clear-cut division of the play-texts and fragments in English that survive from before 1500 is between the very large group of those intentionally and explicitly concerned with Christian observance and doctrine, and the very small group of those not so concerned. Though such a scant and random remnant of what is known once to have existed, the smaller group of texts represents so wide a diversity of traditions – folk, popular, courtly, academic – that only by relatively extended treatment of each can the whole be viewed in a true perspective. The larger group also contains only an accidentally assembled proportion of the body of material known to have existed; but what we have can be arranged and discussed with comparative assurance.

Within the framework of professedly Christian drama, four clusters of plays are easily recognizable: plays based on events of the Old or New Testaments, plays about the lives of saints, plays about miraculous happenings ascribed to Divine Providence, and plays expounding points of moral doctrine. Although the main types of play here set out can be much more copiously illustrated from the vernacular drama of continental Europe than from English material, all four are known to have been familiar in England. The term 'miracle' was traditionally used across the whole spectrum, and is retained in this wide sense by some modern scholars; but it is perhaps best reserved for that third type – now represented in English only by the fifteenth-century *Croxton Play of the Sacrament* – which is a dramatized account of miraculous happenings not recorded in the Bible, not performed by a saint, and not allegorical in treatment.[1]

Most of the surviving English plays belong to the first type, the biblical, and of these most form part of one or other of the great Creation to Doomsday cycles performed by guilds in large town. By too ready an association with such phrases as 'secrets of the Faith' and 'mysteries of the Christian religion', the terms 'mysteries' and 'mystery-cycles', which derive from the word 'mystery' for 'a trade or craft, French *métier*', have gained currency in a wider and vaguer sense, and the term 'guild-cycle' is also freely used. Because not all guilds were craft guilds, and because some guilds which were not craft guilds performed plays which were neither biblical nor parts of cycles (the York fraternity of *Oratio Domini*, for example, with its play setting forth the goodness of the Lord's Prayer),[2] the clearest usage is to avoid 'mystery' and 'guild-cycle' altogether, and to adopt the term 'craft-cycle' for the plays which showed God's scheme of salvation from Alpha to Omega and which were performed by trade guilds at York and elsewhere in England.

Not all the plays within the craft-cycles were, however, based on biblical narrative, whether because (like the plays of Judgement Day) they dealt with events still far in the future, or because (like the York play of the Blessed Virgin's appearance to St Thomas)[3] they made use of popular but apocryphal material. In particular, the plays of the surviving N-town cycle, which was not a craft-cycle, and the records of performances at Lincoln – two sides of the same coin? – show a heavy dependence on material which is not within the confines of the Vulgate canon. Since only the earliest Christians figure in the New Testament, the same is true of most plays on the lives of saints; but (not by chance, in all probability) the two saint-plays which survive in English, both in the sixteenth-century Digby manuscript, have a biblical narrative as their basis, and one of them – *The Conversion of St Paul* – keeps fairly close to its source.[4] The other, *Mary Magdalen*, is not preponderantly apocryphal, but significantly deserts the narrative

---

[1] *NCPF*, 55–89, lxx–lxxv.
[2] See Karl Young, 'The records of the York play of the Paternoster', *Speculum*, VII (1932), 540–6.
[3] York Weavers' Play, ed. L. Toulmin Smith [1885]; in *York Plays* (New York, 1963), 480–90.
[4] Baker, *Digby Plays*, 24–95.

tradition: its characters include the Seven Deadly Sins and the Four Daughters of God.[1]

This brief review of the first three overlapping but recognizable clusters of plays within the framework of professedly Christian drama has thus brought us to the edge of a gulf which separates them all from the fourth cluster, that of plays expounding points of moral doctrine – a gulf over which the author of *Mary Magdalen* and a few other writers chose to cast a bridge. It is apparent that the craft-cycles, the saint plays and the miracle plays have something important in common: they are based on chronicles of events. The fourth cluster has a different basis. Though comparatively little material survives in English, the tradition from the *Pride of Life* fragment through *The Castle of Perseverance* and *Mankind* to *Everyman* is clearly marked, and involves a quite distinct principle of organization: the allegorical.[2] Conformably with a well-established medieval fashion in preaching and literature, the morality plays use the method of *Piers Plowman* rather than that of *The Prioress's Tale*.

The difference between the biblical tradition in medieval drama and the morality tradition is the difference between commemorative reconstruction and hortatory exposition. In essence, both the Latin liturgical drama and the vernacular Creation to Doomsday cycles are commemorative reconstructions of events regarded as historical: so too, in essence, are plays on the lives of saints, and representations of miraculous happenings within space and time invoked by saints or interposed by Divine discretion. By contrast, the moral plays are designed to convey and comment upon a selection of doctrine, and to recommend certain patterns of choice and action to members of the audience. Precept, example and exhortation provide the organizing principles of each moral play in itself and of each incident within it. For this reason, though the happenings displayed in a moral play are fictitious, in the sense that they represent no historical event, the shaping impulse behind the fiction is not life-experience, nor yet creative imagination, but a sense of decorum based on a large body of pre-analysed doctrinal material already familiar to the audience in the same way as the biblical narratives, that is to say, through the instruction of churchmen.

It is worth noting at this point that neither within the tradition of dramatized narrative nor within the tradition of exemplary imperative was there much room for the two elements most characteristic of drama from

---

[1] See D. L. Jeffrey, 'English saints' plays', in *Medieval Drama*, Stratford-upon-Avon Studies, XVI (1973), 68–89.

[2] See Bernard Spivack, *Shakespeare and the Allegory of Evil* (New York and London, 1958).

the Renaissance to the present day – for the unexpected turn of events within the play, or for the deliberate manifesto through the play of the unique individual who created it. Medieval drama was remembrancing drama, and its substance could be only relatively unfamiliar: the rules of its game were accepted by all concerned, and a prime object with the makers of medieval plays was that they should be seen – by God and by the audience – in the very process of keeping the rules effectively. For this reason, the distinction between 'religious' and 'secular' drama in England before 1500 is (like the distinction between 'dramatic' and 'semi-dramatic' performances in this period) rather the product of modern modes of thought than a reflection of different attitudes and standards in the playmakers. The same men of education and aptitude used their talents from occasion to occasion for sundry purposes: now one method of presentation seemed to them appropriate, now another.

To see the matter in terms of 'playmakers' is itself misleading: the 'York Realist' and the 'Wakefield Master' did not themselves impress title or name on their contributions to the general endeavour, and the huge bulks of *The Castle of Perseverance* and the Cornish *Ordinalia* survive in copies which have room for stage plans and stage directions but none for indications of authorship.[1] It is true that the tendency to seek limited personal fame as the deviser of a costumed performance or a spectacle with verses for a particular (often a courtly) occasion is documented throughout the fifteenth century. John Lydgate, monk and courtier, used biblical, classical, moral and topical frameworks for occasional entertainments of which the texts survive alongside his more obviously professional under- takings like the pageant *Procession of Corpus Christi* and lengthy translation of the French Dance of Death verses.[2] At the end of the century, Henry Medwall, in his capacity of clerk to Cardinal Morton, devised both the allegorical morality *Nature* and the dramatized narrative with Renaissance moral, *Fulgens and Lucres*.[3] In the same tradition, as the sixteenth century dawned, John Skelton the married priest, tutor to the future Henry VIII, devised the topical morality play *Good Order* in the old vein and the great moral and political play of *Magnificence* in the new.[4] Neither Medwall,

---

[1] *The Castle of Perseverance*, ed. Mark Eccles in *Macro Plays*, EETS, CCLXII (1969); stage-plan from Macro MS f. 191ᵛ transcribed p. 1. See Plates 4 and 5.

[2] A good introduction to the range of Lydgate's work is Derek Pearsall, *John Lydgate* (London, 1970).

[3] *The Plays of Henry Medwall*, ed. A. H. Nelson (Cambridge and Totowa, N.J., 1980).

[4] *Magnificence*, ed. R. L. Ramsay, EETS, e.s. XCVIII (1906); *Good Order*, see Bibliography, p. 330.

however, nor Skelton (whose abundant personal vitality his poems elsewhere attest) sought to reveal in his plays any of the qualities which separated him as an individual from other men of Christian learning and common sense.

Magnificence, though essentially a lesson for a king, has universal applications. The words used by Skelton to describe this play are important: he calls it a 'processe brefly compylyd / Comprehendynge the worlde casuell and transytory' (2505–6) and 'A playne example of worldly vaynglory' (2509), adding: 'A myrrour incleryd [*shining*] is this inter-lude, / This lyfe inconstant for to beholde and se' (2519–20). This language, which harks back to the unctuous gloom of Chaucer's Monk and the *de casibus* tradition, has to be modified by Skelton to allow for the admixture of topical foolery and the happy ending: 'This treatyse, deuysd to make you dysporte, / Shewyth nowe adayes howe the worlde comberyd is' (2533–4), and finally 'This matter we haue mouyd, you myrthys to make, / Precely [*Expressly*] purposyd vnder pretence of play' (2547–8), go straight to the heart of Skelton's intention, to present his selection of wholesome doctrine in a suitably sugared pill.

The earliest surviving title-page of *Everyman*, from John Skot's edition (*c*.1528), describes this anonymous piece in much the same way: 'Here begynneth a treatyse...in maner of a morall playe.'[1] Though this prose description and the opening Messenger speech (with its 'By fygure a morall playe' and 'The story sayth...', 1–21; 3, 10) may be sixteenth-century writing, the Doctor's conclusion belongs to the early Dutch and English substance of *Elckerlijc/Everyman*,[2] and to the same tradition as that within which Skelton worked: 'This morall men may haue in mynde. / Ye herers, take it of worth, olde and yonge' (902–3). The combination of precept, example and exhortation is the hallmark of a moral play, whether ascribed or anonymous.

To understand how the unexpected event and the individual voice did at last find their place in English plays, it is necessary to turn back to the basic distinction between the biblical tradition and the morality tradition, and to remember how the useful concept 'commemorative reconstruction of events regarded as historical' breaks down even within the cycles: since Doomsday has not yet occurred, plays on the subject are not reconstructing any happening in space and time, so hortatory exposition of received

[1] Reproduced as frontispiece to *Everyman*, ed. A. C. Cawley (Manchester, 1961).
[2] See E. R. Tigg, *The Dutch Elckerlijc is Prior to the English Everyman* (London, 1981), esp. 12.

doctrine is *de rigueur*. The concept of audience familiarity with narrative must also be modified in respect of plays about miracles, or on the lives of saints, if these are based on non-biblical material. It can be shown from many instances in the English cycles that a rich vein of legendary and apocryphal material provided supportive details and sometimes whole narrative units to supplement and link biblical episodes,[1] and it seems fair to assume that whether or not such accretions were already familiar from vernacular preaching to the greater part of a given local audience, they would soon become so by repeated annual performance. In the same way the salient events in the lives of certain saints were supported by legend beyond the limits of biblical narrative: the figure of Mary Magdalen, for example, subsumed several distinct personages from the Gospel accounts of Christ's ministry, and was elaborated from legend.[2] Making every allowance for popular interest in hagiography and attested miracles, for local cults, and for the iteration of legend by topical preaching as the church calendar revolved, we must still conclude that when a clerical author attempted a saint-play or a miracle play he could not expect from his audience such a detailed familiarity with his material as he could if he attempted almost any subject, short of the Last Judgement, based on the biblical narrative of God's plan for Man's salvation.

From this conclusion two insights may be derived, which between them account for most of the developments in dramatic technique before the end of the fifteenth century in England. The first is that the quest for clarity of exposition common to writers of Doomsday plays, moral plays, and plays on relatively unfamiliar saints and miracles, led to the adoption of similar methods across this field, including the use of type-characters, of allegory as an organizing device, and of visual emblems and suggestions derived from other areas of medieval art and from secular presentations. The second is that the process above described continued separately from and independently of the biblical tradition, which offered the quite distinct problem of keeping the familiar – indeed the over-familiar – fresh and full of interest.

When medieval drama first became the subject of modern scholarship, it was too readily assumed that the great English craft-cycles had in fact

[1] For an example see Carolyn Wall, 'The apocryphal and historical background of *The Appearance of Our Lady to Thomas* (Play XLVI of the York Cycle)', *Mediaeval Studies*, XXXII (1970), 172–92.

[2] See Clifford Davidson, 'The Digby *Mary Magdalene* and the Magdalene cult of the Middle Ages', *Annuale Mediaevale*, XIII (1972), 70–87.

lost their vitality by the middle of the sixteenth century, and that the morality tradition was a healthy offshoot which somehow survived its parent. Both these assumptions have since been proved fallacious. It is now sufficiently attested that after Henry VIII's breach with Rome the extent to which the craft-cycles enshrined the old religion rendered them so suspect to Protestant governments that by the middle of Elizabeth's reign a determined onslaught of inhibitory legislation had taken full effect. That there was a sharp struggle at the last might indicate no more than the reluctance of civic authorities to lose a profitable festival institution, were it not for evidence, derived from close analysis of the surviving texts and performance records, that a good deal of re-arrangement and new writing of cycle-plays went on throughout the fifteenth century (in some towns well into the sixteenth), and that some of the new writing incorporated successful dramatic techniques from the non-biblical tradition. As late as 1565, for example, the Norwich Grocers provided a completely new text for their play of Adam and Eve, adding parts for two allegorical characters, Dolour and Misery, besides one of the rare speaking parts for the Holy Ghost.[1] On the question of priority in composition, moreover, the survey of extant manuscripts, in the light of many extended studies of linguistic and other dating evidence, has shown that the fragment of a morality play which we call *The Pride of Life* dates from before 1400, and that *The Castle of Perseverance* belongs to the first quarter of the fifteenth century.[2] Both plays are thus substantially earlier than much of the extant work within the cycles, a fact more telling in view of the 'Mors', 'Contemplacio' and Parliament of Heaven passages in the N-town cycle.[3]

What used to be the established view of this matter can be quoted from a scholar whose pioneer editions of many early plays endear his memory – F. J. Furnivall:

> In the progress of the drama, Moralities followd [*sic*] Mysteries, and were succeeded by Interludes. When folk tired of Religion on the Stage, they took to the inculcation of morality and prudence; and when this bored them, they set up Fun.[4]

Effectively as this is phrased, there is scarcely a grain of truth in it. The

[1] *NCPF*, 8–18, xxii–xl.

[2] *Pride of Life* in *NCPF*, 90–105, lxxxv–c: for *Castle of Perseverance* dating, see *Macro Plays*, ed. Eccles, x–xi.

[3] See pp. 279–80, 287.

[4] Intro. to *Digby Plays*, ed. F. J. Furnivall, EETS, e.s. LXX (1896), xiii.

moral plays grew up side by side with the biblical drama, and were equally devoted to the promotion of the Christian religion: the morality and doctrine they inculcated were central to that religion. Long moral plays with large casts were indeed succeeded by shorter moral plays with as many characters but smaller casts: the practice of doubling parts which made this possible belongs to the sphere of professional acting, and (as we shall see, p. 235) the term 'interludes' was regularly applied to such shorter pieces in the repertory of Tudor acting groups before the opening of the first London playhouse in 1576. Moral plays were thus succeeded by moral interludes; but interludes of anything but a moral nature had amused English audiences from at least the end of the thirteenth century, to which in a context both of 'Fun' and professional playing the extant minstrel-farce *Interludium de Clerico et Puella* belongs.[1]

On the right occasions a light-hearted alternative to religious drama seems always to have been available. Quite apart from collaborative group amusements like singing-games and dancing-games, as also from celebratory seasonal undertakings of a dramatic kind, like Plough Monday plays and May-games, there were entertainments by individuals and groups to while away the leisure of the rich man in his castle, and to brighten the infrequent off-duty hours of the poor man at his gate (see pp. 225 f., 232).

The sequence of reactions to drama which Furnivall suggests is also faulty. So far from tiring of the religious plays, Englishmen kept them going until Elizabeth I put them down, while new plays and interludes on controversial religious topics appeared against odds well into the sixteenth century. Far from being bored with the didactic weight of the morality tradition, English audiences went on expecting and accepting moral advice from their playwrights in the public theatres till long after the death of Elizabeth.

It will be useful briefly to review here the nine allegorical plays with English affiliations which can reasonably be assigned a performance date before 1500. Eight of these texts as we have them are in English, though the oldest, *The Pride of Life*, may have been composed (as its manuscript was certainly copied) in Ireland, and one of the latest, *Everyman*, seems to have been derived from a Dutch original. The remaining piece, dating from about 1460 and in Latin, is by Thomas Chaundler, an Oxford academic and divine whose career is on record.[2] Except for Chaundler and

---

[1] BL Add. MS 23986, ed. Bruce Dickens and R. M. Wilson, *Early Middle English Texts* (London, 1951), 132–5.

[2] *Liber Apologeticus de Omni Statu Humanae Naturae*, ed. D. Enright-Clark Shoukri (London and New York, 1974).

Henry Medwall, the lawyer in minor orders who wrote *Nature* towards the end of the fifteenth century, the authors of these texts are unknown.

There can be no doubt that besides being allegorical in treatment each of these plays is truly moral in the sense that a substantial body of its lines expounds moral doctrine. The two texts commonly regarded as our earliest in this field both contain elaborate passages of instruction. *The Pride of Life*, though incomplete, contains a whole sermon delivered by a bishop on the 'worse was it never' theme, beside other improving discourses.[1] *The Castle of Perseverance* crowns a series of moral harangues from Virtues with a protracted theological debate between the Four Daughters of God.[2]

The unique manuscript of *The Castle of Perseverance* belongs to the first quarter of the fifteenth century, and shows the morality tradition already in full flower, amply expressed in over thirty *dramatis personae* on the one hand and in an impressive range of staging techniques on the other. Its power to instruct is much greater than the impact of its explicit sermonizing, because there are within its 3649 lines several passages and incidents of enduring dramatic value.

The fragmentary play which was entitled by its first editor *The Pride of Life* survives only in partial facsimile and print. Its manuscript has, however, been reliably assigned to the dawn of the fifteenth century, and the play of which it contains the prologue and opening may well have been performed several decades earlier than *The Castle of Perseverance*. Luckily the whole action of the piece is outlined in its prologue (1–112). Though on a somewhat smaller scale than *The Castle of Perseverance*, because the fortunes of its protagonist are traced only from zenith to nadir, not from cradle to tomb, before he faces ultimate judgement, *The Pride of Life* seems to have required a similar version of the place-and-scaffold system of outdoor staging and, with its large cast and pivotal scene of battle, to demand comparable outlay on costumes and effects. This play has likewise a power to prompt serious reflection which has little to do with the earnest homilies of Regina and Episcopus.

From the middle of the century come two recently edited allegorical pieces, known from their provenance as the Winchester dialogues.[3] *Lucidus and Dubius* has little action and lacks a formal conclusion. *Occupation and*

---

[1] *NCPF*; sermon in *Pride of Life*, 327–90; parallels discussed lxxxvii ff.

[2] *Castle of Perseverance*, 1602–66, 3129–560.

[3] Winchester College MS 33; ed. Norman Davis in *Non-Cycle Plays and the Winchester Dialogues* (Leeds: University of Leeds School of English, Medieval Drama Facsimiles V, 1979), 135–78; transcript 179–208. See also B. S. Lee, 'Lucidus and Dubius: a fifteenth century theological debate and its sources', *Medium Aevum*, XLV (1976), 79–96.

Idleness has a greater range of style and very occasionally requires some stage business. Though both are saturated with sermon material, the sporadic attempts at colloquial interchange between their abstract characters make these two English pieces the forerunners of sixteenth-century didactic interludes.

Three allegorical plays of differing magnitude survive from the third quarter of the fifteenth century, two in English and one in Latin. The English pair are strongly contrasted, *Wisdom* tending to the sublime and *Mankind* to the ridiculous; but each contains long and serious exposition of moral doctrine and can appeal to an audience at more than one level, *Wisdom* (as described, pp. 251–8) offering pageantry and dance, *Mankind* knockabout farce and rowdy song.[1] Among the many and important differences between *Mankind* and the other moral plays of its century is that the action covers only a limited period in the life of the protagonist, presenting neither his immaturity nor his death and judgement. He is adult, conscious of weakness and anxious for counsel when we first meet him (186–216), suffers in the cross-fire between good and evil during the play, and is left sobered and well-intentioned to live out his days. This of course makes of him a figure closer to the experience of an audience, medieval or modern, than other types of central character whose articulateness is not in tune with their alleged physical condition – Humanum Genus in *The Castle of Perseverance* delivers himself of rounded stanzas while still a naked new-born babe (275 ff.), while Anima in *Wisdom* is presented as a girl of marriageable age who has never sinned in mind, will or understanding before the play opens (16 ff.), and Everyman continues to hold discourse with his own faculties even as they desert him. Whether it is this more homely aspect of Mankind or the black comedy of his tempters which has made modern revivals of *Mankind* successful, the play has in fact proved worth reviving.[2]

The Latin piece, Thomas Chaundler's *Liber Apologeticus de Omni Statu Humanum Naturae*, has more in common with *Wisdom* than with *Mankind*. It is solemn, learned and lengthy, without *Wisdom*'s admixture of topicality, and its action has the complete lifespan-and-beyond scope of *The Castle of Perseverance*, with the extra premise that Homo the protagonist is not born but created, Adam in all but husbandhood, during Act I. This ostentatiously literary piece (the initial letters of its stanzas are even arranged

[1] *Wisdom* in *Macro Plays*, ed. Eccles, 113–52; *Mankind*, 153–84.
[2] Notably at the University of Toronto in 1966, in Bristol by the Bristol Old Vic Theatre School in 1971, and by the Mediaeval Players on tour in 1981.

to form an acrostic) has four acts and announces them as such. It is the forerunner of many academic plays (in Latin, Greek or English) which smell too strongly of the lamp to tempt performance; yet it may well have been presented, at least as a rehearsed reading, by Chaundler's pupils at New College, Oxford.[1]

It is difficult to assign priority between *Everyman* and Medwall's *Nature*. Neither play survives in manuscript, and almost thirty years of the sixteenth century elapsed before either was printed in an edition destined to reach the hands of modern scholars as a complete text.

Everyman exists in four printed editions, all independent, two being mere fragments from the press of Richard Pynson, and two (slightly later but complete) bearing the imprint of John Skot.[2] It has been convincingly demonstrated that the same (lost) English manuscript was the grandfather of all the extant English editions: that whoever prepared the text of *Everyman* available in this lost ancestral manuscript translated it from the Dutch text of *Elckerlijc* offered by an Antwerp publisher, Willem Vorsterman, at a date between 1518 and 1525; and that Vorsterman's edition of *Elckerlijc* is the third Dutch edition with surviving copies, the earliest we possess having appeared at Delft in about 1495.[3] The conclusion that *Everyman* as we have it is junior to and derived from *Elckerlijc* is inescapable; but the question of English influence on the author of *Elckerlijc* will remain open until the full story of the Dutch play's source-material can be told.

Medwall is said on the title-page of *Nature*, in William Rastell's edition of about 1530, to have written it while chaplain to John Morton, Archbishop of Canterbury: the same allegation had been made about his *Fulgens and Lucres*, a secular play, when John Rastell had printed it some twenty years earlier. We know that Medwall was in Cardinal Morton's service, as legal secretary rather than chaplain, throughout the last decade of the fifteenth century, and that there was a link between him and the Rastells through Sir Thomas More which makes their testimony valuable.[4]

In type, however, *Everyman* is an intensely solemn play which recalls the earliest period of moral drama: it is wholly an effectively dramatized sermon, besides which Medwall's set passages of explicit moralizing

---

[1] *Liber Apologeticus*, Intro.; 24, 14–16.
[2] See *Everyman*, ed. Cawley, ix–x.
[3] See E. R. Tigg, (I) 'Is *Elckerlijc* prior to *Everyman*?', *JEGP*, 38 (1939), 568–96; (II) *The Dutch Elckerlijc is Prior to the English Everyman*.
[4] See Nelson (ed.), *The Plays of Henry Medwall*, 9–14, 17.

appear conventional and jaded. The essence of Medwall's *Nature* is the informed, high-spirited satire of his low-life vignettes, which point forward to Dame Quickly's tavern in Eastcheap.

These nine texts are the main source of our information about the morality tradition in England. There are in addition some allegorical personages and sections in religious plays of other kinds, and a number of moral interludes printed in the early sixteenth century which seem to be reworkings of older pieces.[1] Because the moral plays are part of a didactic crusade which made use of many media, light on their techniques and implications can frequently be obtained from homiletic literature and from the iconography of manuscript illuminations, church murals, stained glass and carvings.[2] For a true perspective on the morality tradition as a whole, however, and a preparation for the study of its employment to promote sectarian and political as well as ethical ends in English drama of the sixteenth century, it is essential to set the moral plays not only in the context of religious drama but in the context of their audience's experience of theatre and expectation from the playwright and his art.

---

[1] The sixteenth-century texts *Mundus et Infans*, *Hickscorner* and *Youth* are discussed below, pp. 258 ff.; for a complete survey of later work, see T. W. Craik, *The Tudor Interlude* (Leicester, 1958).

[2] See M. D. Anderson, *Drama and Imagery in English Medieval Churches* (Cambridge, 1963), also Clifford Davidson, *Drama and Art* (Kalamazoo, Mich., 1977).

2 The earliest secular drama: mirth and solace

The recreational uses of drama were well known to the ancient world. Besides the dramatic forms which are enshrined in surviving literature – the high festival tragedy and comedy of Athens, the urbane holiday comedy of Rome – there existed in classical times a wide range of entertainments which left no literary records but are known to have been based on various combinations of the performance arts. From Sicily and southern Italy in particular comes the evidence that hours of leisure were frequently beguiled by persons whose function was to exhibit their skills in music-making, song and recitation, dance, acrobatics and imitation of life and manners. It is of course this last branch of entertainment which required the techniques we recognize as those of the actor – mime, impersonation, speech and movement in costume – and it is in this context that early vase paintings attest collaborative groups of performers engaged in what may fairly be termed 'putting on a show'.[1] Such performances may well have used improvised dialogue, along a pre-arranged story-line, rather than a set script: we know from the tradition of *commedia dell'arte* playing in Renaissance Europe that very elaborate and satisfactory entertainment can

[1] Margarete Bieber, *The History of the Greek and Roman Theater* (Princeton, N.J. [1939], 2nd edn, rev. 1961; London, 1961), 129–46.

be achieved in this way.[1] As far as the subject matter of such shows is known to us, it appears to lie in the territory later occupied by the dramatic forms farce and burlesque, though it is worth remembering that vestiges of religious belief and ritual often shape theatrical conventions, as we shall see in the medieval period. The vase paintings also show a distinctive style of costume for the players and a neat platform stage backed by curtains which bears an uncanny resemblance to the booth stages of street and fairground to be seen in illustrations of travelling players from sixteenth-century Europe.[2] Into the arguments which link the stagecraft of professional players from the pre-Christian era with traditions of popular entertainment in the Middle Ages and Renaissance there is no need to enter here: since what has been once devised to answer a given purpose may be independently devised again in similar circumstances, it will suffice to analyse the terms of demand and response, and to see how far the pattern seems to have been repeated.

What was wanted from the drama of entertainment in the centuries preceding the birth of Christ? There seem to be three requirements: that it should be available when leisure served its patrons; that its mood should be relaxed; and that it should be more or less unedifying. Those who rose to the need were professionals with developed skills, willing to disguise their everyday selves in special array and to work in teams to secure their effects.

The drama of entertainment becomes institutionalized if the use of leisure becomes a public concern and if those in authority begin to extend patronage as officials rather than individuals.[3] Most of the enjoyable types of show had found their way to Rome by the time of Caesar Augustus, and new permanent theatres had been built for *ludi scenici*, though itinerant groups still raised their platform stages for scattered audiences outside the great cities of the Empire and for private patrons at request.[4] Standard tragedy and comedy were not the staple repertory even at the theatres, and the touring companies offered even more unedifying material than their forebears. Serious writers kept clear of the stage, though some poets of standing provided texts for the fashionable development of dumb-show

[1] Allardyce Nicoll, *Masks, Mimes and Miracles* (London, 1931), stresses the affinities between Atellan farce and the *commedia dell'arte* tradition: see esp. 214–33.

[2] See Richard Southern, *The Seven Ages of the Theatre* (London [1962], 1968), 159–62, and Plate IV, of Pieter Balten's Dutch fair scene, *c.*1550, in the Rijksmuseum, Amsterdam. Booth stages are also shown in Plates 6 and 7 of *The Revels History of Drama in English*, Vol. II.

[3] For the *tribuni voluptatum*, see Chambers, II, 229–30.

[4] Chambers, I, 4, 7; Bieber, op. cit., 227–53, reviews all the evidence about plays of the Roman Empire.

dance to a choral accompaniment which was known as pantomime.[1] The *pantomimus* was a solo performer who acted and danced his way through the story with which the choir's song was concerned: without speaking a word, but helped by a selection of masks, he took all the parts in turn and interpreted them by gesture and movement. The Latin phrase expressing 'to present the tales' is *saltare fabulas*, and the *fabulae salticae* were mainly on indecent mythological subjects.[2] It is to the *pantomimi*, who included men of great personal fame, that the term *histriones* began to attach itself in particular: *histrio* was the Etruscan for 'actor', and is used in a wide sense by Tacitus to include performers of Atellan farce and the variety artistes known as mimes.[3] It is useful to note here that *ludius* is the regular Latin word for 'actor': *actor* is indeed a Latin term, but used alone means the leader of a company, otherwise *dominus gregis*.[4] The word *mimus* applies to the comedian and to his show: since there were women among the mimes, *mimae* was used to designate them. The general word for 'performers' was *scenici*: among their ranks were also the *rhapsodes*, who gave straight performances of chants from tragedies, the *scurrae* and *sanniones*, who were jokers and buffoons, and the jugglers, rope-walkers, tumblers and weight-lifters whose 'acts' amused the public in variety shows which seem to have their parallels in every age.[5] We meet many of these entertainers, and the terms which identified them, in the records kept in Latin by those responsible for expenditure on revels during the medieval period.

Though certain Roman actors were idolized by several classes of society, the graver thinkers and the law-givers of Rome were hostile to the profession as a whole, even before the rise of Christianity brought ardent opponents into league against it. Good sense and good feeling were alike insulted by some of the words and actions permitted in stage shows as a matter of course, while some of the excesses of blood and sex when *spectacula* lost their fictitious element were an outrage to public decency.[6]

---

[1] Chambers, I, 6.

[2] Nero himself impersonated Canace in labour, with recitation: Suetonius apparently considered this theme tragic (*Life of Nero*, cap. xxi). Lucian remarked that the themes of tragedy and pantomime were alike; but Leda, Europa and Danaë were all subjects for pantomime. See Nicoll, *Masks, Mimes and Miracles*, 131–4.

[3] Tacitus, *Annales*, I, lxxvii; IV, xiv.

[4] Chambers, I, 6, n. 3.

[5] J. D. A. Ogilvy, '*Mimi, scurrae, histriones*; entertainers of the early Middle Ages', *Speculum*, XXXVIII (1967), 608–19.

[6] Chambers, I, 4–5; for the excesses of Heliogabalus, see Nicoll, *Masks, Mimes and Miracles*, 134. See also T. Frank, 'The status of actors at Rome', *Classical Philology*, XXVI (1931), 11–20. Plates 25 and 26 give medieval artists' impressions of Roman actors.

To a general moral repugnance, however, Christians added a metaphysical objection: acting is a kind of lie, because the actor who escapes from his everyday self into disguise and fiction is shirking his personal responsibility to live entirely in and for the Way, the Truth, and the Life. Such deep-rooted antipathy naturally expressed itself in ordinances against commerce between Christians and actors, at first from within the early Church and binding only on Church members, but increasingly finding a counterpart in civil legislation.[1] After AD 378, when Christianity became the official religion of the State, the stringency of Church regulations against actors kept pace with a progressive curtailment of their rights by imperial edict from both Constantinople and Ravenna; but a fury of pulpit denunciation of the disobedient suggests that there had been no change of heart in the public at large.[2]

Certainly it was neither Church nor State which finally closed the theatres. War, the enemy of leisure, and financial crisis, the fruit of defeat, brought ruin to one great city after another during the fifth century. The barbarians whose ravages brought the institutionalization of Roman actors to an end were not themselves partial to drama. Though the Ostrogoth king Theodoric found it politic to retain the *spectacula* in Rome when he was responsible for its government in the early sixth century, and though he gave orders for the theatre which Pompey had erected in 55 BC to be repaired, he seems to have taken a disparaging tone towards the *histriones*, in whose ranks he included the *aurigae* who raced chariots in the arena.[3] The last reference to *spectacula* at Rome is in AD 533:[4] by the end of the sixth century there was not a theatre in Europe. It would, however, be rash to suppose that there were no actors.

Purpose-built theatres and official subsidies are no more essential to the actor than concrete terraces and fixed feeding-times to the penguin; the creature in its native element accepts different standards of security and comfort. Though after the collapse of Roman civilization the literary drama of the ancient world rested on its laurels until Renaissance scholarship put classical theatre-architecture back on the map, the heterogeneous class of entertainers went on being available to patrons with leisure, whether the rich at marriage feasts or the poor in market squares. We have no means of numbering the entertainers in Christendom during the seventh and eighth centuries; but that they existed, and that among them were people

[1] Chambers, I, 8–9, 12–13.
  Chambers, I, 13–19.
[3] Chambers, I, 20.
[4] Chambers, I, 21.

whose skills drew them the old labels for actors, can be established from the hostile references and prohibitions recorded by churchmen who wished to limit their activities.[1]

The old term *ludus* had meant 'game' or 'sport' in so wide a sense that it had needed qualification before it indicated gladiatorial combats, athletic exhibitions or stage plays. *Ludus* went forward into the vocabulary of the Middle Ages with a wide significance across a range of recreations: with it in much the same contexts was used another Latin term, *iocus*, and its associates. From *iocus* the modern English 'joke' is derived, and we have 'jocular' from its adjective *jocularis* as well as 'jocose' from *jocosus*. The original sense of 'a verbal jest' shaded into 'a mirthful ploy' and the *ioculator* who began as a quipster or dealer in pleasantries soon became a general merrymaker. *Iocus* itself moved into the romance vernaculars of Europe to take over the wide senses of *ludus*. The Italian *giuoco*, the Spanish *juego* and the Catalan *joch* are used for 'game' and 'sport' over a range of activities: the French *jeu*, and the verb *jouer*, often need 'play' somewhere in their translation into English. It is the French version of *ioculator*, 'merrymaker', that most requires attention: *jougleur* was a term with a wide meaning, much wider than that of modern English 'juggler'. The safest rendering of *ioculator* and *jougleur* is 'entertainer', though the word which most often conveys the required sense in the fourteenth century and beyond is 'minstrel', a household entertainer who may or may not be musical.[2]

English clergy were admonished by the Council of Rome in AD 679 that the practice of maintaining musicians and that of countenancing *iocos vel ludos* should be discontinued.[3] The latter phrase seems to mean something more specific than 'fun and games': 'acts' of revelry and 'pieces' of play are suggested, and a 'performance' with the clergy as audience is envisaged by the stricture. Over two centuries later, the same King Edgar who set St Ethelwold to rationalize the observances of the diocese of Winchester, and thus became responsible for our earliest sighting of Easter drama in England, gave his views on the degeneracy of English monks in terms which afford us a glimpse of secular performance.[4] So notoriously immoral was monastic life, he declared, that *mimi cantant et saltant in triviis* on the theme. At mimicry and pantomimic dance-action (note the old Latin term *saltare*) people at street-corners could laugh whatever their native tongue. But *cantant* implies a text, and in England more than a hundred years before

---

[1] Chambers, I, 35–6.
[2] Chambers, II, 230–3.
[3] Ogilvy, op. cit., 607.
[4] Ogilvy, op. cit., 614.

the Norman Conquest, an Old English text. We must not press this inference too closely, however, as the skit may have used or parodied snatches from liturgical chant, so that Latin, dog-Latin or nonsense-patter composed the song-text. The *mimi* may have improvised afresh for each performance, and in any case need never have made or carried about any written records of what they played. But the secular drama in England has its foot in the door.

One point to be kept in mind when considering the origin of secular drama in England is that the earliest court entertainers after the Conquest used French as a medium: there is a certain amount of evidence towards establishing a date for habitual use of English at public gatherings. The earliest piece of an English play to survive has come to rest in Cambridge University Library and is known as the Cambridge Prologue.[1] Twenty-two lines of French followed by twenty-two lines of English in a hand of not later than 1300 are squeezed as far as possible to the left on an odd leaf which was originally the last of its manuscript and from which a corner has already been cut away – presumably the intention was to cut off the Prologue strip and use it as an actor's 'part' (such as the 'Dux Moraud' fragment discussed on pp. 289 f.). The double text remains, however, containing French and English to the same general effect – the request for silence and attention made by the herald of a pagan emperor to the company gathered to witness what the English version calls a 'game' (8). The interesting thing is that though both versions threaten punishments for defiant members of the audience, and both heralds swear by 'Mahun' (Mahomet), like many a Herod and Pilate after them, the two admonitions appear to have been separately composed, with different details: neither is a literal translation of the other.

Another scrap of parchment from the early fourteenth century, known as the Rickinghall Fragment because there are some Latin accounts of that Suffolk manor on the back, shows the same phenomenon:[2] a boastful king summons the nobility into his presence in two stanzas of French, which are followed by nine lines of English to the same effect, picking up two rhyme-words but omitting to translate about half the first stanza. After the direction *Tunc dicet nuncio*, the French speech proceeds for three lines and breaks off.

Probably neither of these plays was secular in content; but together these fragments establish that two kinds of audience had to be provided for. A

---

[1] *NCPF*, 114–15, cxi–cxiv.
[2] *NCPF*, 116–17, cxiv–cxv.

mixed audience would get both French and English, or a select text could
be given in either language as required. How long this transitional period
lasted is suggested by a Yorkshire lawyer, William Nassington, when he
translated a Latin work into English in about 1375:

> Some cane franche and na latyn,
>> that used has court, and dwelled therin.
> And some cane of latyn a party
>> that cane franch but feberly.
> And some undirstandye ynglych
>> that nouther can latyn ne franche.
> Bot lerede and lewed, alde and yonge,
>> all undirstandys ynglych tonge.[1]

Though it was necessary for a courtier to command the French tongue
until well into the fifteenth century, the status of English at court was
confirmed by the eminently satisfactory example of Geoffrey Chaucer's
poems. That Chaucer took the pains to translate *Le Roman de la Rose* is
an indication that some of his public were prepared to enjoy a French classic
at second hand; but the exquisite workmanship of his own verse composition
left no doubt that English was a vernacular capable of serving a writer of
the first magnitude in the Renaissance mode. Chaucer was, however, a
luminary without peer, and without successor before the sixteenth century.
A more representative man of letters, John Gower, carefully hedged his
bids for fame by providing three major works, one in French, one in Latin
and one in English: his effigy still rests his head on them in Southwark
Cathedral.[2] None of them was a play: to write a secular play was not yet
appropriate to an aspiring poet in England. It is ironic that a kind of play
which might have tempted Chaucer in his less courtly moments was already
established in France before his death: in 1398 the Provost of Paris issued
an edict to prohibit the performance of 'jeux de personnages par manière
de farces, de vie de sains, ne autrement' in Paris or its environs without
special warrant.[3] The tradition of French farce was not checked by this
measure, but took till 1465 or so to produce its finest medieval example,
Maître Pierre Pathelin.[4] If it had been Chaucer's duty to prepare 'jeux de

---

[1] In his translation of John Waldby's *Speculum Vitae*, preserved in BL MS Royal 17 c
viii, f. 3: see Janet Coleman, *English Literature in History, Medieval Readers and Writers*
(London, 1981), 173–4.
[2] See John H. Fisher, *John Gower* (London, 1965), 37–9, for an account of tomb and effigy.
[3] See Grace Frank, *The Medieval French Drama* (Oxford, 1954), 245.
[4] ibid., 253–9.

personnages par manière de farces' for Richard II, some of the rowdier of the Canterbury tales might never have been written, but England would not have had to wait for John Heywood to turn *fabliaux* into literary drama for court entertainment.[1]

Farcical dialogue without literary pretension and *fabliau*-type narrative arranged for solo performance were, however, staples of entertainment in the repertory of minstrels long before Chaucer was born, and (by an accident the more remarkable because in the nature of things such skits were jealously guarded against would-be copyists) one example of each kind survives in English from the end of the thirteenth century. The Latin title of the first, *Interludium de Clerico et Puella*, suggests that the piece was either composed or copied by a rootless scholar, 'clerc fayllard', like its hero, who is rejected by the Girl, Malkyn, and resorts to a procuress – whose name of Eloise suggests that an Anglo-Norman source is not far behind.[2] Though only two scenes remain, the display of unctuous piety by Mome Helwis when first approached links her with a long folk tradition of hypocritical old witches whose best-known literary embodiment, the monstrous Spanish bawd La Celestina, rears her ugly head again in one of the earliest secular interludes to be published in England, *Calisto and Melebea* (*c*.1525).[3]

It has generally been assumed that Mome Helwis is also a sister-ship to Dame Sirith in the solo performer's narrative, which is the only Middle English *fabliau* (outside of Chaucer's work) to survive. The plot of *Dame Sirith* concerns the trick by which yet another reluctant girl, Margeri, is persuaded to accept the advances of clerk Wilekin. The bawd's ploy – and perhaps that of Mome Helwis – is to feed pepper and mustard to a pet dog until tears run out of its eyes, and then to terrify her victim by alleging that the animal is really a girl punished by witchcraft for offending the clerk.[4] This unedifying folk-motif of course provided an opening for the talents of the minstrel's own pet when such pieces were performed. This feature, the use of English so early, and the indecency of the text, all suggest a popular rather than a courtly audience: so does the concluding offer to act as bawd for anyone present if remuneration is adequate (no doubt the collecting bowl went round at that point).[5]

[1] T. W. Craik, 'The true source of John Heywood's "*Johan Johan*"', *MLR*, XLV (1950), 289–95.

[2] See Dickens and Wilson, *Early Middle English Texts*, 132; this text is also edited by J. A. W. Bennett and G. V. Smithers, *Early Middle English Verse and Prose* (Oxford, 2nd edn, 1968), 196–200.

[3] See *Three Rastell Plays*, ed. Richard Axton (Cambridge and Totowa, N.J., 1979), 15–16.

[4] See J. A. W. Bennett and G. V. Smithers, ed. cit., 77–95.

[5] See Richard Axton, *European Drama of the Early Middle Ages* (London, 1974), 19–23.

Though we cannot prove that popular skits with the 'weeping bitch' motif went on being performed during the fourteenth and fifteenth centuries, one odd piece of evidence suggests that they did. It is that whoever quarried the interlude *Calisto and Melebea* out of the celebrated Spanish novel-in-dialogue (which once bore that title) associated the bawd Celestina so strongly with a whimpering bitch that he introduced the animal as an image of the bawd in a warning dream related by Melebea's father – and this although no such passage occurred in the text he was translating, which in any case he intended to alter so radically that the heroine's repentance came in time to forestall her loss of virginity.[1]

It is worth noting in this connection that the unedifying outcome of the action in *Dame Sirith* was as characteristic of popular minstrelsy as the godly conclusion of *Calisto and Melebea* in its humanist English dress is characteristic of early sixteenth-century secular interlude. John Rastell, who certainly published and perhaps adapted *Calisto and Melebea* as 'A new commodye in Englysh in maner of an enterlude', was Thomas More's brother-in-law and dedicated to the inculcation of high principles and sound learning.[2] The plays he wrote and published were part of this humanist programme, but their earnestness is matched by that of the great majority of the three dozen or so English interludes which survive from the first half of the sixteenth century.[3] Only John Heywood's court *divertissements* of the decade after 1520 and the academic comedy *Thersites* of 1537 (a Latin school-dialogue adapted, possibly by Nicholas Udall)[4] point forward to a drama as truly secular in theme and treatment as the light-hearted work of the thirteenth-century minstrels had been.

In order to interpret the scanty evidence about secular drama between the thirteenth century and the humanist period, it is essential to consider the prejudice against professional players and the very limited toleration for amateur theatricals which were freely expressed by prominent members of the clergy on numerous occasions. Such pronouncements as that by Hugh de Wells at Lincoln against *ludi seu Placita Secularia* in 1230,[5] by Walter de Chanteloup, Bishop of Worcester, against the *ludus de Rege et Regine* in 1240,[6] or of Robert Grosseteste at Lincoln against miracles, May-games

[1] *Three Rastell Plays*, ed. Axton; *Calisto and Melebea*, 950–68. See also Axton's Introduction, p. 17.
[2] ibid., 4–10.
[3] See Craik, *The Tudor Interlude*.
[4] Marie Axton (ed.), *Three Tudor Classical Interludes* (Cambridge and Totowa, N.J., 1982).
[5] See R. S. Loomis, 'Lincoln as a dramatic centre', in *Mélanges d'histoire du théâtre du Moyen-Age et de la Renaissance offerts à Gustave Cohen* (Paris, 1950), 241–7
[6] Chambers, I, 91–2.

and mell-suppers[1] in 1244, are principally intended to restrain the
involvement of clerical actors in folk, or degraded 'religious', pieces; but
a new note was struck in 1250, when the University of Oxford was obliged
to forbid its scholars to wander about in masked and garlanded bands,
creating a disturbance in churches and public places of the city.[2] Here we
are confronting the phenomenon later known as 'revels', where people of
education conspire to take up theatrical trappings for their own amusement
and relaxation, always on an agreed occasion and for a pre-arranged period.
Another example of this, which vexed the Bishop of Exeter in 1348, was
the infamous doings of a sect of malign men who called themselves the
Order of 'Brothelyngham' and went round the streets dressed as monks,
blowing horns, and forcibly abducting passers-by for ransom.[3] We would
call this a 'rag' of an unpleasant nature: the members of the group – on
a par with such *sociétés joyeuses* as the Cornards of Rouen under their Abbé
in fifteenth-century France[4] – called it a *ludus*. What Bishop Grandisson
called it is best left beneath the veil of Latin. All this is essentially amateur
activity, and while it may attach itself to festive occasions like May Day
or Twelfth Night and provide a context for rehearsed entertainment by
professional players, it is in itself a form of merry-making rather than
secular drama.

When we come to the ecclesiastical view of professional entertainers,
however, we find that the range of minstrelsy was wide, and that only a
part of it lay within the confines of dramatic art. Thomas de Cabham, who
died in 1313, gave an account of minstrels in the *Penitential* he wrote when
he was sub-dean of Salisbury.[5] He calls them *histriones*, but divides them
into three groups according to pursuits well beyond acting. The first two
groups, both sure to be damned, are those who disfigure themselves with
indecent clothing, horrible masks and wanton movements, and those who
hang about at court making topical fun and currying favour by blackguarding
absentees. The words that come to mind as we survey these pursuits are
fools, tumblers, buffoons and jesters rather than players: and the third
group, who make use of musical instruments, seem to be solo performers
considered collectively, not members of acting companies. Some of these
are also damnable – those who sing suggestive songs (such as *Dame Sirith?*)

---

[1] Loomis, op. cit., 241–7.
[2] Chambers, I, 92.
[3] Chambers, I, 383, n. 2.
[4] Chambers, I, 375 ff.
[5] Chambers, I, 59; II, 262–3.

at wine-bibbings: in fact the only minstrels in heaven will be those who sing about the noble deeds of princes and the lives of saints, and these deserve to be known as *ioculatores*.

The musical instruments proper to Cabham's last group deter us from recognizing either the damnable vocalists or the elect bards as actors. It is useful to remember, however, that the origin of the term 'minstrel' is a medieval diminutive – *ministrallis* – of the classical Latin *minister*, a household attendant. The group of servants within a great household whose duty it was to entertain its master came in the course of the Middle Ages to have the term reserved for them, however various their talents. Glancing over the many surviving accounts of payment to the minstrels of royal, noble and even ecclesiastical households, we readily form two conclusions: first, that a lot of money regularly went their way: secondly, that their services were required indoors and at seasons of festivity, in particular during the twelve days of Christmas.[1]

The next clue to guide us through the scattered records is the word 'interludium', which we met in the title of *Interludium de Clerico et Puella*. Though of disputed origin, and by no means limited in its earlier usage to secular pieces (as E. K. Chambers pointed out long ago, it 'appears to be equally applicable to every kind of drama known to the Middle Ages'),[2] it became the standard term for plays of whatever nature performed indoors at the feasts of rich households. In about 1360 the author of *Sir Gawain and the Green Knight* associated Christmas festivities with 'layking of enterludez' (472). During the twelve days of Christmas in 1427, Henry VI was amused by two groups of players: 'Jakke Travail et ses compaignons' received four pounds for 'diverses jeuues et entreludes', and 'autres jeweis de Abyndon feisantz autres entreludes' got twenty shillings.[3] As we shall see when we consider the court entertainments of John Lydgate, not all the pieces devoted to brightening royal Christmases were called interludes. In 1463, however, a very revealing exception to an Act of Apparel concerned not only minstrels but 'players in their interludes'.[4] This linking of terms was repeated when the Act of Apparel was continued at three separate dates in the reign of Henry VIII, and became a commonplace. Both terms referred to specialist entertainers who were by choice under the protection of various great men, wore a livery, and if playing away from

[1] Chambers, II, 231–3; I, 46–53.
[2] Chambers, II, 182.
[3] Chambers, II, 256–7.
[4] Chambers, II, 186, n. 3.

home carried some form of licence.[1] In 1572, at the point when Elizabeth I's government was suppressing the religious drama but no public playhouse had yet opened in London (James Burbage built The Theatre in 1576 for a wholly secular repertory), a statute directed against vagrancy throws the history of professional playing into perspective: persons to be whipped as rogues, vagabonds and sturdy beggars include 'all Fencers Bearewardes Comon Players in Enterludes & Minstrels, not belonging to any Baron of this Realme or towards any other honourable personage of greater Degree; all Juglers Pedlars Tynkers and Petye Chapmen; whiche said Fencers Bearewardes comon Players in Enterludes Mynstrels Juglers Pedlars Tynkers & Petye Chapmen shall wander abroade and have not Lycense of two Justices of the Peace at the leaste'.[2]

Looking back from this vantage-point at the reign of Edward IV, we see not only the linking of minstrels with interlude players, but an important step towards the creation of the two classes of entertainers envisaged by Elizabeth's statute: the protected and the whippable. In 1469 Edward IV granted a charter to his own household minstrels which in the first place incorporated them under their own elected marshal and in the second place put them at the head of a fraternity or guild of minstrels to which a couple of existing groups already belonged, and which all other minstrels in the country (except those of Chester, protected by the Dutton family) were to join or be suppressed.[3] Edward's motive for this legislation, as stated in the preamble, was that certain 'rudes Agricolae et Artifices' had been setting up as minstrels and raking in profits under false colours, to the decay both of minstrelsy and husbandry and the injury of his own royal servants. Henceforward, it would appear, Bottom the Weaver was in peril.

Seldom do the accounts in Latin, French or English of payments to minstrels or interlude players give any hint of the nature of their entertainment. An exception is *ly Cape mayntenawnce*, for which Magdalen College, Oxford, paid nine pence in 1486-7.[4] This title suggests a topical satire, but to judge by the way the abuse of maintenance had been handled in the moral play of *Wisdom* some twenty years earlier (see pp. 251 f.), the piece may have been allegorical. Unmistakably direct and personal satire against the leather-dressers of Exeter in the shape of a 'noxious and blameworthy play, or rather buffoonery' had provoked Bishop Grandisson

[1] Chambers, II, 186-9; I, 54-5.
[2] Chambers, I, 54, n. 4.
[3] Chambers, I, 55; II, 259-61.
[4] Chambers, II, 248.

in 1352, but this may have been a recrudescence of the Brothelyngham
trouble (see p. 234) rather than a professional performance.[1] A hint that
the vast resources of verse romance, always dear to minstrels, were not left
untapped by players is given by a record of *Eglemour and Degrebelle* at St
Albans and *A Knight cleped Florence* at Bermondsey in 1444.[2]

From about 1475 dates a manuscript fragment of forty-two lines from
a play about Robin Hood:[3] because it is associated with the Pastons of
Norfolk, and Sir John Paston referred in a letter of 1473 to a servant whom
he had kept 'thys iij yer to pleye Seynt Jorge and Robyn Hod and the Shryff
of notyngham', the inference is often drawn that Sir John was the patron
of players to whom this copy once belonged. The servant in question,
however, one Woode, was employed in the Paston stables, and the life of
the household was disrupted by a local feud in a manner which makes
hall-plays unlikely during the three years of his service. The linking of St
George and Robin Hood in Paston's reference suggests folk-plays in due
season: probably Woode had indeed taken the lead in these, and
retrospectively his master was angry enough to say that this was all he had
done for his keep.[4]

Given the dearth of direct evidence about the subjects of secular drama
during the fifteenth century, it is helpful to go about the enquiry in another
way, by looking at what was acceptable to the great patrons and their guests
in hall, so far as that may be judged from the surviving compositions used
for this purpose. Most of these are by John Lydgate, a monk of (but
infrequently at) Bury St Edmunds. Lydgate's literary output was immense
and varied: the small portion of it which was presented, rather than read
aloud or circulated in manuscript, is of great interest. The texts he devised
for the entertainment of various companies of nobles on festival days belong
to the years 1427 to 1435, and our knowledge of the way in which they
were presented comes from two sources, internal evidence for one and the
editorial matter of a prominent London scribe called John Shirley for the
other.[5]

Shirley was a contemporary of Lydgate, and a substantial businessman;
we have no means of knowing whether the long titles he gives to Lydgate's
texts contain any part of Lydgate's own titles in the manuscripts copied,

[1] Chambers, II, 190, n. 4.
[2] Chambers, *English Literature at the Close of the Middle Ages* (Oxford, 1945), 65.
[3] N. Davis (ed.), *Non-Cycle Plays and the Winchester Dialogues* (Leeds: University of
Leeds School of English, Medieval Fascimiles V, 1979), 75–8.
[4] ibid., 75–6.
[5] See Derek Pearsall, *John Lydgate* (London, 1970), 73–5.

and very few means of checking the enormously circumstantial detail about the provenance of each work. Shirley certainly does his best to give the impression that he was deep in the poet's confidence. A study of his titles, however, reveals that he does not really know what to call the seven texts which later editors have decided to class as 'mummings'. He tries a different description each time: 'a balade'; 'a balade...for a momyng'; 'þe maner of a bille by wey of supplicacion putte to þe kyng...as in a disguysing...devysed by Lydegate'; 'þe deuyse of a desguysing'; 'þe devyse of a momyng'; 'a lettre made in wyse of balade...brought by a poursuyaunt in wyse of mommers desguysed'; and, most cumbrous of all, 'a lettre made in wyse of balade...of a mommynge whiche þe goldesmythes of þe Cite of London mommed in right fresshe and costele welych desguysing to þeyre Mayre Eestfeld'.[1]

There is some excuse for Shirley. Disguisings and mummings were both varieties of merrymaking under the general heading of revels, involving dressing-up, particularly in masks. Christmas at the English court throughout the fourteenth century saw expenditure by the Wardrobe on sets of costumes and visors – animal heads, linen coifs for twenty-one counterfeit lawyers[2] – to be worn by courtiers in something very like a fancy-dress ball with a prescribed theme. Dancing in masquerade is of course the activity from which the elaborate masques of later periods derived, but there is no record of texts associated with the make-believe element in such revelling.

Mummings, which (as the very name suggests) were dumbshows at least in origin, were by the fifteenth century associated with going about the streets and visiting houses to challenge their masters to games of dice. Obviously folk custom has been assimilated here, but we learn from a fragment of English chronicle once owned by Stowe that in 1377 a great company of the citizens of London took this way of making a presentation to Prince Richard, three months before he ascended the throne as Richard II.[3] Disguised as emperor, pope, cardinals, devilish legates, knights and squires, the mummers arrived on horseback in a long torchlit procession, entered the royal hall on foot, and in dumbshow invited the prince and other notables to a game with loaded dice. When the royal party had won all the rich stakes provided, the mummers accepted refreshments, and then ordered the musicians who had accompanied the procession to strike up

---

[1] *The Minor Poems of John Lydgate*, ed. H. N. MacCracken, EETS, CXCII (1934) [*Part II*], 668; 672; 675; 682; 695; 698.
[2] Chambers, I, 392–3.
[3] Chambers, I, 394–5.

for a dance: the prince and his lords danced on one side and the mummers on the other. Several other mummings of this general type – complimentary games in costume for grandees – are recorded before the seven efforts by Lydgate which gave Shirley as editor so much trouble to classify. The feature which Lydgate's seven have in common is the awkward one: each has a substantial set of verses to accompany the actions of the mummers.

Lydgate's devices (to adopt the most neutral term) are thus of key importance in the transitional period of court presentations, and lie both in manner and matter somewhere between dumbshow with recited commentary and impersonation with dialogue. Each piece was made to measure for its occasion, and one – the *Mumming at Hertford* – has a true dramatic effect. These pieces are, however, neither plays nor interludes, and while we must look at them carefully for the clues they afford to their patrons' taste, it is well to bear in mind that both plays and interludes did already exist and were felt to be of a distinct kind. A proclamation of 1418 seems to envisage all the types of costumed entertainment as taking to the streets in the Christmas season, since it provides that 'no manere persone, of what astate, degre, or condicioun that euere he be, duryng this holy tyme of Cristemes be so hardy in eny wyse to walk by nyght in any manere mommyng, pleyes, enterludes, or eny other disgisynges with eny feynyd berdis, peyntid visers, diffourmyd or colourid visages in eny wyse'.[1] It is hard to doubt that the drama here prohibited was secular; but lacking the texts we must make do with Lydgate.

The child Henry VI and his French mother, the widowed Queen Catherine, frequently provided occasions for Lydgate's poems and devices. For the royal Christmas at Eltham in 1424, a single speaker (possibly Lydgate himself) presented Bacchus, Juno and Ceres, who bore olive boughs in token of peace to ensue between England and France: the ritual gifts of corn, wine and oil were offered to the King.[2] For Christmas at Windsor in 1429, when Henry was about to be crowned King of France at Rheims, Lydgate provided what was in essence a mimed miracle play: a versified account of how King Clovis obtained the fleur-de-lys shield of France and the golden coronation ampulla of Rheims (through the good offices of St Clothilda, St Remigius and the holy hermit of Joye-en-Vale) preceded a dumbshow of these events.[3]

Four more devices made by Lydgate for civic occasions show little

[1] Chambers, I, 394, n. 3.
[2] *Minor Poems*, ed. MacCracken, EETS, cxcii (1934) [*Part II: Secular*], 672–5.
[3] ibid., 691–4.

originality in subject. A banquet for May Day was allotted Flora leading on
Ver and May.[1] Another, for Christmas, had Dame Fortune and the Four
Cardinal Virtues.[2] The Mercers' Twelfth Night celebration in 1429
featured a messenger from Jupiter, poets at the Muses' Well, a crystal rock,
two fishing-boats and a merchant-ship unloading silks.[3] At the Goldsmiths'
Candlemas feast the same year a herald called Fortune introduced King
David and Hebrews from each of the twelve tribes, with a golden Ark of
the Covenant as a gift for the guest of honour.[4]

Minimal acting ability was required from these mummers. The Presenter
in each case did all the talking, while the rest displayed emblems, bowed,
or offered gifts to guests on the dais when appropriate. The Levites who
bore the Ark had, however, to break into song,[5] and so did the Four
Cardinal Virtues.[6] Fortune wore a double mask to signify her double face,
and sported her famous Wheel:[7] she was probably trundled into the hall
on a wheeled rostrum, upon which her curious double-sided dwelling,
palace reversing to hovel, was erected, together with her two tuns of
contrasted beverages, sweet wine and gall.[8]

Such scenic emblems were commonplace at high-class revels even in
Chaucer's day, and no doubt the shipping Lydgate ordained for the Mercers
in 1429 was of a similar type, moving on wheels like the Noah's Arks of
the craft-cycles.[9] One point of interest is that the large vessel was painted
with a moral maxim in French, and the labours of the two fishermen were
pointed up by French proverbs, engraved on the crystal rock and
embroidered on a hanging 'nor fer froo'.[10] Nothing in the four civic
mummings, however, suggests that in his last device, for the young King
at Hertford Castle in 1430, Lydgate could triumphantly dispense with
stock figures and hackneyed effects.

The Mumming at Hertford[11] has two features which are startlingly akin
to those of much later work of an undoubtedly dramatic kind. The first

[1] ibid., 668–71.
[2] ibid., 682–91.
[3] ibid., 695–8.
[4] ibid., 698–701.
[5] ibid., 699–700, ll. 29–35.
[6] ibid., 691, ll. 338–41.
[7] ibid., 682, l. 5; 685, ll. 129, 138.
[8] ibid., 683, ll. 38–48; 684, ll. 83–9.
[9] See Plate 29; also L. H. Loomis, 'Secular dramatics in the royal palace, Paris, 1378, 1389,
and Chaucer's "Tregetoures"', *Speculum*, XXXIII (1958), 242–55.
[10] *Minor Poems*, ed. MacCracken, EETS, CXCII (1934) [*Part II*], 697, ll. 61–3; 698, ll. 89–91.
[11] ibid., 675–82.

is that it involves the King and company in its fiction: what happens seems to be an actual incident of that selfsame Christmas-gathering in hall, where all present knew their own place and function. Into the hall as suppliants come a group of poor liegemen, whom Lydgate calls 'Certayne sweynes' and Shirley 'rude vpplandisshe people': they bring a petition of complaint against their wives, and crave the King's safe-conduct and protection. As with the apparently casual opening conversation of the pages A and B in Medwall's *Fulgens and Lucres* at the end of the century, only the rhyming verse would assure the quick-eared spectator that this was an arranged entertainment. The entry of the wives, however, gives the game away: if the suggestion 'distaves' made marginally by Shirley can be relied upon, they march in fully armed with women's weapons when they offer to 'darrein it in chaumpcloos by bataylle' (156, 166). The cross-petition of the wives is conducted with great vigour and telling reference to the Wife of Bath's example, a joke for the educated. A spokesman for the King (who was too young to join the game by casting a verdict) postpones final judgement for a year, during which the women are still to enjoy their mastery. This last speaker was probably Lydgate himself, who could proceed with the impunity of his cloth to warn the still-laughing assembly against ever entering the bonds of marriage.

The second forward-looking feature is that the names of the warring villagers and their occupations are up-to-date and English, like those of the characters in *Gammer Gurton's Needle* and *Ralph Roister Doister* over a century later. The henpecked husbands and their shrewish spouses are spoken for by the leaders of each group. The six wives are called Beatrice Bitter-sweete (married to Robin the Reeve); Cecely Soure-chere (married to Colin Cobbler); Pernelle (married to Bartholomew the Butcher); Tybot Tapister (married to Tom Tinker); Phelyce (married to Colle Tyler); and Mabel, who is mentioned (79) in such cringing terms that she is obviously the partner of the group-spokesman himself. The latter points out and names his fellows as he describes their sufferings, but in his humility before the King speaks in a politely impersonal way without naming himself. Presumably it is Mabel who speaks for the women.

Lydgate's ingenuity in managing without a Presenter gives this piece much more vitality than is usual in his devices, and the accounts of conflict lend themselves to accompanying dumbshow even before the embattled approach of the wives on hearing themselves described as 'wolfesses' (155). Even without the Wife of Bath reference, it would be clear that Lydgate had Chaucer's uncourtly customers in mind. This satirical convention continued in English poetry, and is met at much the same level in Skelton's *Tunnyng of Elynour Rummyng*.[1] Lydgate himself often chose to chronicle such squalid goings-on in his verse: witness the frowsty verisimilitude of his *ballade* 'froward Maymound'.[2] We are here within touching distance of anecdotal confessions from the Sins and Vices of moral drama on the one hand and the *fabliau*-type personages of French farce on the other – John Heywood was to work this vein in the next century. Noah and his wife in legend and cycle-play are also close at hand. But the *Mumming at Hertford* is a pastime, not a play, and we find nothing nearer to secular drama within the next sixty years.

Much more typical of a fifteenth-century hall-entertainment is a mumming of the Seven Philosophers for the 'kyng of Crystmas' in some revels at Trinity College, Cambridge:[3] though a Nuncius and the Philosophers severally proffer ethical advice, and conclude with a song, the style is pedestrian and the precepts flat. Suitably for scholars in a vacation, however, the seventh philosopher suggests that work and play by turns give best results: 'Ye may the better labour at the long, / When ye haue myrthe your besynes among' (76–7). This is the true charter of secular drama.

A most solemn piece of work from the second half of the fifteenth century is 'Maister Benet's Cristemasse Game', twelve stanzas of invocation addressed to each of the Apostles in turn by a Presenter who is evidently Christ, though such is the reverence of the copyist that only the saints' names are used for prefixes.[4] The imagined occasion of this ceremony seems to be Judgement Day, for each saint's whole life is rehearsed before he is bidden to his seat in bliss. The author was Benedict Burgh († *c*.1483), a cleric, sometime tutor to Lord Bourchier. Though his pious composition is hardly a game or a play in the modern sense, it is an excellent example of the overlapping of religious and secular traditions.

A third version of the speeches-from-a-fixed-group formula is the kind of show Shakespeare made Holofernes organize in *Love's Labour's Lost*, that of the Nine Worthies. A surviving example which happens to be precisely dated is the text for a series of street pageants along the route of Queen Margaret's entry to Coventry in 1455:[5] Hector of Troy, Alexander the

---

[1] R. S. Kinsman (ed.), *John Skelton, Poems* (Oxford, 1969), 53–70.

[2] *Minor Poems*, ed. MacCracken, EETS, cxcii (1934) [*Part II*], 445–8.

[3] Trinity College Cambridge MS 599; R. H. Robbins (ed.), *Secular Lyrics of the XIVth and XVth Centuries* (Oxford, 2nd edn, 1955), 110–13.

[4] BL MS Harley 7333, f. 149 ff.: F. J. Furnivall (ed.), *Notes & Queries*, s. iv, I (16 May and 6 June 1868), 455–6, 531.

[5] Coventry Leet Book: see R. S. Loomis, 'Verses on the Nine Worthies', *MP*, xv (1917–18), 19–27; text at 25–6.

Great, Joshua, David, Judas Maccabeus, Arthur, Charlemagne, Julius Caesar and Godfrey of Boulogne were the 'ix conqueroures' selected. Each of their complimentary stanzas is in the first person, and most contain hints of action – bowing, kneeling – which suggest that the Worthies actually spoke their lines on this occasion. Another example (of unknown auspices) has the same choice of champions but verses so short that a dumbshow with inscriptions seems more probable – King Arthur's couplet is

> The round Tabyll I sette with Kynghtes strong
> ȝyt shall I come agen, thow it be long.[1]

A third example, with the same Worthies, looks like the record of a *tableau*, because the writer has noted not only the third-person quatrains ('Lo, alexander...') but the coats-of-arms proper to each Worthy: King David is of 'Iherusalem.he bere gold iij harpys sabyll in large'.[2]

The thing which all these exhibitions have in common is that they contain no element of surprise: it is the principle of decorum, of providing exactly what chimes with expectation, which governs their composition. The reason that Lydgate was called upon to write so many semi-dramatic pieces is that he was expert in telling people very neatly what they took for granted already. Only a short step, however, lies between this and the kind of bland didactic piece which tells people what they do not know already but need to know – which contains instruction not in ethics but in subjects like astronomy, meteorology and geography. There is a sense in which Lydgate's helpfully pedantic *Pageant of Knowledge*,[3] with its careful guide to zodiacal medicine ('Aries ys hoot, & also coleryk / And in þe hede kepeþ hys dominacion', 139–40) and Rastell's *Four Elements*,[4] with its tedious demonstration that the earth is round, belong to different worlds: Lydgate was dead by 1450, and the next half-century brought England into a Tudor age in which new learning, printed books and the discovery of America put innovation, exploration, and the spirit of rational enquiry to the fore. Rastell himself got only as far as Waterford when he set sail for Newfoundland in 1517, to which year his frankly didactic interlude probably belongs, twenty years after Cabot's successful voyage.[5]

---

[1] In the Reynes MS (Bodleian Tanner MS 407, f. 32); for dating and refs. see *NCPF*, cxx–cxxi.
[2] F. J. Furnivall, 'The Nine Worthies and the heraldic arms they bore', *Notes and Queries*, s. vii, VIII (13 July 1889), 22–3.
[3] *Minor Poems*, II, 724–34, 734–8.
[4] *Three Rastell Plays*, ed. Axton, 29–68.
[5] ibid., 5–7.

What the pieces have in common is the desire to propagate knowledge: they differ in that to Lydgate even secular matters are part of an accepted, God-centred Truth, on which he was an authority, whereas Rastell knew that he must sugar the pill of fact with dancing, cross-talk, riotous no-goods and the parody of a song of Robin Hood.

It is, however, in the context of the morality tradition that Rastell's *Four Elements* should be discussed, for it is to allegorical personages like Studious Desire and Sensual Appetite that Rastell turned for the slight fiction and standard light relief of his educational interlude. Both as playwright and publisher, John Rastell is a key figure in the story of English drama, but not till after 1500. To conclude the long chapter of fifteenth-century mirth and solace and open the account of secular drama in the Renaissance mode we must look at Henry Medwall's *Fulgens and Lucres*.[1]

Though John Rastell elected to print *Fulgens and Lucres* about twenty years earlier than his son selected *Nature* for publication, there is no reason to believe it the earlier of Medwall's plays. Both belong to the last decade of the fifteenth century, when Medwall lived in Cardinal Morton's household at Lambeth Palace; each is arranged in two parts so that it can be played as banquet entertainment on two successive occasions; and neither has incontrovertible internal dating evidence. The testimony of William Roper, Sir Thomas More's son-in-law, that More stepped in among the players and made a part for himself extempore 'at Christmas tyde sodenly sometimes' when he was a young page in Morton's household,[2] has often been linked with the way A and B emerge from the lower ranks of the assembled company when *Fulgens and Lucres* is about to begin, and seem to work themselves by degrees from well-informed bystanders to participants in the action. More was a page at the very beginning of the decade, but such a household joke would not readily stale. Certainly the antics of A and B when they compete for the love of Ancilla, Lucrece's maid, are of a grossness that suggests older and coarser players than the fourteen-year-old More.

The main plot of *Fulgens and Lucres*, which the A and B intrigue in part parallels, is taken from a Latin treatise, *De Vera Nobilitate*, which was written by an Italian humanist, translated into English and into French, and printed in its English dress by Caxton.[3] Medwall was at King's College,

---

[1] A. H. Nelson (ed.), *The Plays of Henry Medwall* (Cambridge and Totowa, N.J., 1980), 31–89.

[2] *The Lyfe of Sir Thomas Moore, Knight*, ed. E. V. Hitchcock, EETS, CXCIX (1935), 5.

[3] Buonaccorso da Montemagno, *c.* 1428. Trans. French by Jean Mielot, before 1460: see R. J. Mitchell, *John Tiptoft* (London, 1938), 177–8. Trans. English by John Tiptoft, *c.* 1460; pub. Caxton in Cicero, *Tulle of Old Age*, 1481; text ed. Mitchell, op. cit., 215–41.

Cambridge, by 1481, when Caxton's edition appeared: the original by Buonaccorso had been in existence for half a century or so, and Eton scholars like Medwall were excellent Latinists, so he may well have met the text as improving literature long before he chose to use its very clear moral in a hall-play. The action is simple: Fulgens, a Roman senator, wishes to find a suitable husband for his daughter Lucrece: he is inclined to favour a patrician, Publius Cornelius, but agrees to give Lucrece her free choice between this suitor and another, Gaius Flaminius, of established position and respectable means, but of common blood. Because the suitor who is noble by birth is ignoble in conduct, and the suitor of lowly birth is noble in virtue, Lucrece decides that rank alone cannot make a nobleman: she chooses 'Gayus', as Medwall spells him.

Very great care is taken in the interlude to avoid the extrapolation that simple faith is *per se* more than Norman blood: Lucrece tells Cornelius

> Yf ye wyll the title of noblenes wynne
> Shew what have ye done your self therfore (II, 620–1);

but she honours the noble family of which he is an unworthy scion (II, 759–65). It is to the well-born that the moral is addressed, as B explains in his final speech,

> that suche as be gentilmen of name
>   May be somwhat movyd
> By this example for to eschew
> The wey of vyce and favour vertue;
>   For syn is to be reprovyd
> More in them, for the degre,
> Than in other parsons such as be
>   Of pour kyn and birth (II, 891–8).

The doctrine of *noblesse oblige* is not egalitarian, except in the sense that Gayus invokes when he says of his rival: 'both he and I cam of Adam and Eve' (II, 665). In the sight of God, however, virtuous conduct makes a difference between man and man: Medwall encourages the audience to share God's point of view by dressing Cornelius like the Sin of Pride in a moral play – exactly like Pride in Medwall's own *Nature*, indeed, down to the variegated stripes of his hose.[1]

No Christian father, whatever his private views on giving a girl some

---

[1] *Nature*, I, 747–70, 1055–81; *Fulgens and Lucrece*, I, 717–50 (both ed. Nelson, *Plays of Henry Medwall*).

voice in choosing her bridegroom, could repudiate a moral so cunningly qualified: too immediate an application was moreover precluded by the Cardinal's celibacy and the special considerations attending the matches of royalty. Many of those present probably received it as pious sentiments are usually received, politely but without urgent interest: for these people the horse-play and dirty jokes of the sub-plot, together with the music and dancing, would bring the entertainment to an acceptable level. It is salutary to remember that in practice the precise claims of rank were well understood by the company at large, and in particular by minor officials of the household like the hall-marshal, whose duty it was to seat the guests in the right order of precedence. One such, John Russell, who served Humphrey of Gloucester earlier in the fifteenth century, provided in his *Boke of Nurture* a descending table, in which cardinal is fourth (to pope, emperor and king), and 'Kyngis sone' ties with archbishop for fifth place: Medwall's master was definitely high in the tree-top.[1] Russell goes on to consider some cases by which 'a merchalle is put oft tymes in gret comberaunce' (1086) – how to settle the point of precedence between a poor princeling and a wealthy commoner (blood has it), what to do with the pope's parents (give them a private dining-room), where to place a lady who has married beneath her (let her keep her former rank). In such a context of jealously scrutinized social mobility, the extra strain of determining comparative virtue is not widely feasible: the Gayus/Lucrece match becomes one more headache for hall-marshals.

That Medwall himself foresaw the reaction of at least part of his audience, and that *Fulgens and Lucres*, for all its Renaissance flavour, is squarely in the tradition of 'Both gode examples and right honest solace' (I, 153), is indicated early in the play when B says:

> How be it, the matter touchith me never a dell,
> For I am nether of vertue excellent
> Nor yet of gentyl blode.
>
> 　　　we come to see this play
> As farre as we may by the leve of the marshall.
> I love to beholde suche myrthes alway. (I, 140–9)

---

[1] Ed. F. J. Furnivall in *Education in Early England*, EETS, LII (1868), 117–99, civ–cxv.

3 Allegory into drama: souls in jeopardy

Allegory is a form of rhetoric, a special way of calling attention to a pattern of ideas. It is used by people who know all the answers, to enlighten those who might otherwise neglect to ask all the questions.

That the impulse to present ethical doctrine in allegorical terms was regularly and repeatedly satisfied in writing from early in the history of western literature is fully documented, and much scholarship has been expended on charting the origins and developments of allegory as a literary genre. Frequently the sources of allegory as a dramatic mode are considered solely in relation to the same body of material, and the point of stimulus for translating a description of allegorical action into a scenario for a piece of drama is taken to be the early illustrations of the literary work in question. The best-known example of this misconception is the specific and close linking of the *Psychomachia*, a fourth-century allegorical poem by the Christian Prudentius about the conflict of good and evil, with sundry episodes in Holy Wars which occur in plays of the late Middle Ages.[1] Prudentius indeed wrote with great imagination and zest: his accounts of hand-to-hand combats between personified Virtues and their counterpart

[1] For a sympathetic account of the poem and references see C. S. Lewis, *The Allegory of Love* (Oxford, 1936; New York, 1958), 66–73.

Vices (while the general battle rages Roman-fashion on the body as a plain) lent themselves splendidly to the illuminators whose vignettes of the duels adorn surviving copies of his poem.[1] In the excitement of detecting pairs of adversaries familiar from later homiletic tradition and from some vernacular plays of the fifteenth century, certain critics hailed Prudentius as Father of the Moral Drama. The term *psychomachia* has established itself as a *sine qua non* of criticism, identifying whole schemes of analysis of the morality tradition.[2]

Perhaps the simplest way to appreciate the weakness of this putative link is to envisage the effect of staging the *Psychomachia* of Prudentius as a whole. The snag would not lie in the scale and properties of the conflict. One of the earliest European plays to survive, the twelfth-century Latin *Antichristus* from Tegernsee in Bavaria, employed more than sixty actors (including several who represented personifications, for example Mercy, Justice, Heresy, Hypocrisy, the Church, the Spirit of the Gentiles) to figure forth national and cosmic confrontations in a way involving four full-scale battles.[3] In our own day the readiest medium to do justice to the details of the *Psychomachia* would be cine-photography: a faithful rendering of its action could be produced as a side-project to the filming of some such epic of the cinema as *Ben Hur*. The more faithful the version, however, the less satisfactory would be the result, for a reason inseparable from the nature of dramatic as distinct from literary allegory.

The reason is that once an abstract noun borrows flesh and blood from a player with full physical being, its actions appear to be those of a real person, and as such provoke associations and expectations which cannot be bounded by considerations of allegorical significance. The embodied characters look like real people, and real people are providing a connection between one action and the next; but their motivation and process of behaving are — and have to be — in the strictest sense inhuman. Only at moments of crisis (such as those selected with unerring tact by the illuminators) is it possible to recognize a gesture that is at once allegorically meaningful and humanly probable. In between such moments, the action seems shocking, or laughable, or both.

The *Psychomachia* would suffer badly in this way. Because abstract nouns

[1] See Plate 27; also Adolf Katzenellenbogen, tr. Crick, *Allegories of the Virtues and Vices in Mediaeval Art* (London, 1939).
[2] See Bernard Spivack, *Shakespeare and the Allegory of Evil* (New York and London, 1958), 60–95.
[3] Young, II, 371–87.

in Latin take the feminine gender, all the Virtues and Vices are represented by Prudentius as female. Though the illuminators cheat a little by showing some of the Vices as harpies, the spectacle of their virago Virtues in helmets and drapery, brandishing gory weapons in a riot of carnage, does not edify even in miniature. Such sequences as the entrance of the lady Luxuria in a golden chariot, scattering petals over ranks of swooning females, would be both silly and distasteful in dramatic form.

This is not to say that some aspects of the allegorical action in the *Psychomachia* and other writings of its genre did not furnish very telling precedents for devisers of moral plays. When the Vice Avarice puts on the guise of Thrift in order to seduce by stealth where open assault has failed, she anticipates by a thousand years the action of the Deadly Sin Covetise in *The Castle of Perseverance*, who succeeds in luring the aged Humanum Genus from the refuge which has withstood direct siege:

> þi purs schal be þi best frende...
> If þou be pore and nedy in elde
> þou schalt oftyn euyl fare (2521, 2529–30)

Covetise is, however, male, and supported by a large male cohort – World, Flesh, Devil, Bad Angel, and five Deadly Sins. Only Luxuria, whom Covetise calls his sister, 'swete Lecherye' (1020), retains her feminity in the army of sin, and she uses her wiles plausibly enough to make Humanum Genus in youth her 'leue lemman' (1189). The Virtues who inhabit the Castle of Perseverance are indeed a band of lovely ladies, matched exactly against their counterpart sins; but they are dressed as winged angels (if Bad Angel's disparaging reference to their 'hakle', feathers [2650], can be trusted), and they use measures of defence that are neither unbecoming to their sex nor derogatory to their dignity. From the battlements of the Castle they toss red roses, emblems of Christ's Passion, which have the effect of heavy missiles on the male sins and lie as spilt Blood on the battlefield. Chastity, however, deals with Lechery by other means: invoking the Blessed Virgin, she sprinkles the foul-mouthed meretrix with water from the well of grace, and conquers, quenching lust's fire (2387–90). Whoever wrote *The Castle of Perseverance* may well have read Prudentius, together with some of the allegorical works from later centuries which featured castles under siege by evil powers.[1] What makes his treatment satisfactory as drama is that he understood and applied the basic rule for allegory intended to be staged: 'use commonplace with commonsense'.

[1] See Roberta Cornelius, *The Figurative Castle* (Bryn Mawr, Penn., 1930).

A notable example of sustained dramatic allegory on the theme of Virtues Triumphant is preserved from the twelfth century: it is the abbess Hildegard of Bingen's *Ordo Virtutem*, a Latin piece with music and dancing, which not only expresses the saintly vision of its composer but reveals a firm grasp of visual and dramatic effect.[1] A peculiarity of the text is that though several crucial actions can be inferred from the dialogue, there are no stage directions as such: the mood of the singer is, however, prescribed in the speech-prefixes. Thus the central character, 'Anima' or the Soul, is at first 'Felix Anima', but is later 'gravata', heavy with her sense of impatience. She stands at audience-level with a chorus of aspirant souls: seated high above her is Humility, queen of the Virtues, who surround her throne at the level of Paradise. A flight of steps links the two levels, and is ascended by a group of patriarchs; but Anima's attempt to climb is hindered and discouraged by the Devil, who croaks out worldly wisdom as he guards the lowest step. Because Anima in her zeal for immortal bliss has not reckoned with the inevitable struggle, while life endures, against carnal temptations, the Devil's reminder that she is only human deflects her from the ascent, and she looks to the world for honour, placing herself thereby in the Devil's power. He now taunts the Virtues with having no separate being: they are all aspects of Godhead, whereas he, by his rejection of God's service, has attained unique personal identity. His brief speeches are contrasted with the slow monodic chanting of the Virtues.

The next section is of astonishing sophistication: what amounts to a holy *carole* is danced by the Virtues, each taking her turn to call the rest into a circle, to mark their coronation in the blessed state of perseverance. The formation has unmistakable analogues not only with folk-dance and singing-game figures but also with that eternal circular dance of the blessed spirits which (according to the apocryphal *Acts of John*)[2] Christ taught His loyal disciples after the Last Supper:

> He bade us therefore make as it were a ring, holding one another's hands, and himself standing in the midst he said, Answer Amen unto me.... Thou that dancest, perceive what I do, for thine is this passion of the manhood, which I am about to suffer.... I would keep tune with holy souls. (pp. 253–4)

In the *Ordo Virtutem*, the round dance reaffirms the order of eternity

[1] See Peter Dronke, *Poetic Individuality in the Middle Ages* (Oxford, 1970), 168–79; Latin text, 180–92.
[2] See *The Apocryphal New Testament*, ed. M. R. James (Oxford, 1953), 228 ff.; 253–4.

and provides the basis for the next movement of the drama, the defeat of the Devil and salvation of Anima. When she creeps back in penitence to cry for mercy, the Virtues come down to snatch her from the clutches of the Devil and bind him in his own chains. In a tableau strangely akin to one of the *Psychomachia*'s vignettes, Chastity takes the victorious stance assigned to the Blessed Virgin Mary when depicted as reversing the trespass of Eve: she sets her heel on Satan the Serpent's head, and sings of the Virgin Birth. Scotched but not killed, the Devil continues to blaspheme; but Chastity goes on to proclaim the full meaning of the Incarnation, and the piece ends with choruses of praise and thanksgiving for the process of Redemption.

This remarkable church-drama handles with tact and assurance themes which were to recur in vernacular plays throughout the Middle Ages. It offers a different kind of satisfactory experience from any surviving English play in the allegorical mode, though something of the same intense union of doctrine, visual symbolism and movement to music is achieved in the best moral masques of the Stuart period. Let us remember that the theme of Anima and the Devil is capable of allegorical treatment to such stunning effect, for we meet it in fifteenth-century England with a very different emphasis. One of the moral plays in the Macro manuscript has been published under editorial titles derived from its *dramatis personae*, Wisdom (who is Christ) and the trio of human faculties proper to the Soul, by name Mind, Will and Understanding; but Lucifer's corruption of Anima and her redemption by Christ make up the action. It is worth looking closely at *Wisdom*, which dates from about 1465, because the play is not only a good example of the strengths and weaknesses of allegorical drama but a transitional type in the development of moral drama in England.[1]

Wisdom is probably the least likely of the fifteenth-century moral plays to find favour with a modern audience.[2] It is scrupulously didactic, and seems to be intended for performance indoors to an educated company (perhaps of church dignitaries, undergraduates, lawyers or senior schoolboys) who are accustomed to hearing long discourses punctuated by passages of Latin and will accept a generous helping of pageantry, music and dancing to augment a most meagre allowance of dramatic action. None the less, *Wisdom* repays close analysis: lacking the art that conceals art, its structure is a clear guide to what its learned author considered proper to the form.

[1] Eccles (ed.), *Macro Plays*, 113–52.
[2] But it has been revived successfully: see Avril Henry's review, *METh*, 3 (1981), 53–5, of a production at Winchester cathedral by King Alfred's College.

There are four phases of the Soul's progress to be displayed, and each is allotted what is in effect a self-contained scene. The first imparts the doctrine of Christ's provision for the Soul of Man; the second shows the process by which Lucifer brings about a fall from grace; the third shows the faculties of the Soul in degradation and bondage to deadly sin; the fourth shows Christ's recall of the faculties to a sense of responsibility for the Soul's corruption, and the consequent cry for mercy, contrition and submission to the ministrations of the Church, which duly bring the Soul through confession, penance and absolution to reunion with Christ and all the brightness of her former state. All this matter was not only standard but very familiar teaching: the audience was sure to recognize framework and detail. The point of presenting it in dramatic form was to bring the moral home in a more beguiling way than by giving a sermon.

The play opens with the entry and enthronement of Christ in full majesty as Divine Wisdom: when Anima kneels in worship, Wisdom counsels her in stately stanzas on the mystic bliss of a soul's experience of God's love. The tone is high, though the writer has borrowed his own wisdom from the works of mystics rather than arrived at it by personal experience. The Soul, whose costume is carefully prescribed in a long English stage direction, appears as a richly dressed virgin; but she is cloaked in black. Wisdom explains this mixed fashion with reference to the doctrine of original sin. Through Christ's sacrifice, grace was made available to the Soul in the Sacraments, of which Baptism has already reformed her to God's likeness. Reason, however, the image of God, can control only part of the Soul, her five inner wits. Over her five outer wits – the five senses – Sensuality still holds sway.[1] The black cloak betokens an inborn impulse to sin, the white garments reveal Reason's perception of God. The five inner wits enter as virgins in white, and sing in Latin a couple of verses from the *Song of Songs* – Solomon's dealings with the Queen of Sheba are plainly in the writer's mind beside the imagery of Solomon's love-song. After introducing the Soul in her state of grace ('For þe clene sowll ys Godys restynge place', 176) to the three faculties of every Christian Soul, Wisdom instructs her in their duties: Mind keeps God the Father ever in memory, and will nurture Anima in Faith; Will is the intention to do good which is inspired by the Holy Spirit and issues in Charity; Understanding gives Hope in the mercy of God the Son. She has also Free Will, and must take care to keep it pure. Wisdom then warns Anima to keep her five wits safe from the Three Enemies, the World, the Flesh and the Devil, so that

[1] For the five wits, outer and inner, see *The Lay Folks Catechism*, ed. T. F. Simmons and H. E. Nolloth, EETS, CXVIII (1901), 19.

sensuality does not hinder her. Dismissed to fight the good fight, the Soul with glad submission moves away in her wedding procession, preceded by her virgins singing a Trinity Sunday antiphon ('Thou art all fair, my love, there is no spot in thee', *Song of Songs* 4: 7). Wisdom the Bridegroom follows, together with the Three Faculties, richly dressed. So ends the first part of this play, which in its orthodoxy, aureate language, solemn verse movement and expensive costuming has made a high bid to be worthy of its theme. It is slow-moving and heavy-handed, but not unimpressive.

So far *Wisdom* has proceeded in a timeless and unlocated world: in the second and third sections it is anchored in fifteenth-century England. The writer introduces Lucifer in an established mode, giving him the 'Owt harow' cry frequently ascribed to devils, together with the correct 'dewyllys aray' and manner (roaring and louring); but there is no trace of indecency or low language in this figure, who concentrates on explaining his own theological context and announcing his strategy for the corruption of mankind. This involves choosing the psychological moment to offer temptation –

> I know all compleccyons of a man
> > Werto he ys most dysposyde;
> Ande þerin I tempte ay-whan (343–5)

and also a reassuring disguise: 'Her LUCYFER dewoydyth and cummyth in ageyn as a goodly galont' (380ᵇ). His quick change is achieved by removing his outer clothes, since he is already dressed 'wythin as a prowde galonte' (325 SD). Mind, Understanding and Will appear, deep in sober conversation, and still in 'syde aray' (509), the long garments of dignified old age. Lucifer, however, does not talk like a man of fashion: he argues from the scriptures, with some display of Latin learning, against the contemplative life – if Christ himself chose a *vita mixta*, why should his followers cloister themselves? 'Lewe, lewe, suche syngler besynes. / Be in þe worlde, vse thyngys nesesse' (441–2). Mind gives ground by degrees and is persuaded. Lucifer then makes much shorter work of Understanding and Will, hinting to both that pleasures lie in worldly advantage and sensual gratification. As soon as they yield to his suggestion, their language drops from the aureate to the gross: when bidden 'euer be mery: let reuell rowte!', they reply

> MYNDE   Ya, ellys I beschrew my snowte!
> WNDYRSTONDYNGE   And yff I care, cache I þe gowte!
> WILL   And yff I spare, þe Dewyll me spede! (505–8)

Lucifer sends them off to change their clothes to a worldly fashion, and in solemn stanzas explains how their imminent plunge into pride, avarice and lechery will suffice to damn the Soul. He cannot be said to gloat; but there is still one trick up his sleeve – at the end of this speech 'he takyt a schrewde boy wyth hym and goth hys wey cryenge' (550[b]). Was the naughty boy planted in readiness among the audience, or did our writer know very well that there would be children present?

In the third section, Mind, Will and Understanding show themselves in fashionable clothes and share out the fashionable vices: Mind intends to cultivate pride, envy and wrath; Understanding chooses avarice; and Will takes the fleshly trio of lechery, gluttony and sloth. After joining as 'tenowr', 'mene' and 'trebull' in a song which was apparently too worldly to be set down for posterity, the three compare notes about the evils of the age which they are now enjoying. Each introduces a dumbshow dance of supporters. Mind, who has become 'Maintenance' (the equivalent of modern American 'graft'), joins the 'Deuellys dance' with Indignation, Sturdiness, Malice, Hastiness, Revenge ('Wreche') and Discord, to the popular tune of 'Madam Regent' on trumpets. Understanding, who has used his new riches to corrupt the course of justice, dances as Perjury to bagpipe music, leading a venal jury of six from Middlesex, 'þe quest of Holborn'. Will's dumbshow dancers are female, according to the stage direction 'Here entreth six women', and Will's own word for them 'þis damesellys'; but they dance (to the hornpipe, with a pun on cuckolds' horns) in couples, three of them dressed as gallants and three as matrons, 'wyth wondyrfull vysurs congruent'.

This is of course an odd point: unless the parts of Recklesshead, Idleness (two for Sloth), Surfeit, Greediness (two for Gluttony), Adultery ('Spousebreche') and Mistress (two for Lust) were in fact to be played by women – which would suggest a noble household rather than a celibate establishment as the intended environment for performance – the costumes and visors which gave the audience to understand that three of the six male actors should be viewed as women-dressed-as-men must have been wonderful indeed. The obvious explanation is that Anima and her train of five virgins are meant to be played by women, who since they will not be needed again till the last section can double as 'harlottys' here; but it is possible that what is in question is the 'hermaphrodite' costume with double mask and lateral combination of petticoat and breeches which was later affected by certain masquers, Harlequins and Venetian courtesans.[1]

---

[1] See for example Daniel Rabel's costume-designs for 'Les Androgines' in 'La Douarière de Billebahaut', Paris, 1629, which are reproduced by Cyril W. Beaumont, *Ballet Design Past and Present* (London, 1946), 3.

The instant shock and hostility displayed by Mind and Understanding suggest that though Will does not explicitly lay claim to the seventh name mentioned, 'jentyll Fornycacyon', he does tear off his clothes and dance so lasciviously as to earn it. Mind threatens to penalize the dancers for their 'French' manners (767–8), and Understanding chastises Will until the order to expel them has been given:

WNDYRSTONDYNGE þi longe body bare
       To bett I not spare.
       Haue the ageyn!
WYLL   Holde me not! let me go! ware!
       I dynge, I dasche! Þer, go ther! (770–4)

Having thus illustrated Mind's comment 'Wer [where] vycys be gederyde, euer ys sum myschance' (766), the three begin to plan a further career of sin which is inseparable from the legal quarters of London. Understanding will practise corruptly in the courts of Westminster, Mind tout for clients outside St Paul's between two and three of an afternoon. Will has a more relaxed programme: 'Met and drynke and ease, I aske no mare, / Ande a praty wenche, to se here bare' (814–15). He does, however, wish to put a spoke in the wheel of a jealous churl who is married to one 'Jenet N.', Will's 'cosyn' (834–5). Among the expedients suggested by Mind and Understanding are pieces of legal chicanery like indicting the churl in another shire, a common but excommunicable offence. 'Þe crose and þe pyll' on the two sides of a coin will ward off all possible repercussions, for 'Mede stoppyt, be yt neuer so allyede' (862) – bribery blocks legal action, however well-connected the plaintiff. With a snatch of light song, the three make towards an evening at the tavern –

WYLL   Mery, mery, all mery þan be we!
       Who þat ws tarythe, curs haue he and myn! (871–2)

Will has called Christ's curse on whoever delays the rioters; ironically, it is Christ Himself who bars their way, as He comes in the shape of Wisdom to open the fourth section with a version of *memento mori*:

WYSDOM Dethe to euery creature certen ys.
        They þat lyue well, þey xall haue blys;
        Thay þat endyn yll, þey goo to hell. (876–8)

Mind is moved; Understanding does not want to listen – 'I wyll no wndyrstondynge xall lett my pley' (887); Will is culpably slothful. When the warning is repeated, Wisdom accompanies it with an object-lesson: 'Here ANIMA apperythe in þe most horrybull wyse, fowlere þan a fende' (at 902). From beneath her repulsive tatters run seven small boys dressed as devils to represent the deadly sins which have reduced her to this graceless state: they return to her as Wisdom begins His complaint against the Soul's ingratitude and criminal folly. It is enough: the work of redemption begins. Reverting to aureate language, Mind and Understanding acknowledge their offence, and Will resolves to turn back to God. Anima can now throw herself on Christ's mercy, and accept his advice to show true contrition. As she begins to weep for her sins, the devils who represent them are seen to leave her. Singing a penitential text, Anima goes out with her contrite attendants to become reconciled with Holy Church by confession and the sacrament of penance.

Wisdom now delivers a set sermon on the nine principal ways to please God. The original audience may not have realized that the whole sermon was a versified translation and expansion of a Latin treatise once ascribed to Richard Rolle, *Novem Virtutes*,[1] but cannot have failed to notice that sixty-seven lines on end are given by one speaker without the slightest pretext for more than oratorical action. Of course Anima has to change into her former costume during this monologue: she returns in procession with all her train wearing triumphal crowns and singing a psalm of gratitude. Wisdom greets her in the language of the *Song of Songs* as His sister and His spouse, describes His own Passion, and urges her never again to decline from this state of grace and glory. With a fine display of macaronic verse, the three faculties chime in, and Anima points several morals before urging every soul in the audience to fear the Lord and follow the same path through Wisdom to perfection.

This laborious analysis of *Wisdom* begins to yield useful insights as soon as the right questions are put. If we insist on asking why so much is said and so little happens, the answer can only be given in terms of the writer's conviction that the doctrinal material on which the play is based ought to be of urgent and compelling interest to every human being: only the frailty of mankind gives reason to try to bring the argument home by dividing its expression between costumed players. A better question is whether any of the things which do happen in the play make a point more clearly than a stanza on their implications could. Once granted that tableaux and processions catered to a well-established taste by no means confined to the medieval period, the author's claim to have used essentially dramatic means rests on the employment of costume conventions and a few surprise effects.

[1] See W. K. Smart, *Some English and Latin Sources and Parallels for the Morality of Wisdom* (Menasha, Wisconsin, 1912), 34–7.

That Lucifer should disguise himself to begin his temptation, that the change of heart in the three faculties should be marked by change of costume, and Anima's fall from grace be reflected in her ruined appearance, are commonplaces which are used effectively. The kind of decorous imagination which inspired masques and disguisings at court for so many generations of monarchs can be seen at work in the way that the dumbshows are described: 'Here entur six dysgysyde in þe sute of MYNDE, wyth rede berdys, and lyouns rampaunt on here crestys, and yche a warder in hys honde: her mynstrallys, trumpes. Eche answere for hys name' (691 SD). The livery of fierce uncharitableness shows the red of war and the proud rage of the king of beasts, and those who wear it come armed with batons of authority: the trumpets also sound. This is a traditional kind of effect, but not a weak one: when the names of Indignation and the rest are acknowledged by these shapes of anger, the moral point is well made.

Three incidents that involve fast and initially startling action are the snatching up of the boy by Lucifer, the ugly little struggle which breaks up Will's dance of harlots, and the issue of the deadly sins from Anima's mantle. The author has taken care to reserve his grandest verse and Latin texts for the doctrinal scenes, his colloquial language and proverbial tags for the scenes with contemporary references. None of all this shows much bent for drama: as ever, the writer has used what he happens to know as well as he can. But if we ask whether there is anything in the moral play of *Wisdom* which points forward to that combination of thought and action, of word and visual effect, which makes a moment of spiritual insight important and memorable, or a dialogue cumulatively telling, the answer must be yes. Lucifer as he seduces the three faculties is excellently well-conceived, clever and shallow and patronizing as ever a power of real evil could be. The zest of a few speeches, moreover, carries its own conviction:

WNDYRSTONDYNGE   We woll be fresche, hanip la plu joly!
['Bottoms up!']

Farwell penance! (511–12)

But the greatest moment of this play comes at its turning-point, and makes a breaking of mood and contrast of tone to match the visual and ethical confrontation. The three revellers are seeking wine, but it is the cup of mortality which Wisdom extends to them:

WYSDOM   O thou Mynde, remembyr the!
Turne þi weys, þou gost amyse.

Se what þi end ys, þou myght not fle:
Dethe to euery creature certen ys. (873–6)

As we shall see (pp. 282 f.), the moment of confrontation with Death, which Wisdom here evokes without presenting, was important in many of the moral plays which survive from fifteenth-century England. It is essential to the action of *The Pride of Life*, though the manuscript of that play breaks off before this point; to *The Castle of Perseverance*, though the action of that play is prolonged far beyond this point; to Thomas Chaundler's *Liber Apologeticus*; and above all to *Everyman*.

The pattern of *Wisdom*, which shows the representative of humankind reclaimed from degradation, restored to grace and surviving to live acceptably, forms one phase only of the action of *The Castle of Perseverance*, but exactly parallels that of its own near contemporary, *Mankind* (*c.*1466).[1] The same pattern is twice repeated in Henry Medwall's backward-looking *Nature* (see pp. 259–61), which makes use of Lydgate's poem *Reason and Sensuality*, and is echoed in a group of moral interludes printed early in the sixteenth century, *Mundus et Infans*, *Hickscorner* and *Youth*.[2]

Wisdom has, however, one feature which is unmatched in any play from the repent-and-survive group: God in one of His Persons has a speaking part. The values of Heaven are represented by Christ and the Blessed Virgin in *The Pride of Life*: by God the Father and His Four Daughters in both *The Castle of Perseverance* and *Liber Apologeticus* (which last also introduces Christ Incarnate); and by God the Father and an Angel in *Everyman*. In *Mankind*, however, the priest Mercy is the sole supporter of morality; in *Nature* the brunt of instructing Man is borne by Reason until the Seven Virtues rally round at the close of Part II; *Mundus et Infans* (printed 1522) has Conscience and Perseverance on the side of the angels; *Hickscorner* (written between 1497 and 1512)[3] has Pity, Contemplation and Perseverance; *Youth* (printed *c.*1520) has Charity and Humility.

In much the same way, the infernal powers made fewer appearances as

---

[1] D. C. Baker, 'The date of *Mankind*', *Philological Quarterly*, XLII (1963), 90–1. See also T. J. Jambeck and Reuben R. Lee, '"Pope Pokett" and the date of *Mankind*', *Mediaeval Studies*, XXXIX (1977), 511–13.

[2] See H. N. MacCracken, 'A source of *Mundus et Infans*', *PMLA*, XXIII (1908), 486–96; E. T. Schell, '*Youth* and *Hyckescorner*: which came first?', *Philological Quarterly*, XLV (1966), 468–74.

[3] After 1497, because Hickscorner has been in 'the newe founde island': before 1512, because the *Regent*, mentioned in his ship-catalogue, was sunk in that year. But see Ian Lancashire, 'The sources of *Hyckescorner*', *Review of English Studies*, n.s. XXII (1971), 257–73.

the fifteenth century advanced. It would seem that a gaping hell-mouth temporarily accommodated the soul of Rex Vivus in *The Pride of Life*; the Devil incarnate, Belial, has a scaffold in *The Castle of Perseverance* and a Bad Angel to fetch the soul of Humanum Genus away; and *Wisdom*'s own Lucifer is a less grotesque figure than the 'invisible' fiend Titivillus with his net in *Mankind*.[1] The seven small boys dressed as imps who run from beneath Anima's cloak in *Wisdom* stand for the seven sins into which she has fallen: the scriptural source of the incident seems to be Mark 16: 9, where Mary Magdalen is the female sinner in question. Though in *Liber Apologeticus* the evil Fear-of-Death brings a letter from Hell, Satan as Death's secretary does not appear. Everyman fears 'paynes huge and grete' (191), but there are neither devils nor intrinsically evil characters in the solemn play which bears his name.

Evil powers rather than devils are used by Medwall and in the early printed group. World, Flesh and the Seven Sins who support Belial in *The Castle of Perseverance* are all revived by Medwall, though Flesh has been translated into Sensuality and Covetise is discussed but not presented. In *Mundus et Infans*, which bears the marks of adaptation for two actors from an older and longer play,[2] World has some effective speeches, but all possible sins and errors are rolled up into the single figure of Folly. In *Hickscorner* and *Youth*, all the libertines talk like fifteenth-century Londoners, whether they are presented as sins, human beings or general nuisances.

It should be noted that *Wisdom*'s method of analysing the representatives of human character into four speaking parts, Anima and her own three Faculties, is more elaborate than that of any other extant moral play before *Everyman*. In *The Pride of Life*, though it seems likely that two actors were needed for Rex Vivus (one playing his body-and-soul in life, the other his soul after death, as with Humanum Genus in *The Castle of Perseverance*), only Health is a simple attribute: Strength and Mirth are partly aspects of the King's ebullient personality but partly also external forces, his army and his jester. This is not a trio of good – even of neutral – qualities; in the context of a soul's salvation, the possession of physical and nervous vigour is a positive hindrance to taking at all seriously the urgent necessity of acquiring spiritual resources against the crisis of death. Mirth in particular is the first of a long line of equivocal characters in moral plays

---

[1] *Mankind*, ed. Eccles, *Macro Plays*, 153–84; see esp. ll. 460–1, 529–31, and refs. at p. 220, n. 301.
[2] MacCracken, 'A source of *Mundus et Infans*', 486–96.

and interludes whose devil-may-care lightness is expressed in song. He tells the Queen:

> For I am Solas, I most singe
> Oueral qwher I go.   *Et cantat.* (321–2)

His song is not preserved, but the door has been set ajar for Autolycus.

The Castle of Perseverance presents all the pressures upon Humanum Genus as external to his consciousness. Good Angel is a spirit deputed to counsel him, not 'Conscience': the Seven Virtues and the Seven Sins are absolute powers, independent of his petty stake in each. The Castle stands centrally in the plain whether he perseveres or not. He becomes a miser, repenting only with his last breath, but Covetise remains throughout the root of all evil.

Mankind and *Liber Apologeticus* also show external pressures only. In the latter piece, 'Homo' does not speak after Death's stroke; but there is perhaps a hint in an illustration of the Four Cardinal Virtues arraying him for eternal life that a second actor, with trimmed hair and beard, took over the role at this point.[1]

Towards the end of the century, Medwall uses two facets of Man's character in addition to Man himself – Man's Innocency and Man's Worldly Affection. Medwall represents Innocency, Man's nurse, as female (I, 505, 511), but Innocency, Man's dismissed servant, as male (I, 641–3). Far from being a slip, this neatly illustrates the difference between an abstract quality and a human characteristic. Lady Innocency is an eternal Virtue: Man's native innocence, properly masculine, is limited to his own boyhood.

Everyman shows four aspects of the protagonist as well as himself. Strength, Beauty, Discretion and Five Wits, recognized by him in the second half of the play, stand for his own holdings of these qualities, not for absolutes. In contrast, Goods and Good Deeds, though personal to him, are not part of his nature: they stand respectively for his treasure on earth and his treasure in Heaven. Knowledge represents the power within his soul to recognize the way to God, which is a free gift from God not proportioned to desert. Knowledge will thus remain with him while he lives, but must be transcended in Heaven, where he is to know even as he is known.

Two of the early sixteenth-century publications present the protagonist

---

[1] Thomas Chaundler, *Liber Apologeticus*, ed. D. Enright-Clark Shoukri, Plate XIV.

in a new way – according to his stage of development. Though Humanum Genus in *The Castle of Perseverance* speaks first as a new-born baby and last as an old man, his complete life-span forms a part for a single actor. In the seven ages of *Mundus et Infans*, however, the Child heads the procession of Wanton, Lust-and-Liking (a compound name also found in *The Castle of Perseverance*), Manhood, Shame, Age and (at long last) Repentance. Youth in the play of that name is shown revelling in the sins that beset his phase of existence in particular.

The most interesting treatment is that of *Hickscorner*, which dispenses with a central 'Homo' figure in favour of two already corrupt beings, Free Will and Imagination: these sound like aspects of a single character but behave much more like individual human villains. Both, however, undergo rather sudden conversion when threatened with death and Hell, whereas the title-character, most wicked of them all, roisters off to Shooter's Hill and escapes retribution. Hickscorner, whose name means 'an ignorant scoffer', is closely related both to Mischief in *Mankind*, who works with the devil Titivillus and the three ruffians Naught, New-Guise and Nowadays, and to Riot from Newgate in *Youth*, with his typical gallant's cry 'huffa! huffa!'. Both Hickscorner and Riot are voluble no-goods who clap one of the remonstrant virtues in irons. They are forerunners of a type of tempter frequently found in sixteenth-century interludes and named on title-pages as 'the Vice'.[1] Perhaps a hint of how this term came to be applied to such figures may be found in the words of Hickscorner's mentor Contemplation, who visited England

> For to preche and teche of goddes soth sawes
> Aȝenst vyce yt doth rebell aȝenst him & his lawes. [Aii^v]

Though the choice between good and evil is the predominant concern in all the early moral plays, a military *psychomachia* occurs only in *The Castle of Perseverance*. Medwall indeed in *Nature* with great ingenuity sets up an expectation of conflict in the traditional seven duels, but avoids confrontation on the plea that Man's advanced age destroys without a struggle all the Sins except Covetise. In *Mary Magdalen*, however, a two-part play extant only in the early sixteenth-century Digby manuscript, a miracle-studded presentation of the saint's life is combined with an allegorical section which in part reflects the taste of a previous generation.[2] The Three Enemies and

---

[1] See Spivack, *Shakespeare and the Allegory of Evil*, 130–50, and, for list of Vice plays, n. 10 on 466.
[2] Baker, *Digby Plays*, 24–95; allegorical section, 34–49.

the Seven Sins lay siege to the Castle of Maudleyn, inherited by Mary from her father King Cyrus: they, however, succeed by guile rather than by force, as Lady Lechery and Bad Angel infiltrate the castle and persuade Mary to seek amusement in Jerusalem. There she is plied with wine by Lechery and a Taverner, and meets her well-dressed seducer, whose cry 'Hof, hof, hof' aligns him with the Vice types (492). His name, Curiosity, indicates the delicate truth that Mary's own interest in sex led to her downfall. Her subsequent loose life is not acted out, but is suggested in two contrasted pieces of allegory. First, in the old style, Bad Angel accepts the Devil's commission to confirm her in the laudable life of lechery: the Three Enemies then go home, while the Seven Sins repair secretly to the House of Simon the Leper. Next, with a new subtlety of technique, Mary is seen to enter an arbour, where she dreamily soliloquizes about her 'valentynes' (564), and falls asleep awaiting a lover. It is, however, Good Angel who comes to her, with such powerful remonstrances that she repents her sin and leaves the arbour to seek her true Lover, Christ. When she has anointed His feet at the House of Simon the Leper, His words of absolution cast out the Seven Sins, now dressed as devils: they retire with Bad Angel in a clap of thunder to Hell, where they are soundly beaten for their failure. Belphagor and Beelzebub set fire to Simon's house, presumably so that its last state should be worse than its first (Matthew 12: 45). The allegorical action ceases at this point, though another devil and a number of angels appear later in the play.

It is interesting that the anonymous writer of *Mary Magdalen* chose to use allegory as well as the traditional serio-comic devil-lore in his presentation of the saint's life. That a play could deal directly and effectively with fornication is shown by the N-town 'Woman Taken in Adultery' (Block, pp. 200 ff.), where realism is achieved without undue sacrifice of modesty. It would seem that allegory had its own positive attraction for audiences – it posed a kind of riddle, which lively (and trained) minds could gleefully solve, just as they solved many another verbal and visual rebus in the world around them. The slower-witted could be sure of a sufficient exposition from the text – or from their peers – in time to gain the moral benefit which full understanding was supposed to confer.

4 Sermon into drama: borrowed gear

Nearly every critic who has discussed the origin of moral plays in England has concluded that the link between early continental allegorical pieces, in Latin or a vernacular, and the well-developed fifteenth-century examples of allegorical plays, in English, is to be looked for in a special type of guild-play recorded at York and at Lincoln before 1400 and known as the Paternoster play. E. K. Chambers states the widely accepted position:

> The first English moralities seem to have been known as Paternoster plays.... Although all these Paternoster plays are lost, their general character can be made clear...a dramatization of the struggle of the vices and the corresponding virtues for the soul of man. (II, 154)

The evidence on which this opinion was based has not been discredited, except in one small particular mentioned below; but it has been put in an entirely different perspective by fifty years' work on the civic records of York and Lincoln, and the materials for a very different conclusion are now available. The clearest way towards the truth is a review of the evidence as it now stands.

The first evidence for English plays not based on a narrative belongs to the third quarter of the fourteenth century, when no less able a witness than John Wycliffe referred to a play performed at York '& in many oþere cuntreys' which made use of the Lord's Prayer in English:[1]

> & her fore freris han tauȝt in englond þe paternoster in engliȝcsh tunge, as men seyen in þe pley of ȝork, & in many oþere cuntreys, siþen þe paternoster is part of matheus gospel, as clerkis knowen, why may not al be turnyd to engliȝcsh trewely, as is þis part? (429)

The York Paternoster play, to which this is the earliest preserved reference, was undoubtedly designed to inculcate a moral truth, that the Lord's Prayer is of central importance to the Christian. Though Wycliffe ascribes its origin to the teaching friars, whose translation of the prayer he seems incidentally to countenance, we hear of it again about ten years later as the proud responsibility of a religious guild, specially founded to perpetuate it because it had proved such a salutary and popular institution. From the Latin return made by the Pater Noster Guild of York to Richard II's council in 1388–9, the general subject of the play emerges: it concerned the usefulness of the Lord's Prayer, and in it many vices and sins were condemned as well as virtues commended.[2] It is because a Pater Noster Guild account-roll of 1399, now missing, yielded one transcriber the reading 'ludum Accidie', a play of Sloth, that a connection with the Seven Deadly Sins was assumed as confidently for York's Paternoster play as for that of the neighbouring town of Beverley, where that connection was clearly established. Another transcriber however read 'ludum doctorum', a play of the doctors, at the same point in the roll before it was lost, and the reference to Sloth is to that extent discredited.[3]

The records of Beverley for 1469 do plainly reveal a show of Paternoster pageants for all seven of the Deadly Sins and an eighth pageant for 'viciose'. This, in combination with the York records, is the basis for assuming that the Yorkshire Paternoster plays were allegorical and presented a *psychomachia*. The link with the prayer was explained by E. K. Chambers as 'the mediaeval notion that each clause of the Lord's Prayer was of specific merit against one of the deadly sins' (II, 155). It is worth noting that although the publication in recent years of many Middle English sermons and

---

[1] In 'De Officio Pastorali', Ashburnham MS XXVII: ed. F. D. Matthew, *The English Works of Wyclif*, EETS, LXXIV (1880), 405–57.
[2] P.R.O. C47/454: Englished by L. Toulmin Smith in *English Gilds*, EETS, XL (1870), 137–40.
[3] For reading 'ludum Accidie' by L. Toulmin Smith, see *York Plays*, xxix: for reading 'ludum doctorum', see Angelo Raine, *Mediaeval York* (London, 1955), 91–2.

homilies has only strengthened the general proposition that a notion of this kind existed, the scheme of correspondences varies from sermon to sermon.[1]

The records of performance of the Paternoster play at York cover the next two centuries, and it was actually the last of the city's plays to roll along the streets, in 1572; but the text has been missing since the Archbishop of York ignored the city's request to return its impounded playbooks in 1575.[2] The Beverley Paternoster is likewise missing, and though the records of Lincoln show eight performances of a Paternoster play, the earliest in 1397–8, the last in 1521–2,[3] the text has vanished with every clue to its nature.

It has, however, emerged that the York Creed play, an institution first mentioned in 1446 in the will of the priest who may have written it, William Revetour, was a didactic piece of some length in English, presented every ten years or so for the benefit of the citizens of York, the last performance taking place in 1535. Elaborate plans to revive it in 1568 are on record, and clearly envisage its presentation in a series of pageants in the same manner as the York Corpus Christi plays, which it was to replace for that year. Objections to the (by then controversial) doctrine inculcated by the play prevented the carrying out of this project, and the text seems to have shared the fate of York's other civic plays. A careful examination of all the references to the Creed play has led to the conclusion that it was not only mounted and performed in the same way as the Corpus Christi cycle but made use of the very wagons and gear which were regularly used by the craft-guilds.[4]

The nature of the Creed play and the conditions of its performance seem to cast some light on the York Paternoster play. There can be no doubt that inscribed scrolls and banners were used in the presentation of the Creed play, and the inference is that (unlike the scroll-texts held by patriarchs in some of York's stained glass windows) the inscriptions were in English. Did the York Paternoster play use similar banners? There are indications

[1] See, for instance, *Middle English Sermons*, ed. W. O. Ross, EETS, CCIX (1940), 46–59, as against *Mirk's Festial*, ed. Theodor Erbe, EETS, e.s. XCVI (1905), 282–8.
[2] See Alexandra F. Johnston, 'The plays of the religious guilds of York: the Creed play and the Pater Noster play', *Speculum*, L (1975), 89–90, 75–6.
[3] Stanley J. Kahrl, *Records of Plays and Players in Lincolnshire 1300–1585* (MSC, VIII, 1969 [1974]), 27, 28, 30, 32 (*bis*), 37, 38, 50.
[4] See Johnston, 'The plays of the religious guilds of York', 55–90: documents on Paternoster play edited 86–90.

that it did: the Pater Noster Guild in 1389 owned a wooden chest in which to keep properties that were not valuable except for the play's purposes,[1] and in 1558 (the first year that the city rather than a religious guild presented the play) a painter called Ametson was paid 'liij s iiij d' for 'certayn bannar clothes for pater noster playe'.[2]

The Pater Noster Guild merged with the St Anthony's Guild in 1446 (the year the Creed play passed to a religious guild), and the only evidence about the play's length is a codicil of 1464–5 to the will of a St Anthony's Guild chaplain: 'Item ego Willelmo Ball omnes libros meos de ludo de pater noster', which suggests that the books in question were copies of separate episodes in a substantial composition.[3]

This is supported by the arrangements for the last presentation of the play in June 1572, when thirteen 'Places for hearyng of Pater Noster Play' were appointed in various quarters of the city, and the pageant-masters of 'such pageantes of certayne Occupacions of this Citie as shall be occupied in Pater Noster play' were directed to attend their own pageant with two of their guildsmen apiece, 'and see good ordre kept'.[4] The records of the Bakers show that their pageant of the Last Supper was among the wagons involved, together with its 'gear'.[5]

We seem to be dealing with a didactic play which used banners, and which borrowed costumes and properties from the craft-guild Corpus Christi cycle-plays to eke out its limited collection of special properties. That the Creed play, which by definition existed to draw attention to biblical events mentioned in the Creed, should borrow in this way is understandable; but why should a play based on the seven petitions of the Lord's Prayer, and devoted to the reprobation of sins and commendation of virtues, require biblical pageants such as the Bakers'? And granted that it did, what else did it require?

The answer which suggests itself is that (as Chambers pointed out) each clause of the Lord's Prayer can be understood as a specific defence against one particular sin: the regular use of the Paternoster in devotion repels the seven sins as a group and inculcates the seven virtues. Most of the biblical episodes dramatized in the craft-cycle of York are excellent illustrations of sins and virtues in action: the Fall of Lucifer is for example a standard

[1] ibid., 86–7: note 'vna cista lignea' in Latin text [one wooden chest], but left out of translation given.
[2] ibid., 88, item 9.
[3] ibid., 87, item 2.
[4] ibid., 89, item 13.
[5] ibid., 90, item 16.

type of Pride, and Christ, washing the disciples' feet, of Humility. The Last Supper shows Christ giving his disciples bread, and is thus linked with the petition 'give us this day our daily bread' in a way obvious even to modern readers unfamiliar with medieval modes of exegesis.

Though no proposed reconstruction of the York Paternoster play is completely acceptable in detail, it has become evident that only those discussions which account for the use of craft-cycle subjects are on the right lines. It is possible that the text was no more than a long edifying harangue on the spiritual benefits of the Paternoster, pointing the moral of such scenes as the Entry into Jerusalem and the Agony in the Garden within a scheme of correspondences laid out sermon-wise by an expositor. If 'ludum Accidie' was a mistaken reading, the play may not even have introduced the sins as characters. Because more than one scheme of exegesis is available, indeed, the suggestion of suitable pageants for illustrative tableaux is strictly an academic exercise.

When we turn to the Beverley Paternoster play, we find that the evidence for its existence, structure and management lies in an entry, partly in English and partly in Latin, in a Minute Book of 1469 (f. 150), which was described and summarized in an essay of 1901 by A. F. Leach, who had worked extensively with the Beverley records.[1]

A few comments on this entry are necessary before its implications are drawn out. First, thirty-six craft-guilds are mentioned in it, as well as Gentlemen, Clerks and Valets: if the last three groups are the same extra three to which copies of the play are said to have been distributed, twice as many guilds shared financial responsibility as were required actually to perform. Further, the play used mobile pageants and a processional system like the Beverley Corpus Christi cycle, but of the eight pageants listed, one was assigned two aldermen and the rest only one apiece. Finally, the names of the *lusores* – the parts, not the actors – are given, and are identical with the names of the pageants, but the pageants are listed in a different order, each with the group of guilds financially responsible for it. 'Viciose' is dealt with first, and the Seven Deadly sins follow – *superbie, luxurie, accidie, gule, invidie, avaricie* and *ire*.

It would seem that whatever went on at York – or at Beverley itself – nearly a hundred years earlier, the Beverley Paternoster play of 1469 had seven allegorical roles, those of the Deadly Sins. There has, however, been great difference of opinion as to the eighth of the *lusores*, Vicious, and the

---

[1] Arthur Leach, 'Some English plays and players 1220–1548' in *An English Miscellany presented to Dr Furnivall* (Oxford, 1901), 205–34; Beverley Paternoster, 220 ff.

pageant of 'viciose'. This was the premier pageant, maintained by the gentlemen, merchants, clerks and valets, and was allotted two aldermen – we know that one of them, John Copy, was himself a merchant, because he is recorded as such on 6 August 1469, when he was heavily fined for belligerence towards the players and others.[1] The 'digniorae villae' had been formed into a guild of gentlemen in 1411, and are assigned the 'Castle of Emaut' (Christ's Resurrection appearance to the disciples on the road to Emmaus) in a list of the Beverley Corpus Christi plays which survives from about 1520.[2] The Clerks are presumably the 'Prestes' responsible for the 'Coronacion of Our Lady' on the same list. These two groups and the Merchant Adventurers were outstandingly rich and prestigious – *venerabiles* indeed.

Whether the pageant of 'Viciose' is listed first because it was first to be played, or because its sponsors were so distinguished, is as much a matter of opinion as whether its protagonist was a 'typical representative of frail humanity', as E. K. Chambers thought (II, 154), or an abstract embodiment of Vices as distinct from Sins, as many other critics seem to assume. There can be no doubt that *vitia*, defects of character or bad habits of a less desperate nature than *peccata*, sins of consent, were severally embodied in fifteenth-century plays of earlier date than 1469 – Backbiting (Detraccio) in *The Castle of Perseverance* is one example. It is also true that figures called 'The Vice', with names of very wide import such as 'Iniquity', are to be found in many interludes of the sixteenth century.[3] The idea that the pageant of 'Viciose' showed a group of Vices – Flattery, say, and Folly and Immodesty – seems unlikely, since 'Vicious' is named among the *lusores* as a single entity. On the other hand, the concept of generalized Vice of the 'Iniquity' type does not fit in very well with the hint from York that selected biblical tableaux from the Corpus Christi pageants were used as examples in discussion of the separate sins. As will be seen later, the idea that Vicious was a weak, sinful human being has a good deal to recommend it.

Pride is named first among the Seven Deadly Sins on both the *lusores* list and the groups-of-guilds list. The pageant of *superbie* was assigned to the shoemakers, goldsmiths, glovers, glaziers, skinners and fishmongers: of these all but the glaziers figure in the 1520 list of Corpus Christi pageants. We therefore have some guide to what settings and costumes were available

[1] ibid., 222.
[2] ibid., 218–19.
[3] For list see Spivack, *Shakespeare and the Allegory of Evil*, 466, n. 10.

for the Pride pageant out of Corpus Christi stock: the plays which this group of guilds undertook in 1520 dealt with the Massacre of the Innocents, the Magi, Cain, Christ's entry into Jerusalem and the Presentation in the Temple.

It is perhaps a coincidence that the guilds assigned to the *luxurie* pageant are connected with clothing: the cardmakers, weavers, fullers and dyers all contributed to the processing of cloth, the pinners and wiredrawers made fastenings. The first, and the last two, of these guilds had no play in 1520: the others did the Piercing of Christ's side, the Creation of Adam and Eve, and the Agony in the Garden. These are all, of course, outdoor scenes.

To the pageant of Sloth no fewer than eight guilds were assigned, of which only the 'furbishours' (armour-polishers) had no pageant in 1520. The rest of the group comprises physically taxing crafts: watermen, husbandmen and labourers, creelmen (porters by basket) and millers certainly needed strength of arm, saddlers and ropemakers worked with tough materials. Their plays were those of Noah's Ark, the Nativity, Christ's Temptations, Adam and Eve unparadised, the Raising of Lazarus, the Creation of the World, and the Fall of Man.

Four of the Gluttony group have obvious connections with that sin: the innkeepers, who do not figure in the 1520 list, and the bakers, vintners and cooks who do. The tilers, with no apparent link, had the Fall of Lucifer play: the others had the Last Supper, the Adoration of the Shepherds, and the Harrowing of Hell.

Envy had the butchers, wrights, coopers, arrowmakers and 'patyners' (makers of wooden clogs): the last had no play in 1520, and the others had the Scourging of Christ, the Resurrection, the Flight into Egypt and (with the bowmakers) Abraham and Isaac.

To Avarice were assigned the tailors, masons, braziers, plumbers and cutlers. The masons and plumbers were well-established guilds who had appeared in a list of crafts responsible for plays in 1390;[1] but they are not listed in 1520. The braziers appear in neither list, but seem to have had affiliations with the cutlers. The only two plays we can thus associate with this group are 'Slepynge Pilate', the tailors' play of the First Trial before Pilate, and 'the Stedynynge', or Crucifixion, done by the cutlers and the potters.

Last come the Ire contingent, for some reason apparently listed in Latin. The tanners were an old guild, and though they do not figure in 1520 are

---

[1] Chambers, II, 340.

probably there included with the barkers, who by then had the Descent from the Cross. The barbers and smiths had John the Baptist and the Ascension respectively. The painters were fined in 1520 for doing a Magi play badly, but are unlikely to have challenged the goldsmiths' right to crown the Three Kings of Cologne in 1469.[1]

In this state of evidence, all conclusions about the contents of the Beverley Paternoster play must be tentative: I put forward my own for what they may be worth. As I see it, the reason that the pageant of Vicious needed two aldermen, and is mentioned first in one list and last in the other, is that it was presented in two episodes, introducing and concluding the central exhibition of the Seven Deadly Sins. The double expense would fall on the richest groups, who (in my view) turned out two pageant-wagons for each episode. In the first, very plainly-appointed, wagon, provided by the Valets, the Sinful Man, Vicious by name, vitiated by his sins, would be confronted by a priest or some other figure of authority, who would direct his thoughts towards repentance. The first step, a reverential recognition of God, would be taken by Vicious as he was taught to repeat the first clause of the Lord's Prayer ('Our Father, which art in Heaven, hallowed be Thy name'), and shown how Christ taught his disciples on the Road to Emmaus and was recognized by them at last in the breaking of bread – the Gentlemen's 'Castle of Emaut' pageant.

Next, by both reckonings, comes the pageant of Pride. Through this episode must be taught the clause 'Thy Kingdom come', so it needs to make clear the vanity of worldly kingship and the humility of Christ the King during his life on earth. For this purpose the three Kings kneeling before the Christ-child, the tyranny of Herod the King, the presumption of Cain, the meek entry of Christ into Jerusalem and Simeon's acknowledgement of the infant Jesus as Messiah can all provide useful illustrations, and the figure of Pride could be used to link the tableaux or provide contrasting monologues.

I follow the list of groups in taking the Lechery pageant next. This must teach 'Thy will be done', and certainly the dyers' play 'prainge at the Mounte', which shows Christ's agonized submission to His Father's will in the Garden of Gethsemane, is germane to this lesson. The piercing of Christ's side makes the same point, but if the Beverley play on this subject covered the same ground as York's,[2] it also provided two Romans in armour – Longinus who received his sight from Christ's blood, and the

---

[1] Leach, op. cit., 217.

[2] The York Butchers' 'Mortificacio Cristi' [XXXVI]; for 'piercing' episode, see *York Plays*, ed. cit., 368–9.

Centurion who from the darkening of the sky judged that Christ had been falsely condemned. With these two a different point about obedience could easily be arranged – the incident of that Centurion who being himself under orders took it for granted that Christ had but to speak for his servant to be healed. It may be that the fullers' cast for their 'makinge of Adam and eve' could be used to show the chaste love of man and woman before the Fall; but there are three gaps in our information here which might cover a play of the Woman taken in Adultery, or of Salome before Herod, to point the case against Lechery.

We now arrive at the only pageant where clause and sin really do seem to have a traditional link: 'Give us this day our daily bread' is a specific against Sloth. I believe, however, that this clause at Beverley was illustrated both by the Sloth episode and by the Gluttony episode. Christ resisting the temptation to turn stones into bread, and Adam and Eve 'gravynge and spynnynge', earning bread by the sweat of their brows, have an obvious affinity: Noah by his industry avoided the fate of the apathetic. The Creation of the World, the Nativity and the Raising of Lazarus all show God at work – the vital energy of the Almighty manifest on earth, the very antithesis of Sloth. To the same clause, but to the sin of Gluttony, the bakers' play of the Last Supper has obvious appropriateness – Christ shows how to gain spiritual strength by regular partaking of the sacramental food when he distributes the Bread of Life to His disciples. The Cooks with their hell-mouth could readily show the fate of gluttonous men and wine-bibbers. The Fall of Lucifer shows the fate of the spiritually greedy, and the Shepherds in Bethlehem's stable are a witness to plain living and high thinking.

In my view the next clause, 'And forgive us our debts as we forgive our debtors', was illustrated both by the Envy pageant and the Avarice pageant: both sins spring from lovelessness and self-centred discounting of the welfare of others. Most of the plays on the life of Christ could be expounded to show His sacrificial love, and the Abraham play has the same moral; but there are too many guilds whose subject is unknown to us in the Avarice group for much speculation to be profitable. No lesson could, however, be more apt to the theme of forgiveness than Christ's prayer for His executioners, which must have formed part of the 'Stedynynge' play. York of course had a group of Judas plays, of which neither the ironmongers' 'Christ at the House of Simon the Leper' nor the saucemakers' 'Suspencio Jude' survive:[1] if the Beverley cycle had a similar group in 1469, the

[1] ibid., xxii, 'Irenmangers' and n. 3; xxiv, n. 1.

resentment of Judas over the 'wasted' box of ointment, his selling of his Master for thirty pieces of silver, and his remorse, would fit Envy and Avarice very well.

The Ire pageant must have illustrated 'Lead us not into temptation' as well as the contrast between irascibility and long-suffering. Though John the Baptist was indeed a victim of vengeful ire, the barbers' play showed him at Christ's Baptism; he could certainly prophesy the wrath of God, on the one hand, and indicate Christ as the Lamb of God, the pattern of patience, on the other. But the real link with this clause and with the lesson of the smiths' Ascension play is the descent of the Holy Spirit as a dove, witnessed at the Baptism and promised by the ascending Christ in his farewell to the disciples. It is the Holy Spirit who wards off temptation, and His seven Gifts that furnish all the help a contrite soul requires to live in peace. An Ascension play recorded at Bury St Edmunds in 1477 linked the 'ȝiftis of the Holy Gost' with the portrayal of the Ascension itself,[1] and the York Ascension play shows Christ first promising the disciples that they shall suffer for the truth, next reprobating their mistrust and disputes one with another, and finally describing the help and comfort which only the descent of the Holy Spirit can bring.

So we come to the last clause, 'but deliver us from evil': for this I suggest that the 'Viciose' group brought out their second episode, using the great Doomsday pageant of the merchants along with the priests' Coronation of the Virgin to show not only Christ's power to deliver but the truth of the Paternoster's conclusion, 'For Thine is the Kingdom, the Power and the Glory, for ever and ever. Amen'. Vicious, the Sinful Man whose need for repentance had introduced the whole play, would not be required in the pageants of universal significance which follow, particularly not in the scene of the Last Judgement, where every member of the audience would be faced with the question of whether he personally belonged to the sheep or the goats.

These suggestions are necessarily open to criticism, and may yet be irrefutably set aside if more evidence comes to light. Two conclusions are, however, inevitable: first, that the Beverley Paternoster play dealt with the Lord's Prayer in a didactic manner; next, that in 1469 it made use of at least seven allegorical personages.

There can be no doubt, then, that the late fourteenth century and the fifteenth century brought forth some special examples of dramatized

[1] Chambers, II, 343–4.

sermon in English. The York Paternoster play and the York Creed play were vehicles of moral instruction which used methods of bringing home their morals which were openly didactic, like the display of signs and banners. Though we cannot estimate the proportion of their texts which explicitly related such costumed players as were grouped on their pageant-wagons to the particular lesson on hand, we can see that such explanations would be essential, and could not be much abbreviated without impairing the clarity of the doctrine. It would seem, however, that neither of these plays was a *psychomachia*, and that they had few allegorical roles. They cannot be denied the title of early moral plays, but they are not morality plays of the type familiar to us where the preponderance of characters are either allegorical or supernatural. Even the Beverley Paternoster play, with its Seven Deadly Sins and latish fifteenth-century evidence for their distribution between different pageants, is not a morality play in that sense – the Sins on different wagons cannot converse together.

The existence and success of these plays is, however, exactly the encouragement that somebody who really did want to use allegory as a way of calling attention to his message would readily accept. Because established techniques for mounting plays were available in the last three decades of the fourteenth century, they were borrowed for didactic drama: because they went on being effective for both biblical and moral (not yet allegorical) plays, they lent something to allegorical drama when that kind was attempted.

5 Sermon into allegory: shared concepts

It has long been recognized that the Persons of the Trinity and all the hosts of Heaven were presented in the allegorical moralities in the same way as in other religious drama, and that this mode of presentation is based on the Bible, apocryphal tradition and church ritual. The discovery that costumes and settings of guild-plays were literally borrowed for use in Paternoster plays only strengthens the view that an audience experienced in interpreting wall-paintings and stained glass windows had a settled and detailed expectation of what dress and properties befitted each well-known character. A special point about the Godhead is suggested by an iconographical tradition in illuminated Bibles which shows God in Trinity as a man-sized being, having two faces inside one aureole (the Father full-bearded, the Son with centrally-parted smooth hair) and the Spirit as a dove (with His own aureole and outspread wings) clinging to the left shoulder.[1] That elaborate (often gilded) masks of this type were used in plays explains many instances where the single speech-prefix 'Deus' heralds expressions appropriate to now one, now another Person of the Trinity. A good example occurs in

[1] A good example is the Genesis of the fourteenth-century 'Naples' Bible now in the Austrian National Library, Vienna (Codex 1191): see *The Illuminated Naples Bible*, ed. Eva Irblich (Fribourg, 1979; Geneva, 1979), 17 (from f. 4ʳ), 119.

the Digby *Conversion of St Paul*,[1] where the source (Acts 9: 4, 17) specifies the voice of Jesus on the Road to Damascus and the appearance of Jesus to Ananias. The words of 'Deus' when 'Godhed spekyth in heuyn' are

> I am þi Savyour that ys so trwe,
> Whych made heuyn and erth, and eche creature. (185–6)

and though the stage-directions '*Cryst apperyth to Annanie*' and '*et exiat Deus*' frame the interview, 'From Almyghty God sertanly to the sent I am' is the way Ananias reports his commission. It is also noteworthy that a stage-effect is used to show Saul's illumination by the Holy Spirit: '*Hic aparebit Spiritus Sanctus super eum*', probably as a hovering dove on golden rays of the sort shown in pictures of the Annunciation. Since Ananias proceeds to 'crysten' Saul '*In nomine patris et filij et spiritus sancti*', it is no wonder that Poeta closes this section of the play by recommending the audience to the Trinity (353).

Though *The Conversion of St Paul* uses no abstract characters, it does contain two non-biblical episodes of a popular stamp: in the first (85–119), Saul's servant exchanges filthy insults with an Ostler, and in the other (412–502) the devils Belial and Mercury lament Saul's defection with the thunder-claps, flashes of fire, crying and roaring which were standard in scenes of Hell. No doubt, like Belial in *The Castle of Perseverance* a century before,[2] these demons concealed gunpowder in pipes disposed strategically about their persons. The devil-scene was probably added to the play as late as 1530,[3] a concession to unsophisticated taste which foreshadows the Robin and Ralph episode in Marlowe's *Doctor Faustus*.

It is significant that Belial and Mercury conclude their conversation by rejoicing that the Seven Deadly Sins are so rampant among men that Saul's defection will hardly be felt: they mention all except Sloth by name (489–95). The position of the Devil at the head of an unholy trinity, responsible with World and Flesh for all the sins that beset mankind, is stock sermon material. Grosseteste was one among many notable expositors when he wrote: 'The demons fight against the soul's rationality by pride... the world

---

[1] Baker, *Digby Plays*, 1–23.

[2] See Plate 5 for stage-plan of *Castle of Perseverance*: for fireworks, note SD on plan, 'and he þat schal pley belyal loke þat he haue gunnepowdyr brennynge in pypys in hys handys and in hys erys and in his ars whanne he gothe to batayl', transcribed by Eccles, *Macro Plays*, 1.

[3] D. C. Baker and J. L. Murphy, ''The late medieval plays of MS Digby 133: scribes, dates, and early history', *RORD*, x (1967), 153–66.

against its sensible part by cupidity...the flesh against its vegetative part by lechery',[1] an alignment akin to that found in *The Castle of Perseverance*. It is not a coincidence that the converted Saul goes straight on to preach against the sins – including 'slugyshness' (510–37). An exact parallel can be found in the elaborate Prologue of Demon which forms a link between the Raising of Lazarus and the Passion sequences of the N-town cycle (Block, pp. 225–9): Lucifer here counters Christ's sending out of the twelve disciples by displaying and freshly naming his own little flock of servants, all the sins except (again) Sloth. He mimics the elevated tone of a preacher –

> Gyff me your love·grawnt me myn Affeccion
> And I wyl vnclose·þe tresour of lovys Alyawns [*alliance*]
> (p. 227, 61–2)

– comments on the fashionable, worldly dress of a gallant (Pride) and a whore (Lechery), and calls the pair Honesty and Natural Kind. His parting words are a blasphemous parody of Christ's at Matthew 28: 20: 'I am with ʒow at all tymes·whan ʒe to councel me call' (p. 229, 123). Once again, a monition against the sins immediately follows, this time from John the Baptist:

> I councel þe ʒe reforme all wronge
> in ʒour concyens of þe mortall dedys·sevyn (p. 229, 5–6)

and once again the villainy of Annas and Caiaphas ensues.

Lucifer's association of evil-doing with the latest style in dress is a good example of a sermon theme prevalent in the moral plays. Pride in *The Castle of Perseverance* instructs Humanum Genus:

> Loke þou blowe mekyl bost
> Wyth longe crakows on þi schos
> Jagge þi clothis in every cost
> And ell men schul lete þe but a goos. (1058–61)

The combination of long, pointed shoes and fancy-cut edges belongs to early fourteenth-century fashion: Lucifer's 'long pekyd schon' and 'hosyn enclosyd' (p. 227, 69–70) would have been worth remark between 1400 (when joined hose – 'tights', as we call them – came in) and 1410 (when long, pointed toes went out); but the lice-infested 'side lokkys' of his page-boy hair-style (p. 227, 85–6) and his 'hey smal bonet' (p. 228, 87)

---

[1] 'Treatise for Confessors', BL MS Royal 7 Fii, f. 89ᵛ⁻ᵛ. Quoted by Siegfried Wenzel, 'The three enemies of Man', *Mediaeval Studies*, XXIX (1967), 47–66; esp. pp. 48–9.

place this passage between 1460 and 1480, when 'peaked' shoes were in again and Turkish bonnets were newly in vogue.[1] Lechery's widely-spread collar trimmed with fur was a new style in 1475 or so (p. 228, 105).[2] The indecently short 'joly jakett' to which New Guise and Nought reduce Mankind's dignified long gown (*Mankind*, 718) is the same fashion which the Lucifer of *Wisdom* recommends (*Wisdom*, 510): it was often satirized in verse of the period:[3]

> They be cutted on the buttok even aboue the rompe.
> Euery good man truly such shappe lothes. (Idley, II, B, 44–5)

A close link between the fashions of a gallant and the sins, especially lechery, is made later in the century by the *Treatyse of a Gallant* –

> As in this name Galaunt / ye may expresse
> Seuen letters for some cause in especyall
> That fygureth the vii deedly synnes & theyr wretchednes,[4]

and by Medwall in *Nature*, who uses Pride's advice that Man change to the latest style as a device to link the two parts of the play.[5] Pride describes what he orders for Man from the tailor (I, 1060–75), and though Man repents and relapses again before Pride can report 'All thyng ys redy' (II, 425), he changes into the new clothes and returns with Bodily Lust, a male incarnation of Lechery, to receive the compliments of his retinue of sins (II, 563 ff.). It is implicit that when at last Man is converted and leaves to seek Repentance (II, 1364–70), he uses the three stanzas of Reason's address to the audience to conceal his shameless dress beneath a penitential garment – he comes back to report that he has been to Confession and now knows Heart's Contrition (II, 1397–8). Everyman is given the garment of contrition, wet with his tears, at the same stage in his restoration to grace;[6] but Everyman's absolution and penance are swiftly followed by his death, whereas Man with Reason at his side means to continue in 'good perseveraunce' and pass to his reward after a worthier phase of life.

[1] C. W. Cunnington and P. Cunnington, *Handbook of English Mediaeval Costume* (London, 2nd edn rev. 1973), 108–9, 147, 150.
[2] ibid., 155.
[3] See for instance the discourse on Pride by Peter Idley in 'Instructions to his Son' (1440–50) in Cambridge University Library MS Ee 4.37: the work is edited by Charlotte d'Evelyn (Boston: Modern Language Association of America, 1935); see esp. 159.
[4] See V. J. Scattergood, *Politics and Poetry in the Fifteenth Century* (London, 1974), 343–4.
[5] *The Plays of Henry Medwall*, ed. Nelson, 91–161.
[6] See *Everyman*, ed. Cawley, 638–47; also n. to p. 35, and p. xxiv with its n.

Though the agents of evil in *Mankind* express themselves in so many fifteenth-century colloquial obscenities, the protagonist's father-confessor Mercy relates them firmly to the traditional pattern:

> The New Gyse, Nowadayis, Nowgth, þe World we may hem call;
> And propyrly Titiuillus syngnyfyth the Fend of helle:
> The Flesch, þat ys þe vnclene concupissens of ʒour body...
> Þei browt ʒow to Myscheffe. (885–9)

Titivillus seems to be presented as a grotesquely large-headed demon like the Big-Head of later mummers' plays (461), but his function as tempter is serious enough, and there is a point in his strategy which is worth special attention, as it helps explain the omission of Sloth in the sin-lists so far discussed. Devils are not themselves lazy, but they make the sinner so, in a spiritual sense above all. In *Mankind*, Titivillus places a board in the earth to make digging too difficult. Mankind has already used his spade to beat the three worldlings, but gives up cultivation when he finds hard ground and contaminated seed (530–50). The spade is at once an emblem of labour and a reminder that Adam was condemned to dig because of his Fall, so when Titivillus carries it off, Mankind sinks into a sloth the more culpable because he imagines he can pray instead of working. As he tells his beads, Titivillus whispers three dissuasions – short prayers pierce heaven, Mankind is already the most pious of his family, and nature calls. Mankind goes out to ease himself, returns only to fall asleep, and so becomes the picture of Sloth. The crowning irony, which only those dieted on medieval sermons can relish, is that the spade is also a distinguishing property of Sloth, who was supposed to use it to channel away the water of grace from the moats surrounding allegorical castles. Sloth in *The Castle of Perseverance* joins the siege with 'Ware, war, I delue wyth a spade...Fro þe watyr of grace þis dyche I fowe' (2326–9). Besides being yet another reason for taking the ditch in the stage-plan of this play to be part of the setting, the Castle's moat, the speech is a reminder of why *accidia*, sloth of spirit, is so disabling: the lazy soul does not seek cleansing by absolution. Sloth's opposed Virtue, Solicitudo (whose name means rather more than Busyness, perhaps 'Spiritual Awareness'), goes on to point this out (2345–55), in the spirit of a popular pastoral handbook of the early fourteenth century, *Oculus sacerdotis*:[1] 'In the army of the devil, pride carries the banner...then

---

[1] BL MS Royal 6E, f. 46ʳ; see Siegfried Wenzel, *The Sin of Sloth* (Chapel Hill, N. Carolina, 1967), 148.

Accidia empties the ditches of the water of grace, for "a sad mind dries up the bones"' (Proverbs 17: 22).

A valuable clue to the way in which plays designed to present incidents essential to the doctrine of salvation moved effortlessly into allegory is afforded by a solitary part for an actor playing God the Father. Preserved by a sixteenth-century copyist who endorsed it 'old verses / Fro limebrook', the part records not only God's speeches but the tags from other named speakers which served as cues, as well as some stage directions.[1] The action opens on the basis of the fifth chapter of Revelation; but just as Christ Victorious is about to unclasp the Book of Seven Seals, Satan intervenes to allege 'Villeny and wronge' (17), by which he means the redemption from Hell of the 'synners' (71) now sanctified by the Blood of the Lamb (31–4). Restraining St Michael from smiting Satan, God hears the complaint and offers 'commissioners' to try it impartially (76). Satan repudiates the advocacy of several patriarchs before electing 'Verite and Justice', whom God appoints, together with their sisters Mercy and Peace (116, 131–2). God then apparently relaxes for 'an houre space' (149) while the debate proceeds. When the 'Courte celestiall' adjourns, God follows up a speech by Christ with such massive supporting testimony that the murmuring Fiend is at last bereft of arguments. Both vocabulary and style suggest that the original of this piece was of fifteenth-century workmanship: W. W. Greg edited the part as *Processus Satanae*.

The Heavenly Sisters selected as commissioners are of course the Four Daughters of God who figure so often in medieval literature and whose genesis was in Hebrew scripture. 'Mercy and truth are met together: righteousness and peace have kissed each other' (Psalm 85: 10) is a text from which the two contrasted pairs of God's attributes, the stern and the gentle, fairly step forth to debate. In the Midrash, a rabbinical commentary of the tenth century, their debate preceded the creation of man: in Christian homiletic, a version of this Parliament in Heaven prefaced sometimes the redemption of mankind and sometimes specifically the Annunciation.[2] In the N-town cycle, the episode is introduced by the 'exposytour in doctorys wede' (Block, p. 271, SD at 1) called Contemplacio, who first appears after the section of prophetic prophecies to act as guide through the early life of the Blessed Virgin (pp. 62–97): after Mary's betrothal, Contemplacio reports a general cry in Heaven for mercy on the sins of mankind, the debate ensues, and concludes in the reconciliation of

[1] Welbeck Abbey MS: ed. W. W. Greg, *MSC*, II, iii (London, 1931), 239–50.
[2] Hope Traver, *The Four Daughters of God* (Bryn Mawr, Penn., 1907).

the Four with their ritual kiss (pp. 97–103), whereupon Gabriel is despatched to Nazareth. This is late work, like Chaundler's Latin version in the *Liber Apologeticus* (see next paragraph); but the long section in *The Castle of Perseverance* where the Four debate the dying plea of Humanum Genus for mercy (3129–560) shows that they were *dramatis personae* in England even before their famous French incarnations in the *Passions* of Mercadé (pre-1440) and Gréban (*c*.1452).[1] Two Anglo-Norman dialogues of the twelfth century show the Four debating the guilt of Adam: both are purely literary compositions, but they seem to stem from Stephen Langton, Archbishop of Canterbury,[2] and Grosseteste's *Château d'Amour*, equally literary, carried the motif into the thirteenth century with the authority of a Bishop of Lincoln:[3] it became stock material for English preachers. That both Langland and Lydgate made use of it in poems is not surprising; but it was also used in 1445 for one of the street-pageants to welcome Margaret of Anjou to London.[4] The choice illustrates very neatly the utter accessibility of moral allegory to the fifteenth-century public.

It is worth taking a close look at the *Liber Apologeticus* for several reasons, in spite of its limited circulation in its own day. For one thing, it can be dated on irrefutable evidence: it belongs to the years when Chaundler held his first chancellorship of Oxford University, 1457 to 1461. For another, its action constitutes a selection from the stock of characters and themes most frequent in allegorical drama. For a third, its unique manuscript contains fourteen elegant and detailed illustrations, which yield much more than moral instruction.[5]

The action when briefly summarized does not sound lively, and indeed very little happens in the piece compared with the very much which is spoken. Newly created Man, first of mankind, makes the wrong choice between sober Dame Reason and sly Lady Sensuality. He falls from grace, is exiled from his throne, enjoined mortality, discipline and hard labour, and arraigned by two of God's Four Daughters, Truth and Justice. God, however, chooses to accept the pleas of His other two daughters, Mercy and Peace, becomes incarnate, and hails Man as brother. To keep Man in the way of salvation, God-as-Christ before ascending to Heaven gives him four servants: they are the Four Cardinal Virtues, Justice (a second

---

[1] See Grace Frank, *The Medieval French Drama*, 179–87; esp. 180, n. 1.

[2] See Peter Dronke, *Poetic Individuality in the Middle Ages* (Oxford, 1970), 169, n. 2.

[3] See *The Middle English Translations of Robert Grosseteste's 'Château d'Amour'*, ed. Kari Sajavaara (Helsinki, 1967).

[4] BL MS Harley 3869: ed. Carleton Brown, *MLR*, VII (1912), 225–34. See also Gordon Kipling, 'The London Pageants for Margaret of Anjou' *METh*, 4 (1982), 5–27.

[5] *Liber Apologeticus*, ed. D. Enright-Clark Shoukri, 25–6; Plates I–XIV; 41–4.

embodiment), Temperance, Fortitude and Prudence, and between them they so support Man that he can bear to admit Fear-of-Death, who announces the imminent and terrible arrival of Death his master.

Heavenly Love promptly brings a message promising eternal life beyond the grave, so Fear-of-Death is cast out. Man is able to give a dignified welcome to Death, who strikes him and strips away his mortal part. The Cardinal Virtues carry Man up to receive a crown and to rejoice for ever in God's sight among the hosts of Heaven.

The source which Chaundler was quarrying for this piece, Hugo of St Victor's *De Anima*,[1] had already lent the Cardinal Virtues and Fear-of-Death episode to one of the earliest extant prose homilies in English, *Sawles Warde*, and the material was familiar in other English versions.[2] Chaundler, however, worked directly from the Latin of this influential Christian book and of several other such texts.[3]

Conformably with the eminence of this author, the *Liber Apologeticus* proceeds with a pomp of Latin phrase and a panoply of rhetorical ornament which have no connection with vulgar speech or popular entertainment. We know that Chaundler inflicted a set of Latin dialogues in honour of William of Wykeham upon his college as a Christmas revelry, and that he caused a lengthy Latin verse debate on the respective merits of Bath and Wells (written by himself as between St Peter and St Andrew) to be read aloud in public for the general edification:[4] he would hardly have blenched at setting up the *Liber Apologeticus* in the same way, and is unlikely to have intended this elaborate work for the eye of its dedicatee, Bishop Beckington, alone. Those who took part and those who watched would, however, have needed a firm grasp on their classical and theological erudition to make sense of the long speeches, and it must have seemed an interminable evening.

Nevertheless, the beautifully prepared manuscript which was presented to Beckington contains in its fourteen illustrations many details of the action in progress (such as the dart with which Death strikes Man – see Plate 30) which are not mentioned in the text or its rubrics. Whether the illustrator had witnessed a performance or not, he was obviously in no doubt about how the characters should look and what gestures they must be seen to make.

It is obvious that Chaundler was drawing upon a stock of imagery which

---

[1] ibid., 21, 188–92.
[2] See R. M. Wilson, *Early Middle English Literature* (London, 3rd edn, 1968), 119–21.
[3] *Liber Apologeticus*, 18–20.
[4] ibid., 4, 14–16, 37, n. 15.

was the common property of learned divines like himself, parish priests who gave sermons to the lewd, and the lewd who recognized the sermon-images when they met them embodied in the action of religious plays. Newly created Man is called a prince, and invested by God with a mantle of immortality, a sceptre of justice, and an orb which represents lordship of the globe. To these regal insignia the artist adds a canopied throne, and he trims the robe of immortality with the ermine of an earthly monarch. But Man is not pictured with a crown until the last of all the illustrations, when the crown of an eternity in God's presence after death makes him king indeed. With a decorum which is characteristic of medieval iconography, Man before his fall is shown with a simple circlet: it is Dame Reason who wears the crown.

Many symbolic actions – pieces of business from a theatrical point of view – are woven into the illustrations upon slight hints in the text. The fact that Sensuality is a young woman, a blind handmaid, whose offering of the forbidden fruit equates her with an Eve otherwise missing from the story, is elaborated by the artist into a tableau of shame and seduction on a peculiar long seat resembling both bed and tomb, where Man realizes in horror that his sceptre is broken and orb rolled away, as he rises from the lap of the temptress to see himself naked and ugly in Reason's mirror. Death's looks are not described in the text beyond his 'horrible countenance', but the artist presents him as a naked cadaver striking Man with a long dart. Because Man triumphs over Death in the sense that he receives immortality, he is shown in the last picture trampling the kneeling cadaver beneath his feet as he sits enthroned.

The moment of confrontation with Death is of course an important and popular topic in the art and literature of the medieval period. Because one of the latest and best-known morality plays in English, *Everyman*, makes so much of Death as a mighty messenger from God Himself, and in that text (as we have it) there is dignity rather than grisly circumstance in the presentation of Death as a character, it is easy to assume that grotesquerie formed no part of the usual way of presenting the fatal confrontation. Such an assumption is false. The blackened skeletons brandishing spears which menace brightly dressed men, women and children in so many manuscript illuminations of the fourteenth and fifteenth centuries frequently have jubilant or vindictive expressions and poses.[1] The word 'macabre' seems

[1] For refs. see James M. Clark, 'The Dance of Death in medieval literature', *MLR*, XLV (1950), 336–45: some pictures of interest are reproduced by T. S. R. Boase, *Death in the Middle Ages and the Renaissance* (London, 1972), 104–7. Two Dance of Death pictures may also be found in Vol. II of the Revels History of Drama (Plates 8 and 9).

to have entered the French language (perhaps from a personal name) in the late fourteenth century, as an epithet for that gruesome procession of men in every rank of life being tugged to the grave by skeletal or devisicerated cadavers which is known as the *danse macabre*.[1] Whether or not an actual dance or mime preceded pictorial representation of this theme is debatable: it is, however, clear that wall-paintings of the grim dancers and their reluctant human partners were to be found in a number of churches of western Europe during the fifteenth century. Some – for example that of La Chaise-Dieu, Haute Loire – still survive, a monument to a peculiarly repellent sensibility;[2] but the two examples most germane to the present purpose, that of the cemetery of the Innocents Church in Paris, and the copy of it in a cloister of St Paul's Cathedral for which John Lydgate translated the verse-inscriptions, have long since perished.

Woodcuts of the series of pictures at the Innocents, and copies of the inscriptions, do, however, survive in several French editions, of which the oldest, extant in only one copy, is of 1485.[3] It is immediately obvious from both text and illustrations that the imperative summons to join the dance is offered not by 'Death', a personification, but by a number of dead men – a variety of skeletal figures, differently equipped with dart or pick-axe or shovel, some partially shrouded, many with worms preying on their vestigial flesh, all maliciously grinning as they sink their bony grip into their victims. The verses begin with a warning that 'Mort n'espargne petit ne grant', but this theme is taken up not by 'La Mort' but by four dead men, speaking in turn and represented as playing on instruments – bagpipes, portative organ, harp, fife and drum – to accompany the dance. The first summons is offered by 'Le mort' to 'Le Pape', the next by 'Le Mort' to 'L'Empereur', and so on via cardinal and king in a grotesque echo of the precedence manuals (see p. 246) through all the walks of life down to the 'petit enfant, n'a guere né', with his 'A.a.a je ne sçay parler'. The moral is pointed by 'Le roy mort' – the dead king, not the King of Death – who tells us (in Lydgate's version)[4]

3e folke that loken | vpon this purtrature
Beholdyng here | all the estates daunce
Seeth what 3e ben | & what is 3owre nature
Mete vnto wormes | not elles yn substaunce (p. 74, 633–6)

[1] See Beatrice White, Intro. and Apps. to *The Dance of Death*, ed. Florence Warren, EETS, o.s. CLXXXI (1931), xvi–xvii, 98–100.
[2] See Boase, op. cit., fig. 89.
[3] Edward F. Chaney (ed.), *La Danse Macabré des Charniers des Saints Innocents à Paris* (Manchester, 1945).
[4] Lydgate's text ed. Florence Warren, *The Dance of Death*, EETS.

A crowned corpse bearing a warning scroll and leaning over the tripartite banner of King René of Anjou survives in a Book of Hours now in London:[1] it was painted, perhaps by King René himself, in about 1435, a generation earlier than the printed versions of the *danse macabre*. Earlier still may be found representations of the confrontation of three living men with three dead men – themselves as they must shortly be. This motif – known in France as 'les trois morts et les trois vifs' – proved popular in other parts of Europe, and may have given rise to the 'pairing' of cadaver and victim in the deadly dance.[2] The literature of this subject is extensive, and there is no need to follow it further here than to note that we have scattered references to actual performances by players of pieces based on the *danse macabre*. At Bruges in 1449 a 'jeu, histoire et moralité sur le fait de la danse macabre' was presented before Philip the Good of Burgundy, and at Besançon the same sort of thing was done in 1453.[3] The *memento mori* aspect of the whole theme slides into social satire very readily, and it was presumably the concept of Death the Leveller which appealed to the poor of Paris so strongly that they resorted to the cloisters of the Innocents for holiday entertainment.

Though an apparent reference to the well-known theme is made by Death in *Everyman* –

> I set not by golde, syluer nor rychesse,
> Ne by pope | emperour | kynge | duke, ne prynces (125–6),

the universality of the play's application precludes the precise ranking of the central character. Everyman seems to be of middle years and middle class; he is a Christian who has lapsed from grace, he has valuable possessions by which he sets too much store, he has family and friends who are carnally-minded, but has himself in his time performed some good actions. It is the sheer ordinariness of Everyman which gives his fate such impact; but the Death who confronts him with such composure and majesty has little in common with the worm-eaten cadavers of the *danse macabre* woodcuts. It is ironic that the woodcut of Death chosen for *Everyman* by John Skot[4] should have derived from the French tradition rather than the play itself: a tall skeleton holding a coffin-lid stands amid memorial crosses on an open grave. Death in *Everyman* carries a dart (76), and at the close

[1] BL Egerton 1070, f. 53: repro. Boase, op. cit., fig. 108.
[2] E.g. Campo Santo fresco, Pisa: repro. Boase, op. cit., fig. 90.
[3] See Beatrice White, Intro. to *The Dance of Death*, ed. Warren, xi.
[4] Reproduced as frontispiece to *Everyman*, ed. Cawley: see also 39–40 of that edition.

of his warning visit announces that he will smite with it (178–9); but since Everyman does not recognize his visitor at first (113–14), it would seem that at least a cloak and hood disguise the King of Terrors until the proclamation, 'I am Dethe that no man dredeth' [who is afraid of nobody] (115), sets Everyman trembling and trying to bargain. When Everyman approaches his grave at the end of the play, Death is not among the speakers, and there is little wormy circumstance: Everyman indeed mentions that he must turn to earth, which precipitates the flight of Beauty, disinclined to consume away and stifle in the 'cave' he shows her, but the emphasis is on his progressive loss of faculties and the loyalty, up to the moment of dissolution, of the sisters Knowledge and Good Deeds. There is perhaps a hint that Death makes his appearance with a trumpet to herald that instant (843); but Everyman makes a good end, having been fortified by the rites of Holy Church (773–4) after arranging the restitution of his ill-gotten gains and leaving the other half of his goods as alms (699–702).

We shall see that Everyman is the only character left to us in the moral plays who makes such a good end: in the hybrid play of *Mary Magdalen*, indeed, angels convey a priest to administer the last rites to the dying saint, who manages to recite a little more of the mandatory text 'In manus tuus, Domine' (Luke 23: 46) than Everyman did, before she expires.[1] Two angels then receive her soul, there is jubilation in Heaven, and the Priest says he will hand the body over to the local bishop for burial (2119–30). Death does not appear as a character in this play, though the saint's father 'takyt his deth' – feels the throes and is helped off to bed – early in the story (265 ff.), and both Lazarus and the Queen of Marseilles have death-bed speeches (819 ff., 1753–65). It is perhaps because both the last-named characters are to be resurrected within the play that the question of whether angels or devils bear away their souls is not raised. In many extant pictures of death-bed scenes, the soul of the newly dead is seen like a small child issuing from the mouth of the corpse, while winged angels and demons wait to secure it: sometimes the soul is seen aloft, torn between opposing forces.[2]

A particularly valuable illustration in the early fifteenth-century Rohan Book of Hours shows the dead man lying lightly shrouded on an embroidered vestment spread among skulls and bones: from his mouth issues the Latin text of 'In manus tuus...' on a scroll. His tiny, naked soul, unbearded and with bright hair, is in the clutches of a flying, shaggy demon, who is being vigorously attacked by St Michael and a troop of other

[1] *Mary Magdalen*, ed. Baker, *Digby Plays*; death of saint, 2094–118.
[2] Examples in Boase, op. cit., 39 and fig. 28; figs. 103–5.

Heaven-dwellers. God the Father in person, crowned and with cross-nimbus, leans down holding sword and orb to address the decedent in French, urging penance and promising relief on Judgement Day.[1] This grouping is very much nearer the serious, deeply compassionate anxiety for the soul's future shown in several moral plays than any of the *danse macabre* woodcuts.

As it happens, though the stroke of Death is seen in the action of *The Castle of Perseverance* (2840), a page of the manuscript is missing just after Humanum Genus dies (3007), at the point where his soul, Anima, who has been hidden under a bed since the beginning of the play, begins a complaint against the body and an appeal to his Good Angel. The rival Angels have been wrangling over the hero's fate since the play began, and they are at it again when the text resumes, Bad Angel in the ascendant. Because Humanum Genus died the prey of Covetousness, the soul is hauled off to the torments of Hell, whence he is to be exhaled in due course by the Four Daughters of God. About one hundred lines of text are missing here, and naturally some of them must have been concerned with the early stages of the Angels' argument, but at least a stage direction and perhaps some dialogue should have disposed of the body. Since the ill-conditioned servant of World, Garcio, who was sent to vex the death-bed by announcing himself as the heir 'I Wot Neuere Whoo', has already made the threat 'Into a lake I schal hym lyfte' (2915), it seems likely that he came back at some point in the missing passage to heave the corpse into the ditch and possess himself of the money-bags kept in 'Covetyse copbord be þe beddys feet' (stage-plan; see Plate 5).

The figure of Death in *The Castle of Perseverance* appears after Humanum Genus has left the Castle at the instigation of Covetyse and settled down as a miser. There is no element of surprise in his appearance, as several references to the approach of death have been made in the preceding stanzas (2734, 2759, 2772). Death's boast is on standard lines until, with a change of emphasis appropriate to the case in hand, he remarks that modern men are so avaricious that they have even forgotten to be afraid of him (it was otherwise 'In þe grete pestelens'), and he soon expects to broach them on the point of his lance (2779–842). He makes a start on Humanum Genus, and goes his way. As solemn but less stern, the Death of *Everyman* replies to Everyman's questions and even offers him good advice. The cynical and cruel tone of *les morts* in the *danse macabre* is taken by World and Garcio in *The Castle of Perseverance* when Humanum Genus lies dying: the play is probably older, however, than the sequence in the

---

[1] Bib. Nat. Paris MS lat 9471, f. 159: repro. Boase, op. cit., fig. 102.

cemetery of the Innocents. The gloating of Goods in *Everyman* (454–6) is in the tradition of World's 'I wolde þou were in þe erthe beloke/And anoþyr hadde þyne erytage' (2871–2).

One of the most frightening things about Death in *Everyman* is the way he confronts the careless worldling so unexpectedly ('O Dethe, thou comest whan I had the leest in mynde', 119). This effect was avoided in *The Castle of Perseverance*, and it seems unlikely that the King of Death in *The Pride of Life* arrived unheralded at the trial by combat; but a parallel irony is found in the N-town cycle, where Herod's pomping is interrupted by the advent of Mors, armed with a spear, 'Ow se how prowdely ʒon kaytyff sytt at mete./of deth hath he no dowte[;] he wenyth to leve evyr-more' (Block, p. 175). The initial boast of Mors ('I am deth goddys masangere', p. 174, 177 ff.) is also parallel with the *Everyman* treatment, but Mors is allowed three additional stanzas after he has killed Herod and the two knights, whom Diabolus bears off to 'showe such myrthe as is in helle' (p. 176, 232 SD). Possibly Diabolus took small naked images to brandish as the three souls, for Mors makes it clear that Herod's body is still in sight of the audience – 'he lyth now ded here on his syde' (249) – and that Herod's soul has left it:

Now is he as pore as I
wormys mete is his body
his sowle in helle ful peynfully
of develis is al to-torn (p. 177, 255–8)

We learn also from this last speech that Mors here really was presented like one of the *danse macabre* skeletons:

Thow I be nakyd and pore of array
and wurmys knawe me al a-bowte
ʒit loke ʒe drede me nyth and day. (272–4)

It is apparent that the embodied figure of Death has a longer and more distinguished ancestry than is implied by loose references to the Dance of Death tradition. One of the earliest records of court revels in Scotland, the chronicler John of Fordun's description of Alexander III's wedding-feast at Jedburgh in 1285, mentions the interruption of a martial evolution to music by the sudden entry of a spectral shape, something between man and phantasm, in whose presence 'risum dolore miscetur' [laughter was mingled with grief]: because the King was killed within the year, a retrospective extra shudder is demanded by the account.[1]

---

[1] A. J. Mill, *Mediaeval Plays in Scotland* (Edinburgh, 1927), 48.

It is a coincidence that in *The Pride of Life* Death also comes to a king with a lovely young wife, and a coincidence in another sense that the pages of this play in which the confrontation actually occurs, the King dies, and the fiends seize upon the soul, have not survived. It is however evident from the Prologue and the opening pages that, after repeated warnings of the power of Death, the King of Life issues a presumptuous challenge, is defeated in combat by the King of Death and given his death-wound.

> Qwhen þe body is doun ibroȝt [brought down]
>   þe soule sorow awakith:
> þe bodyis pride is dere aboȝt,
>   þe soule þe fendis takith. (93–6)

The implication of the next stanza is that just as Mercy and Peace in *The Castle of Perseverance* plead with their sisters and their Father for the soul of Humanum Genus, the Blessed Virgin will intercede for the soul of the King of Life:

> And throgh priere of Oure Lady mylde
> þe soule and body schul dispyte;
> Scho wol prey her son so mylde,
>   Al godenisse scho wol qwyte [i.e., she will request her son to let her compensate for the goodness which the sinner lacks]. (97–100)

What seems to be gained by her intercession is a Debate between the Body and the Soul – a version of a theme very well known in Old and Middle English.[1] In the earliest treatments the soul has its melancholy say without contradiction, but a late thirteenth-century poem preserved in no fewer than six manuscripts shows the lines on which the debate ran, once the Body was allowed to reply.[2] The dead man here had been a proud knight: as he lies on his bier, the Soul laments that it has been condemned to Hell on account of the Body's sins, and blames the Body for neglecting spiritual matters and dying unrepentant. The Body ripostes by upbraiding the Soul for not imposing stricter discipline before it was too late. Hideous prognostications of the torments of Hell are realized in this version when, after a ghastly ride on horseback, yelling demons thrust the still-complaining

---

[1] See R. M. Wilson, *Early Middle English Literature* (London, 3rd edn, 1968), 170–2, and J. D. Bruce, 'A contribution to the study of "The Body and the Soul" poems in English', *Modern Language Notes*, v (1890), 385–401.

[2] Bodleian Laud MS 108 [*inter alia*]: ed. O. F. Emerson, *A Middle English Reader* (New York, 1905), 47–64, 266–70.

Soul into a smoky hell-mouth, which closes on the whole troop. An excellent carving of Pride, in the full chain-mail of a twelfth-century knight, shows such a culmination in the Last Judgement tympanum of the Benedictine monastery-church of Sainte Foy at Conques: propelled by demons, the knight plunges helmet-first from horseback into the gaping earth.[1]

It is plain that the besetting sin of Rex Vivus in *The Pride of Life* is in fact Pride – revealed in his boastful euphoria, his maintenance of flatterers, his rejection of sage counsel, and above all his deliberate issue of a futile general challenge. The iconography of Pride's Fall is thus appropriate to him; but because Rex Vivus was not Pride Incarnate, only a proud king, his story was capable of continuation after this *débâcle*. After severe suffering the Soul was to be weighed, and with Our Lady to turn the scale, saved from the fiends and left in her custody (105–8). This type of incident is not uncommon in illustrations of St Michael weighing the souls at the Last Judgement: sometimes devils try to pull down the scale on their side, sometimes the Blessed Virgin places her rosary in the scale to assist a soul.[2]

Interestingly enough, the banns to *The Castle of Perseverance*, a kind of synopsis intended as advertisement for the touring version of the play, can be so read as to suggest that in that version the Blessed Virgin rather than the Four Daughters of God appeared as advocate for Humanum Genus, and secured him not immediately Heaven, but purgatory, a 'ful bytter place' (124–30), but one where he can expiate his sins until the final welcome to God, 'Cum syt at my ryth honde', which does occur in the text we have (3599). Since in our text the soul has by this time been tormented until it is 'Lyter þanne lef is on lynde', it is fortunate that the weighing motif is not used.

It has also been argued that the mid-fifteenth-century actor's part known from its speaker as *Dux Moraud* is the vestige of a Miracle of the Virgin, a type of play which has no English example available for comparison.[3] The action of *Dux Moraud*, readily to be inferred from the surviving part, has two features in common with that of the only extant English miracle, *The Croxton Play of the Sacrament*: it is sensational and has folk-analogues.[4]

[1] The Last Judgment *tympanum* over the west portal of Sainte-Foy is clearly seen in Paul Deschamps, *French Sculpture of the Romanesque Period* (New York, 1972), Plate LVII.

[2] W. L. Hildburgh, 'Iconographical peculiarities in English alabaster carvings', *Folk-Lore*, XLIV (1933), 32–57: Boase, op. cit., figs. 22–3.

[3] C. B. Hieatt, 'A case for *Duk Moraud* as a play of the miracles of the Virgin', *Mediaeval Studies*, XXXII (1970), 345–51.

[4] *NCPF*, 106–13, c–cxi.

Dux Moraud seduces his daughter, and incites her to murder first her mother and then the child of incest. He goes travelling, hears a church-bell, repents (perhaps after a sermon, arguably through a vision of hell-pains), confesses to a priest, accepts penance (apparently total renunciation of his estate and perpetual pilgrimage), and volubly presses similar reform upon his daughter. When she beats him over the head, he expires on a note of forgiveness, intercession, and trust in his own salvation. It seems unlikely that the play concluded with his reception into the next world, because the fate of his Incestuous Daughter is of urgent interest. The suggestion that in contrast she became an Awful Warning, carried away by demons amid showers of squibs, has at least an aesthetic propriety. No surviving moral play from fifteenth-century England has this ending, but it is reported that *The Cradle of Security*, a morality performed at Gloucester by travelling players when Shakespeare was a boy, brought the prince who stood for the wicked of the world to such a fate,[1] and it is of course an essential of the folk-stories behind the ending of Marlowe's *Doctor Faustus*. Certainly it would take a most spectacular intervention by the Blessed Virgin to pluck this particular sinner from the burning. Whether the writer of *Dux Moraud* managed to make his moral point without the help of allegory is moot, but a devil or two probably figured in the piece.

A doctrine censured by a committee of theologians in 1368 had so much popular appeal that it is worth considering in the context of dying calls for God's mercy in medieval plays thereafter. It was fathered by Uthred of Boldon, a Benedictine preacher who was allowed to retire to Finchale Priory near Durham while the views he had promulgated were discredited by order of Stephen Langton and taken up, to some extent, by Wycliffe.[2] Uthred's doctrine of *clara visio* was that every human soul, whatever the race, creed or age of its mortal body, enjoyed one moment of clear sight just before death, in which it was free to choose or reject God: upon this moment depended irrevocably its portion in eternity. This glimpse of God was not the Beatific Vision of the just in Paradise, but an intellectual vision of the kind survived by Moses, Elijah and St Paul: the text adduced in support of the doctrine was 'all flesh shall see the salvation of God' (Luke 3: 6). Uthred seems to have felt a kindly concern for such hard cases as still-born infants and the righteous heathen; but he held that a baptized child in a state of both grace and innocence might none the less make the wrong choice

---

[1] R. Willis, *Mount Tabor: or Private Exercises of a Penitent Sinner* (London, 1639), 110–14; reprinted by J. D. Wilson, *Life in Shakespeare's England* (Harmondsworth, 1944), 40–2.
[2] See Janet Coleman, *English Literature in History, 1350–1400* (London, 1981), 250.

in his moment of vision and be for ever damned.[1] Some of the arguments against this view as applied to ordinary sinful Christians are voiced by Justice and Truth in *The Castle of Perseverance*: the strongest is that to adopt it opens the door to a sin worse than the seven deadly, the sin against the Holy Ghost:

> Late repentaunce if man saue scholde,
>> Wheyþyr he wrouth wel or wyckydnesse,
> Þanne euery man wold be bolde
>> To trespas in trost of forȝevenesse.
> For synne in hope is dampnyd, I holde;
>> Forgevyn is neuere hys trespase.
> He synnyth in þe Holy Gost manyfolde. (3275–81)

There can be little doubt that all the fifteenth-century English moral plays were written by clerks, men with a grounding in theology. The pains that are taken by them all to emphasize the importance of holy living as well as holy dying, and the explicit warnings against sinning in hope of mercy, show the orthodox condemnation of Uthred's dangerous belief. Even in *Mankind*, with its high proportion of knockabout farce, the point is stressed:

> Synne not in hope of mercy: þat ys a cryme notary (845)...
> Aske mercy and hawe [*receive it*], whyll þe body wyth þe sowle hath hys annexion;
> Yf ye tary tyll your dyscesse, ȝe may hap of your desyre to mysse.
> Be repentant here, trust not þe owr of deth. (863–5)

The purpose and message of the early moral plays is best summarized in the words which conclude *The Castle of Perseverance*: God the Father's part here concludes, and the actor who played it becomes spokesman for the cast in a final, earnest exhortation –

> All men example here-at may take
>> To mayntein þe goode and mendyn here mys.
>>> Þus endyth oure gamys.
>> To saue ȝou fro synnynge
>> Evyr at þe begynnynge
>> Thynke on ȝoure last endynge!
>>> Te Deum laudamus! (3644–9)

[1] See M. D. Knowles, 'The censured opinions of Uthred of Boldon', *Proceedings of the British Academy*, XXXVII (1951), 305–42.

Appendix: manuscripts and contents of the extant English cycles

David Mills

The Chester Cycle

Text The cycle is extant in three single-play manuscripts and five manuscripts containing all or most of the cycle. Two cyclic manuscripts also contain all or part of the banns to the cycle used after the Reformation (BL Harley 2013 and Bodley 175 – see below); the banns are also independently attested (Chester City Archives MS and BL Harley 1944), and a version of the pre-Reformation banns also survives (BL Harley 2150). All the cyclic manuscripts are later than the date of the last recorded performance of the cycle, in 1575.

1 Manchester Fragment: MS 822 11C2 (15th century?). Contains part of *The Resurrection*.
2 Peniarth 399 (*c*.1500?). Contains *Antichrist*.
3 Huntington 2 (1591), by Edward Gregory. Contains the complete cycle with the exception of play 1 and possibly the banns, since the opening pages have been lost.
4 BL Additional 10305 (1592), by George Bellin. Contains the full cycle.
5 Chester Coopers' Guild (1599), by George Bellin. Contains *The Trial and Flagellation of Christ*.

6 BL Harley 2013 (1600), by George Bellin. Contains the banns and the full cycle.

7 Bodley 175 (1604), by William Bedford. Contains part of the banns and the full cycle.

8 BL Harley 2124 (1607), by James Miller and two other scribes. Contains the full cycle.

For further information about manuscripts and scribes, see the standard EETS edition and facsimile editions of Huntington 2 and Bodley 175 by Lumiansky and Mills in the Bibliography.

CONTENT

Although the cyclic manuscripts contain substantially the same material, they diverge at one point in its organization. Harley 2124 presents the Trial and Flagellation and the Passion of Christ as a single play, numbered 16; the other four manuscripts present it as two separate plays, the Trial and Flagellation of Christ and the Passion of Christ, but give no separate number for the second play. Consequently all manuscripts number the plays 1–24, but four of them contain twenty-five plays. In the listing below, the plays are numbered 1–25. In the Lumiansky-Mills EETS edition the two parts of the Harley 2124 Play 16 are numbered 16 and 16A, which correspond to 16 and 17 on the list below.

The titles used are from the list of 1539–40, with the titles from the Lumiansky-Mills edition, which give a clearer guide to content, in brackets. The name of the performing guild is also given.

1 *The Falling of Lucifer* (*The Fall of Lucifer*) – The Tanners
2 *The Creation of the World* (*Adam and Eve; Cain and Abel*) – The Drapers
3 *Noah and his Ship* (*Noah's Flood*) – The Waterleaders and Drawers of Dee [carters of water and carriers from the River Dee]
4 *Abraham and Isaac* (*Abraham, Lot, and Melchysedeck; Abraham and Isaac*) – The Barbers
5 *King Balaack and Balaam with Moses* (*Moses and the Law; Balaack and Balaam*) – The Cappers[1]
6 *The Nativity of Our Lord* (*The Annunciation and the Nativity*) – The Wrights [carpenters]
7 *The Shepherds' Offering* (*The Shepherds*) – The Painters
8 *King Herod and the Mount Victorial* (*The Three Kings*) – The Vintners

9 *The Three Kings of Cologne* (*The Offerings of the Three Kings*) – The Mercers

10 *The Slaying of the Children of Israel by Herod* (*The Slaughter of the Innocents*) – The Goldsmiths

11 *The Purification of Our Lady* (*The Purification*; *Christ and the Doctors*) – The Blacksmiths

12 *The Pinnacle with the Woman of Canaan* (*The Temptation*; *The Woman Taken in Adultery*) – The Butchers

13 *The Raising of Lazarus from Death to Life* (*Blind Chelidonius*;[2] *The Raising of Lazarus*) – The Glovers

14 *The Coming of Christ to Jerusalem* (*Christ at the House of Simon the Leper*; *Christ and the Money-lenders*; *Judas' Plot*) – The Corvisors [shoemakers]

15 *Christ's Maundy where He Sat with His Apostles* (*The Last Supper*; *The Betrayal of Christ*) – The Bakers

16 *The Scourging of Christ* (*The Trial and Flagellation*) – The Fletchers, Bowyers, Coopers and Stringers [arrowmakers, bowmakers, caskmakers and bowstringmakers]

17 *The Crucifying of Christ* (*The Passion*) – The Ironmongers

18 *The Harrowing of Hell* (*The Harrowing of Hell*) – The Cooks

19 *The Resurrection* (*The Resurrection*) – The Skinners[3]

20 *The Castle of Emmaus and the Apostles* (*Christ on the Road to Emmaus*; *Doubting Thomas*) – The Saddlers

21 *The Ascension of Christ* (*The Ascension*) – The Tailors

22 *Whitsunday, the Making of the Creed* (*Pentecost*) – The Fishmongers

23 *Prophets Before the Day of Doom* (*The Prophets of Antichrist*) – The Clothworkers

24 *Antichrist* (*Antichrist*) – The Dyers

25 *Doomsday* (*The Last Judgement*) – The Websters [Weavers]

NOTES

1 In Harley 2124 Play 5 includes, as a sequel to Balaam's prophecy, a Procession of Prophets.

2 The Lumiansky-Mills title to Play 13, *The Blind Chelidonian*, is corrected to *Blind Chelidonius* in the forthcoming notes to the text.

3 The two Harley manuscripts conclude *The Resurrection* with the appearance of Christ to Mary Magdalen, to the Maries and to Peter. The play breaks off before these episodes in the other manuscripts.

The Wakefield (Towneley) cycle

Text   One manuscript, Huntington 1, is the sole evidence for this cycle. The manuscript was apparently the civic register of the cycle. The most recent description, the Cawley–Stevens facsimile edition (see Bibliography), sets the earliest date for the manuscript as 'certainly not earlier than the 1480s and perhaps not earlier than 1500' (p. xvii) and offers a range between 1480 and the early sixteenth century. One scribe wrote out the first thirty-one plays of the extant text; another added a further play out of sequence.

CONTENT

Twenty-eight leaves are missing. Consequently some plays must have been lost, including some three or four between Plays 29 and 30, and possibly also prefatory Banns; and Plays 1, 4, 5, 17, 18, 29 and 30 are incomplete. Plays 7, 8, 31 and 32 are out of sequence. In only five instances are the crafts responsible for the plays indicated. In the following list the titles are those proposed by Ian Lancashire, with the manuscript titles used in the standard England–Pollard edition (see Bibliography) in brackets.[1] The performing guild is noted where known.[2]

1   *The Creation (The Creation)* – The Barkers[1] [tanners]
2   *The Killing of Abel (Mactacio Abel)* – The Glovers
3   *Noah and the Ark (Processus Noe Cum Filiis)*
4   *Abraham (Abraham)*
5   *Isaac ([Isaac])*[1]
6   *Jacob (Iacob)*
7   *The Prophets (Processus Prophetarum)*
8   *Pharaoh (Pharao)* – The Litsters or Dyers
9   *Caesar Augustus (Cesar Augustus)*
10   *The Annunciation (Annunciacio)*
11   *The Salutation of Elizabeth (Salutacio Elezabeth)*
12   *The First Shepherds' Play (Una Pagina Pastorum)*
13   *The Second Shepherds' Play (Alia Eorundem)*
14   *The Offering of the Magi (Oblacio Magorum)*
15   *The Flight Into Egypt (Fugacio Josep & Marie In Egyptum)*
16   *Herod the Great (Magnus Herodes)*
17   *The Purification of Mary (Purificacio Marie)*
18   *The Play of the Doctors (Pagina Doctorum)*
19   *John the Baptist (Iohannes Baptista)*

20 *The Conspiracy (Conspiracio [Et Capcio])*[1]
21 *The Buffeting (Coliphizacio)*
22 *The Scourging (Fflagellacio)*
23 *The Crucifixion (Processus Crucis [Et Crucifixio])*[1]
24 *The Talents (Processus Talentorum)*
25 *The Deliverance of Souls (Extraccio Animarum)*
26 *The Resurrection of the Lord (Resurreccio Domini)*
27 *The Pilgrims (Peregrini)* – The Fishers
28 *Thomas of India (Thomas Indie [Et Resurreccio Domini])*[1]
29 *The Lord's Ascension (Ascencio Domini)*
30 *The Judgement (Iudicium)*
31 *Lazarus (Lazarus)*
32 *The Hanging of Judas (Suspencio Iude)* – The Lysters

NOTES

1 The England–Pollard titles are sometimes supplied by the editors without manuscript authority. Play 1 has no title. The title for Play 5 has been lost together with the opening of the play, but is supplied from the *explicit* at the end. In Play 20 *et capcio* is added to the manuscript title because there is an isolated *c* after the title and because the *explicit* reads *Explicit Capcio Iesu*. At Play 23, *et crucifixio* is added to the title because the *explicit* reads *Explicit Crucifixio Domini*. In Play 28 England–Pollard misleadingly include the erroneous *Resurreccio Domini*; the play was originally wrongly titled and the error was subsequently corrected to *Thomas Indie*.
2 The guild-names have been added beside or below the titles in a different hand. That for Play 32 is, however, beside the *finis*.

The York cycle

Text The York cycle as we know it survives in BL Additional MS 35290; at the time of the Toulmin Smith standard edition (see Bibliography) the manuscript was still owned by the Earl of Ashburnham and it is often referred to as the Ashburnham manuscript. It evidently represents a civic register of the cycle, compiled from individual play-texts and changed from time to time in minor details. The main scribe's work has been assigned to 1463–77. A sixteenth-century manuscript of Play 42, the Scriveners' play of the Incredulity of Thomas, known as the Sykes manuscript after its last owner, also survives; it has been edited by A. C. Cawley in *LSE*, 7–8 (1952), 45–80.

CONTENT

The manuscript contains forty-eight plays together with a fragment of another play written in a hand possibly of the late fifteenth century. Forty-eight of the 270 leaves are blank, and there are indications in five places of pages having been torn out. In some cases space was left for play-texts which were never submitted; after Play 22, *The Temptation*, are four blank pages, with the heading 'The Vinteners' and two lines of their play on the Marriage of Cana, and after Play 23 there are five blank pages with the opening heading 'Ironmongers', awaiting their play of Jesus eating with Simon the Leper and Mary Magdalen. Other plays were copied in after the main manuscript was written. That the cycle now extant was not the same as that seen in York in the early fifteenth century is indicated by the two play lists by the Town Clerk, Roger Burton, in the York Memorandum Book (see *REED, York*, 1, 17–26), one of which is used by Ian Lancashire in his *Guide to Dramatic Texts and Records* (Toronto, 1981. Since the list does not correspond to the extant text, the titles and ascriptions below are taken from the Toulmin Smith edition only.

1 *The Creation, Fall of Lucifer* – The Barkers
2 *The Creation to the Fifth Day* – The Plasterers
3 *God Creates Adam and Eve* – The Cardmakers
4 *Adam and Eve in the Garden of Eden* – The Fullers
5 *Man's Disobedience and Fall* – The Coopers
6 *Adam and Eve Driven from Eden* – The Armourers
7 *Sacrificium Cayme et Abell* – The Glovers
8 *Building of the Ark* – The Shipwrights
9 *Noah and the Flood* – The Fishers and Mariners
10 *Abraham's Sacrifice* – The Parchmenters and Bookbinders
11 *The Israelites in Egypt, The Ten Plagues, and The Passage of the Red Sea* – The Hosiers
12 *Annunciation, and Visit of Elizabeth to Mary* – The Spicers
13 *Joseph's Trouble About Mary* – The Pewterers and Founders
14 *Journey to Bethlehem: Birth of Jesus* – The Tilemakers
15 *The Angels and the Shepherds* – The Chandlers
16 *Coming of the Three Kings to Herod* – The Masons
17 *Coming of the Three Kings, The Adoration* – The Goldsmiths
18 *Flight into Egypt* – The Marshals
19 *Massacre of the Innocents* – The Girdlers and Nailers
20 *Christ with the Doctors in the Temple* – The Spurriers and Lorimers [spurmakers and workers in small ironware]

21 *Baptism of Jesus* – The Barbers
22 *Temptation of Jesus* – The Smiths
23 *The Transfiguration* – The Curriers [leather-dressers]
24 *Woman Taken in Adultery. Raising of Lazarus* – The Capmakers
25 *Entry into Jerusalem* – The Skinners
26 *Conspiracy to Take Jesus* – The Cutlers
27 *The Last Supper* – The Bakers
28 *The Agony and Betrayal* – The Cordwainers [workers in cordovan leather, shoemakers]
29 *Peter Denies Jesus: Jesus examined by Caiaphas* – The Bowers and Fletchers [arrowmakers]
30 *Dream of Pilate's Wife: Jesus Before Pilate* – The Tapiters and Couchers [tapestrymakers and beddingmakers]
31 *Trial Before Herod* – The Litsters [dyers]
32 *Second Accusation Before Pilate: Remorse of Judas: Purchase of Field of Blood* – The Cooks and Waterleaders [water-carriers]
33 *Second Trial Continued: Judgement on Jesus* – The Tilemakers
34 *Christ Led Up to Calvary* – The Shearmen
35 *Crucifixio Christi* – The Pinners and Painters
36 *Mortificacio Christi* – The Butchers
37 *Harrowing of Hell* – The Saddlers
38 *Resurrection: Fright of the Jews* – The Carpenters
39 *Jesus Appears to Mary Magdalen After the Resurrection* – The Winedrawers
40 *Travellers to Emmaus* – The Sledmen [sledge-hauliers]
41 *Purification of Mary* – The Hatmakers, Masons and Labourers
42 *Incredulity of Thomas* – The Scriveners
43 *The Ascension* – The Tailors
44 *Descent of the Holy Spirit* – The Potters
45 *The Death of Mary* – The Drapers
46 *Appearance of Our Lady to Thomas* – The Weavers
47 *Assumption and Coronation of the Virgin* – The Hostlers
48 *The Judgement Day* – The Mercers
Fragment   *Coronation of Our Lady* – The Innholders

The N-town cycle (*Hegge Plays, Ludus Coventriae*)

Text   BL Cotton Vespasian D VIII, which contains this cycle, is predominantly the work of one scribe whose hand is accepted to be of the later fifteenth century. The date of 1468 at the end of Play 18 may indicate the date of copying; but, as Meredith–Kahrl state in their facsimile edition (see Bibliography), it must at least indicate the earliest possible date for the manuscript's compilation. Three other scribes are represented in the manuscript, one of whom wrote out the whole of Play 40, *The Assumption of the Virgin*, which the main scribe interpolated into his text. Of the three titles for the cycle, *Ludus Coventriæ* – that used by Block for the standard edition (see Bibliography) – is the title included in the descriptive note on the fly-leaf which was written by Richard James, librarian to Sir Robert Cotton in the seventeenth century, in the mistaken belief that the cycle was that of Coventry; *Hegge Plays* incorporates the name of the first known owner of the manuscript, Robert Hegge; and *N-Town*, preferred by W. W. Greg, derives from the lines in the Banns:

> At vj of þe belle we gynne oure play
> In N.town wherfore we pray
> That god now be ȝoure Spede.

where *N* presumably stands for *nomen*, 'name', and requires the name of a town to be supplied. The location of the cycle has been much debated; see pp. 22–3.

CONTENT

The banns which preface the cycle describe forty plays. The cycle diverges from this description in a number of places and has clearly been revised, including the creation of several 'self-contained' plays covering a variety of events. Numbers have been set in the right-hand margin to divide the text into separate actions; these numbers run from 1 to 42, omitting numbers 17 and 22 in the sequence but duplicating 10. Greg, 'Bibliographical and Textual Problems', and Block, introduction, discuss the problems of revision involved, which are complex. There are few titles for individual plays in the text.

The lack of a clear scheme of play-division and of titles for most plays presents problems in listing contents. In the following list, the titles and divisions proposed by Meredith–Kahrl, viii–xiii, are adopted, but with references to the page and lines in Block, and to the numbers allocated to those sections in the manuscript text. 'Self-contained' sequences are indicated in the notes which follow the list.

1 *The Creation, and Fall of Lucifer* (p. 16, line 1–p. 19, line 82; the manuscript 1)

2 *The Creation, and Fall of Man* (p. 19, line 1–p. 29, line 416; the manuscript 2)

3 *Cain and Abel* (p. 29, line 1–p. 35, line 195; the manuscript 3)

4 *Noah, and Lamech* (p. 35, line 1–p. 43, line 253 + SD; the manuscript 4)

5 *Abraham and Isaac* (p. 43, line 1–p. 51, line 264; the manuscript 5)

6 *The Ten Commandments* (p. 51, line 1–p. 57, line 194; the manuscript 6)

7 *The Tree of Jesse* (p. 57, line 1–p. 62, line 134; the manuscript 7)

8 *The Conception of Mary* (p. 62, line 1–p. 71, line 226; the manuscript 8)

9 *Mary in the Temple* (p. 71, line 1–p. 82, line 17; the manuscript 9 with the erroneously duplicated 10)

10 *The Betrothal of Mary* (p. 83, line 1–p. 97, line 486; the manuscript 10)

11 *The Parliament of Heaven and the Annunciation* (p. 97, line 1–p. 108, line 340 + SD; the manuscript 11)

12 *Joseph's Trouble About Mary* (p. 109, line 1–p. 115, line 224; the manuscript 12)

13 *The Visitation* (p. 115, line 1–p. 122, line 36; the manuscript 13, including the Contemplacio epilogue)[2]

14 *The Purgation of Mary and Joseph* (p. 123, line 1–p. 135, line 372; the manuscript 14)[1]

15 *The Birth of Christ* (p. 135, line 1–p. 145, line 320; the manuscript 15)

16 *The Shepherds* (p. 146, line 1–p. 151, line 154; the manuscript 16)

17 *The Magi* (p. 151, line 1–p. 162, line 334; the manuscript 18)

18 *The Purification* (p. 162, line 1–p. 169, line 206; the manuscript 19)

19 *The Slaughter of the Innocents* (p. 169, line 1–p. 177, line 284; the manuscript 20)

20 *Christ and the Doctors in the Temple* (p. 178, line 1–p. 187, line 288; the manuscript 21)[1]

21 *The Baptism* (p. 188, line 1–p. 193, line 182; unnumbered)[1]

22 *The Temptation* (p. 193, line 1–p. 200, line 221; the manuscript 23)

23 *The Woman Taken in Adultery* (p. 200, line 1–p. 209, line 296; the manuscript 24)[1]

24 *The Raising of Lazarus* (p. 210, line 1–p. 225, line 456; the manuscript 25)[1]

NOTES

1 The following plays have titles: nos. 14, 20, 21, 23, 24, 37, 38, and 39. In several instances a division is marked by a stage direction, but in other cases the stage direction is more transitional than divisive and cannot accurately be apportioned to one play or another. The final play is incomplete.

2 Meredith–Kahrl do not number, but list separately the 'Doctors' Prologue',

p. 269, line 1–p. 270, line 40. Block numbers the 'Contemplacio Epilogue' to Play 13 separately from the rest of the play, p. 121, line 1–p. 122, line 36. Block prints, without line number, 'what appears to be a roughly scribbled copy of part of Magdalene's speech', pp. 336–7, between Plays 36 and 37.

3 Three important 'self-contained' groups of episodes can be clearly discerned in the manuscript, forming extended independent plays:
  (*i*) The 'Contemplacio' group, Plays 8–13,
  (*ii*) The First Passion Play, Plays 25–27,
  (*iii*) The Second Passion Play, Plays 28–34.

Texts of the other fragments in Part III

Although the other plays mentioned in Part III are sufficiently brief for their content to be given there, it may be helpful to list below details of the manuscripts in which they occur:

The Coventry cycle   The Shearmen and Tailors' Pageant survives through Thomas Sharp's transcript of the play published in 1817 and 1825, the manuscript having been subsequently destroyed. The manuscript of the Weavers' Pageant, written by Robert Croo in 1534, survives at Coventry.

The Newcastle cycle   The Shipwrights' 'Noah's Ark' play survives in a transcript by Henry Bourne published in 1736.

The Norwich cycle   The Grocers' play of the 'Creation and Fall' was known to Robert Fitch in 1856 and to Osborn Waterhouse in 1909 through eighteenth-century copies, now lost, of John Kirkpatrick's transcript of the Grocers' Book, made in the 1720s.

The Northampton 'Abraham'   The play is extant in fols 59–85 of Trinity College, Dublin, D.4.18, and is written in a mid-fifteenth-century hand.

The Brome 'Abraham'   The play occupies fols 15^r–22^r of the 'Book of Brome', owned by Yale University Library, and is written in a late fifteenth-century hand.

The Digby 'Candelmes: Killing of the Children'   The plays are in Bodley Digby 133; the manuscript bears the date 1512.

The Digby 'Conversion of St Paul'   The play is in Bodley Digby 133; the paper watermarks 'are attributed to the first three decades of the sixteenth century, and all are French' (Baker–Murphy facsimile, p. x).

The Digby 'Mary Magdalen'   The play is in Bodley Digby 133, dated by Baker–Murphy *c.*1515–20.

Bibliography

Abbreviations

EETS	Early English Text Society
ELN	*English Language Notes*
JEGP	*Journal of English and Germanic Philology*
LSE	*Leeds Studies in English*
METh	*Medieval English Theatre*
MLN	*Modern Language Notes*
MLQ	*Modern Language Quarterly*
MLR	*Modern Language Review*
MP	*Modern Philology*
MSC	Malone Society Collections
NCPF	*Non-Cycle Plays and Fragments*, ed. N. Davis
PMLA	*Publications of the Modern Language Association of America*
PQ	*Philological Quarterly*
REED	*Records of Early English Drama*
RES	*Review of English Studies*
RORD	*Research Opportunities in Renaissance Drama*
SP	*Studies in Philology*
TN	*Theatre Notebook*

I The staging of medieval drama

(I) BIBLIOGRAPHIES

The basic bibliographies for medieval drama are: R. W. Ackerman, 'Middle English Literature to 1400', in *The Medieval Literature of Western Europe: A Review of Research, mainly 1930–1960*, ed. J. H. Fisher (New York, 1966), 73–123; *The New Cambridge Bibliography of English Literature*, ed. George Watson, 5 vols (Cambridge, 1969–77); C. Brown and R. H. Robbins, *The Index of Middle English Verse* (New York, 1943) – *Supplement*, ed. R. H. Robbins and J. L. Cutler (Lexington, Kentucky, 1965); A. Harbage, *Annals of English Drama 975–1700*, rev. S. Schoenbaum (London, 1964); *A Manual of the Writings in Middle English 1050–1500*, ed. A. E. Harting: vol. 5, XII, 'Dramatic pieces', by A. J. Mill, S. Lindenbaum, F. L. Utley and B. Ward (New Haven, Conn., 1975), 1315–84, 1557–1629; M. Henshaw, 'A survey of studies of medieval drama: 1935–50', *Progress of Medieval and Renaissance Studies in the United States and Canada*, Bulletin No. 21 (Boulder, Colorado, 1951), 7–35; B. Salomon, 'Early English drama, 975–1585: a select, annotated bibliography of full-length studies', Medieval Supplement to *RORD*, XIII–XIV (1970–1), 267–77; C. J. Stratman, *Bibliography of Medieval Drama*, 2 vols, 2nd edn (New York, 1972); and J. E. Wells, *A Manual of the Writings in Middle English 1050–1400*, and *Supplements* I–IX (New Haven, Conn., 1916–51).

Information about more recent work can be found in the annual bibliographies published by the Modern Humanities Research Association, the Modern Language Association, *The Year's Work in English Studies*, *Research Opportunities in Renaissance Drama* [*RORD*] (which has carried a medieval supplement since 1970), and the twice-yearly *Newsletter* of REED (*Records of Early English Drama*). *Medieval English Theatre*, published twice yearly since 1979, is a journal specializing in this period.

(II) EDITIONS

For Latin liturgical plays, see Karl Young, *The Drama of the Medieval Church*, 2 vols (Oxford, 1933), the definitive collection and study. David Bevington, *Medieval Drama* (Boston, Mass., 1975), includes an excellent selection of liturgical plays, with Latin text and translation. *The Play of Daniel: A Thirteenth-Century Musical Drama*, has been edited by N. Greenberg, with a translation by Jean Misrahi (New York, 1959), and *The Son of Getron*, another music drama, has been transcribed and edited for modern performance by C. C. Sterne (Pittsburgh, Penn., 1962).

There are a number of editions of selected religious plays in the vernacular. Those which have been to some extent modernized and/or annotated include: Bevington, *Medieval Drama* (see above), with its wide selection of biblical and moral plays; A. C. Cawley, *Everyman and Medieval Miracle Plays* (London, 1956; rev. edn, 1977), with marginal glossing of difficult words and footnote translations of difficult passages; R. T. Davies, *The Corpus Christi Play of the English Middle Ages* (London, 1972); Peter Happé, *English Mystery Plays* (Harmondsworth, 1975); and R. G. Thomas, *Ten Miracle Plays* (York Medieval Texts, London, 1966). Individual cycles are represented by Maurice Hussey's edition of sixteen pageants from *The Chester Mystery Plays* (London, 1957); J. S. Purvis, *The York Cycle of Mystery Plays* (London, 1957); and Martial Rose, *The Wakefield Mystery Plays* (London, 1961), which has a scholarly and stimulating introduction.

The more advanced student will look to the editions of the Early English Text Society. These include: *The Chester Plays*, first edited in two parts by H. Deimling (London, 1892) and Dr Matthews (*sic*) (London, 1916), and, more recently, as *The Chester Mystery Cycle*, vol. I: Text, by R. M. Lumiansky and David Mills (London, 1974); *Two Coventry Corpus Christi Plays*, ed. Hardin Craig (London, 1902; 2nd edn, 1957); *The Digby Plays*, ed. F. J. Furnivall (London, 1896), and the more recent edition by D. C. Baker, J. L. Murphy and L. B. Hall, Jr, called *The Late Medieval Religious Plays of Bodleian MSS Digby 133 and E Museo 160* (Oxford, 1982), containing *The Conversion of St Paul, Mary Magdalen, Killing of the Children, Wisdom, Christ's Burial* and *Christ's Resurrection; Ludus Coventriae or the Plaie called Corpus Christi*, ed. K. S. Block (London, 1922); *Non-Cycle Plays and Fragments*, ed. Norman Davis (London, 1970); and *The Towneley Plays*, ed. G. England and A. W. Pollard (London, 1897). A new edition of the Towneley Plays, by A. C. Cawley and Martin Stevens, is to be published by EETS.

Other editions of religious plays include: *The Play of Antichrist from the Chester Cycle*, ed. W. W. Greg (Oxford, 1935); *The Wakefield Pageants in the Towneley Cycle*, ed. A. C. Cawley (Manchester, 1958), which contains the *Murder of Abel, Noah, First and Second Shepherds' Plays, Herod the Great*, and the *Buffeting; York Plays*, ed. Lucy Toulmin Smith (Oxford, 1885), and ed. Richard Beadle (York Medieval Texts, 2nd ser., London, 1982).

For collections of moral plays, see *The Macro Plays*, ed. Mark Eccles

(London, EETS, 1969), which comprise *The Castle of Perseverance*, *Wisdom*, and *Mankind*; *English Moral Interludes*, ed. Glynne Wickham (London, 1976), containing *Mankind*, Medwall's *Fulgens and Lucres*, *The Conversion of St Paul*, Bale's *Temptation of Our Lord*, *Nice Wanton*, and Merbury's *Marriage between Wit and Wisdom*; *Four Morality Plays*, ed. Peter Happé (Harmondsworth, 1979), viz, *The Castle of Perseverance*, Skelton's *Magnyfycence*, Bale's *King Johan*, and Sir David Lindsay's *Satire of the Thrie Estaitis*; and *Three Late Medieval Morality Plays*, ed. G. A. Lester, which contains *Mankind*, *Everyman*, and *Mundus et Infans* (London and New York, 1981). Lindsay's *Satire* is available separately in *The Works of Sir David Lindsay* (Edinburgh and London, Scottish Text Society), vols II (1931) and IV (1936). *Everyman* has been edited by A. C. Cawley (Manchester, 1961) and, as *The Summoning of Everyman*, by G. Cooper and C. Wortham (Nedlands, W. Australia, 1980).

(III) FACSIMILES

Many of the later plays of the period are available in Tudor Facsimile Texts, ed. J. S. Farmer *et al.*, in 151 vols (London, 1907–14). *The Macro Plays* have been edited by David Bevington (New York, 1972). The Newcastle play of *Noah's Ark* is reproduced by John Anderson and A. C. Cawley in *REED Newsletter* 1 (1977), 11–17.

The series of Medieval Drama Facsimiles, ed. A. C. Cawley and S. Ellis (Leeds, 1973–), includes: I. *The Chester Mystery Cycle* (MS Bodley 175), introduction by R. M. Lumiansky and David Mills; II. *The Towneley Cycle* (MS Huntington HM 1), introduction by A. C. Cawley and Martin Stevens; III. *The Digby Plays* (MSS Digby 133 and e Museo 160), introduction by D. C. Baker and J. L. Murphy; IV. *The N-town Plays* (MS Cotton Vespasian D VIII), introduction by Peter Meredith and Stanley J. Kahrl; V. *Non-Cycle Plays and The Winchester Dialogues*, introduction by Norman Davis; VI. *The Chester Mystery Cycle: a reduced facsimile of Huntington Library MS 2*, introduction by R. M. Lumiansky and David Mills; and VII. *The York Plays* (MS Additional 35290), with *Ordo Paginarum* section of the A/Y Memorandum Book, introduction by Richard Beadle and Peter Meredith, note on the music by Richard Rastall.

(IV) RECORDS

The main sources of information about the staging of plays in medieval England are the texts themselves (including the stage directions and staging plans), the Chester *Breviary*, municipal and guild records, churchwardens' accounts, and contemporary descriptions of tournaments and royal entries. Among the earliest publications of municipal and guild records, special mention should be made of Thomas Sharp's *A Dissertation on the Pageants or Dramatic Mysteries, Anciently performed at Coventry, by the Trading Companies of that City; Chiefly with Reference to the Vehicle, Characters, and Dresses of the Actors*... (Coventry, 1825; repr. 1973). This book has become the original source of information about many Coventry guild records owing to the destruction of the manuscripts by fire and bombs. Unfortunately, there is no extant English dramatic document corresponding to the directors' copies used for Passion plays performed in France, Germany and Switzerland, such as the *Abregiés* of Mons (ed. Gustave Cohen, Strasbourg and Paris, 1925), the Frankfurt *Dirigierrolle* (ed. R. Froning, *Das Drama des Mittelalters* [Stuttgart, 1891], II, 340–73), or the Director's copy of the Lucerne Passion Play (see H. Wyss (ed.), *Das Luzerner Osterspiel*, 3 vols [Bern, 1967], and M. Blakemore Evans, *The Passion Play of Lucerne* [New York, 1943]).

However, the *REED* project (*Records of Early English Drama*, directed by A. F. Johnston, University of Toronto) hopes eventually to publish dramatic records from all parts of England. Four volumes have so far been published by the University of Toronto Press: *York*, ed. A. F. Johnston and M. Rogerson, 2 vols (Toronto and Buffalo, N.Y., 1979); *Chester*, ed. L. M. Clopper (Toronto and Buffalo, N.Y., 1979); *Coventry*, ed. R. W. Ingram (Toronto and Buffalo, N.Y. 1981), and *Newcastle-upon-Tyne*, ed. J. J. Anderson (Toronto, Buffalo, and Manchester, 1982).

(V) GENERAL STUDIES

The following are useful introductions to medieval drama in England and include discussion of its staging: E. K. Chambers, 'Medieval Drama', in *English Literature at the Close of the Middle Ages* (Oxford, 1947), 1–65, Bibliography, 206–18; Francis Edwards, *Ritual and Drama: The Mediaeval Theatre* (Guildford and London, 1976); Stanley J. Kahrl, *Traditions of Medieval English Drama* (London, 1974); A. M. Kinghorn, *Mediaeval Drama* (London, 1968); J. S. Purvis, *From Minster to Market Place* (York, 1969); Glynne Wickham, *The Medieval Theatre* (London, 1974); Arnold Williams, *The Drama of Medieval England* (Michigan State University Press, 1961); and D. M. Zesmer, 'Medieval drama', in *Guide to English Literature* (New York, 1961), 266–86 (with an annotated bibliography by S. B. Greenfield, 376–81).

The standard histories of early drama are E. K. Chambers, *The Mediaeval Stage*, 2 vols (Oxford, 1903); Anna J. Mill, *Mediaeval Plays in Scotland* (Edinburgh and London, 1927); W. S. Clark, *The Early Irish Stage* (Oxford, 1955); Hardin Craig, *English Religious Drama of the Middle Ages* (Oxford, 1955), which includes a valuable chapter on medieval staging (115–50); D. M. Bevington, *From 'Mankind' to Marlowe: Growth of Structure in the Popular Drama of Tudor England* (Cambridge, Mass., 1962); and Robert Potter, *The English Morality Play: Origins, History, and Influence of a Dramatic Tradition* (London and Boston, Mass., 1975). H. C. Gardiner, *Mysteries' End: An Investigation of the Last Days of the Medieval Religious Stage* (New Haven, Conn., 1946), attempts to show how 'the spirit of the Reformation caused the authorities, lay or ecclesiastical, to suppress the plays'. R. M. Wilson, *The Lost Literature of Medieval England* (London, 1952), contains an interesting chapter on lost and fragmentary plays (215–40). *Christian Rite and Christian Drama in the Middle Ages*, by O. B. Hardison, Jr (Baltimore, Md., 1965), is an authoritative study of Latin liturgical drama, beginning with an analysis of the conceptual framework of Chambers' *The Mediaeval Stage* and concluding with a consideration of the vernacular dramatic tradition. See also Karl Young, *The Drama of the Medieval Church*, 2 vols (Oxford, 1933). A. P. Rossiter, *English Drama from Early Times to the Elizabethans* (London, 1950), is an eccentric but very readable book. Murray Roston's *Biblical Drama in England: From the Middle Ages to the Present Day* (London, 1968) contains a chapter on 'The medieval stage'. For a wide-ranging account, see Richard Axton, *European Drama of the Early Middle Ages* (London, 1974).

A general study which deals mainly with staging is Bamber Gascoigne, *World Theatre: An Illustrated History* (London, 1971). Allardyce Nicoll, *The Development of the Theatre: A Study of Theatrical Art from the Beginnings to the Present Day*, 5th edn (London, 1966), and Richard Southern, *The Seven Ages of the Theatre* (London, 1962), are also good, succinct histories, with excellent illustrations. Glynne Wickham, *Early English Stages 1300 to 1660*: I (*1300–1576*), II, Pts 1 and 2 (*1576–1660*), and III (*Plays and their Makers to 1576*) (London, 1959, 1963, 1972 and 1981), offers a learned and humane history of staging during the medieval and later periods. See also Sumiko Miyajima, *The Theatre of Man: Dramatic Technique and Stagecraft in the English Medieval Moral Plays* (Clevedon, Avon, England, 1977); A. M. Nagler, *The Medieval Religious Stage: Shapes and Phantoms* (New Haven, Conn., and London, 1976); W. Tydeman, *The Theatre in the Middle Ages: Western European Stage*

Conditions c.800–1576 (Cambridge, 1978); and Rosemary Woolf, *The English Mystery Plays* (London, 1972), V. A. Kolve's *The Play Called Corpus Christi* (London, 1966) is a masterly study of the English Corpus Christi plays which, among many other things, advances some stimulating ideas about staging conventions as one aspect of medieval theatre considered as 'a theatre of game'. The complexity of the concept of theatre in this period is also illustrated in Mary H. Marshall, 'Theatre in the Middle Ages: evidence from dictionaries and glosses', *Symposium*, IV (1950), 1–39, 366–89.

(VI) PAGEANT STAGING AND THEATRE-IN-THE-ROUND

The controversy over the staging of the Corpus Christi pageants can be pursued through a number of works: see R. J. Pentzell, 'The Medieval Theatre in the Streets', *Theatre Survey*, XIV (1973), 1–21, and Alan H. Nelson, *The Medieval English Stage: Corpus Christi Pageants and Plays* (Chicago and London, 1974). Also valuable are Richard Hosley, 'Three kinds of outdoor theatre before Shakespeare', *Theatre Survey*, XII (1971), 1–33, and Alan H. Nelson, 'Some configurations of staging in medieval English drama', in *Medieval English Drama: Essays Critical and Contextual*, ed. Jerome Taylor and Alan H. Nelson (Chicago and London, 1972), 116–47.

Richard Southern's brilliant reconstruction of the staging of *The Castle of Perseverance* in a medieval circular theatre – *The Medieval Theatre in the Round: A Study of the Staging of 'The Castle of Perseverance' and Related Matters* (London, 1957; 2nd edn, 1975) – has proved equally controversial. Works stimulated by it include P. D. Arnott, 'The origins of medieval theatre in the round', *TN*, XV (1960–1), 84–7; A. Freeman, 'A "round" outside Cornwall', *TN*, XVI (1961–2), 10–11; Merle Fifield, *The Castle in the Circle* (Muncie, Indiana, 1967), and 'The arena theatres in Vienna Codices 2535 and 2536', *Comparative Drama*, 2 (1968–9), 259–82; Alan H. Nelson, 'Early pictorial analogues of medieval theatre in the round', in the Medieval Supplement to *RORD*, XII (1969), 93–106; and R. W. V. Elliott, 'The topography of *Wynnere and Wastoure*', *English Studies*, XLVIII (1967), 1–7. See also Stephen Joseph, *Theatre in the Round* (London, 1967), chapter 2: 'The early story'. Southern's thesis has been most forcibly attacked by Natalie C. Schmitt, in 'Was there a medieval theatre in the round?', *TN*, XXIII (1968–9), 130–42 and XXIV (1969–70), 18–25; reprinted in Taylor and Nelson (eds), *Medieval English Drama*, 292–315. John R. Elliott, 'Medieval rounds and wooden O's: the medieval heritage of the Elizabethan theatre', in *Medieval Drama*, ed. N. Denny, Stratford-upon-

Avon Studies 16 (London, 1973), 223–54, stresses theatrical continuity from medieval to Renaissance times.

(VII) SPECIAL TOPICS

More specialized aspects of medieval theatre are considered in the papers collected in J. Dutka (ed.), *Proceedings of the First Colloquium at Erindale College, University of Toronto, 31 August to 3 September 1978* (Toronto, REED, 1979). See also David Bevington, 'Discontinuity in medieval acting tradition', in *The Elizabethan Theatre*, V, ed G. R. Hibbard (Hamden, Conn., 1975), 1–16; Hans-Jürgen Diller, *Redeformen des englischen Misterienspiels* (Munich, 1973). Costume is discussed in James Laver, *Drama: Its Costume and Décor* (London, 1951), and in chapter 3 ('Mysteries, miracles, and moralities') of his *Costume in the Theatre* (London, 1964); props and costumes in Peter Happé, 'Properties and costumes in the plays of John Bale' and John Wasson, 'The *St George* and *Robin Hood Plays* in Devon', in *METh*, II (1980), 55–65 and 66–69 respectively. See also Meg Twycross and Sarah Carpenter, 'Masks in medieval English theatre: the mystery plays', *METh*, III (1981), 7–44 and 69–113.

Useful studies of specific works include Martial Rose, 'The staging of the Hegge Plays', in *Medieval Drama*, ed. Denny, 197–222; Eleanor Prosser, *Drama and Religion in the English Mystery Plays: a Re-evaluation* (Stanford, Calif., 1961), contains a perceptive commentary on the staging of the N-town Passion sequence (124 ff.). F. M. Salter's *Mediaeval Drama in Chester* (Toronto, 1955) makes good use of the early records of the Chester plays, while David Mills's 'Stage directions in the MSS of the Chester mystery cycle', *METh*, III (1981), 45–51, draws attention to the remarkable amount of information which they supply. A number of scholars have written on the Wakefield cycle: in particular, Arnold Williams, *The Characterization of Pilate in the Towneley Plays* (1950); John Gardner, *The Construction of the Wakefield Cycle* (Carbondale and Edwardville, Ill., 1974); Jeffrey Helterman, *Symbolic Action in the Plays of the Wakefield Master* (Athens, Georgia, 1981); while Cynthia Tyson, in *The Staging of the Towneley Plays* (unpublished PhD thesis, University of Leeds, 1971), argues, from close textual examination, for the greater likelihood of fixed-place than of processional production. An interesting study, for comparative purposes, is the edition and translation, by John R. Elliott and Graham A. Runnalls, of *The Baptism and Temptation of Christ: The First Day of a Medieval French Passion Play* (New Haven, Conn., and London, 1978).

(VIII) DRAMA AND THE VISUAL ARTS

Because of the incompleteness of the documentary evidence for the drama of this period, it is especially valuable to follow the lead of art historians who have studied its possible influence on the visual arts. These include E. Mâle, *L'Art Religieux de la Fin du Moyen Age en France* (Paris, 1908; 5th edn, 1949); W. L. Hildburgh, 'English alabaster carvings as records of the medieval religious drama', *Archaeologia*, XCIII (1955), 51–101; Otto Pächt, *The Rise of Pictorial Narrative in Twelfth-Century England* (Oxford, 1962); and M. D. Anderson, *Drama and Imagery in English Medieval Churches* (Cambridge, 1963).

Useful reference works are Clifford Davidson, *Drama and Art: An Introduction to the Use of Evidence from the Visual Arts for the Study of Early Drama* (Kalamazoo, Mich., 1977), and Clifford Davidson and David E. O'Connor, *York Art: A Subject List of Extant and Lost Art, including Items relevant to Early Drama* (Kalamazoo, 1978). 'The Princeton Index of Christian Art' is described by Isa Ragusa in *METh*, IV (1982), 56–60. See also A. M. Nagler, *The Medieval Religious Stage*, 89–105, and Pamela Sheingorn, 'On using medieval art in the study of medieval drama', *RORD*, XXII (1979), 101–9. A bibliography of iconographic sources, compiled by Theodore De Welles, is printed as an appendix to Theresa Coletti and Kathleen M. Ashley, 'The N-Town Passion at Toronto and late medieval Passion iconography', *RORD*, XXIV (1981), 181–92.

Of outstanding importance are the medieval miniatures representing scenes from the plays. In addition there are many interesting parallels to the drama to be found in the woodcuts and ornamental borders of early printed books: see Peter Meredith and J. L. Marshall, 'The wheeled dragon in the *Luttrell Psalter*', *METh*, II (1980), 70–3. There are also some thirty nineteenth-century engravings copying William Boonen's drawings of scenes from the Louvain Procession of Our Lady, 1594: these are reproduced by E. van Even, *L'Omgang de Louvain* (Brussels and Louvain, 1863); see also G. R. Kernodle, 'The Medieval Pageant Wagons of Louvain', *Theatre Annual*, X (1952), 71–5. James Laver, *Isabella's Triumph* (London, 1947), reproduces in colour the pageant cars taking part in the Brussels 'Triumph' for the Archduchess Isabella, 1615, as painted by Denis van Alsloot. See also Meg Twycross, 'A pageant-litter drawing by Dürer', *METh*, I (1979), 70–2, and 'The Flemish *Ommegang* and its pageant cars', *METh*, II (1980), 15–41 and 80–98: a very full bibliography is given at the end of this article.

(IX) MISCELLANEOUS

Works whose relationship to medieval drama is more tangential include Erich Auerbach, *Mimesis: The Representation of Reality in Western Literature* (tr. Trask, Princeton, N.J., 1953). For Auerbach, the medieval conception of reality, figurally structured and bounded by a Christian view of world-history, finds full expression in religious drama. See also C. A. Patrides, *The Grand Design of God: The literary form of the Christian view of history* (London, 1972), and W. Moelwyn Merchant, *Creed and Drama: An Essay in Religious Drama* (London, 1965), which includes a chapter on 'Medieval liturgical drama'. G. R. Owst, *Literature and Pulpit in Medieval England* (Cambridge, 1933; 2nd edn, Oxford, 1961), draws attention in chapter 8 ('Sermon and drama') to a number of striking resemblances between sermon and vernacular religious drama. Notwithstanding his excessive enthusiasm for the sermon, he demonstrates a parallel development of sermon and drama, and probably a considerable amount of interaction.

Finally, two introductions to some special problems of the subject may be mentioned: Arthur Brown, 'The study of medieval drama', in *Medieval and Linguistic Studies in Honor of Francis Peabody Magoun, Jr*, ed. J. B. Bessinger and R. P. Creed (London, 1965), 265–73; and Ian Lancashire, 'Medieval drama', in *Editing Medieval Texts*, ed. G. Rigg (New York, 1978), 58–85.

II The drama of religious ceremonial

(I) THE LANGUAGE OF MEDIEVAL DRAMA

Chapters 5–8 of A. C. Baugh's *A History of the English Language*, 2nd edn (London, 1959), readably survey the main developments in the English language for the period covered here. Norman F. Blake, *The English Language in Medieval Literature* (London and Totowa, N.J., 1977), is a stimulating account of the linguistic component in medieval literature. The *Middle English Dictionary* (*MED*) is in progress (at the time of writing, it has reached O1); it is the best reference guide to spelling and meaning, but should be supplemented for its unpublished material by the *Oxford English Dictionary* (*OED*) and, on occasions, by Joseph Wright, *English Dialect Dictionary*, 6 vols (1898–1905), although the spelling-forms of the latter often require the user to postulate a number of possible spellings before finding the entry he requires. Joseph and Elizabeth Wright, *An Elementary Middle English Grammar*, 2nd edn (London, 1928), is helpful for morphology and syntax, but Tauno F. Mustanoja, *A Middle English Syntax: Part I. Parts of Speech* (Helsinki, 1960), is a fuller account of syntax. Thorlac Turville-Petre has recently written authoritatively on *The Alliterative Revival* (Woodbridge, Suffolk, and Totowa, N.J., 1977), and registers are among the topics considered by R. W. V. Elliot in *Chaucer's English* (Language Library, London, 1974).

(II) TEXTS

The following standard editions of play-cycles have been used: George England, *The Towneley Plays*, with side-notes and introduction by Alfred W. Pollard (London, EETS, e.s. 71, 1897); K. S. Block, *Ludus Coventriæ, or The Plaie Called Corpus Christi* (London, EETS, e.s. 120, 1922); Hardin Craig, *Two Coventry Corpus Christi Plays* (London, EETS, e.s. 87, 2nd edn, 1957); R. M. Lumiansky and David Mills, *The Chester Mystery Cycle*, vol. I, *Text* (London, EETS, s.s. 3, 1974); Lucy Toulmin Smith, *York Plays: The Plays Performed by the Crafts or Mysteries of York on the day of Corpus Christi in the 14th, 15th, and 16th Centuries* (Oxford, 1885; re-issued New York, 1963). Norman Davis, *Non-cycle Plays and Fragments* (London, EETS, s.s. 1, 1970) includes the Shrewsbury Fragments, the Norwich Grocers' Play, the Newcastle Play, the Northampton and the Brome Plays of Abraham and the Croxton *Play of the Sacrament* among its texts and supersedes O. Waterhouse, *The Non-Cycle Mystery Plays* (London, EETS, e.s. 104, 1909). Donald C. Baker, John L. Murphy, and Louis B. Hall, Jr, *The Late Medieval Religious Plays of Bodleian MSS Digby 133 and E. Museo 160* (Oxford, EETS, 1982), which replaces Furnivall's edition of 1896, contains *The Conversion of St Paul, Mary Magdalen, Killing of the Children, Wisdom, Christ's Burial*, and *Christ's Resurrection*. Use has also been made of the 'standard' anthology of texts, David Bevington, *Medieval Drama* (Boston, 1975), which contains *inter alia* liturgical and Latin texts with accompanying translations and the *Ordo Repraesentationis Ade* with translation; the anthology replaces the still useful J. Quincy Adams, *Chief Pre-Shakespearean Dramas* (Boston, 1924) which contains the text of the Revesby play (see below).

The complete text of the Lollard *Tretise of Miraclis Pleyinge* is in Thomas Wright and James Orchard Halliwell, *Reliquiae Antiquae. Scraps from Ancient Manuscripts, Illustrating Chiefly Early English Literature and the*

English Language, 2 vols (London 1841–3; 2nd edn, 1845), Vol. II, 42–57, and has been edited by Clifford Davidson as *A Middle English Treatise on the Playing of Miracles* (Washington, D.C., 1981); a new edition by Nicholas Davis is in preparation. Sir Richard Morison's *Discourse Touchinge the Reformation of the Lawes of England* is published in Sydney Anglo, 'An Early Tudor Programme for Plays and Other Demonstrations against the Pope', *Journal of the Warburg and Courtauld Institutes*, 20 (1957), 176–9.

Other documents are cited from Chambers, Mill, Nelson and Toulmin Smith below. For other play-texts, see Brody and Young below and the editions cited above for Part I.

(III) GENERAL WORKS

The most influential and comprehensive survey of medieval drama is E. K. Chambers, *The Mediaeval Stage*, 2 vols (Oxford, 1903). Earlier studies, of which Chambers is justly critical, include J. P. Collier, *The History of English Dramatic Poetry to the Time of Shakespeare: and Annals of the Stage to the Restoration*, 3 vols (London, 1831; new edn, 1879); William Hone, *Ancient Mysteries Described, Especially the English Miracle Plays, Founded on the Apocryphal New Testament Story, Extant among the Unpublished Manuscripts of the British Museum, Including Notices of Ecclesiastical Shows* (London, 1823); and Thomas Warton, *The History of English Poetry from the Twelfth to the Close of the Sixteenth Century*, edited by W. C. Hazlitt, 4 vols (London, 1871), especially Vol. 2. Chambers' evolutionary approach crystallizes in Hardin Craig, *English Religious Drama of the Middle Ages* (Oxford, 1955). The approach is examined by O. B. Hardison, *Christian Rite and Christian Drama in the Middle Ages* (Baltimore, 1965).

Glynne Wickham approaches the field of medieval drama from the standpoint of theatre history and stage production in his books *Early English Stages 1300–1660*, Vol. I, *1330–1576* (London, 1959; rev. edn, 1980), *Shakespeare's Dramatic Heritage* (London, 1969), and *The Medieval Theatre* (London, 1974). Stanley J. Kahrl, *Traditions of Medieval English Drama* (London, 1974), evaluates texts from the point of view of their intended theatre. Alan H. Nelson, *The Medieval English Stage: Corpus Christi Pageants and Plays* (Chicago and London, 1974), and Anna J. Mill, *Mediaeval Plays in Scotland* (Edinburgh and London, 1927), contain useful transcripts of records and, together with the REED volumes (see above), have been cited in the chapter; Nelson should be read with an awareness of the controversial nature of his theories – see, for example, the review of his book by L. M. Clopper, Martin Stevens and Stephen Spector in *JEGP*, 75 (1976), 403–7.

Arnold Williams, *The Drama of Medieval England* (Michigan, 1961), is a stimulating attempt 'to get at the dramatic essentials' of medieval plays. Richard Axton, *European Drama of the Early Middle Ages* (London, 1974), attempts a new synthesis of the different traditions and affirms the vitality and pervasiveness of the folk-drama.

Much important discussion of medieval drama is in learned journals, including the specialist periodicals listed in the Part 1 bibliography. Jerome Taylor and Alan H. Nelson, *Medieval English Drama: Essays Critical and Contextual* (Chicago and London, 1972; hereafter Taylor–Nelson), anthologizes some of the most important and stimulating. Neville Denny, *Medieval Drama* (London, Stratford-Upon-Avon Studies 16, 1973) is a collection of original essays. *The Drama of the Middle Ages: Comparative and Critical Essays*, edited by Clifford Davidson, C. J. Gianakaris and John H. Stroupe (New York, 1982) reprints a number of the important studies from *Comparative Drama*.

General works on the criticism of medieval literature are important but would require a separate bibliography. Norman F. Blake, *The English Language in Medieval Literature* (Totowa, N.J., 1977), mentioned above on p. 312, raises interesting general issues, and Pamela Gradon, *Form and Style in Early English Literature* (London, 1971), looks at many central problems. Erich Auerbach, *Mimesis: The Representation of Reality in Western Literature*, translated from the German by Willard Trask (Princeton, N.J., 1953), has been particularly influential. Specific reference in this Part is made to L. D. Benson, *Malory's 'Morte Darthur'* (Cambridge, Mass., 1976); D. S. Brewer, *Chaucer: the Critical Heritage*, 2 vols (London, 1978); Douglas Kelly, '*Matière* and *genera dicendi* in Medieval Romance', *Yale French Studies* (1974), 147–59; and Arthur K. Moore, 'Medieval English Literature and the Question of Unity', *MP*, 65 (1968), 285–300. More specific discussions are listed below.

The economic, political, religious and social background similarly requires a separate bibliography. A standard account of fourteenth-century England is May McKisack, *The Fourteenth Century, 1307–1399* (Oxford History of England, vol. 5; Oxford, 1959); the discussion of 'Trade, Industry and the Towns' in chapter 12 is particularly relevant to the drama. The rise of the towns, their social structure and government are usefully surveyed by Colin Platt, *The English Medieval Town* (London, 1979) and, with a wider geographical range, Fritz Rörig, *The Medieval Town* (London,

1967 (English translation); reprint, 1979). Important articles by D. M. Palliser, 'The trade guilds of Tudor York', and by Charles Phythian-Adams, 'Ceremony and the citizen: the communal year at Coventry', both cited in this Part, are in P. Clark and P. Slack, *Crisis and Order in English Towns, 1500–1700* (London, 1972). Reference is also made to Walter Ullmann, *A History of Political Thought: The Middle Ages* (Harmondsworth, 1965). See also under sections vi and viii, below.

(IV) THE LITURGY

The Study of Liturgy, ed. Cheslyn Jones, Geoffrey Wainwright and Edward Yarnold (London, 1978), is a general historical introduction, with classified bibliographies. Theodor Klauser, *A Short History of the Western Liturgy* (London, 1979), a translation by John Halliburton of *Kleine abenländische Liturgiegeschichte* (1965), is a brief and clear history, but should be supplemented with Jean Daniélou, *The Bible and the Liturgy* (London, 1960), and Louis Bouyer, *Rite and Man. The Sense of the Sacral and Christian Liturgy* (London, 1963), and *Life and Liturgy* (London, 1956; reprinted 1965), the latter being especially useful for its discussion of liturgical studies and liturgical history. *A Dictionary of Liturgy and Worship*, ed. J. G. Davies, appends short but valuable bibliographies to the principal entries. Gerhard Podhradsky's *New Dictionary of the Liturgy* (London, 1967) contains material not found in the original German, supplied by the author for this English edition.

Any Roman Catholic missal designed for use by the laity, containing brief commentaries and English translations, and published before the Second Vatican Council (1962–5), will give an impression of the richness of material, scriptural and non-scriptural, and the elaboration of ceremony of the Roman liturgy; but the Roman liturgy after the Council of Trent (1545–1563) was different from the medieval liturgy, and modern missals provide only an introduction and a starting-point. The publications of the Henry Bradshaw Society are comprehensive editions of medieval service books, including ones used in England.

Karl Young's *The Drama of the Medieval Church*, 2 vols (Oxford, 1933; reprinted 1962), remains indispensable as an anthology of liturgical texts, but the presentation is so heavily determined by older views of the origin of the drama that it must be used with great caution. Diane Dolan, *Le Drame liturgique de Pâcques en Normandie et en Angleterre au Moyen âge* (Paris, 1975), also has a full bibliography.

Although biblical references in this volume are to the Authorized Version of the Bible, the middle ages used the Vulgate, and so the translation of the Bible by Ronald Knox (London, 1955), which is of the Vulgate, can be useful. Leonard Johnston and Aidan Pickering, *A Harmony of the Gospels* (London, 1962), is based on the Knox translation. Jean Leclercq's evocation of monastic culture and its influence, *L'Amour des lettres et le désir de Dieu*, translated into English as *The Love of Learning and the Desire for God* (New York, 1962), is particularly valuable on the assimilation into original writings of the spirit and formulas of the scripture and the liturgy.

(v) MUSIC

The New Oxford History of Music, Vol. II: *Early Medieval Music up to 1300*, ed. Anselm Hughes (London, 1954; reprinted 1976), covers the period; *The History of Music in Sound*, Vol. II: *Early Medieval Music* (HMV HLP 3: record 1 of a set of two) includes a version of the *Quem Quaeritis*. *The Pelican History of Music*, Vol. I: *Ancient Forms to Polyphony*, ed. Alec Robertson and Denis Stevens (Harmondsworth, 1960; reprinted 1966), is also valuable. Gerald Abraham's *Concise Oxford History of Music* (London, 1979) has a more recent bibliography.

W. L. Smoldon's *The Music of the Medieval Church Dramas* (Oxford, 1980) and his 'Liturgical Music-Drama' in *Grove's Dictionary of Music and Musicians*, 5th edn, by Eric Blom (London, 1954), Vol. V, 317–43, are a necessary reminder that the dramatizations were music-drama. *Studies in Medieval Drama in Honour of William L. Smoldon on his 82nd Birthday* is a reprint of a special issue of *Comparative Drama*, VIII, 1 (1974).

The Oxford Anthology of Music: Medieval Music, ed. W. Thomas Marrocco and Nicholas Sandon (London, 1977), is supplemented by two records, *Medieval Music: Sacred Monophony* (OUP 161) and *Medieval Music: Ars Antiqua Polyphony* (OUP 164). Modern recordings of medieval music are subject to limitations similar to modern productions of medieval plays, but both, within those limitations, are essential. *Jubilate Deo: Pièces simples du répertoire grégorien* (Decca Aristocrate 7552) is designed to present simple pieces of Gregorian chant for congregational singing in modern Roman Catholic worship and does not aim at historical reconstruction. The *Archiv* series (Deutsche-Grammophon: *Archiv* 2533 131, 2533 158, 2533 163, 2533 284, 2533 320, 2533 359) is a survey-anthology of the three traditions of Gregorian chant, the principal liturgical forms, and the different styles of singing. Decca issue a series of such records, including *Chant Grégorien: La Dédicace des Églises* (Decca 7.521 A) and *Chant Grégorien: Semaine Sainte* (Decca 278.054/55).

(VI) FOLK-DRAMA

Alan Brody, *The English Mummers and Their Plays: Traces of Ancient Mystery* (London, n.d.), written in 1969, classifies and analyses the various types of folk-drama and gives specimen texts. Older studies include R. J. E. Tiddy, *The Mummers' Play* (Oxford, 1923; reprinted 1972), and E. K. Chambers, *The English Folk Play* (Oxford, 1933); see also Axton, above. C. R. Baskervill's articles, 'Dramatic Aspects of Medieval Folk Festivals in England', *SP*, 17 (1920), 19–87, and 'Mummers' Wooing Plays in England', *MP*, 21 (1924), 225–72, are important surveys of material, the latter including texts. E. C. Cawte, Alex Helm and Norman Peacock, *English Ritual Drama* (London, 1967), provides Brody's classification and examines distribution of the plays. Christina Hole, *A Dictionary of British Folk Customs* (London, 1976; paperback, 1978), is a useful popular guide to folk-practice surviving today. Numerous articles on folk-customs, -dances and plays appear in journals such as *Notes and Queries*, *Folklore*, *Folk-Life*, *Journal of the English Folk Dance Society*, *Journal of the English Folk Dance and Song Society*. In this section particular reference is made to Alex Helm, 'In Comes I, St. George', *Folklore*, 76 (1965), 118–36; and to Susan Pattison, 'The Antrobus Soul-caking play: an alternative approach to the Mummers' play', *Folk-Life*, 15 (1977), 5–11.

In addition to the texts cited above under Anglo and Adams respectively, the Scots 'Pleugh Song' is in *Music of Scotland* (*Musica Britannica* 15), no. 30, and R. B. Dobson and J. Taylor give ballad and play-texts for Robin Hood in their *Rymes of Robin Hood: an Introduction to the English Outlaw* (London, 1976). Axton, op. cit., pp. 40–2, discusses the 'Pleugh Song'; additional background to the Robin Hood ballads is provided by Maurice Keen, *The Outlaws of Medieval England* (London, 1961) and J. C. Holt, 'The origins and audience of the Ballads of Robin Hood', *Past and Present*, 18 (1960), 89–110, together with the ensuing correspondence in *Past and Present*, 19 (1961). N. Davis, *The Paston Letters*, 2 vols (London, 1971), prints Sir John Paston's letter concerning W. Woode in Vol. I, 460–1. Reference is also made to Priscilla Heath Barnum, *Dives and Pauper* (London, EETS, e.s. 275, 1976), and to F. J. Child, *The English and Scottish Popular Ballads* (Boston and New York, 1886–98; reprinted, 1965). In *The Early Plays of Robin Hood* (Cambridge and Totowa, N.J., 1981) David Wiles traces the folk-play origins and development of the Robin Hood plays and includes documents, gazetteer maps and original play texts in his appendices.

Evaluations of the influence of folk-drama on other modes can be found in the surveys listed above. Other aspects are discussed in P. Happé, 'The Vice and the folk-drama', *Folklore*, 75–6 (1964–5), 161–93; M. Dean Smith, 'Folk-play origins of the English masque', *Folklore*, 65 (1954), 74–86; W. K. Smart, '*Mankind* and the Mumming plays', *MLN*, 32 (1917), 21–5.

(VII) SAINTS' PLAYS

E. Catherine Dunn, 'French medievalists and the saint's play: a problem for American scholarship', *Medievalia et Humanistica*, n.s. 6 (1975), 51–62, proposes new sources for the genre. Other studies include David L. Jeffrey, 'English saints' plays', Denny, 69–90, and Glynne Wickham, 'The staging of Saints' Plays in England', *The Medieval Drama*, ed. Sandro Sticca (New York, 1972), 99–119. The Digby *Mary Magdalen* is the subject of John W. Velz, 'Sovereignty in the Digby *Mary Magdalene*', *Comparative Drama*, 2 (1968), 32–43; Clifford Davidson, 'The Digby Mary Magdalen and the Magdalen cult of the Middle Ages', *Annuale Medievale*, XII (1972), 70–87; and Theresa Coletti, 'The design of the Digby play of *Mary Magdalen*', *SP*, 76 (1979), 313–33.

(VIII) PLAY-CYCLES

W. W. Greg's *Bibliographical and Textual Problems of the English Miracle Cycles: Lectures Delivered as Sandars Reader in Bibliography in the University of Cambridge, 1913* (London, 1914), a series of articles originally published in *The Library* (third series) 5 (1914), deals authoritatively with the manuscripts of the cycles and transmission of texts. It should be supplemented by the introductions to the Leeds series of Medieval Drama Facsimiles listed above. Selected guild-ordinances are printed in *English Gilds. The Original Ordinances of More Than One Hundred Early English Gilds: Together with ye olde Vsages of ye Cite of Wynchester; The Ordinances of Worcester; The Office of the Mayor of Bristol; and the Customary of the Manor of Tettenhall-Regis. From Original Manuscripts of the Fourteenth and Fifteenth Centuries, Edited with Notes*, with an introduction and glossary by Lucy Toulmin Smith and preliminary essay by Lujo Brentano (London, EETS, o.s. 40, 1870; reprinted 1963). Harold C. Gardiner, S.J., *Mysteries' End: An Investigation of the Last Days of the Medieval Religious Stage* (Yale Studies in English 103, New Haven and London, 1946; reprinted 1967), deals with the circumstances of the suppression of the cycles;

William Tydeman, *The Theatre in the Middle Ages: Western European Stage Conditions, c.800–1576* (Cambridge, 1978), in his 'Epilogue', gives some account of the importance of neo-classical concepts of drama in the cycles' decline. Rosemary Woolf, 'The influence of the mystery plays upon the popular tragedies of the 1560s', *Renaissance Drama*, n.s. 6 (1973), 89–105, examines one aspect of the cycle-drama's influence upon other dramatic forms, while Anne Righter, *Shakespeare and the Idea of the Play* (London, 1962), prefaces her discussion of Shakespearian drama with a perceptive account of medieval theatre and its implications.

The most important discussion of the Corpus Christi play as genre is V. A. Kolve, *The Play Called Corpus Christi* (London, 1966), which has also proved seminal in its use of game-paradigms in its sensitive criticism of the drama. Jerome Taylor, 'The dramatic structure of the Middle English Corpus Christi, or Cycle, plays', Taylor-Nelson, 148–56, was an earlier attempt to trace a link between play-cycle and feast. Some objections to such an approach are set out in Nelson, op. cit., Chap. 1, 'Introduction: historical inquiry and formal criticism'. A different approach is adopted by Rosemary Woolf in her article 'The effect of typology on the English mediaeval plays of Abraham and Isaac', *Speculum*, XXXII (1957), 805–25, and in her book, *The English Mystery Plays* (London, 1972). The usefulness of typology to the critic of medieval drama is considered by Arnold Williams, 'Typology and the cycle plays: some criteria', *Speculum*, XLIII (1968), 677–84, and Patrick J. Collins, 'Typology, criticism, and medieval drama: some observations on method', *Comparative Drama*, 10 (1976–7), 298–313.

The specific aspect of characterization is the main concern of Eleanor Prosser, *Drama and Religion in the English Mystery Plays: a Re-Evaluation* (Stanford, 1961). Those interested in tracing the traditions available to a dramatist in constructing a character will find it helpful to look the character up in the *Jewish Encyclopaedia*, the *Catholic Encyclopaedia* and a Bible dictionary such as W. Smith, *Dictionary of the Bible*, 3 vols (London, 1860–3); these works will also often indicate the sources of other non-biblical material in the cycles. Lawrence M. Clopper, 'Tyrants and Villains: Characterization in the Passion Sequences of the English Mystery Plays', *MLQ*, 41 (1980), 3–20, is concerned with specific examples of the technique of characterization. The composite origins of certain figures have attracted particular attention. Herod is the subject of R. E. Parker, 'The Reputation of Herod in Early English Literature', *Speculum*, VIII (1933), 59–67; S. S. Hussey, 'How many Herods in the Middle English drama?', *Neophilo-*

logus, 48 (1964), 252–9; chapter 3 of Penelope B. R. Doob, *Nebuchadnezzar's Children: Conventions of Madness in Middle English Literature* (New Haven and London, 1974); and David Staines, 'To out-Herod Herod: the development of a dramatic character', *Comparative Drama*, 10 (1976), 29–53. Pilate is considered in Arnold Williams, *The Characterization of Pilate in the Towneley Plays* (East Lancing, 1950), and Robert A. Brawer, 'The characterization of Pilate in the York Cycle Play', *SP*, 69 (1972), 289–303.

Waldo F. McNeir, 'The Corpus Christi Passion plays as dramatic art', *SP*, 48 (1951), 601–28, was an early attempt to view the plays as drama and is still important. Aspects of cycle-drama are discussed in Arnold Williams, 'The comic in the cycles', Denny, 109–24, and T. W. Craik, 'Violence in the English Miracle plays', Denny, 173–96. Influences from contemporary religious thought and teaching are considered in A. C. Cawley, 'Middle English metrical versions of the Decalogue with reference to the English Corpus Christi cycles', *LSE*, n.s. 8 (1975), 129–45; J. W. Robinson, 'The late medieval cult of Jesus and the mystery plays', *PMLA*, 80 (1965), 508–14; and Lauren Lepow, 'Middle English elevation prayers and the Corpus Christi cycles', *ELN*, 17 (1979), 85–8. Rosemary Woolf, 'The theme of Christ the lover-knight in medieval English literature', *RES*, n.s. 13 (1962), 1–16, is also relevant to the drama. R. W. Ingram, 'The use of music in English miracle-plays', *Anglia*, 75 (1957), 55–76, and John Stevens, 'Music in medieval drama', *Proceedings of the Royal Musical Association*, 84 (1958), 81–95, deal with an important and often neglected aspect of medieval drama; a book on music in the cycles by Richard Rastall is in preparation.

Among the many comparative studies of episodes in the cycles may be noted Lynette Muir, 'The Fall of Man in the drama of medieval Europe', *Studies in Medieval Culture*, 10 (1977), 121–31; Robert A. Brawer, 'The form and function of the prophetic procession in the Middle English cycle play', *Annuale Medievale* 13 (1972), 88–123; M. M. Morgan, '"High fraud": paradox and double plot in the English Shepherds' Plays', *Speculum*, XXXIX (1964), 676–89; David L. Wee, 'The Temptation of Christ and the motif of divine duplicity in the Corpus Christi cycle drama', *MP*, 72 (1974), 1–16; Robert A. Brawer, 'The Middle English Resurrection play and its dramatic antecedents', *Smolden Festschrift*, 77–9; David J. Leigh, 'The Doomsday mystery play: an eschatological morality', Taylor-Nelson, 260–78.

Each cycle attracts its own critics. On the Chester Cycle, F. M. Salter, *Mediaeval Drama in Chester* (Toronto, 1955), is the culmination of that critic's earlier scholarship, seen notably in W. W. Greg, *The 'Trial and*

Flagellation' with Other Studies in the Chester Cycle (Oxford, Malone Society, 1935), and 'The Banns of the Chester Plays', *RES*, 15 (1939), 432–57, and 16 (1940), 1–17, 137–48. Salter's views have been re-examined and tellingly modified in Lawrence M. Clopper, 'The Rogers' description of the Chester plays', *LSE*, 7 (1974), 63–94, and 'The history and development of the Chester cycle', *MP*, 75 (1978), 219–46. *REED*'s volume of *Records* (see above) is essential background reading, and valuable historical information may also be found in George Ormerod, *The History of the County Palatine and City of Chester* (London, 2nd edn, ed. T. Helsby, 1882). On sources, see A. C. Baugh, 'The Chester Plays and French influence', *Schelling Anniversary Papers* (New York, 1923), 35–63; Robert H. Wilson, 'The *Stanzaic Life of Christ* and the Chester Plays', *SP*, 28 (1931), 413–32; and J. Burke Severs, 'The relationship between the Brome and Chester plays of *Abraham and Isaac*', *MP*, 42 (1945), 137–51. Nan Cooke Carpenter discusses 'Music in the Chester Plays', *Papers in Language and Literature*, 1 (1965), 195–216. A concern with thematic integrity underlies R. M. Lumiansky, 'Comedy and theme in the Chester *Harrowing of Hell*', *Tulane Studies in English*, 10 (1960), 5–12; David Mills, 'The two versions of Chester Play V: Balaam and Balak' in Beryl Rowland, *Chaucer and Middle English Studies* (London, 1973), 366–71; and Lawrence M. Clopper, 'The principle of selection of the Chester Old Testament plays', *Chaucer Review*, 13 (1979), 272–83. Recent new approaches to the cycle are made in Kathleen Ashley, 'Divine power in the Chester cycle and late medieval thought', *Journal of the History of Ideas*, 39 (1978), 387–404, and John J. McGavin, 'Sign and transition: the *Purification* Play in Chester', *LSE*, 11 (1980), 90–104. A new book-length study is by Peter W. Travis, *Dramatic Design in the Chester Cycle* (University of Chicago Press, Chicago and London, 1982). The essays in *The Chester Cycle: Essays and Documents* (Chapel Hill, N. C., 1983) by R. M. Lumiansky and David Mills review the questions of text, sources and development; Richard Rastall contributes an essay on music in the cycle.

Wakefield has gathered the largest corpus of criticism. A. C. Cawley's scholarly student-anthology, *The Wakefield Pageants in the Towneley Cycle* (Manchester, 1958), provides the best introduction to the Master and his work. Book-length studies are provided by Walter E. Meyers, *A Figure Given: Typology in the Wakefield Plays* (Pittsburgh, 1970), and John Gardner, *The Construction of the Wakefield Cycle* (Carbondale, Ill., 1974). Marie C. Lyle, *The Original Identity of the York and Towneley Cycles*

(Minneapolis, 1919), assesses Wakefield's debt to the York cycle, and Martin Stevens discusses 'The missing parts of the Towneley cycle', *Speculum*, XLV (1970), 254–65; see also the Cawley–Stevens facsimile edition of the manuscript above. Stylistic elements are sensitively discussed by E. Catherine Dunn, 'Lyrical form and the prophetic principle in the Towneley plays', *Mediaeval Studies*, 23 (1961), 80–90, and 'The literary style of the Towneley plays', *American Benedictine Review*, 20 (1969), 481–504; Martin Stevens builds upon her insights in 'Language as theme in the Wakefield plays', *Speculum*, LII (1977), 100–17. Of the numerous studies of the Wakefield Master and his work, that by Hans-Jürgen Diller, 'The craftsmanship of the Wakefield Master', Taylor–Nelson, 245–59, is particularly perceptive; the same volume contains Lawrence J. Ross, 'Symbol and structure in the *Secunda Pastorum*', 177–211, and Nan Cooke Carpenter, 'Music in the *Secunda Pastorum*' (from *Speculum*, 26 (1951), 696–700). Among studies of specific plays or groups of plays may be noted John Gardner, 'Theme and irony in the Wakefield *Mactacio Abel*', *PMLA*, 80 (1965), 515–21; Martin Stevens, 'The dramatic setting of the Towneley *Annunciation* play', *PMLA*, 81 (1966), 193–8; Maynard Mack, Jr, 'The *Second Shepherds' Play*: a reconsideration', *PMLA*, 93 (1978), 78–85; Robert A. Brawer, 'The dramatic function of the Ministry Group in the Towneley cycle', *Comparative Drama*, 4 (1970), 166–76; George A. West, 'An analysis of the Towneley play of *Lazarus*', *PQ*, 56 (1977), 320–8; and Theresa Coletti, 'Theology and politics in the Towneley *Play of the Talents*', *Medievalia et Humanistica*, n.s., 9 (1979), 111–26; and Jeffrey Helterman, *Symbolic Action in the Plays of the Wakefield Master* (1981). See also Williams, *The Characterization of Pilate*, above. John Speirs, 'The Towneley *Shepherds' Plays*', though accessible in *The Age of Chaucer*, in *The Pelican Guide to English Literature*, Vol. I (Harmondsworth, 1954; rev. edn, 1959), 167–74, should be read with an awareness of alterative approaches, as should the same author's articles, 'The mystery cycle, 1: some Towneley plays', *Scrutiny*, 18 (1951), 86–117, and 'Some Towneley cycle plays. Part III', *Scrutiny*, 18 (1952), 246–65.

On the sources and analogues of the York cycle, see W. A. Craigie, 'The gospels of Nicodemus and the York mystery plays', *An English Miscellany: Presented to Dr Furnivall* (Oxford, 1901), 52–61; Francis A. Foster, 'The mystery plays and the Northern Passion', *MLN*, 26 (1911), 169–71 and Francis H. Miller, 'The Northern Passion and the mysteries', *MLN*, 34 (1919), 88–92; Eleanor G. Clark, 'The York plays and The Gospel of

Nicodemus', *PMLA*, 43 (1928), 153–61. On background, see *REED Records* and Palliser above; on relations with Wakefield, see Lyle above. The work of the York Realist is discussed by J. W. Robinson, 'The art of the York Realist', Taylor–Nelson, 230–44, and metrical criteria are examined in Jesse Byers Reese, 'Alliterative verse in the York cycle', *SP*, 48 (1951), 639–68. Effie MacKinnon, 'Notes on the dramatic structure of the York cycle', *SP*, 28 (1931), 433–49, and Clifford Davidson, 'After the Fall: design in the Old Testament plays of the York cycle', *Medievalia*, 1 (1975), 1–24, examine aspects of structure, and Davidson also discusses 'The realism of the York Realist and the York Passion', *Speculum*, L (1975), 270–83. Richard J. Collier, *Poetry and Drama in The York Corpus Christi Play* (Hamden, Conn., 1977), is a study of the various poetic modes used in the cycle. Alexandra F. Johnston, 'The plays of the religious guilds of York: the Creed play and the Pater Noster play', *Speculum*, L (1975), 55–90, looks at other kinds of religious drama in the city and their possible affinities with cyclic drama. Peter Meredith, 'John Clerke's hand in the York Register', *LSE*, n.s. 12 (1981), 245–71, throws light on an important figure in the city's theatrical history. A new edition of the York cycle, by Richard Beadle (London, 1982), has appeared in the York Medieval Texts series.

On the location of N-town, see Craig, op. cit., 265–80; Kenneth Cameron and Stanley J. Kahrl, 'The N-Town Plays at Lincoln', *TN*, 20 (1965), 61–9; and Mark Eccles, '*Ludus Coventriæ*: Lincoln or Norfolk?', *Medium Ævum*, 40 (1971), 135–41. Block's edition is an excellent review of sources, and the Meredith–Kahrl facsimile edition, above, deals with problems of the manuscript. The cycle is the subject of a book-length study, C. Gauvin, *Un Cycle du Théâtre Réligieux Anglais au Moyen Age* (Paris, 1973). Timothy Fry, 'The unity of the *Ludus Coventriæ*', *SP*, 48 (1951), 527–70, finds the basis of the play in the 'abuse of power' thesis; see Prosser's comments, op. cit., 194–5. H. R. Patch, 'The *Ludus Conventriæ* and the Digby Massacre', *PMLA*, 35 (1920), 324–43, and Martial Rose, 'The staging of the Hegge plays', Denny, 197–222, examine other aspects of the cycle. Specific issues are discussed in Sr Mary Patricia Forrest, O.S.F., 'The role of the Expositor Contemplacio in the St. Anne's Day plays of the Hegge cycle', *Mediaeval Studies*, 28 (1966), 60–76, and Daniel P. Poteet, 'Condition, contrast and division in the *Ludus Coventriæ* "Woman Taken in Adultery"', *Medievalia*, 1 (1975), 78–92.

Reference is made in this section to R. W. Ingram, '"To find the players and all that longeth thereto": notes on the production of medieval drama in Coventry', *The Elizabethan Theatre V* (Ontario and London, 1975), 17–44; see also his '"Pleyng geire accustumed belongyng & necessarie": guild records and pageant production in Coventry', *Proceedings of the First Colloquium at Erindale College, University of Toronto, 31 August – 3 September 1978* (Toronto, *REED*, 1979), 60–100.

III Early moral plays and the earliest secular drama

(a) TEXTS AND COMMENT ON TEXTS

(i) *Anonymous moral drama with sustained use of allegory*

1 *The Pride of Life*'s manuscript was lost when the Dublin Public Record Office was destroyed in 1922. It had been transcribed and edited by James Mills, who published the incomplete play in 1893 under the title by which it is known in the best modern edition, that of Norman Davis in *Non-Cycle Plays and Fragments* (London: EETS, s.s. 1, 1970), 90–105, lxxxv–c.

To the bibliography provided by Davis may be added (with a caution against pressing parallels with folk-drama to extremes) the account of Robert Potter, *The English Morality Play* (London and Boston, 1975), 14–15.

2 *The Castle of Perseverance* is one of the manuscript plays formerly owned by Cox Macro, and now in the Folger Shakespeare Library, Washington, D.C. The Early English Text Society have twice published it: the best modern edition is their second, by Mark Eccles, in *Macro Plays* (London: EETS, CCLXII, 1969). Eccles adds a good introduction and notes to his edition of the text.

Much of the criticism of this play has turned on the interpretation of its stage-plan: see A. C. Cawley, 18–19, above. In addition to material listed by Eccles (xlix–l), there is a useful article by Edgar T. Schell, 'On the Imitation of Life's Pilgrimage in *The Castle of Perseverance*', *JEGP*, LXVII (1968), 235–248.

3 'Lucidus and Dubius', a dialogue in Winchester College MS 33, has been edited in facsimile and transcribed with comment by Norman Davis in *Non-Cycle Plays and the Winchester Dialogues* (Leeds: University of Leeds School of English, Medieval Drama Facsimiles V, 1979), 135–60, 179–91.

4 'Occupation and Idleness', from the same Winchester College MS,

appears after [3] above, 161–78, 192–208. An edition of both the
Winchester Moralities by Richard Beadle is in preparation and to be
published by D. S. Brewer. In addition to the useful introduction to the
Dialogues by Norman Davis in his edition, his article 'Two unprinted
dialogues in Late Middle English and their language', *Revue des Langues
Vivantes*, XXXV (1969), 461–72, is of interest: see also B. S. Lee,
'Lucidus and Dubius: a fifteenth-century theological debate and its
sources', *Medium Aevum*, XLV (1976), 79–96.

5 *Wisdom* is another of the Macro plays: like *The Castle of Perseverance*,
it has been edited by Mark Eccles in *Macro Plays* (see [2] above).

Especially useful among the critical works listed by Eccles is W. K.
Smart, *Some English and Latin Sources and Parallels for the Morality
of Wisdom* (Menasha, Wisconsin, 1912).

6 *Mankind* is the third Macro play, and edited by Mark Eccles in the same
Early English Text Society volume as *The Castle of Perseverance* and
Wisdom (for reference see [2] above).

To the material listed by Eccles should be added the account of Glynne
Wickham in his preface to the modern-spelling text of the play edited
by him in *English Moral Interludes* (London and Totowa, N.J., 1976).
The article by Paula Neuss, 'Active and idle language: dramatic images
in *Mankind*', Stratford-upon-Avon Studies XVI (*Medieval Drama*),
(London, 1973), 41–67, is of interest.

7 *Everyman* does not survive in manuscript: there are extant four different
early printed texts, two complete, two fragmentary, which are listed and
described by A. C. Cawley in his introduction to what is incomparably
the best modern edition (Manchester, 1961).

Most of the best material on *Everyman* and *Elckerlijc* is listed by
A. C. Cawley in his bibliography: to this must be added the conclusive
pamphlet by the late E. R. Tigg, *The Dutch Elckerlijc is prior to the
English Everyman* (London, 1981). Three articles are worth consulting:
that by Lawrence V. Ryan, 'Doctrine and dramatic structure in *Everyman*', in *Speculum*, XXXII (1957), 722–35; that by T. F. Van Loon,
'*Everyman*: a structural analysis', in *PMLA*, 78 (1963), 465–75; and that
by V. A. Kolve, '*Everyman* and the Parable of the Talents' in *The
Medieval Drama*, ed. Sandro Sticca (Albany, N.Y., 1971).

8 *Mundus et Infans* does not survive in manuscript: the text published by
Wynkyn de Worde in 1522 as 'a propre newe Interlude of the Worlde
and the chylde' is reprinted in the series Tudor Facsimile Texts [TFT].
A valuable article is by H. N. MacCracken, 'A source of *Mundus et
Infans*', *PMLA*, XXIII (1908), 486–96.

9 *Hickscorner* was also printed by de Worde, but not dated by him: this text is available in TFT. Another early edition is reconstructed by W. W. Greg in 'Notes on some early plays: *Hycke Scorner*', *The Library*, s. iv, XI (1930), 44–56. References are to Farmer's TFT edition of 1908. Much of the criticism concerns this play's relation to *Youth* (see [10] below). The priority of *Youth* is argued by E. T. Schell in '*Youth* and *Hyckescorner*, which came first?', *Philological Quarterly*, XLV (1966), 468–74. Another useful article is by Ian Lancashire, 'The sources of *Hyckescorner*', *Review of English Studies*, n.s. XXII (1971), 257–73.

10 *Youth* was printed, without a date, by John Waley: this text is in TFT. For Schell's article arguing the priority of *Youth* to *Hickscorner*, see [9] above.

(ii) *Anonymous religious drama with allegorical elements*

1 *Mary Magdalen* is one of the plays in Bodleian MS Digby 133: it has been edited in facsimile by D. C. Baker and J. L. Murphy (Leeds: University of Leeds School of English, Medieval Drama Facsimiles, III, 1976), and the same editors with L. B. Hall have prepared an edition for the EETS, 1982.

    D. L. Jeffrey, 'English Saints' Plays', in *Medieval Drama*, Stratford-upon-Avon Studies XVI (London, 1973), discusses this play, 68–89. A useful account of the temptation by Curiosity is given by Robert H. Bowers, 'The tavern scene in the Middle English Digby play of *Mary Magdalene*', in *All These to Teach: Essays in Honor of C. A. Robertson* (Gainesville, Florida, 1965), 15–32.

2 *Processus Satanae* is W. W. Greg's edition of the 'old verses/Fro limebrook' in the Welbeck Abbey MS: see *MSC*, II, iii (London: Malone Society, 1931), 239–50. God's part only is preserved, but the Parliament in Heaven between the Four Daughters of God (see b-iii below) was evidently an allegorical section of the same drama.

3 *Ludus Coventriae*, the N-town Cycle, was edited by K. S. Block from BL MS Cotton Vespasian D viii: this edition, EETS, e.s. CXX (1922 for 1917) is cited as 'Block' throughout the present work. The allegorical section shows the Parliament in Heaven between the Four Daughters of God (Block, 97–103), and is introduced by 'Contemplacio', dressed as a university doctor.

4 The Norwich Grocers' play of Adam and Eve is edited by Norman Davis, *NCPF*, 8–18, xxii–xl. The two allegorical speakers are Dolour and Misery.

(iii) *Other anonymous religious drama cited in Part III*

1 *The Cambridge Prologue*: see Norman Davis, *NCPF*, 114–15, cxi–cxiv.
2 *The Rickinghall Fragment*: see Norman Davis, *NCPF*, 116–17, cxiv–cxv.
3 *The York Cycle*: ed. L. Toulmin Smith, *York Plays* (1885; New York, 1963).
4 *The Croxton Play of the Sacrament*: ed. Norman Davis, *NCPF*, 55–89, lxx–lxxxv.
5 *Dux Moraud*: ed. Norman Davis, *NCPF*, 106–13, c–cxi. On this actor's part see the excellent argument by C. B. Hieatt, 'A case for *Duk Moraud* as a play of the miracles of the Virgin', *Mediaeval Studies*, XXXII (1970), 345–51. See also the *Durham Prologue*, ed. Norman Davis, *NCPF*, 118–19, cxv–cxviii.
6 *The Conversion of St Paul*: ed. Baker, Murphy, Hall, for EETS, CCLXXXIII (1982), 1–23. An important article which establishes the date of the devil scenes in this play is by D. C. Baker and J. L. Murphy, 'The late medieval play of MS Digby 133: scribes, dates and early history', *RORD (Report of the MLA Conference)*, X (1967), 153–66.

(iv) *Anonymous secular entertainment 1350–1500*

1 *Interludium de Clerico et Puella*: this text has been well edited from BL Add. MS 23986 by Bruce Dickens and R. M. Wilson, *Early Middle English Texts* (London, 1951), 132–5, and is given with marginal glosses by Glynne Wickham in an appendix to *English Moral Interludes* (London and Totowa, N.J., 1976), 199–203.
2 *Dame Sirith*: impeccably edited by J. A. W. Bennett and G. V. Smithers, *Early Middle English Verse and Prose* (Oxford, 2nd edn, 1968), 77–95, this thirteenth-century *fabliau* is tellingly discussed by Richard Axton, *European Drama of the Early Middle Ages* (London, 1974), 19–23.
3 *Robin Hood fragment*: ed. N. Davis, *Non-Cycle Plays and the Winchester Dialogues* (Leeds: University of Leeds School of English, Medieval Facsimiles V, 1979), 75–8.
4 *Mumming of the Seven Philosophers*: edited from Trinity College Cambridge MS 599 by R. H. Robbins, *Secular Lyrics of the XIVth and XVth Centuries* (Oxford, 2nd edn, 1955), 110–13.
5 Show of *Nine Worthies* at Coventry, 1455: edited from Coventry Leet Book by R. S. Loomis, 'Verses on the Nine Worthies', *MP*, XV (1917–18), 25–6; also *REED, Coventry*, 29–34.
6 'ix Worthy' from Reynes MS (Bodeian MS Tanner 407, f. 32): quoted

and discussed by Norman Davis, *NCPF*, cxx–cxxi. For full text see *The Parlement of the Three Ages*, ed. I. Gollancz (London, 1917), 135–6.

7 'ix^e Worthy' from BL MS Harley 2259, f. 39^v: ed. F. J. Furnivall in 'The Nine Worthies and the heraldic arms they bore', *Notes and Queries*, s. vii, VIII (13 July 1889), 22–3.

(v) *Work of a dramatic or semi-dramatic kind by known authors*

JOHN LYDGATE

Most of Lydgate's voluminous works have found their way into volumes of the Early English Text Society: those which contain his semi-dramatic writing, and material referred to in this section, are the two collections of his *Minor Poems* edited by H. N. MacCracken; I (Religious Poems) in EETS, o.s. CVII (1910); II (Non-Religious Poems) in EETS, o.s. CXCII (1934). The translation of the French *danse macabre* verses from the Innocents Church in Paris which Lydgate made for the cloisters of Old St Paul's is edited by Florence Warren, *The Dance of Death*, EETS, o.s. CLXXXI (1931), with valuable introduction and appendices by Beatrice White. Glynne Wickham reprints the *Mumming at Hertford* and *Mumming at Bishopswood* with marginal glosses in an appendix to *English Moral Interludes* (London and Totowa, N.J., 1976), 204–13.

A good introduction to Lydgate with full bibliographical reference and fair treatment of his Mummings is Derek Pearsall, *John Lydgate* (London, 1970).

BENEDICT BURGH

'Maister Benet's Cristemasse Game' was edited from BL MS Harley 7333, f. 149 ff. by F. J. Furnivall in *Notes and Queries*, s. iv, I (1868), 455–6 (16 May), 531 (6 June). Burgh cuts a modest figure in the *D.N.B.*: he was dead by 1483, when Caxton mentions him in the preface to *Cato Magnus*.

THOMAS CHAUNDLER

Liber Apologeticus de Omni Statu Humanae Naturae [A Defence of Human Nature in Every State], has been elaborately edited by Doris Enright-Clark Shoukri with a full translation, introduction, notes and bibliography: she also reproduces the fourteen illustrations of the unique MS (London: Modern Humanities Research Association, 1974; New York, Renaissance Society of America, 1974).

HENRY MEDWALL

The Plays of Henry Medwall have been carefully edited by Alan H. Nelson (Cambridge and Totowa, N.J., 1980). *Nature* first appeared in William Rastell's edition of about 1530; this edition is reprinted in the series Tudor Facsimile Texts.

W. R. MacKenzie, 'Source for Medwall's *Nature*', *PMLA*, XXIX (1914), 189–99, is of interest. Nelson provides full critical treatment and references in his edition cited above.

Fulgens and Lucres was printed by John Rastell in about 1510, and edited by F. L. Boas and A. W. Reed (London, 1926). A useful modernized text is given by Wickham, *English Moral Interludes. Fulgens and Lucres* has received more critical attention than *Nature*, and Nelson gives full references in his edition of Medwall's plays (see above). Essential to the understanding of the play's sources is Rosamond J. Mitchell's *John Tiptoft* (London, 1938), which reprints the Earl of Worcester's translation of Buonaccorso's *De Vera Nobilitate*, 215–41. A stimulating discussion by Robert C. Jones, 'The stage world and the "real" world in Medwall's *Fulgens and Lucrece*', *Modern Language Quarterly*, XXXII (1971), reinforces the personal experience of everyone concerned with the revival of the play in hall-banquet setting at Bristol University in 1964: photographs and other material about the revival can be consulted in the Theatre Collection of the University of Bristol by arrangement with the Keeper.

JOHN SKELTON

The edition of *Magnificence* by R. L. Ramsay, EETS, o.s. XCVIII (1906), was reprinted in 1958: a useful edition in modern spelling is by Paula Neuss (Manchester and Baltimore, 1980).

Ramsay's seminal introduction to his edition has come under fire from many subsequent critics: W. O. Harris, *Skelton's 'Magnificence' and the Cardinal Virtue Tradition* (Chapel Hill, N.C., 1965), and A. R. Heiserman, *Skelton and Satire* (Chicago, Ill., 1961), are of special value.

The fragment of a morality play called *Good Order* which William Rastell printed in 1533 has been attributed to Skelton on grounds set out by Ray Nash in 'Rastell fragments at Dartmouth', *The Library*, s. iv, XXIV (1943), 66–73, and argued by him and G. L. Frost in '*Good Order*: a morality fragment', *Studies in Philology*, XLI (1944), 483–91. Light on a reference in the fragment to the banishment of Riot and Gluttony, cross in hand, is thrown by N. M. Trenholme, *The Right of Sanctuary in England* (Columbia, Mo, University of Missouri Studies I, 1903), esp. 24, 28–9, 40–1.

A good selection of Skelton's poems, from which his personal style and the racy observation which characterizes *The Tunnyng of Elynour Rummyng* can be sampled, is edited by R. S. Kinsman, *John Skelton: Poems* (Oxford, 1969). *The Complete English Poems* are ed. John Scattergood (Harmondsworth, 1983).

JOHN RASTELL

Three plays from John Rastell's press which are held to be by him or sponsored by him are edited by Richard Axton, *Three Rastell Plays* (Cambridge and Totowa, N.J., 1979). All seem to be sixteenth-century work but reference for purposes of comparison is made in this section to both *The Four Elements* and *Calisto and Melebea* (facsimiles available in TFT). A useful starting-point for criticism of *Calisto and Melebea* is H. D. Purcell's 'The *Celestina* and the Interlude of *Calisto and Melebea*', *Bulletin of Hispanic Studies*, XLIV (1967) 1–15.

M. E. Borish, 'Source and intention of *The Four Elements*', *Studies in Philology*, XXXV (1938), 149–63, raises questions further treated by Elizabeth Nugent, 'Sources of Rastell's *Four Elements*', *PMLA*, LVII (1942), 74–88, and by Johnstone Parr, 'More sources of Rastell's *Interlude of the Four Elements*', *PMLA*, LX (1945), 48–58. The connection between Rastell, More and Medwall is illuminated by Pearl Hogrefe, *The Sir Thomas More Circle* (Urbana, Ill., 1959). C. R. Baskervill's 'John Rastell's dramatic activities', *MP*, XIII (1916), 557–60, is still of interest.

JOHN HEYWOOD

Though all Heywood's entertainments belong to the sixteenth century, reference is made in the text to his version of French farce, *Johan Johan, Tib his Wife and Sir Johan*, which is available in TFT, and was revived with hilarious effect at Bristol University in 1965. T. W. Craik corrects earlier accounts of Heywood's sources for this play in 'The true source of John Heywood's *Johan Johan*', *MLR*, XLV (1950), 289–95.

(b) BACKGROUND MATERIAL

(i) *The theatrical tradition*
The tradition of entertainment in classical times and the dark ages is well documented by Margarete Bieber, *The History of the Greek and Roman Theater* [1939] (Princeton, N.J., 2nd edn, rev. 1961 and London, 1961). Allardyce Nicoll is concerned in *Masks, Mimes and Miracles* (London, 1931) to trace the acting style and material of popular entertainment from Atellan

farce to the *commedia dell'arte* tradition of the Renaissance. Richard Southern's particular interest in the form of platform-stage backed by curtains which appears in vase paintings of *phlyax* plays, Atellan farces and also illustrations of popular theatre from sixteenth-century Europe is developed in *The Seven Ages of the Theatre* (London, 1962, etc.), under the heading 'booth-stage'.

Valuable tools towards understanding the origin of the minstrel tradition are T. Frank's 'The status of actors at Rome', *Classical Philology*, xxvi (1931), 11–20, and J. D. A. Ogilvy's '*Mimi, scurrae, histriones*: entertainers of the early Middle Ages', *Speculum*, xxxviii (1963), 608–19. See also M. H. Marshall, 'Theatre in the Middle Ages: evidence from dictionaries and glosses', *Symposium*, iv (1950), 1–39, 366–89.

An important article on entertainment during courtly feasts is by L. H. Loomis, 'Secular dramatics in the royal palace, Paris, 1378, 1389, and Chaucer's "Tregetoures"', *Speculum*, xxxiii (1958), 242–55: this is reprinted in *Medieval English Drama: Essays Critical and Contextual* (Chicago and London, 1972).

E. K. Chambers, *The Mediaeval Stage* (Oxford, 1903) is still in its two volumes an indispensable reference guide to the period. Valuable for an intelligent reconstruction of early performances is Richard Axton, *European Drama of the Early Middle Ages* (London, 1974). Sections of the field are reviewed by Grace Frank, *The Medieval French Drama* (Oxford, 1954), and Anna J. Mill, *Mediaeval Plays in Scotland* (Edinburgh, 1927). The range of English moralities and interludes is analysed by T. W. Craik, *The Tudor Interlude* (Leicester, 1958).

(ii) *The homiletic tradition*

(a) Texts

Two useful manuals of parochial instruction are Archbishop Thoresby's *Lay Folks Catechism*, ed. T. F. Simmons, EETS, o.s. cxviii (1901), and John Mirk's *Instructions for Parish Priests*, ed. Edward Peacock, EETS, o.s. xxxi (1868). *Mirk's Festial* was edited by Theodor Erbe, EETS, e.s. xcvi (1905), and a valuable collection of *Middle English Sermons* by W. O. Ross, EETS, o.s. ccix (1940). Other useful treatises are *Speculum Christiani*, ed. Gustaf Holmstedt, EETS, o.s. clxxxii (1933), and *The Book of Vices and Virtues*, ed. W. N. Francis, EETS, o.s. ccxvii (1942).

(b) Comment

The Apocryphal New Testament, a collection edited and translated by M. R. James (Oxford, 1953), provides source-material for many incidents in medieval drama and iconography. An instance cited on p. 218 is discussed by Carolyn Wall, 'The apocryphal and historical background of *The Appearance of Our Lady to Thomas* (Play XLVI of the York Cycle)', *Mediaeval Studies*, XXXII (1970), 172–92. A most valuable article is Clifford Davidson's 'The Digby *Mary Magdalene* and the Magdalene cult of the Middle Ages', *Annuale Mediaevale*, XIII (1972), 70–87.

On the doctrine of *clara visio*, M. D. Knowles in 'The censured opinions of Uthred of Boldon', *Proceedings of the British Academy*, XXXVII (1951), 305–42, provides information and further references.

A sound survey of many topics connected with literacy and education is by Janet Coleman, *English Literature in History, 1350–1400, Medieval Readers and Writers* (London, 1981). Fifteenth-century attitudes are well illustrated by V. J. Scattergood, *Politics and Poetry in the Fifteenth Century* (London, 1971).

(iii) *The allegorical tradition*

Classic in his analysis of Prudentius and with full reading references, C. S. Lewis has made *The Allegory of Love* (Oxford, 1936; New York, 1958) an indispensable tool. Another important study which treats the allegorical tradition among others is Peter Dronke, *Poetic Individuality in the Middle Ages* (Oxford, 1970).

Special figures of allegory have been considered at length by many writers and only a brief selection can be given here.

Castles Roberta Cornelius, *The Figurative Castle* (Bryn Mawr, Penn.,1930), gives a wide range of reference to the use of this motif. Also of value is Kari Sajavaara's *The Middle English Translations of Robert Grosseteste's Château d'Amour* (Helsinki: Société Néophilologique, 1967).

The Four Cardinal Virtues This group, which has Justice only in common with the group known as *Four Daughters of God* (see below), is found in the early prose homily *Sawles Warde*: for account and references see R. M. Wilson, *Early Middle English Literature* (London, 3rd edn, 1968). F. S. Boas discusses '*The Four Cardynall Vertues*, a fragmentary moral interlude' [*c*.1540] in *Queen's Quarterly* [Kingston, Ontario], LVIII (1951), 85–91.

The Four Daughters of God Hope Traver wrote the standard study of this motif: *The Four Daughters of God* (Bryn Mawr, Penn., 1907). Kari Sajavaara gives a good account of Grosseteste's use and its influence (ref. cited under *Castles* above). Reference should also be made to Samuel Chew, *The Virtues Reconciled: an Iconographic Study* (Toronto, 1947).

Psychomachia The works of Prudentius in two volumes have been translated by H. J. Thomson in the Loeb series (London, 1949 and 1954; Cambridge, Mass., 1949–1954): *Psychomachia*, I, 274–345. See also Thomson's 'The *Psychomachia* of Prudentius', *Classical Review*, XLIV (1930), 109–12, and C. S. Lewis, *The Allegory of Love*. It is Bernard Spivack in *Shakespeare and the Allegory of Evil* (New York and London, 1958) who has pressed the interpretation of the whole morality tradition in terms of this motif (esp. 60–95). See also Adolf Katzenellenbogen (b iv below).

Seven Deadly Sins The standard work on the formation of this group is by Morton W. Bloomfield, *The Seven Deadly Sins*, 'an introduction to the history of a religious concept with special reference to mediaeval English literature' (East Lansing, Michigan, 1952 and 1967). A useful supplement to this is Siegfried Wenzel's 'The Seven Deadly Sins: some problems of research', *Speculum*, XLVII (1968), 1–22. Wenzel has made a special study of *The Sin of Sloth: acedia in medieval thought and literature* (Chapel Hill, N. Carolina, 1967).

Seven Virtues One group so designated is made up of the Four Cardinal Virtues (see above) with Faith, Hope and Charity. Another, more frequent in medieval literature, is a group of remedial virtues, specific against the Seven Deadly Sins. See Adolf Katzenellenbogen under b iv below.

Three Enemies The World, the Flesh and the Devil as a group are discussed by Siegfried Wenzel, 'The Three Enemies of Man', *Mediaeval Studies*, XXIX (1967), 47–66.

Vices Because the Vice as a special incarnation of evil is a notable dramatic tradition in sixteenth-century interlude, and because 'Viciose' in the Beverley Paternoster play records (see b v below) is a point of controversy, there has been much throwing about of brains on Vices. Bernard Spivack in *Shakespeare and the Allegory of Evil* (ref. under *Psychomachia* above) lavishly develops his view that what Coleridge called 'motiveless malignity' in Iago should be understood in the context of the Vice tradition. The well-known study by L. W. Cushman, 'The Devil and the Vice in the English dramatic literature before Shakespeare', *Studien zur englischen Philologie*, ed. L. Morsbach, VI (Halle, 1900) has still some points of interest; but a view which distinguishes the Vice as demi-devil from the Vice as Fool was persuasively argued by F. H. Mares, 'The origin of the figure called "the Vice" in Tudor drama', *Huntington Library Quarterly*, XX (1958–9), 11–29. Robert Withington has written frequently on this subject, but it suffices to mention here his 'Braggart,

Devil and "Vice", a note on the development of comic figures in the early English drama', *Speculum*, XI (1936), 124–9. For devil-tempters akin to Vices, such as Titivillus in *Mankind*, see Eccles, *Macro Plays*, EETS, CCLXII (1969), 220, n.M 301.

(iv) *The iconographical tradition*

An excellent guide to medieval religious iconography is Clifford Davidson's *Drama and Art*, 'an introduction to the use of evidence from the visual arts for the study of early drama' (Kalamazoo, Michigan, 1977). M. D. Anderson's *Drama and Imagery in English Medieval Churches* (Cambridge, 1963) is of value, and Adolf Katzenellenbogen's *Allegories of the Vices and Virtues in Mediaeval Art, from early Christian times to the thirteenth century* (London, 1939) begins an account which Samuel Chew's *The Virtues Reconciled: an Iconographic Study* (Toronto, 1947) does something to continue.

The iconography of death has received special attention: many useful illustrations are reproduced with comment by T. S. R. Boase, *Death in the Middle Ages* (London, 1972), and the whole set of woodcuts of *La Danse Macabré des Charniers des Saints Innocents à Paris* is provided by Edward F. Chaney in his reprint of the 1485 edition of their inscriptions (Manchester, 1945). Both James M. Clark in 'The Dance of Death in medieval literature', *MLR*, XLV (1950), 336–45, and Beatrice White in her introduction and appendices to Florence Warren's edition of *The Dance of Death* in Lydgate's translation, EETS, o.s. CLXXXI (1931), supply a good guide to the location of Dance of Death material. Clifford Davidson's bibliography to *Drama and Art* (ref. in the para. above) is a repository of references to specialized work on this motif among others. Two useful articles by W. L. Hildburgh are 'English alabaster carvings as records of the mediaeval English drama', *Archaeologia*, XCIII (1955), 51–101, and 'Iconographical peculiarities in English alabaster carvings', *Folk-Lore*, XLIV (1933), 32–56, 123–50.

(v) *Paternoster plays*

In view of the fact that no Paternoster play survives, the volume of writing on this subject is very large. The documents in respect of York were printed by Karl Young, 'The records of the York Play of the Paternoster', *Speculum*, VII (1932), 540–6, and *in extenso* (from newly collected material as well as old) by Alexandra F. Johnston, 'The plays of the religious guilds of York: the Creed Play and the Pater Noster Play', *Speculum*, L (1975), 55–90. Arthur F. Leach's study 'Some English plays and players,

1220–1548', in *An English Miscellany presented to Dr Furnivall* (Oxford, 1901) remains the basic source on the Beverley Paternoster play (220–34), though a list of Beverley guilds responsible for craft plays in 1390 (also unearthed by Leach, and printed by Chambers, II, 340) is necessary in addition if the argument in the present text is to be followed. Stanley J. Kahrl's carefully edited *Records of plays and players in Lincolnshire, 1300–1585* (Oxford: MSC, VIII, 1969 [1974]) establishes the dates of performance of the Lincoln Paternoster play.

A determined attempt to link the Vice tradition with Beverley's 'Viciose' was made by Tempe E. Allison, 'The Paternoster Play and the origin of the Vices', *PMLA*, XXXIX (1924), 789–804. An equally ingenious attempt to link the Beverley Paternoster with a little-known French play involving the conversion of the Seven Deadly Sins is made by Robert Potter in *The English Morality Play* (London, 1975), 25–9; but the discovery, given prominence by Alexandra F. Johnston (ref. in the paragraph above), that craft-play gear was borrowed for Paternoster play performances rules out such theories in favour of some such interpretation as her own or the one argued on pp. 270–3, above.

(vi) *The morality tradition*
The general books on early moral plays in England are listed last because their scope is best understood in relation to views already mentioned in this bibliography. Bernard Spivack's *Shakespeare and the Allegory of Evil* (see *Psychomachia*, above) has been an influential promoter of the '*psychomachia* to Vice' school of thought. Robert Potter's *The English Morality Play* (London and Boston, 1975) is an ambitious and lively work which shows a commendable interest in the effect of plays in performance: it is, however, unreliable on such points as the folk-analogies of *The Pride of Life*, the priority of the Dutch *Elckerlijc* over *Everyman*, and the theme of the Paternoster play of Beverley. Merle Fifield's *The Rhetoric of Free Will* (Leeds, 1974) is a brisk Procrustean attempt to demonstrate 'five-action structure' in English morality plays. A useful though not always accurate work is Peter J. Houle's *The English Morality and Related Drama: A Bibliographical Survey* (Hamden, Conn., 1972): it is an alphabetical guide to fifty-seven moral plays and interludes, with extensive references. The most recent book on the subject is W. A. Davenport, *Fifteenth-Century English Drama. The Early Moral Plays and their Literary Relations* (Cambridge and Totowa, N.J., 1982).

Index

Abbot of Bonacord, 135
Abbot of Marham, 135
Abbot of Narent, 135
Abbot's Bromley, Staffordshire, Horn
  Dance, 126, 128–9
Aberdeen, 22, 135, 165; performing
  guilds, 165
Abraham and Isaac: Brome play, 145, 170,
  193–4, 195, 204, 302; Northampton
  play, 302
academic drama, 223, 233
Act of Apparel, 235–6
acting: compared to children's play, 90;
  compared to preaching, 87–8; doubling
  of parts, 38–9, 39n, 220; prohibition of,
  124–5, 130–1, 135, 136, 228, 231;
  regulation of, 38–9, 51–2, 55, 58
actors, 4, 11, 12, 48–9, 210, 227–30;
  attacks on, 34, 85–7, 227–9, 233–5;
  Corpus Christi plays, 30, 38–41; Greek
  and Roman, 225–9, 227n; names for,
  227–9, 234–5; place-and-scaffold
  productions, 17–19; professional, 32–5,
  41, 220, 226–7; statute against vagrants,
  236; touring companies, 19, 33, 145–6,

201–2, 204; women performers, 227,
  254; women played by men, 49
*Adam, Jeu de, Mystere de, see Ordo
  representacionis Ade*
allegorical characters, 248, 333–4; in
  mystery plays, 198–9, 219, 224, 287; in
  psychomachia, 248–9; *Accidia, see* Sloth;
  Adultery, 254; Age, 261; *Anima*: in
  Wisdom, 222, 250–9, in *Castle of
  Perseverance*, 286; Avarice, 249, 269,
  271–2; Backbiting, 268; Beauty, 260,
  285; Bodily Lust, 277; Body, 288;
  Charity, 258; Chastity, 249, 251;
  Church, 248; Confession, 277;
  Conscience, 258, 260; Contemplacio,
  198, 200, 219, 279; *Contemplation*, 258,
  261; Covetise, 18, 249, 259, 260, 261,
  286; Curiosity, 262; Death, 258, 259,
  281–8, 335; Discord, 254; Discretion,
  260; Dolour, 219; Envy, 269, 271–2;
  Fear-of-Death, 259, 281; Five Wits,
  252 and n., 260; Flesh, 18, 249, 252,
  259, 275; Folly, 259; Fornication, 255;
  Fortune, 240; Free Will, 261; Gluttony,
  254, 269; Good Deeds, 260, 285;